PLATO'S *TIMAEUS* AND THE LATIN TRADITION

This book focuses on the development of Platonic philosophy at the hands of Roman writers between the first century BCE and the fifth century CE. It discusses the interpretation of Plato's *Timaeus* by Cicero, Apuleius, Calcidius, and Augustine, and examines how these authors created new contexts and settings for the intellectual heritage they received and thereby contributed to the construction of the complex and multifaceted genre of Roman Platonism. It takes advantage of the authors' treatment of Plato's *Timaeus* as a continuous point of reference to illustrate the individuality and originality of each writer in his engagement with this Greek philosophical text. Each chooses a specific vocabulary, methodology, and literary setting for his appropriation of Timaean doctrine. The authors' contributions to the dialogue's history of transmission are shown to have enriched and prolonged the enduring significance of Plato's cosmology.

CHRISTINA HOENIG is an Assistant Professor of Classics at the University of Pittsburgh. Her academic research specializes in the cross-cultural and cross-linguistic transmission of philosophical concepts and ideas in Greco-Roman antiquity, with a focus, specifically, on the role of Greek–Latin translation as an exegetical tool in the history of Roman Platonism.

T0384606

CAMBRIDGE CLASSICAL STUDIES

PLATO'S *TIMAEUS* AND THE LATIN TRADITION

CHRISTINA HOENIG
University of Pittsburgh

CAMBRIDGE
UNIVERSITY PRESS

Shaftesbury Road, Cambridge CB2 8EA, United Kingdom

One Liberty Plaza, 20th Floor, New York, NY 10006, USA

477 Williamstown Road, Port Melbourne, VIC 3207, Australia

314–321, 3rd Floor, Plot 3, Splendor Forum, Jasola District Centre, New Delhi – 110025, India

103 Penang Road, #05–06/07, Visioncrest Commercial, Singapore 238467

Cambridge University Press is part of Cambridge University Press & Assessment, a department of the University of Cambridge.

We share the University's mission to contribute to society through the pursuit of education, learning and research at the highest international levels of excellence.

www.cambridge.org
Information on this title: www.cambridge.org/9781108402392

DOI: 10.1017/9781108235211

First published 2018
First paperback edition 2023

A catalogue record for this publication is available from the British Library

Library of Congress Cataloging-in-Publication data
Names: Hoenig, Christina, author.
Title: Plato's *Timaeus* and the Latin tradition / Christina Hoenig.
Other titles: Cambridge classical studies.
Description: Cambridge: Cambridge University Press, 2018. |
Series: Cambridge classical studies
Identifiers: LCCN 2018013736 | ISBN 9781108415804 (hardback)
Subjects: LCSH: Plato. Timaeus. | Philosophy, Ancient.
Classification: LCC B387.H64 2018 | DDC 113–dc23
LC record available at https://lccn.loc.gov/2018013736

ISBN   978-1-108-41580-4   Hardback
ISBN   978-1-108-40239-2   Paperback

CONTENTS

Contents

TABLES

List of Tables

ACKNOWLEDGEMENTS

Parts of this book originated as a doctoral thesis at the University of Cambridge, UK. I am indebted to all those who gave me advice and guidance during those years. Alongside my peers, I would like to thank James Warren, Malcolm Schofield, Harold Tarrant, and especially David Sedley, who supervised my project, helped me turn it into a book, and remained a steady and patient voice of reason and wisdom throughout. I am greatly indebted, moreover, to Gábor Betegh for his time and advice while I was writing the book. I benefited greatly from the expertise of many other people, such as Gretchen Reydams-Schils, Béatrice Bakhouche, John Magee, John Dillon, Margaret Graver, Federico Petrucci, and Enrico Moro, all of whom have helped me broaden my understanding of the subjects discussed in the various chapters of this study. Early versions of these chapters were presented at the Annual Conference of the Classical Association, the Annual Meeting of the Society of Classical Studies, and at conferences at the University of Notre Dame, the University of Pittsburgh, the University of Edinburgh, Scotland, and the University of Oslo, Norway. I would like to thank the audiences of these meetings for their help and feedback.

I am indebted to the University of Cambridge for supporting my doctoral studies, and to the University of Pittsburgh for providing me with the Richard S. and Jane Edwards Endowed Publication Fund and other resources. I would also like to thank Michael Sharp at Cambridge University Press, Céline Durassier at Out of House Publishing, and Marta Steele for her indefatigable help with the indices. I am grateful to my colleagues at the Department of Classics, the Department of Philosophy, and the Department of the History and Philosophy of Science for their support and camaraderie, and to Ceri Davis from the University of Swansea, who directed my attention to Calcidius when I was still an unassuming undergraduate student. Finally, I would like to thank my husband, Carter, for his unconditional patience and support. This book is dedicated to my parents, Rudolf and Christine.

ABBREVIATIONS

Ancient Sources

Aetius

Plac.	*Placita*

Alcinous

Didask.	*Didaskalikos*

Apuleius

Apol.	*Apologia*
DDS	*De deo Socratis*
DPD	*De Platone et eius dogmate*
Flor.	*Florida*
Met.	*Metamorphoses*
Mund.	*De mundo*

Aristotle

Cael.	*De caelo*
Phil.	*De philosophia*
Gen. an.	*De generatione animalium*
Gen. et corr.	*De generatione et corruptione*
Met.	*Metaphysica*
Phys.	*Physica*
Rhet.	*Rhetorica*

Augustine

Civ.	*De civitate dei*
Contr. Ac.	*Contra Academicos*
Conf.	*Confessiones*
Consens.	*De consensu evangelistarum*
Spir. et. litt.	*De spiritu et littera*
Enn. ps.	*Ennarationes in psalmos*
Gen. litt.	*De Genesi ad litteram*
In Ioh. ev. tract.	*In Iohannis evangelium tractatus*
Quaest. hept.	*Quaestionum in heptateuchum libri septem*
Retr.	*Retractationum libri duo*

Calcidius

Comm. in Tim.	*Commentarius in Platonis Timaeum*
Ep. ad Os.	*Epistula ad Osium*

Cicero

Ac.	*Academica*
Brut.	*Brutus*
De orat.	*De oratore*
Div.	*De divinatione*
Ep. ad Att.	*Epistulae ad Atticum*
Fat.	*De fato*
Fin.	*De finibus bonorum et malorum*
Inv.	*De inventione*
Leg.	*De legibus*
Nat. deor.	*De natura deorum*
Off.	*De officiis*
Opt. gen.	*De optimo genere oratorum*
Or.	*Orator*
Part. or.	*Partitiones oratoriae*
Top.	*Topica*
Tusc.	*Tusculanae disputationes*

Eusebius

Praep. evang.	*Praeparatio evangelica*

Iamblichus

Vita Pyth.	*De vita Pythagorica*

John Philoponus

Aet. mund.	*De aeternitate mundi*

Macrobius

Somn. Scip.	*Commentarii in Somnium Scipionis*

Nemesius

Nat. hom.	*De natura hominis*

Origen

Cant. cant.	*In canticum canticorum*
Contr. Cels.	*Contra Celsum*
Hom. ps.	*Homiliae in psalmos*
Princ.	*De principiis*

Philo of Alexandria

Aet. mund.	*De aeternitate mundi*
Opif. mund.	*De opificio mundi*

Plato

Euthyd.	*Euthydemus*
Leg.	*Leges*
Phd.	*Phaedo*
Phdr.	*Phaedrus*

List of Abbreviations

Phil.	*Philebus*
Plt.	*Politicus*
Soph.	*Sophista*
Rep.	*Respublica*
Symp.	*Symposium*
Tim.	*Timaeus*

Plotinus

Enn.	*Enneads*

Plutarch

E. ap. Delph.	*De E apud Delphos*
Def. or.	*De defectu oraculorum*
Col.	*Adversus Colotem*
Is. et Os.	*De Iside et Osiride*
Plat. quaest.	*Platonicae quaestiones*
Procr. an.	*De animae procreatione in Timaeo*
Quaest. conviv.	*Quaestiones convivales*

Proclus

In Plat. Tim.	*In Platonis Timaeum commentaria*

Ps. Aristotle

Kosm.	*Peri kosmou*

Ps.-Plutarch

Fat.	*De fato*

Quintilian

Inst. or.	*Institutio Oratoria*

xvi

List of Abbreviations

Sextus Empiricus

M.	*Adversus mathematicos*

Theon of Smyrna

Rer. math.	*Expositio rerum mathematicarum ad legendum Platonem utilium*

Theophrastus

Phys. op.	*Physicorum opiniones*

William of Conches

Gloss. sup. Plat.	*Glossae super Platonem*

Reference Works

Dox. Graec.	Diels, H. (ed.) *Doxographi Graeci*. Berlin.
IP 1982	Isnardi Parente, M. (ed.) (1982) *Senocrate e Ermodoro: Frammenti*. Naples.
IP 2012	Isnardi Parente, M., Dorandi, T. (ed.) (2012) *Senocrate e Ermodoro: Testimonianze e Frammenti*. Pisa.
OLD	*Oxford Latin Dictionary*
LS	*Liddell and Scott, Greek–English Lexicon*
SVF	von Arnim, H. (ed.) *Stoicorum Veterum Fragmenta*. Stuttgart.

INTRODUCTION

Plato's *Timaeus*

Plato's *Timaeus* is a dialogue of universal dimensions. It examines the composition and nature of our universe, beginning with its most elementary parts. Such extensive subject matter necessarily branches out into various disciplines: mathematics, harmonics, astronomy, biology, psychology, epistemology, physics, and metaphysics. The dialogue is far-reaching, moreover, in terms of its significance for Western intellectual history. Its dissemination shaped the ensuing philosophical discourse that began with Aristotle and Plato's successors in the Academy and that was enriched by the contributions of the Hellenistic philosophical systems and by the Jewish and Christian scholars of the early centuries CE, until the fascination with this deeply theological text subsided in the course of the rising secularism of the Renaissance.

The dialogue experienced renewed attention in the early decades of the twentieth century, which resulted in the important contributions by A.E. Taylor (1928) and F.M. Cornford (1937). In the subsequent decades the *Timaeus* was at the centre of a chronological controversy sparked by G.E.L. Owen, who rejected its categorization as a dialogue written by the late Plato. Owen's view was based on the similarities, metaphysical and epistemological, with what were perceived to be earlier dialogues: the *Phaedo*, the *Republic*, the *Symposium*, and the *Phaedrus*, as opposed to the 'later' *Theaetetus* and *Parmenides* that are critical of the metaphysical worldview conveyed by the other texts. Owen's view was questioned, in turn, by H.F. Cherniss and it is the traditional chronology supported by the latter that has prevailed up until this point.[1] This episode contributed much to reviving, over the last thirty years, the once sluggish interest in the dialogue, as is reflected by the growing body of modern Timaean scholarship. To name but a few recent studies: T.K. Johansen's *Plato's Natural Philosophy* (2004) is devoted to demonstrating the overall teleological framework, both in content and in structure, of the *Timaeus* and places emphasis on the similarities between the Timaean creation account and Aristotle's natural philosophy. The *Timaeus* in its role as the 'ultimate creationist manifesto' (p. 133) is discussed in the context of a broader study of ancient teleological thinkers and their adversaries in David Sedley's *Creationism and its Critics in Antiquity* (2007). The edited volume *One Book, The Whole Universe: Plato's Timaeus Today* by R. Mohr, K. Sanders, and B. Sattler (2010) examines various approaches to the dialogue, stretching from its immediate reception to modern-day cosmologists, architects, and physicists, and stresses the significance of the *Timaeus* for the wider Western scientific culture. Most recently, Sarah Broadie's *Nature and Divinity in Plato's Timaeus* (2012) has offered a thorough and complex examination of the dialogue that subjects many of its fundamental questions to a rigorous analysis: the nature of the creative divinity, the creation account and its relation to the Atlantis myth, the role of the intelligible forms and the receptacle. A further part of Broadie's study addresses the notorious crux of the Timaean creation story: are we, or are we not, to take the creation account at face value? Undoubtedly, the renewed scholarly interest in Plato's dialogue attests to the perennial significance of the questions and topics it raises.

---

[1] For more recent contributions on the place of the *Timaeus* within the Platonic corpus, see Kahn 2010, who places Timaean cosmology in a wider development of Plato's thought that reaches from the *Phaedrus* to *Laws* 10. Brandwood 1990: 250 and Ledger 1989 steer the discussion away from the relationship between the *Timaeus* and the *Theaetetus/Parmenides* towards texts that are more ambiguous in terms of their dating, e.g. the *Sophist* and the *Philebus*.

The Platonic Tradition

The present examination focuses on the development of Platonic philosophy at the hands of Roman writers between the first century BCE and the fifth century CE. The beginning of this period witnessed a gradual intellectual shift from the Hellenistic philosophical systems, the Stoics, the Academic Sceptics, the Peripatetics, and the Epicureans, to a dogmatist reappraisal of Platonic teaching. Severing the ties with their sceptical predecessors the Platonists, approximately from the first century BCE, absorbed Stoic, Neopythagorean, and Peripatetic nuances on their way towards a harmonizing dogmatism that allowed (Neo)Platonic thought to remain at the forefront of the ideological engagement with the Jewish and Christian scholars of the early centuries CE. Within this dogmatic synthesis, the authors under focus in the present study are witness to the attempt to reconcile and integrate Aristotelian and Stoic materialism with Plato's transcendent realm to arrive at a congruent and coherent analysis of our human existence and its relation to the divine. Perhaps reacting to the evolving Christian intellectual stance, the Platonic focus underwent a subtle reorientation, visible especially in the Middle Platonic thinkers of the second and third centuries CE, away from the intelligible ideas located in a divine transcendent realm, towards a hierarchy of divine agents, led by one supreme god, that was responsible for the creation and administration of the universe.

The rich conversations that accompanied Platonic, Aristotelian, and Stoic material into the early centuries of our era have been the focus of increased attention especially over the past two decades. Harold Tarrant's study *Plato's First Interpreters* (2000) focuses on Plato's Middle Platonic interpreters and sets them in relation to Plato's early successors in the Academy as well as his Neoplatonic successors. Tarrant discusses the concepts of doctrinal content and genre assumed by these authors, and traces the reception of individual dialogues such as the *Gorgias, Parmenides, Sophist, Cratylus,* and *Politicus,* and the *Philebus.* The volume *The Origins of the Platonic System: Platonisms of the Early Empire and Their Philosophical Contexts* (2009) edited by Mauro Bonazzi and Jan Opsomer carefully evaluates the process of doctrinal systemization by philosophical authors from the first century BCE onwards, and emphasizes the emergence of Platonic doctrine as the result of intellectual encounters of Platonic and Platonizing authors with Aristotelian, Stoic, and Pythagorean writings. Discussions on the development of individual philosophical schools are presented in Malcolm Schofield's edited volume *Plato, Aristotle and Pythagoras in the First Century BC* (2013).

With a specific focus on the *Timaeus* as the central point of reference for representatives of the Platonic tradition, Ada Babette Neschke-Hentschke's edited volume *Le Timée de Platon: Contributions à l'Histoire de sa Réception* (2000) sets the interpretations of the dialogue by a range of ancient authors, such as Galen, Calcidius, Proclus, and Boethius, in relation to the views of Marsilio Ficino, A.N. Whitehead, and others. The volume *Ancient Approaches to Plato's Timaeus* (2003), edited by Robert Sharples and Anne Sheppard, explores the dialogue through thematic contexts and through the eyes of individual interpreters such as Theophrastus, Epicurus, Philo, Calcidius, and Proclus. Finally, Francesco Celia's and Angela Ulacco's *Il Timeo: Esegesi Greche, Arabe, Latine* (2012) traces the dialogue's history of reception in the Arabic and Latin world by examining interpretations by Academic, Middle Platonic, and Neoplatonic authors.

At this point, let me add a methodological note. For my discussion of the Timaean doctrine across the centuries I will apply the traditional labels to the periods under focus. I will use the term Middle Platonism when referring to the period from roughly the first century CE until the time of Plotinus, who marks the transition to Neoplatonism. I maintain this traditional chronological division simply to impose a rough framework within which we may situate the authors under focus. I do not wish to suggest that the intellectual development that occurred during this time frame lent itself to as clear-cut and simple a structure as may be implied by this method – indeed, the further we engage with the doctrinal settings of our authors, the more blurred the lines of demarcation appear between what should be considered Hellenistic, Middle Platonic and Neoplatonic, non-Christian and Christian material. While I will, therefore, attempt to place the individual doctrinal elements and influences we encounter in our authors into their appropriate time frames, it is not my primary aim to pinpoint exegetical affiliation. Instead, it is my wish to show that the contributions of each author discussed in the subsequent chapters deserve to be examined as self-contained, coherent, and original approaches to Plato's *Timaeus* in their own right.

Roman Philosophy

A consequence of the increased attention paid to post-Hellenistic philosophy has been the rise in profile also of Roman philosophical writers. Writing philosophy did not come naturally to Roman authors, and we have no knowledge of Latin philosophical writings preceding those of Varro, Cicero, and Lucretius in the first century BCE aside, perhaps, from low-quality manuals without much intellectual and literary pretense that may have circulated in Roman aristocratic settings.[2] The efforts of these Roman authors were encouraged by contemporary historical events that had seen the dissolution of the Greek philosophical schools, accelerated by the newly established Roman empire from 27 BCE, and the spread of philosophers and their ideas away from their centralized Greek institutions towards Rome. The dispersed generation of philosophers relied increasingly on the authority of their masters' writings that now provided a unifying ideological frame of reference where physical cohesion was no longer possible. At the same time, the shift of power towards Rome ensured the continued popularity of Greek philosophy among the Roman educated élite. With Greek philosophical literature and language restricted to upper-class Romans, many of whom held a political office for which they had received a thorough

---

[2] Cf. Chapter 2, n. 1.

rhetorical education, it is no surprise that rhetorical methodology would contribute to the distinctive character of Roman philosophical writing.

The past decades have seen the publication of numerous studies of Roman philosophy, sometimes under the blanket of Hellenistic philosophy, for instance, *The Cambridge History of Hellenistic Philosophy* edited by Keimpe Algra et al. (1999), and *Post-Hellenistic Philosophy. A Study of its Development from the Stoics to Origen.* by George Boys-Stones (2001). Other volumes set Roman philosophy in relation to the Hellenistic systems, for instance, *Philosophy in the Roman Empire* (2007) by Michael Trapp, and *The Cambridge Companion to Greek and Roman Philosophy* (2003) edited by David Sedley. An important contribution that helped stress the distinct character of Roman philosophy is the two-volume study *Philosophia Togata* (1989 and 1997) edited by Miriam Griffin and Jonathan Barnes, and worthy of mention is, moreover, Mark Morford's *The Roman Philosophers* (2002). The most systematic study of the Latin philosophical tradition is Stephen Gersh's *Middle Platonism and Neoplatonism: The Latin Tradition* in two volumes (1986). This exhaustive survey approaches the individual authors by tracing exegetical references under unifying themes such as 'God', 'Form', and 'Nature'.

In the case of the individual authors under focus in the present study, J.G.F. Powell's edited volume *Cicero the Philosopher* (1995) is noteworthy as the first study that reflects the renewed interest in Cicero's *philosophica* during the final decades of the last century in a series of philosophical, historical, and philological investigations that have helped absolve Cicero of the charge of unoriginality and eclecticism. What is more, I owe many insights to David Sedley's 'Cicero and the *Timaeus*' (2013), a study on which I build in Chapter 2. A recent topical contribution to Cicero's philosophical writings is the volume *Cicero's De Finibus: Philosophical Approaches* edited by J. Annas and G. Betegh (2015), which highlights Cicero's authorial role in his portrayal of Hellenistic ethics with the help of philosophical, historical, and methodological approaches to the treatise. Worthy of note here, in particular, is the contribution to the volume by Charles Brittain who, after a careful analysis of evidence in Cicero's *De finibus*, concludes that Cicero may have adopted a rather more radical, Carneadean type of scepticism instead of the probabilist Philonian type that is usually associated with him.

Apuleius' writings are the focus of two examinations that coincide in their aim of placing him in the setting of the Second Sophistic. Gerald Sandy's *The Greek World of Apuleius* (1997) stresses the connection of the Roman author with the Greek sophists and the broader Greek cultural background, while Stephen Harrison's *Apuleius: A Latin Sophist* (2000) considers the Apuleian corpus in its entirety, combining a focus on the specifically Roman aspects of Apuleius' sophistic identity with a rich discussion of testimonia and individual fragments. Three recent studies are noteworthy. Richard Fletcher's contribution *Apuleius' Platonism. The Impersonation of Philosophy* (2014) encourages us to reappraise Apuleius' overall literary and philosophical achievement and what he terms his 'idiosyncratic brand of Platonism' (p. vii). Likewise, Claudio Moreschini's *Apuleius and the Metamorphoses of Platonism* (2015), an accessible and erudite discussion of all aspects of Apuleius' philosophical thought, offers a rather more positive evaluation of the role of rhetoric in Apuleius' Platonism. Finally, in his recent volume *A New Work by Apuleius: The Lost Third Book of the De Platone* (2016) Justin A. Stover argues that a previously unknown Latin work, the *Compendiosa expositio* (*exp.*), which appears in a thirteenth-century manuscript along with other Latin *philosophica*, was composed by Apuleius and intended by him as the third book of the *De Platone et eius Dogmatis*.[3]

In the case of Calcidius Gretchen Reydams-Schils, John Magee and Béatrice Bakhouche have considerably furthered our understanding of this author's underestimated

---

[3] Cf. Chapter 3, n. 1.

contribution to the Platonic heritage, and have sparked a renewed interest in the Calcidian oeuvre. Notable studies are, among others, Professor Reydams-Schils's *Demiurge and Providence: Stoic and Platonist Readings of Plato's* Timaeus (1999), and her edited volume *Plato's Timaeus as Cultural Icon* (2003). Professor Bakhouche's carefully researched approach to Calcidius and the philosophical influences on his thought are summarized in the two volumes of her French edition of Calcidius, *Calcidius: Commentaire au Timée de Platon* (2011). A significant recent advance for Calcidian scholarship is John Magee's first English translation of Calcidius' translation and commentary on the *Timaeus* (2016).

Following the seminal contributions, in the mid-twentieth century, to Augustinian scholarship by P. Courcelle, H. Chadwick, A.H. Armstrong, and J.J. O'Meara, numerous recent investigations offer a narrower topical approach to the subjects touched upon in the present study. Helpful examinations of Augustine's creation narrative and his concept of time are found in S. Knuuttila's 'Time and Creation in Augustine' (2001), and J.W. Carter's study 'St. Augustine on Time, Time Numbers, and Enduring Objects' (2011), both of which build on the important earlier work by Roland Teske in these fields. The study *Christ and the Just Society in the Thought of Augustine* by R. Dodaro (2004) examines Augustine's thoughts on the impact of Christ's mediation against the background of political and ethical views. L. Gioia's *The Theological Epistemology of Augustine's De Trinitate* (2008) studies the epistemological impact of human sinfulness and redemption in the context of the doctrine of soteriology. Worthy of note is, moreover, William E. Mann's edited volume *Augustine's Confessions: Philosophy in Autobiography* (2014), which explores Augustine's concept of the will, his eudaimonism, the role of philosophical perplexity in our ascent to the truth, his theories of time and eternity, and his interpretation of intelligible matter, among other themes that emerge in the *Confessions*.

Plato's *Timaeus* and the
Latin Tradition

The present study discusses the interpretation of Plato's *Timaeus* by Cicero, Apuleius, Calcidius, and Augustine. It is intended to add to the above-named examinations of these authors by developing a more complete and coherent portrayal of each as an interpreter of Plato. I examine how these authors created new contexts and settings for the intellectual heritage they received and thereby contributed to the construction of the complex and multifaceted genre of Roman Platonism. Crucially, I will take advantage of each author's treatment of Plato's *Timaeus* as a continuous point of reference. This approach offers the unique possibility to illustrate the individuality and originality of each writer in his engagement with a Greek philosophical text. Each author chooses a specific vocabulary, methodology, and literary setting for his appropriation of Timaean doctrine such as he finds it in the dialogue or in his exegetical sources. To deliver an authentic portrayal of our Latin interpreters, I will provide a thorough examination of each author's broader intellectual framework, his philosophical method and outlook, as well as his authorial agenda and chosen genre for his treatment of the *Timaeus*. In the case of Cicero, Apuleius, and Calcidius, I will argue, in particular, that Greek–Latin translation and paraphrase takes on the role of an exegetical tool that proves an essential part of these authors' philosophical project. With Plato's *Timaeus* as the unifying reference point, I am able to provide a concrete example that allows us to set an author's work in relation to his Greek primary and secondary sources, and to illustrate noteworthy instances of interrelation and overlap between the Latin authors themselves.

I consider this approach complementary to those studies that assess Roman philosophical writings predominantly according to their value to the Quellenforscher. No doubt, the latter approach remains invaluable for our understanding of the transmission of knowledge and the emergence of a systemized Platonic doctrine. Nevertheless, too strict a focus on the meticulous tracing of doctrinal elements in our Roman authors risks leaving us with the impression of little more than the accumulation of Platonic echoes. The comprehensive nature of my examination, it is hoped, will counteract such a disintegrated view, and show that each author offers a coherent and nuanced treatment of Timaean doctrine that has not yet been appreciated to the full.

In Chapter 1 I sketch out the contents of Plato's *Timaeus* and introduce its central themes. Particular focus is given to a dilemma that has attracted attention from the dialogue's first dissemination and continues to puzzle scholars to the present day: should the Timaean creation account be read in literal or metaphorical terms? My discussion of this apparent interpretative impasse provides the reader with the information necessary to appreciate some of the more complex exegetical responses to Plato's dialogue by our authors. The remainder of this chapter deals predominantly with such interpretative topics as are relevant to my discussion in Chapters 2 to 5.

Each of the subsequent chapters is divided into subsections that examine the author's intellectual background, his Plato and Platonism, and his specific engagement with the *Timaeus*, with the last section discussing the author's interpretation of Timaean motifs or language and his method of incorporating the Platonic material into a new literary setting. Under these headings I allow for considerable flexibility and adapt my focus in each chapter to the individual strengths and interests of the author.

Chapter 2 discusses Cicero's translation of the *Timaeus*, set in relation to his philosophical treatises. Since Cicero's Timaean project is perhaps the most complex compared to the other authors, I will develop this chapter at some length. First discussing his agenda as a translator of Plato, I then focus on Cicero's possible motivation for turning towards the *Timaeus* and, in turn, the reasons he may have had for excluding his translation of the dialogue from his published writings. Furthermore, I show how, with the help of certain terminological modifications, Cicero was able to reframe the Timaean creation account in a manner that would have aligned it with sceptical policy, thereby appropriating the dialogue for the sceptical Academy. In this context, my particular emphasis is on the rhetorical aspects of the Academy's investigative method, which, Cicero recognized, was a tool most formidably suited to philosophical investigation.

Chapter 3 examines Apuleius' attempt to present to his audience a coherent Platonic doctrine by assuming the role of a priest and mediator between Plato's divine authority and the initiates of Platonic wisdom. What is more, I identify several lexical and exegetical items we re-encounter in Calcidius' commentary on the *Timaeus*, discussed in Chapter 4, such as his theories on demons, providence, and fate. The parallels we find in these two authors are examples for the continuity and systemized treatment of specific themes original to Plato's dialogue. Particular focus is given to Apuleius' cosmology, a complex theory that is intended to set out the relations between a transcendent divinity and the sublunary realm, and from which will emerge an interesting dynamic between the author's exegetical stance in his *De Platone et eius dogmate* and his *De mundo*, a translation of the Ps.-Aristotelian treatise *Peri kosmou*. With the help of subtle adjustments, Apuleius balances Platonic and Aristotelian nuances in a manner that leaves us with the impression of a more or less coherent exegetical programme on his part.

With Calcidius, my focus lies on the author's exegetical method. I show that his translation of the *Timaeus* and his commentary on the dialogue form two intrinsically linked components of an exegetical method that is intended to guide the student to the knowledge of the truth. Calcidius' translation aims at the simplification of specialist terminology and at an increased access to Platonic dogma for a non-specialist audience, thereby laying the groundwork for the didactic programme of his commentary. What is more, I examine how Calcidius merges his role as a commentator with that of Timaeus, the narrator of Plato's dialogue, which enables Calcidius to present his exegesis as an authentic insight into Platonic dogma. Additional sections address 'Calcidius the Translator', and the doctrinal parallels between Calcidian and Apuleian exegesis.

Given that Augustine approaches the *Timaeus* through Cicero's Latin translation, one of my aims in Chapter 5 is to illustrate the extent to which specific renderings in Cicero's Latin text impact on Augustine's understanding of Plato's cosmology and metaphysics. Since Augustine often attributes to Plato views that are easily aligned with Christian dogma, he finds himself able to corroborate the Christian stance by drawing on Plato's own words (via Cicero). Individual sections in this chapter discuss the manner in which Augustine's creation narrative has been shaped by the encounters between Neoplatonist and Christian writers, and draw attention to Augustine's polemical treatment of Apuleius' demonology, which Augustine exposes as self-contradictory by pointing, once again, to passages from the *Timaeus*, thereby turning Plato against his own disciple. What is more, Augustine's discussion of matter exhibits several noteworthy parallels to Calcidius' treatment of this topic.

Naturally within the framework of the present study I can do justice neither to every aspect of Plato's *Timaeus*, nor to each of the authors and their vast combined output. What is more, the selective line-up of authors in the present investigation has been determined by various criteria. Firstly, it focuses on those authors whose Timaean exegesis, in my view, results in the most original and distinctive combinations of philosophical and methodological features. Secondly, I aim to exhibit an engagement with the *Timaeus* in a variety of literary settings. The genres chosen by our authors are: translation intended as a part of a philosophical dialogue (Cicero), translation in combination with philosophical commentary (Calcidius), paraphrase, translation, moralizing lecture, and 'textbook' survey of Platonic doctrine (Apuleius), and the autobiographical, often polemical manifesto of Christian doctrine in the case of Augustine.

Finally, it is my aim to showcase Latin interpreters of Plato from various periods. While I consider Cicero's *Timaeus* translation to represent the sceptical Academy, Apuleius offers a 'classic' Middle Platonic approach. Calcidius' stance, even though it strikes me as overall closer to Middle Platonism, shows Neoplatonic tinges. Augustine's Christian outlook, in turn, deeply influenced by Neoplatonic perspectives, makes for a fascinating interplay with the Platonic doctrine he draws from Cicero's translation, which is itself a relict from an earlier period of Platonism, and which is used by Augustine to polemical effect against Apuleius' Middle Platonic stance. As noted previously, the doctrinal similarities between Augustine and Calcidius that emerge in the context of the authors' interpretation of matter make for an intriguing comparison. These and other points of contact, both direct and indirect, between our four authors recommend their writings for a joint analysis of the kind I shall attempt in the present study. Among them, Augustine stands out since, unlike the others, he produced neither a translation of the *Timaeus*, nor longer stretches of recognizable paraphrase. Nevertheless, Augustine's treatment of the dialogue is a crucial witness to the confluence of various terminological and doctrinal features we encounter in Cicero and Apuleius, in particular. Precisely because Augustine could not rely on an extensive knowledge of Greek, these authors counted among the various Latin channels of transmission through which he accessed Platonic philosophy. In Augustine's engagement with the *Timaeus*, therefore, earlier influences come together, resulting in a striking exegetical synthesis.

CHAPTER I

THE SETTING: PLATO'S *TIMAEUS*

The *Timaeus* recounts the coming to be of our cosmos in an exhaustive explanatory account. Given the sheer magnitude of this topic, I am unable to provide here a full summary of the many details contained in the Timaean creation story.[1] I will instead introduce its key elements, draw attention to a number of interpretative matters that have provoked complex responses from the ensuing tradition, and thereby set out the backdrop to the dialogue's treatment at the hands of our Latin interpreters. I will begin with a basic synopsis of the dialogue, followed by an overview of those parts of the text that particularly engaged our authors' minds.

Dialogue Content

At the outset of the *Timaeus* Socrates reminds his interlocutors, Timaeus, Critias, and Hermocrates, of a discussion they had on the previous day (17c). The topic of this discussion was a city's best possible political design, and the city's inhabitants. The type of society discussed included the presence of guardians, men and women who, having undergone training and education that had rendered them 'both spirited and philosophical' (18a),[2] lived separately from the other societal groups and were charged with defending the city in times of war. While these and other references in Socrates' description of the earlier discussion resemble topics that are discussed in the *Republic*, his description is rather too incomplete to allow for the assumption that we ought to consider the *Timaeus* a straightforward sequel

---

[1] For a basic, and succinct survey of the dialogue's contents, along with brief discussions of the various interpretative issues, see Zeyl 2000: xiii–lxxxix. See further Brisson 1974 and the classic commentaries by Taylor 1928 and Cornford 1937.

[2] All translations are my own except where indicated otherwise.

to this dialogue. We may fare best if we assume that the discussion which had preceded the *Timaeus* explored a number of themes that are developed at greater length in the *Republic*, without insisting on a more direct relationship between the two dialogues.[3]

Socrates' starting point for the discussion recorded in the *Timaeus* is the nature of the inhabitants of an ideally structured society. The previous conversation, it appears, had merely described them in theoretical terms. Socrates now expresses the wish to observe these inhabitants in action. Prompted by this request, Critias proposes to relate an account, passed on to him by his famous ancestor Solon, about the inhabitants of primaeval Athens. Victors over mighty Atlantis, these Athenians of old, Critias believes, may be the type of society Socrates has in mind. Short of launching directly into his portrayal of ancestral Athens, however, Critias suggests they start at the very beginning:[4] first, the politician, philosopher, and astronomer Timaeus will describe the coming to be of the universe, leading up to the creation of humans and other living creatures.

At the centre of Timaeus' speaking part is a creation account in which a divine craftsman creates our cosmos by imposing order on chaotic materials. Timaeus initially frames his account with the dualistic metaphysical structure familiar from other dialogues. An intelligible realm of being, *to on* τὸ ὄν[5] ('that which is'), that contains everlasting and immutable forms is distinguished from the sphere of coming to be, *to gignomenon* τὸ γιγνόμενον ('that which comes to be'), in which our universe,

---

[3] Along with many ancient commentators, including Calcidius (*Commentary on Plato's Timaeus*, chapter 5, p. 206, l. 19. All references to Calcidius are according to Bakhouche 2011), Taylor 1928: 46 considered the *Timaeus* to be the sequel to the *Republic*. Against this view see e.g. Cornford 1937: 4–5; see also Gill 1977, and Johansen 2004: 7–23, who argues that the *Timaeus–Critias* is a thematic expansion of the *Gorgias* and the *Republic*.

[4] Foreshadowing Timaeus' methodological programme introduced at *Tim.* 29b2f: 'With regard to every subject matter, it is most important to begin at the topic's natural beginning.'

[5] I will retain the Greek script in quotations and discussions that make reference to specific Greek source texts while transliterating individual terms in the context of more general discussions. I am aware that this distinction is not always clear-cut, and that this policy will, at times, result in a juxtaposition of Greek and English script.

an object of sense perception, is located (27d5ff.). Our physical world is formed by the demiurge from the materials at his disposal in the likeness of an intelligible paradigm, the 'eternal living being', perhaps best understood to represent the totality of intelligible forms whose physical counterparts are to form our universe. These counterparts, the components of our natural world, arise and perish within a substrate or medium that Timaeus terms χώρα, 'space', and ὑποδοχή, the 'receptacle' of physical objects.

Mirroring the intelligible model as far as its physical nature allows, the universe is itself constructed as a divine living creature that possesses soul and intellect. Despite his initial focus on the construction of the cosmic body, Timaeus stresses that the order of his narrative does not reflect the actual order of creative acts. Prior to the formation of the physical universe, the demiurge constructed the cosmic soul, superior to the former in seniority and nobility. The cosmic soul is generated by the demiurge out of the ingredients 'being', 'sameness', and 'difference', which are blended together. These rather obscure ingredients reflect the soul's intellective faculties that allow it to recognize the objects of its thought. In other words, Timaeus establishes an ontological affinity between soul, as the subject engaged in thought, and the objects of its thought.

The cosmic soul is woven into the physical universe and, penetrating the latter from within, steers and regulates the movements of the celestial bodies through its own motions. Simultaneously with the creation of these heavenly bodies the god creates time. The regular orbits of the fixed stars and planets serve as instruments that, from the very start of their existence, determine and safeguard the temporal extensions pertaining to the created universe. Despite the world's own perishability owing to its physical nature, its sempiternity is vouchsafed by the will of its divine creator.

Human soul claims kinship with the cosmic soul. It is constructed by the demiurge out of the same ingredients, albeit of less purity, and thus exhibits the same intellective faculties as its cosmic counterpart. Upon the soul's conjunction with a mortal body that is, in turn, equipped with sense organs adapted to its physical environment, it initially experiences disturbances caused by its exposure to these surroundings. Its potential success in controlling these disturbances would result in its return to the celestial sphere, where it is no longer exposed to the deteriorating influences of an incarnate existence.

The creation of the corporeal parts of the various living creatures that inhabit the universe is delegated to subordinate divine agents, who are themselves created by the demiurge. With regard to the popular divinities familiar from the Olympian stage, Timaeus stresses that any account of their origin is beyond human understanding, a view that resigns us to accepting the accounts propagated by 'the children of the gods', 'even though they speak without plausible or compelling proofs' (40d8–e2). In what follows, Timaeus supplies a divine ancestry that begins with Heaven and Earth, noting that the poets' authority on the subject is based on their professed kinship with the gods.[6] Whether or not we choose to take seriously Timaeus' appeal to their authority, it is clear that the Olympian deities are sidelined in his creation narrative, which, of course, deviates from the traditional theogonies familiar from poetic accounts. Following a detailed description of human physiology, Timaeus concludes his account with remarks concerning the creation of women and of the living creatures inhabiting the remaining parts of our natural world.

The Timaean narrative portrays the universe as a teleologically structured whole. Chaos is transformed into orderly beauty, an aesthetic feature that reflects the purposeful cooperation of the world's harmoniously arranged components. The universe is as beautiful and as good as it can be, exhibiting a kinship of aesthetic and ethical value that coincides in the Greek word καλός (e.g. 29e5). What is more, this twofold value is the design of intellect, represented by the demiurge whose own goodness, which he wishes to bestow upon his creation, is the driving

---

[6] Perhaps a reference to poets such as Musaeus and Orpheus, cf. *Rep.* 346e3–4, where Adeimantus scoffs at those who use the testimony of poets like Musaeus and Orpheus, 'children of the moon and the Muses, as they say', to argue that gods may be swayed by ignoble men through sacrifice and prayer.

force behind the creation process. In order to make the cosmos good, he imposes rationality upon it. He incorporates intellect into the cosmic soul, whose rational activity, through its interconnectedness with the cosmic body, results in the orderly, spherical rotations of the planets. Human soul, through its material kinship with cosmic soul, is the cognitive link that allows us to participate in this cosmic rationality. By aligning our soul's revolutions, our rational activity, with heaven's spherical motions, the manifestation of cosmic soul's engagement in rational thought, we become orderly and good.

Methodology

Our understanding of Timaeus' narrative method hinges on the apparently ambivalent characterization of his account as both μῦθος and λόγος. Are we dealing with a μῦθος of our world's first origins, a mythical tale without any serious claim to coherence or scientific accuracy? Perhaps Timaeus is offering a metaphorical attempt to illustrate the underlying nature of, and relationships among, the various physical components and mechanisms in our world? Or maybe we are dealing with a scientific λόγος after all, with an exposition, albeit in polished prose, of natural philosophy? Alternatively again, our desire to distinguish between both genres may be ill-advised: the dialogue's synthesis of μῦθος and λόγος, far from indicating a deliberate methodological strategy, may carry no great significance, with both terms being used interchangeably. Let us turn to the narrator in search for clarity.

In a notorious passage, *Tim.* 29b2–d3, Timaeus reflects upon the nature and scope of his creation account. We are advised, in the first of many instances, that those λόγοι which offer an interpretation of subject matter pertaining to the physical realm, itself an εἰκών or 'image' formed in likeness of the intelligible model, achieve likelihood with regard to their truth status: 'One ought to determine ... that the accounts concerning that which has been fashioned in the likeness of [the intelligible model], and which is itself a likeness, ought to be [fashioned] in a like manner, in the likeness of those [accounts that treat of the intelligible model itself].'[7] Timaeus' observation rests on the preceding premise that accounts which serve as the 'exegetes' (ἐξηγηταί) of a particular subject matter are akin to the very material they treat: 'In the case of the likeness and its model, [we ought to determine that] the accounts bear a kinship (συγγενεῖς ὄντας) to the subject matter of which they serve as exegetes' (29b3–5). (In the Greek text, we note how the effect of the alike-sounding syllables ἐκεῖνο, ἀπεικασθέντος, εἰκόνος, εἰκότας, and ἐκείνων underlines the statement's very own assertion by heeding its advice.) The kinship Timaeus has in mind is of the following type: accounts that treat of the intelligible realm, in which the everlasting and unchanging forms are located, are themselves 'unshakeable' in their consistency and irrefutable. In turn, accounts that deal with our physical cosmos, itself the 'likeness' (εἰκών) of an intelligible paradigm, are aptly characterized by Timaeus as 'likely' (εἰκότες). Timaeus underlines his train of thought by drawing an analogy between the ontological status, or class, of an account's subject matter and the degree of its epistemological reliability. As the ontological class 'being' (οὐσία) stands to the ontological class 'coming to be' (γένεσις), so the maximum degree of epistemological reliability, 'truth' (ἀλήθεια), stands to the lower degree of epistemological reliability 'convincingness' (πίστις).

Timaeus takes pains to remind his listeners repeatedly[8] that he is offering an εἰκὼς λόγος, or εἰκὼς μῦθος, which suggests that these expressions carry a programmatic function for his investigation and are crucial for our understanding of the dialogue. But what exactly does Timaeus mean by this characterization? Unsurprisingly, the scholarship on the topic is extensive[9] and

---

7 [διοριστέον τοὺς λόγους …] τοῦ πρὸς μὲν ἐκεῖνο [παράδειγμα] ἀπεικασθέντος, ὄντος δὲ εἰκόνος εἰκότας ἀνὰ λόγον τε ἐκείνων ὄντας.
8 Reference to the εἰκὼς λόγος or εἰκὼς μῦθος occurs again at *Tim.* 30b7, 44d1, 48c1, 48d2, 49b6, 53d5–6, 55d1, 56a1, 56d1, 57d6, 59c6, 68d2, 72d7, 90e8.
9 For instance, Baltes 1976, Bryan 2012, Burnyeat 2009, Howald 1922, Donini 1988, and Meyer-Abich 1973.

I shall merely outline some of the most important aspects pertaining to Timaeus' methodology.[10] Εἰκώς as it appears in our dialogue, conveys the sense of 'portraying an image', inasmuch as an εἰκὼς λόγος is identified by Timaeus as the type of account that deals with an image, an εἰκών, such as our universe. This relation is reinforced by the similarity of both terms, εἰκών, 'likeness', and εἰκώς 'likely'.[11] The epistemological status of Timaeus' account is εἰκώς, 'likely', due to the ontological status of its subject matter, the universe, a likeness or a copy belonging to the sphere of change.[12]

The notion of probability conveyed by the term εἰκώς has sometimes been interpreted as that of scientific hypothesis. On this view, the Timaean εἰκώς λόγος is understood to be a provisional or approximate estimation, as opposed to accurate scientific knowledge.[13] Others, as indicated above, emphasize Timaeus' occasional use of the expression εἰκώς

---

[10] The following paragraphs appear in a much condensed and modified form in Hoenig 2013.

[11] Plato plays on this similarity also at *Rep.* 517d1 and *Soph.* 236a8.

[12] Bryan 2012: 114–60, especially 139–60, emphasizes such a meaning of εἰκώς which, she argues, expresses a positive relation between model and likeness. She rejects the notion that Timaeus' εἰκώς λόγος should be considered 'deficient' when compared to accounts that treat of the intelligible realm. Burnyeat 2009: 179–80 suggests 'reasonable' for εἰκώς at *Tim.* 29c2 instead of the commonly accepted 'likely' as an initial interpretation of the text, and 'probable' as the second reading, an inference based on the fact that the most reasonable (in the sense of: 'disclosing the workings of reason in the cosmos') account coincides with that which is most probable. εἰκώς is to be regarded as an 'aspiration' for Timaeus whose task it is to provide a μῦθος that is appropriate to its subject matter (ibid. 178).

[13] See, for instance, Taylor 1928: 59. A clear witness to the association of the εἰκώς λόγος, or μῦθος, with fictitious mythical narrative, as opposed to scientific inquiry, is Susemihl's translation of 1977, in which Timaeus at 29b5ff. declares that accounts dealing with subject matter that is abiding and firm and discernible by intellect (τοῦ μὲν οὖν μονίμου καὶ βεβαίου καὶ μετὰ νοῦ καταφανοῦς μονίμους) are likewise abiding and firm, and 'soweit es überhaupt **wissenschaftlichen Erörterungen** zukommt, unwiderleglich und unerschütterlich zu sein, darf man es hieran in nichts fehlen lassen', translating 'as far as it befits *scientific* **discussions** to be irrefutable and unshakeable ...' for καθ' ὅσον οἷόν τε καὶ ἀνελέγκτοις προσήκει **λόγοις** εἶναι καὶ ἀνικήτοις. At the close of the passage Susemihl's Timaeus warns his listeners that, in the case of those accounts dealing with subject matter pertaining to the sphere of coming to be and change, it is fitting '[sich] damit zu begnügen, wenn **die Dichtung** nur die Wahrscheinlichkeit für sich hat und wir nichts darüber hinaus verlangen dürfen', translating 'it befits us to be content if **the myth** merely holds probability ...' for ἀγαπᾶν χρή ... ὥστε περὶ τούτων **τὸν εἰκότα μῦθον** ἀποδεχομένους πρέπει τούτου μηδὲν ἔτι πέρα ζητεῖν.

Methodology

μῦθος,[14] instead of εἰκὼς λόγος, to describe his own narrative
as indicative of the fact that the dialogue should be read as
a myth, a fictional story or tale that stands in contrast to a
rational, scientific inquiry. This viewpoint complements the
assumption that μῦθος and λόγος should not be understood
as synonyms,[15] but that Plato wished to stress the mythical
character of the Timaean account. Further, μῦθος has been
taken to describe a type of account that relates to the human
sphere and that stands in contrast to a type of knowledge, or
reality, humans cannot attain.[16] Finally, Plato's dialogue has
been interpreted as a combination of both λόγος and μῦθος,
a rationally argued myth centring on the creation of the
universe.[17]

It is precisely the ambiguity of Timaeus' language that
presents an opportunity for our Latin interpreters to put on
display the originality of their own approach to Timaeus' εἰκὼς
λόγος. The choice between the various possible approaches to
the text, a choice faced by the reader of Plato's dialogue and
the Platonic interpreter alike, will to a considerable extent be
influenced by his or her interpretation of several key elements contained in the Timaean cosmology, to which I will
now turn.

---

[14] Apart from its appearance at 29d2, see 59c6 and 69b1.
[15] A viewpoint that rejects the position of Vlastos 1965: 380–3 and, more recently, Rowe 2003.
[16] Johansen 2004: 62–4. Meyer-Abich 1973: 30–1 suggests that the mention of μῦθος at 29d2 echoes Critias' Atlantis story whose contents, Athens's primaeval past, depict a λόγος compared to the μῦθος the Athenians believe to be their past while they remain unaware of prior events erased from their knowledge due to natural catastrophes. Like the Athenians, humans are unaware of the origins of their exist-ence and have access only to mythical self-knowledge as opposed to the true λόγος that reveals the beginnings of human existence. The latter can be attained by philo-sophical investigation.
[17] Johansen 2004: 63 argues that λόγος must be understood as describing the *genus* of accounts in general *as well as* describing a *particular* type of account within the genus λόγος which possesses a higher rationality than another type of account within the same genus: the μῦθος (63). Burnyeat 2009: 168–9 defines as the most important characteristic mark of a μῦθος, which he interprets in the strong sense of the word – 'myth' as opposed to 'story', 'tale' – to be its reference to the divine. The dialogue is a myth inasmuch as it is a theogony describing the coming to be of the created god, the sensible universe. An εἰκὼς μῦθος becomes an εἰκὼς λόγος, being a rational (i.e. 'describing the creator's rational reasoning') account of natural phil-osophy and, at the same time, a myth.

The Setting: Plato's *Timaeus*

An Interpretative Controversy

Any student of Plato's *Timaeus* will have to address an interpretative question of decisive significance for the understanding of the dialogue.[18] Did Plato have Timaeus offer to his interlocutors an actual creation account that identifies the cosmos as generated? Timaeus appears to suggest as much. He draws attention to the createdness of the universe at *Tim.* 27c4–5 where he describes his appointed task as 'producing speeches concerning the All, in what manner it has been created or else is uncreated' (τοὺς περὶ τοῦ παντὸς λόγους ποιεῖσθαί πη μέλλοντας, ἦ γέγονεν ἢ καὶ ἀγενές ἐστιν).[19] He begins this inquiry by drawing a preliminary distinction between the two ontological spheres of being and coming to be: 'what is that which always is and has no coming to be, and what is that which is always coming to be but never is?' (τί τὸ ὂν ἀεί, γένεσιν δὲ οὐκ ἔχον, καὶ τί τὸ γιγνόμενον μὲν ἀεί, ὂν δὲ οὐδέποτε, 27d6). Turning next to the ontological classification of the universe, he asks the all-important question 'whether [the All] has always been, having no origin of coming to be, or whether it has come to be, starting out from some origin' (πότερον ἦν ἀεί, γενέσεως ἀρχὴν ἔχων οὐδεμίαν, ἢ γέγονεν, ἀπ' ἀρχῆς τινος ἀρξάμενος, 28b6–7). The answer comes swiftly: 'it has come to be' (γέγονεν). He reaffirms his statement by declaring that the universe is subject to sense perception, and all things perceptible 'come to be and have been generated' (γιγνόμενα καὶ γεννητά, 28c1–2). As we saw in the previous section, he reminds his listeners, on several occasions, of the fact that his creation account is a likely story, a concession taken by some interpreters to undermine the overall credibility of his

---

[18] The classic study of this topic remains Baltes 1976, 1979. Cf. also Baltes and Dörrie 1998: 375–465.

[19] The accuracy of this reading is disputed and, due to its exegetical relevance, may have been the subject of frequent distortion. The manuscripts list ἦ γέγονεν ἢ καὶ ἀγενές ἐστιν (Burnet's A) and ἢ ... ἢ (F Y); Philoponus reads εἰ ... ἢ, Alcinous ἢ ... ἢ or ἢ ... εἰ, Porphyry, Iamblichus, and Proclus ἢ ... ἢ. It appears that ἢ ... ἢ is the preferred reading, and is, along with ἢ ... ἢ, considered 'neutral' with regard to its exegetical implications by Dillon 1989: 57–60, who discusses this passage and its variant readings in greater detail. See, however, Petrucci 2018: 147–53, who criticizes the notion of 'ideological emendation' in the case of Taurus.

account, instead of merely indicating Timaeus' doubt about the specific details that prompt his recurring reminders. But Timaeus nowhere indicates that the 'convincingness' of his words applies to his entire creation account.[20] Nevertheless, doubts with regard to the validity of a literal interpretation of his account arise from apparent inconsistencies in the narrative that threaten its internal coherence.[21] At 38b6–c3, Timaeus describes the creation of the cosmos as coinciding with the creation also of time (χρόνος δ' οὖν μετ' οὐρανοῦ γέγονεν). Time is created 'in accordance with the paradigm that is of an eternal nature' (κατὰ τὸ παράδειγμα τῆς διαιωνίας φύσεως). In his wish to replicate, as far as possible, the everlastingness of the intelligible model, the demiurge creates fixed celestial bodies whose orbiting movements mark the various extension of time (38c4–6), a perpetual image of eternity. This portrayal of events stands in apparent contradiction to other items in the narrative. Having identified the 'receptacle' as a third cosmological principle alongside being and coming to be, Timaeus describes how there occurred a reciprocal motion between this receptacle and the precursors of the physical elements that were contained in it and were moving in an erratic, disorderly fashion (52d2–53b5). According to Timaeus, these movements preceded the orderly structuring of the physical materials at the hands of the demiurge. If the sequence of events in his narrative were to unfold in chronological succession,[22] we would arrive at a scenario in which the disorderly motions in the receptacle occurred prior to the creation of time, in a time before time. It thus appears that Timaeus' narrative fails to provide a chronological frame in which the events portrayed can be coherently

---

[20] Noted, e.g. by Broadie 2012: 245.
[21] Parts of the following section appear in a much condensed and modified form in Hoenig 2014. See also the summary by Zeyl 2000: xx–xxv.
[22] Petrucci 2016 and 2018 (especially chapter 2) argues that the dilemma should be described as that of a 'sempiternalistic' creation vs. a 'temporal' creation, rather than that of a 'literal' vs. a 'metaphorical' interpretation of the Timaean creation account. More specifically, a 'literal' reading of the dialogue should not automatically be equated with a 'temporal' reading, given that non-temporal, 'literal' interpretations were held by a number of Platonic authors, as he argues.

located. A possible retort, pursued already by the dialogue's readers in antiquity, is to distinguish between pre-cosmic time and measured time that coincided with the creation of the cosmos. Taking the mention of time at 38b6–c3 to refer strictly to measured time avoids the pitfall of chronological inconsistency.[23] Further criticism of Timaeus' narrative has been prompted by the createdness of soul. Before the demiurge set to creating the universe, Timaeus informs us, he created the world soul. In minute mathematical detail, the narrator reconstructs the creation process of this soul which, upon the creation of the world's physical body (36d8–e1), was to permeate the latter in perpetual self-rotating motion. Emphasis is put upon its priority over body in terms of age and excellence: '[the demiurge] constructred soul as prior and more senior to body, both in terms of coming to be and in terms of virtue' (ὁ δὲ [δημιουργὸς] καὶ γενέσει καὶ ἀρετῇ προτέραν καὶ πρεσβυτέραν ψυχὴν σώματος … συνεστήσατο, 34c4–35a1), and on its having been created: it has 'come to be as the most excellent of things that have come to be at the hands of the most excellent of intelligible and eternal things' (τῶν νοητῶν ἀεί τε ὄντων ὑπὸ τοῦ ἀρίστου ἀρίστη γενομένη τῶν γεννηθέντων, 37a1–2). The assumption of a created soul clashes with Plato's description of the soul in the *Phaedrus*, where Socrates convinces Phaedrus that the soul's origin is uncreated (*Phaedr.* 245c9–d1). Such concerns appear less pressing if we desist from a unitarian perspective on Plato's philosophical positions, and allow for a developmental perspective, along with the assumption that the *Phaedrus* predated the composition of the *Timaeus*.

A further discrepancy between the *Timaeus* and the *Phaedrus* is the view, propagated by Socrates in the latter work at 245c9, that self-moving soul is 'the source and origin of motion to all things that move' (τοῖς ἄλλοις ὅσα κινεῖται … πηγὴ καὶ ἀρχὴ κινήσεως), a claim that appears incompatible with the Timaean

[23] Cf. Vlastos 1965: 409–14; Gloy 1986: 52–3. Sorabji 1983: 272–3 analyses the temporal vocabulary in Timaeus' narrative. He points *inter alia* at Plato's use of ποτε, πρίν, πρὸ τούτου, ὅτε, and of frequent past tenses in the passages *Tim.* 28b2–c2, 53a2–b5 and 69b2c2, all of which underline the notion of a pre-cosmic time.

pre-cosmic motion in the receptacle. Similarly, the Athenian of Plato's *Laws* describes the soul as 'identical with the first generation and motion of what is, has been, and will be' and 'the cause of all change and all motion in all things' (896a5–8;[24] cf. 892a2–c7, 899c6–7), a view once again incompatible with the assumption of chaotic, pre-cosmic motion as it is described by Timaeus whose account at no point identifies soul as a further principle alongside being, coming to be, and the receptacle.[25] This problem, however, does not disappear even if we understand the cosmic soul's creation along non-temporal lines. Soul's specific activity of rational thought, which manifests itself as regular, spherical motion, can no more easily be reconciled with the erratic motions in the receptacle. If inclined to press for doctrinal consistency between the *Timaeus* and other dialogues, we may take the references to soul as the origin and cause of all motion in the *Phaedrus* and the *Laws* to describe merely orderly, goal-directed motion, and thereby solve the problem of pre-cosmic erratic motion such as it appears in the *Timaeus*.

These and other arguments *pro* and *contra* a temporal interpretation are still reiterated today, while recent scholarship has seen a reinforcement of the literalist side.[26] Let us review more closely the most influential opinions on either side of the debate, beginning with Plato's own contemporaries. Aristotle addresses the problematic scenario of a 'time before time' at *Met.* 11.6,[27] where he also mentions the difficulties inherent in the assumption of a created time in the context of the creation of the world soul. Given the fact that soul is posterior to (pre-cosmic) motion – a reference to *Tim.* 34c4–35a1 – it must be disqualified as a principle of movement (1072a1–3).[28]

---

[24] ἆρα ἔτι ποθοῦμεν μὴ ἱκανῶς δεδεῖχθαι ψυχὴν ταὐτὸν ὂν καὶ τὴν πρώτην γένεσιν καὶ κίνησιν τῶν τε ὄντων καὶ γεγονότων καὶ ἐσομένων καὶ πάντων αὖ τῶν ἐναντίων τούτοις, ἐπειδή γε ἀνεφάνη μεταβολῆς τε καὶ κινήσεως ἁπάσης αἰτία ἅπασιν;
[25] The specific problems of a temporal reading of the creation account have been set out in greater detail by Baltes 1996: 77–85 and Sorabji 1983: 268–75.
[26] Most recently Broadie 2012, especially chapter 7.
[27] Ar. *Met.* 11.6 1071b6ff., cf. *Phys.* 8 251b10–27; cf. Sorabji 1983: 279–80.
[28] Aristotle incorrectly reports Plato to have maintained that *soul*, rather than time, came to be 'along with the heavens' (1072a2). Cf. Baltes 1976: 8–18 for a more detailed synopsis of Aristotle's arguments against a created universe; further Cherniss 1944: 414–78 and Sorabji 1983: 276–83.

Moreover, Aristotle took issue with the idea of a divine agent that is immediately involved with the creation of the cosmos.[29] Perhaps prompted by Aristotle's criticism, the non-temporal reading of Plato's dialogue found favour with many ancient interpreters, for instance Plato's successor Xenocrates and his Academy.[30] It is again through Aristotle that we learn about their specific position. At *Cael.* 1.10 279b32–280a2 he mocks their claim that Plato had intended his creation account to be read *didaskalias charin*, 'for the sake of instruction', in the same manner as geometers would draw up and construct geometrical figures in order to facilitate their students' understanding of completed structures.[31] In neither case had an actual process of construction taken place. In a classic defence of the creationist interpretation Gregory Vlastos has pointed out, however, that a reading *didaskalias charin* cannot be directly connected with Plato,[32] and argued that the ascription of this position also to his pupil Speusippus and to Theophrastus is doubtful (the latter is reported to have believed that Plato 'perhaps', intended a reading *saphêneias charin*, 'for the sake of clarity', *Phys. op.* 11).[33] Nevertheless, the appeal to didactic or hypothetical method as a way of atoning for the incongruities in Timaeus' creation story gained support from numerous interpreters of Plato. Aetius, Plotinus, and Proclus are all credited with the belief in a creation account that had been set out *epinoiai* (in thought)[34] or *hupothesei* (by hypothesis).[35] Beyond these methodological aspects Platonists such

[29] The details of this charge against the Timaean divinity are discussed in my examination of Cicero's intepretation of Plato's dialogue.
[30] Plut. *Procr. an.* 3.1013A. It is thought by some that this was the position also of Speusippus, cf. fr. 94–5 ed. Isnardi Parente 1982. See, however, Baltes 1976: 19 and more generally 18–22; ibid. 1996: 81; Sorabji 1983: 271 and Broadie 2012: 244 with n. 3. For a critical discussion cf. Petrucci 2018: 45–52.
[31] Aristotle derides their argument, suggesting they had advanced it to vindicate their master's testimony, thereby coming to their own, i.e. the Academy's, help: ἢν δέ τινες βοήθειαν ἐπιχειροῦσι φέρειν ἑαυτοῖς τῶν λεγόντων ἄφθαρτον μὲν εἶναι γενόμενον δέ, οὐκ ἔστιν ἀληθής.
[32] Vlastos 1965 (reprint of Vlastos 1939): 383 n. 2.
[33] As is done by Taylor 1928 and Cherniss 1944.
[34] Reiterated recently by Baltes 1996: 80–2.
[35] Baltes 1976: 82.

26

as Taurus,[36] Crantor, and Xenocrates[37] are reported to have
regarded the overall aim of the dialogue as illuminating in
non-temporal fashion a causal correlation between the intelligent divinity and the mechanical processes at work in the living
cosmos. The efforts undertaken to bolster a non-temporal
reading are famously summarized by the second-century
Middle Platonist Calvenus Taurus. Philoponus at *Aet. mund.*
145.13–147.25 reports that Taurus distinguished four[38] senses
in which the cosmos may be characterized as γενητός, 'having
come to be':[39] γενητός describes (1) an object that, itself not
having come to be, is of the same *genus* as objects that *have*
come to be (i.e. some object may, for whatever reason, forever
be 'unseen' but still remain 'visible' in *genus*); (2) an object that
is composite 'in thought' even though it has never undergone
an actual process of 'being put together'; (3) an object eternally subjected to the process of coming to be and change;
and (4) an object whose existence is dependent on something
external, in the case of the cosmos, a dependency on god as its
causative agent on a higher metaphysical plane. For a non-temporal reading of Plato's terms γέγονεν, 'it has come to be', and
ἀρχή, 'origin', supporting evidence from the dialogue itself was
thought to be at hand. At *Tim.* 28b6, Timaeus asks whether
the cosmos has existed always, having no origin of coming to

---

36 Reported by Procl. *In Plat. Tim.* 1.76,1ff.
37 Plutarch *Procr. an.* 3.1013a ascribes to Crantor and Xenocrates an identical viewpoint. Baltes 1976: 82–3 counts as a variation of this position also what he terms the
  'physical' interpretation that appears, for instance, in Alcinous and Plutarch, and
  according to which Plato classified the cosmos as generated due to the fact that it
  was in a constant state of genesis. Baltes emphasizes as the common factor of both
  interpretations the dependence of the world's coming to be on a causative principle
  that safeguards its continuous state of coming to be, the main difference lying in
  the assumption of an *ongoing* correlative relation between cause and effect that is
  pushed by Baltes's physical interpretation, as opposed to the mere assumption of an
  ontological dependency between causative agent and its effected outcome.
38 Cf. Petrucci 2018: 36–45. Petrucci ascribes to Taurus a literal, sempiternalistic
  reading of the creation account. Cf. further Karamanolis 2006: 180–5, in particular
  181–2. Sedley 2013: 197–8 with nn. 24–5 suggests that Taurus distinguished five
  meanings of γενητός, as opposed to the four meanings usually found in this passage.
  According to the fifth meaning listed by Taurus, γενητός refers to objects that
  possess 'a bodily nature whose being consists in constant becoming', as is explained
  at Philop. *Aet. mund.* 147,21–5.
39 Philop. *Aet. mund.* 145,7–147,13. Cf. Baltes 1976: 106–8; Dillon 1996: 242–4.

The Setting: Plato's *Timaeus*

be, γενέσεως ἀρχὴν ἔχων οὐδεμίαν, or whether it has come to be, γέγονεν, having begun from *some* origin, ἀπ' ἀρχῆς τινος ἀρξάμενος, where the addition of τινος may be taken to sideline a temporal origin of the cosmos.[40] Plutarch and Atticus are known as a proponents of temporal creation[41] against many Platonist voices up until that time.[42] According to the testimony of Proclus, Plutarch assumed that there had been a pre-cosmic 'trace' of time present in the receptacle, the precursor of ordered and created time. Rejecting an uncreated universe Atticus firmly maintained a creation 'according to time', by distinguishing pre-cosmic and disorderly time from orderly time created in conjunction with the cosmos. The distinction between a pre-cosmic and disorderly concept of time as opposed to a post-creation measured type has been reiterated most notably by Vlastos.[43] What is more, Plutarch accounted for pre-cosmic motion by postulating the existence of a prior, irrational state of the world soul that was responsible for the chaotic movement in the receptacle before the creation of cosmos, an event that effected the coming to be of the already existing world soul as a rational and benign cosmic element.[44] Similarly, Plutarch distinguished chaotic matter, which existed prior to its ordering at the hands of the demiurge, from an orderly type of matter that came into being simultaneously with the cosmos. While Plutarch and Atticus are the most widely known adherents to a literal reading, it has been pointed out by Sedley[45] that more

[40] With τινος understood as an *alienans* qualification, denoting 'a beginning of some sort', i.e. a beginning that cannot be identified as such in its full common meaning which usually assumes a temporal aspect. Burnyeat (2002) identifies similar cases in Aristotle's *De Anima*, cf. 36f.
[41] Cf. Procl. *In Plat. Tim.* 2.276,31–277,7; further, Philop. *Aet. mund.* 211,11ff.; 519,22–5.
[42] Cf. Baltes 1976: 38–63; Sorabji 1983: 270.
[43] Vlastos 1965: 409–14. Vlastos' view that no ancient writer appreciated this distinction has been shown to be erroneous by Sorabji and Sedley, who point towards the evidence of Velleius' remarks in Cicero's *Nat. deor.* 1.21 and to the testimonies of Plutarch and Atticus.
[44] Plut. *Procr. an.* 1014b–1016d. Plutarch identified this soul with the evil world soul mentioned in Plato's *Laws* 896df. and with the Timaean ἀνάγκη, 'Necessity' (*Tim.* 56c5f; cf. *Leg.* 741a, 818b); see also Proc. *In Plat. Tim.* 1.382,4.
[45] Sedley 2007: 107 n. 30 with reference to Procl. *In Plat. Tim.* 1.276.30–277.1.

28

ancient authors than has generally been assumed, among them Polemo and Cicero's tutor Antiochus, may have endorsed a creationist reading of the dialogue.

The reader's decision whether or not to interpret the *Timaeus* in a temporal manner has a far-reaching impact upon the manner in which the account's key components are to be understood. I shall now turn to these key themes of the dialogue that will prove significant for our authors.

Demiurge, Cosmic Soul, and Lesser Divinities

Who or what is the demiurge, and what precisely is this divinity's role in the Timaean creation account? According to the narrator's portrayal, the divine craftsman is characterized from the beginning as working with pre-cosmic materials. The actual process of creation that is described by Timaeus is thus not a creation *ex nihilo*, but the harmonic structuring and blending by the demiurge of the materials at his disposal. Does our narrator provide more specific information regarding the divinity's identity? On two occasions, the demiurge is characterized by Timaeus as 'responsible' (*Tim.* 28a4–5 and 28c2–3) for the coming to be of our world. Any hope for a full revelation of his identity is, however, immediately thwarted: 'to discover the maker and father of this All is a difficult task; having discovered him, it is impossible to explain him to the many' (τὸν μὲν οὖν ποιητὴν καὶ πατέρα τοῦδε τοῦ παντὸς εὑρεῖν τε ἔργον καὶ εὑρόντα εἰς πάντας ἀδύνατον λέγειν.)[46] Instead, Timaeus focuses on the god's specific role as the initiator of the cosmogonic process. Why did the demiurge create the orderly universe? His reason for doing so, according to

---

[46] It is possible to assume that Plato wished to express with this statement that a dialogue like the *Timaeus* was not composed in such a manner as to render its contents comprehensible to everybody, in contrast, for instance, to the *Laws*, ultimately intended to be accessible to every citizen of Magnesia. Alternatively, Plato may be alluding to the practice of contemporary mystery cults and the prohibition of revealing a divinity's name, a conjecture advanced by Proclus who associates this with Pythagorean practice. Cf. Procl. *In Plat. Tim.* 2.302,25–303,1. Baltzly et al. 2006–9 point to Iamblichus, *Vita Pyth.* 32.226.8–227.9 as a source for Proclus' explanations.

Timaeus at 29d7–e3, was his inherent goodness. 'He was good, and in the good no envy with regard to anything ever arises.' Free from envy, moreover, the demiurge wanted everything to be like himself, i.e. to be good, as far as this was possible. To this purpose, he concluded that the chaotic pre-cursors of our elemental physical materials, initially, had to be arranged in an orderly structure and then equipped with soul and intellect. Timaeus reconstructs the creator's train of thought as resting on the following premises: 1) Whatever possesses intellect is more excellent than anything lacking intellect; 2) Intellect cannot arise anywhere except in conjunction with soul.[47]

The argument contained in this passage has led some to propose that the divine craftsman, seen as the personification of νοῦς, intellect, must necessarily possess soul. As a consequence, the demiurge has been perceived as identical with the cosmic soul. On this account, the creation of the world soul at the demiurge's own hands is reduced to a narrative strategy, presumably intended to facilitate an understanding of the central role of the cosmic soul in the universe, and to reinforce its divine, immortal nature.[48] The fact that the cosmic soul is made up from the ingredients 'sameness' and 'difference' that enable it to operate as a link between the intelligible and physical spheres may be taken to signify that the demiurge, when

---

[47] Apart from *Tim.* 37a2–4 and 46d5–6, see also Plato's *Phil.* 30a9–10, *Euthyd.* 287d7–e1 and *Soph.* 239a4–8.

[48] An interpretation adapted by Archer-Hind 1888. Cornford 1937 refines this position by identifying the demiurge, specifically, as the rational part of the cosmic soul. See also Carone 2005 esp. 42–6 for a more recent endorsement of this view. Some scholars see a direct link between a 'demythologized' interpretation of the demiurge, i.e. the view that the figure of the demiurge was not intended by Plato as a realistic element in Timaeus' account, and a non-literal reading of Timaean creation story as a whole; cf. Dillon 2003: 81. The 'conflation' of the Timaean demiurge with the cosmic soul, or other elements of the Timaean narrative, is criticized by Broadie 2012. In support of a literal reading of the dialogue, Broadie rejects the identification of the demiurge with the world soul based on the fact that the demiurge is a 'one–many' cause: a craftsman is able to produce more than one creation of the same nature. The world soul, on the other hand, is a one–one cause of the natural universe under its command. What is more, Broadie stresses the importance to see the demiurge as distinct from the world soul and thereby from his creation in order to maintain its authoritative force over the cosmos that can only be maintained by a transcendent creator.

considered identical with the cosmic soul, is a mediating agent that connects the intelligible realm with our sensible world. This interpretation is, however, difficult to square with Timaeus' emphasis on the contrast between the cosmic soul, the 'best of things that have come to be', and the demiurge, the 'best of things eternal and intelligible' (τῶν νοητῶν ἀεί τε ὄντων ὑπὸ τοῦ ἀρίστου ἀρίστη γενομένη τῶν γεννηθέντων [ἡ ψυχή], 37a1–2). Others set the divine craftsman on a par with a further element in the Timaean metaphysical framework, the intelligible forms. However, identifying the demiurge with any one intelligible form, or with the intelligible paradigm, leaves unclear what caused the shift from the pre-cosmic state of affairs, a scenario of intelligible forms and erratic elemental 'traces' in the receptacle, to a cosmos to which orderly and regulated relations between the forms and the elements had given rise.[49] It was to become a most challenging focal point, beginning in particular with the Middle Platonic writers, to explain the divinity's responsibility for creating the sensible universe while maintaining its status as a transcendent being far removed from our human sphere. We shall find that interpreters from the early centuries of our era onwards preferred to associate the creator with the intelligible forms, often conceived of as being located in the creator's mind, instead of identifying him with the cosmic soul that permeated the universe, a development that reflects the increased focus on a divinity whose transcendence must be safeguarded at all costs.

While the demiurge is thus placed into an ontological class that differs from that of his own product, his creative effort is mirrored and continued in the material sphere by lesser divinities that have also been created by him. The dualistic set-up of

---

[49] Hampton 1990 interprets the divinity as identical with the Form of the Good, while Menn 1995 argues for the Form of Intelligence and emphasizes intellect's independence from soul. According to Menn, intellect is the active causal principle of order in the natural world, with the label 'demiurge' merely describing its relational function with regard to the cosmos. Against the specific charge that intellect cannot come to be except in conjunction with soul, Menn holds that, while it cannot arise or come to be without soul in the physical realm, it nevertheless can exist by itself in the intelligible realm. A further alternative is to understand the demiurge as representing a *technê*, a 'manifestation' of craftsmanship, cf. Robinson 2004: 83–6.

the creation account thus remains intact, while the benefi-
cial impact of the intelligible god is carried into the material
realm by various agents. The cosmic soul is merely the first
and eldest of numerous other gods, i.e. the stars and the
planets, that 'have come to be in the heaven' (*Tim.* 40c). As
noted above, Timaeus sidesteps the traditional portrayal of
the descendants of Cronos and Rhea, but soon assigns to
all the divinities that 'rotate visibly', and to 'all that reveal
themselves to the extent that they choose' (*Tim.* 41a3–4) and
that 'have come to be' (*Tim.* 41a5), the task of constructing
the human body (*Tim.* 41a7–d3). Before he retires and his
divine assistants set out to imitate his creative work, the god
himself fashions the human souls which he then places upon
the various heavenly bodies, assigning one to each, and to
whom he explains 'the nature of the All' and announces
the 'laws of fate' (*Tim.* 41e2–3). According to these laws,
irrational behaviour on the part of the human soul has as
its consequence rebirth in a body which ranks lower on the
hierarchy of mortal living beings. Human soul's knowledge
of fate, acquired immediately after its coming to be, places
the responsibility for future evil and misfortune firmly into its
own hands – or rather, into the hands of the living creature
to whom the soul is first assigned once it begins its earthly
existence.

Dualism

We have seen above that, starting from *Tim.* 27d5, Timaeus
frames his creation story with the dualistic metaphysical and
epistemological structure we encounter in Plato's *Republic*
and other so-called 'middle' dialogues. A noetic realm, 'that
which always is' (τὸ ὂν ἀεί), is distinguished from 'what always
comes to be' (τὸ γιγνόμενον ἀεί),[50] our sensible universe.

---

[50] I have retained the ἀεί although I am aware that the evidence supporting it is incon-
clusive. The inclusion of a second ἀεί, one might assume initially, would have been
favoured by those Platonists who endorsed a non-temporal reading and thus an
ongoing process of coming to be. It is, nevertheless, omitted by the vast majority of

Dualism

The ontological planes are associated at *Tim.* 28a1–4 with a corresponding pair of cognitive modes that provide access to them: being is accessible by intelligence, νόησις, with the help of reason (μετὰ λόγου), 'what comes to be', in turn, is 'opined by opinion aided by non-rational sense perception' (δόξῃ μετ' αἰσθήσεως ἀλόγου δοξαστόν). These ontological–epistemological correlations are often associated with the Divided Line in Plato's *Rep.* 6.509d–511 and *Rep.* 7.533d–534a, where the epistemological planes πίστις and εἰκασία are *sub*-divisions of δόξα.[51]

In the *Timaeus*, specifically, τὸ ὄν is described as the model or paradigm, παράδειγμα, which is 'in accordance with itself and selfsame', eternal (*Tim.* 28c–29a), and in whose likeness the divine craftsman fashions the materials at his disposal into an orderly All. As indicated above, the paradigm may be taken to represent the totality of intelligible forms that serve as the blueprints for the many sensible components of the universe.[52]

the Neoplatonist tradition, including Syrianus, Proclus, Simplicius, Olympiodorus, Asclepius, and Joannes Lydus. It is omitted, moreover, by the second-century writers Nicomachus of Gerasa, Numenius, Alexander of Aphrodisias, and Sextus Empiricus. The Christian Philoponus was inconsistent in his omission, as listed by Whittaker 1969: 182. It is retained, oddly, by Eusebius (*Praep. evang.* 11.9) and perhaps also by Plutarch (suggested in *Def. or.* 433e: ἔκγονον ἐκείνου καὶ τόκον ὄντως ἀεὶ γιγνόμενον ἀεὶ τοῦτον ἀποφαίνοντες, a description of the sun as the offspring of Apollo, a possible allusion to the *Timaeus*), both of whom endorsed a temporal creation of the universe. Whittaker, who criticizes Burnet's inclusion of the word in the OCT, argues further that the combination of ἀεί and τὸ γιγνόμενον does not necessarily deny a creation in time since the process of becoming could begin at and continue from the time of creation. Nevertheless, he holds that ἀεί was inserted by Platonists who favoured the Xenocratean interpretation of the *Timaeus*, and who, furthermore, may have been motivated by stylistic balance. Dillon 1989: 62 argues that the reading which retained ἀεί was more widely established among the non-temporal second-century tradition than assumed by Whittaker et al. He re-evaluates evidence from the *Didaskalikos* and several passages in the *Corpus Hermeticum* and points to Plotinus *Enn.* 3.3.7,16–18, καὶ τὰ μὲν ἔμενεν ἀεί, τὰ δὲ ἐγίνετο ἀεί [οἱ καρποὶ καὶ τὰ φύλλα] καὶ τὰ γινόμενα ἀεὶ εἶχε τοὺς τῶν ἐπάνω λόγους ἐν αὐτοῖς οἷον μικρὰ δένδρα βουληθέντα εἶναι, a statement Dillon takes to be deliberately playing on the various meanings of ἀεί that had been established by the Neoplatonist tradition. Dillon concludes that the inclusion of the second ἀεί should not necessarily be accounted for by ideological reasons.

51 Cf. e.g. Cal. *Comm. in Tim.* 342, 568, 17–26, following a common line of exegesis.
52 At *Tim.* 51d Timaeus explicitly refers to the 'forms' whose existence he demonstrates with the help of a syllogism that relies upon the previously introduced association of the two ontological planes and their epistemological correlates.

The distinction between the two ontological realms at the beginning of Timaeus' creation account provides the necessary set-up for his ensuing portrayal of our universe. It is to be located in the sensible realm that, in turn, bears all the characteristic marks of 'what has come to be'. It is perceptible by our senses and perishable in nature.

A closely connected correlative pair that is integral to the dualism of the *Timaeus* is the doublet eternity–time. We saw above that the creation of time coincides with the creation of the celestial bodies whose regular orbiting movements determine the extensions of time familiar to us (38b–39d). Time is a 'moving image of [unchanging] eternity' (*Tim.* 37d5), an image that, in contrast to eternity, which abides in one, moves and changes according to number (*Tim.* 37d6–7). For later Platonic interpreters 'eternity that abides in unity' becomes a characteristic property of the noetic realm that is integrated into its conception to such a degree as to count as a synonym of οὐσία, 'being' itself, perhaps a consequence of the close association of the creator god with intelligible form.

The Receptacle

At *Tim.* 47e3 Timaeus proceeds from the creative activities of intellect, represented by the divine craftsman, to those carried out by intellect in cooperation with 'necessity'. It may be helpful to associate the agent 'necessity' simply with physics, more specifically, with the physical mechanisms to which the material elements in the Timaean cosmos are subjected. The creative acts carried out by intellect in cooperation with necessity are thus steered by intelligent design, while the designer heeds the physical nature of the ordered elements, taking into account the potential effects of the various properties characteristic of them.

As indicated above, the four elements water, fire, earth, and air are identified by Timaeus as three-dimensional compounds formed by the demiurge out of elementary geometric shapes. The elements arise in what is introduced by Timaeus as the *third* principle in his cosmos, alongside the noetic and sensible realms. It is problematic to grasp precisely what this third principle is. Neither intelligible nor physical in its own nature, its function is compared by Timaeus to that of a 'receptacle' or 'wet nurse' in which 'the sensible objects always come to be ... and from which, in turn, they perish' (*Tim.* 49a, e). Further comparisons liken the receptacle to a kind of underlying, malleable, or impressionable stuff (50c, e–51a), and to a neutral ointment base able to take on multiple fragrances (50e). In contrast to sensible objects it is the deserving recipient of the label 'this' and 'that' since it never changes in its essence (*Tim.* 50a). Timaeus likens it to underlying material, such as gold from which a statue is formed (*Tim.* 50a), but the comparison is weak since we are not to conceive of the third kind as a physical material, yet as a base upon which something is imprinted (ἐκμαγεῖον, *Tim.* 50c2). What are imprinted upon it are the 'copies of the everlasting [forms]' (τῶν ὄντων ἀεὶ μιμήματα).[53] The manner in which these copies are imprinted from the forms is 'indescribable and wonderful' (*Tim.* 50c6). Yet it is a 'kind', 'invisible and shapeless, all-receiving, partaking of the intelligible in a baffling and incomprehensible manner' (*Tim.* 51a–b). It is grasped with the help of 'non-sensation, with some type of counterfeit reasoning' (λογισμῷ τινι νόθῳ, *Tim.* 52b). It does not even possess that for which it has come to be (*Tim.* 52c), yet it is listed alongside being and coming to be, wherefore we arrive at 'three different things' (τρία τριχῇ, *Tim.* 52d4).

The image that emerges from these comparisons is that of a basic substrate whose inherent properties are its plasticity or malleability, and its three-dimensional extension. Its lack of any further characteristics serves a specific purpose. In its function as an underlying substrate the receptacle has

---

[53] The μιμήματα are sometimes conceived of as the 'tokens' that transmit the characteristic properties of the intelligible forms into the receptacle. The description of what enters the receptacle as 'bodies' (*Tim.* 50b6), however, suggests that the μιμήματα are simply three-dimensional physical objects.

to remain without essential properties in order to be able to temporarily exhibit the varying elemental natures of the physical objects that come to be and perish in it (*Tim.* 51b4–6). It appears that we ought to adopt a synthetic approach to the different functions of the receptacle. It is the space in which three-dimensional physical objects come to be and perish and, at the same time, the base that underlies the individual characteristics and properties of perishable physical objects.[54] As such, it falls short of explaining precisely how the intelligible forms come to interact with the sensible materials in such as manner as to effect the coming to be of sensible particulars. It merely provides the conditions, or a platform, for this process to come about.

The topics outlined above, along with the possible interpretations given, may be seen as previews or snapshots of the mesmerizingly complex reception of Plato's *Timaeus* at the hands of its interpreters. Weighing up the various interpretative difficulties that emerge in the dialogue, it appears that we ought to take Timaeus at his word in accepting that too close a scrutiny of some of the incongruities in the narrative is ill-advised. Had Plato intended for Timaeus' narrative to serve as a viable explanation of reality, why did he write the dialogue in a manner that is, quite obviously, less than coherent? Would he not have allowed his protagonist to argue his case with rather more convincingness, even if the final truth must escape the mortal reader? Be that as it may, my primary interest in the present study is to examine the responses to the interpretative

---

[54] Zeyl 2000 identifies the receptacle simultaneously as the material substrate from which physical objects are constituted and as the spatial dimension in which these appear, rejecting the idea that these two roles necessarily have to remain distinct. Similarly, Johansen 2004: 133, 'Place and matter coincide in that both are to be understood as the product of abstracting the formal characteristics of a body.' The detailed study of the Timaean receptacle by Algra 1995: 72–120 concludes that such a twofold reading is unconvincing, considering incompatible the different portrayals of the receptacle that emerge from the dialogue: the receptacle as the extension, and thus a constitutive factor, of phenomenal bodies themselves, and the receptacle as the extension or medium through which phenomenal bodies move.

difficulties given by our Latin interpreters, and their strategies for solving them. With our focus thus shifted, we are about to open windows that look out upon divergent stages not only of the dialogue's history of transmission, but of the Platonic tradition in its entirety.

CHAPTER 2

CICERO

Cicero's Plato and Platonism

The Latin Platonic tradition begins with Cicero.[1] The Platonic heritage had passed, by the late second century BCE, into the hands of Philo of Larissa. Chosen as a successor to Clitomachus,[2] he initially continued the line defended by his master, under whom the Academy had subscribed to a radical form of scepticism that had been the trademark also of Arcesilaus and Carneades.[3] These had rejected the possibility that cognition could be attained, and denied that positive doctrines could be drawn from Plato's dialogues. Cicero's statements regarding his affiliation with the sceptical Academy may at times appear confusing. His perspective seems to fluctuate between radical Carneadean scepticism and a probabilist view that encourages the search for the truth, the policy that had been adopted by Philo before he modified his outlook towards a more fallibilist line.[4] Cicero's seemingly contradictory statements concerning his own sceptical stance have been criticized[5] and accounted for by his use of variant sources, or a gradation of his sceptical outlook according to subject matter.[6] It has been proposed, moreover, that Cicero followed

---

[1] Rudimentary Latin translations of Greek philosophical texts were in circulation before Cicero devoted himself fully to this project. He uncharitably describes these Latin texts as either inadequate in content (*Tusc.* 4.6) or deficient in their literary sophistication (ibid. 2.7 cf. 1.6).

[2] Görler 1994b: 916–18; Brittain 2001: 73–128.

[3] Görler 1994b: 796–7, 855–8.

[4] Cic. *Ac.* 2.7, 36, 65, 76; *Div.* 2.28; *Fin.* 1.13, 4.27; *Nat. deor.* 1.11; *Rep.* 3.8.

[5] Cf. Cic. *Off.* 2.7. His apparent volatility has drawn some harsh criticism from Glucker 1988: 63, who describes Cicero's philosophical affiliations as 'flitting from flower to flower'.

[6] Hirzel 1883 vol. 3 attributed to Cicero one probabilist source (Metrodorus, 170–80) and one strictly sceptical source (Clitomachus, 162–70) for his *Academica*. Zielinski 1912 recognized in Cicero a dogmatic viewpoint in the context of moral philosophy.

Antiochus' dogmatist stance in the middle period of his career, into which his *De oratore, De re publica,* and *De legibus* fall, before returning in his later years to Philo's probabilist scepticism he had favoured already as a young man.[7] Against this view, however, there is compelling evidence found in the above-named works for a sceptical position also in Cicero's middle period. Görler argues that Cicero was attracted to sceptical principles of argumentation throughout his life, with a greater or lesser degree of scepticism expressed as appropriate to circumstances such as topic and content, form of presentation, and the literary characters through whom particular viewpoints are advanced.[8] It is crucial to such a perspective to distinguish between Cicero's sceptical methodology in his philosophical treatises, which allowed him to ascribe varying degrees of probability to a particular doctrinal tenet,[9] and the individual contexts in which he presents the philosophy of the Academy.

Cicero differentiates between radical Carneadean policy and his personal stance at *Ac.* 2.66 where he famously describes himself as an *opinator*, falling short of the ideal Academic sage who neither assents to anything nor opines.[10] While his position in the *Academica* is that of a (sometimes unsuccessful) follower of Clitomachus' radical interpretation of Carneades' line, his scepticism elsewhere appears to be of a more positive, probabilist kind along the lines of Philo before his Roman turn.[11]

---

[7] Glucker 1988 and Steinmetz 1989: 1–19, building on Hirzel 1883 vol. 2: 488–9 n. 1.

[8] Cf. Görler's classic defence of this view in Powell 1995: 85–113.

[9] As Long 1995: 41 puts it: 'We must distinguish in Cicero between the *genus philosophandi* and the thesis he finds plausible.'

[10] 'It is, however, not the case that I am someone who never approves anything false, who never assents, who never holds an opinion. But we are inquiring after the sage. In fact, I myself am a great opinion-holder, for I am not a sage' (*nec tamen ego is sum qui nihil umquam falsi adprobem qui numquam adsentiar, qui nihil opiner, sed quaerimus de sapiente. ego vero ipse et magnus quidam sum opinator (non enim sum sapiens)*). Cf. Görler 1995a: 37 with n. 4, who reads in this statement Cicero's admission of his own epistemic limitations.

[11] E.g. *Off.* 2.7., *Fin.* 5.75–6, but see Brittain 2016: 23–5, who does not believe that we should adduce from Cicero's statements at *Fin.* 5.75–6 a 'mitigated' scepticism. Brittain argues against the common perception, also followed in the present study, of Cicero as a mitigated sceptic, in general, and carefully re-evaluates the evidence

Cicero

Cicero associates a more or less radical sceptical outlook
also with Plato. As a spokesperson for Carneadean scepticism
at *Ac.* 1.46, for instance, he downplays the differences between
the Old and New Academies by portraying Plato as a sceptic 'in
whose books nothing is affirmed and there is much discussion
on either side of an argument; one inquires into all possible
subject matters but nothing certain is named'.[12] Where Plato
is ascribed a doctrinal position in Cicero's *philosophica*, it is
often by representatives of those philosophical systems which
claim allegiance to the Old Academy.[13] Cicero's representations
of his own and of Plato's philosophical position must be
considered as context-related viewpoints individually adjusted
to the form, contents, purpose, and the dramatis personae
of his individual works. Before we examine in greater detail
Cicero's translation of Plato's *Timaeus* and his approach to the
work and its original author in terms of doctrine and methodology, let us turn to Cicero's general translation method. In
doing so, we will gain a better understanding of his motivation
for taking on such a challenging project.

concerning Cicero's scepticism in the *De finibus*, which, he suggests, may be representative of Cicero's outlook also in other dialogues. Brittain draws attention to the
fact that Cicero's view of Antiochean ethics in this work is less consistent than is
normally assumed, taking into account the often subtle dialogical set up employed
by Cicero which, according to Brittain, serves to reinforce a rather more radical,
Carneadean type of scepticism instead of the probabilist Philonian type (defended
in Brittain 2001). The evidence adduced for Cicero's position on ethics in the *De
finibus* makes for an intriguing case. Nevertheless, I am hesitant to accept this conclusion wholesale across these writings, and across the various philosophical disciplines covered in them, particularly where Cicero's speaking part is less extensive
than it is in the *De finibus*. I shall be arguing in the course of the present chapter
that the evidence from Cicero's *Timaeus* translation points to a Philonian outlook,
fully aware that the similarities between Cicero and Philo's outlook I illustrate
are predominantly methodological. Nevertheless, while I grant that it is possible
that Cicero adopted the Philonian investigative method while maintaining a more
radical overall outlook, the picture that emerges of Cicero's philosophical stance,
such as I draw it from the evidence of his *Timaeus* translation, is that of Philo's
probabilist scepticism.
[12] [*Plato*] *cuius in libris nihil adfirmatur et in utramque partem multa disseruntur, de
omnibus quaeritur, nihil certi dicitur.*
[13] So, for instance, Antiochus at *Ac.* 1.17, 34; ibid. 1.13–14; the Stoic Balbus at *Nat.
deor.* 1.32.

40

Cicero the Translator

Translation and Rhetoric

Cicero frequently reflects on his work as a translator. He emphasizes the benefits of translation as a tool, available to the student of rhetoric, for developing and refining his individual style.[14] Imitating Greek orators like Aeschines and Demosthenes both in theory (translation) and in practice (declamation),[15] the aspiring orator could adapt the exemplary models of Greek literature for his own purposes. A standard *locus* in Cicero is his *De oratore* 1.155 where, in the person of Crassus, Cicero's own tutor in rhetoric and himself a distinguished orator, he describes the following practice:

'It seemed useful to me – and I made a habit of it as a young man – to set out (*explicarem*) the Greek orations of the most eminent orators. After reading them, I proceeded in such a manner that, in reproducing in Latin what I had read in Greek, I would not only employ the best of those words already in use, but even render (*exprimerem*) some words by means of reproducing (*imitando*) [the Greek] words with such expressions as were new to our audience, provided they were appropriate (*idonea*).'[16]

As a more or less independent rephrasing of the original text the paraphrase was an exercise available to the aspiring orator for the improvement of his literary style. The primary aim of this literary paraphrase was to rephrase the contents of a particular text in different terms and by adding certain stylistic features such as an alternating pattern of synonyms, metaphor, comparisons, and other devices.[17] In a passage of Cicero's *De optimo genere oratorum* he recalls his own schooling:

---

[14] As a young man, Cicero had produced a verse translation of Aratus' *Phaenomena* (cf. *Div.* 2.14 and *Nat. deor.* 2.104ff.). He also translated Xenophon's *Oeconomicus* (*Off.* 2.87) and Plato's *Protagoras*. Cf. Jones 1959: 22f.; Puelma 1980: 143–5; Stemplinger 1912: 118–19, 212.

[15] Stemplinger 1912: 102, 109.

[16] Quintilian was to take up the present passage in his discussion of suitable written exercises (*scribenda*) at *Inst. or.* 10.5.2. Cf. also the helpful discussion in Seele 1995: 76–80.

[17] Fuchs 1982: 10–16 offers an analysis of the various types of paraphrase and their contemporary uses.

I translated (*converti*) the most celebrated orations of two of the most eloquent Attic orators, Aeschines and Demosthenes, delivered against each other … but I did not translate them as an interpreter would do, but in the manner of an orator (*nec converti ut interpres, sed ut orator*), with the same meaning and forms (*sententiis isdem et earum formis*) or, so to say, figures of speech (*figuris*), but with expressions that are in accordance with our own usage.[18]

Crassus and Cicero emphasize the importance of a successful Latin product rather than a close representation of the original. The ultimate aim of translation as a rhetorical exercise was the enhancement of one's artistic expression achieved by the rephrasing of the underlying text in as sophisticated and elegant a fashion as possible.

Roman Translation and the Contest of Cultures

The refinement of an orator's rhetorical style was not the only purpose Cicero attached to the practice of translation. A further aspect came to play a more relevant role in his later years as a writer of philosophy. For this project, the skills he had acquired in his rhetorical training proved an important instrument in the competition for cultural superiority with Greece he so passionately promoted. We encounter this sentiment in the preface to his *Tusculans* where Cicero explains his intention to illuminate the subject of philosophy *Latinis litteris*, not because one could not access the subject via the works of Greek authors, but rather because he is convinced that his fellow Romans 'have shown themselves to possess more wisdom than the Greeks in all matters, both in discovering [novelties] for themselves and in improving upon what they had taken over from them, at least in those matters they had deemed worthy of pursuit'.[19]

He next offers a catalogue listing those areas of expertise in which the Romans, to his mind, have proven superior to their Greek counterparts, while conceding that they have

[18] Cic. *Opt. gen.* 14. Cf. also *Brut.* 310.
[19] Cic. *Tusc* 1.1: *meum semper iudicium fuit omnia nostros aut invenisse per se sapientius quam Graecos aut accepta ab illis fecisse meliora, quae quidem digna statuissent, in quibus elaborarent.*

been outclassed by Greece with regard to intellectual qualities and literature. This defeat, however, Cicero explains with the simple fact that the Romans have up to this point not been competing. Far from being unable to excel in this field, Rome has given Greece a head start simply because their nation did not yet exist when the Greek masters began to write.[20] With the great Roman orators already having matched their Greek rivals,[21] Cicero now announces his intention to set foot on the so-far neglected territory of philosophy, as a service to his fellow countrymen even after his expulsion from the political stage: 'Philosophy has lain dormant until this age, unilluminated through Latin letters. It is my mission to shed light upon and awaken her so I may, if I am able to, be of service to my fellow citizens in my retirement, if I have done so throughout my career.'[22]

To conquer philosophy, the last remaining territory of Greek supremacy, Cicero will avail himself of a powerful weapon: his rhetorical skill. Professing to combine *prudentia* with *eloquentia*,[23] as previously done by Aristotle, he throws into the ring his acclaimed rhetorical skills in order to fit out his native tongue as a worthy contender in philosophical discourse. Challenging the commonplace complaint of his Roman fellow writers regarding the poverty of the Latin language, he can thus argue that 'as concerns the richness of vocabulary we are not only not surpassed by the Greeks but are actually their superior',[24] and that, in addition, it would be a 'noble and glorious [achievement] for the Roman people, in the field of philosophy, not to be dependent on Greek literature'.[25]

---

[20] Ibid. 1.3.

[21] Ibid. 1.5.

[22] *philosophia iacuit usque ad hanc aetatem nec ullum habuit lumen litterarum Latinarum; quae inlustranda et excitanda nobis est, ut, si occupati profuimus aliquid civibus nostris, prosimus etiam, si possumus, otiosi.*

[23] On the combination of philosophy and rhetoric as a means of surpassing Greek philosophy, cf. Cicero's remarks to his son Marcus at *Off.* 1.2.

[24] Cic. *Fin.* 3.5, *Nat. deor.* 1.8, and see his rather dramatic exclamation at *Tusc.* 1.35: 'See how you sometimes are lost for words, Greece, even though you always think you abound in them!' (*O verborum inops interdum, quibus abundare te semper putas, Graecia!*). Cf. ibid. 3.11.

[25] *Div.* 2.5: *magnificum illud etiam Romanisque hominibus gloriosum, ut Graecis de philosophia litteris non egeant.* Cf. *Tusc.* 2.5–7.

An often-cited passage in the preface to Cicero's *De finibus* professes his ambition not merely to perform the role of an *interpres*[26] but to add to the material at hand his own 'judgment and arrangement' (*iudicium et ordo scribendi*), thus producing 'writings that are both stylistically brilliant and not [only] translations from Greek [texts]'.[27] At the same time, however, Cicero reserves for himself the possibility also of producing a more literal type of translation and points to the merit of this exercise in the familiar statement often taken to anticipate his *Timaeus* translation: 'Even if I were to produce a translation (*si plane sic verterem*) of Plato or Aristotle, of the sort our poets have done with plays, I believe I would render a service to my fellow citizens in bringing about their acquaintance with their divine genius. And although I have not attempted this method so far, I believe there is no reason why I should not do so [in the future].'[28] It is precisely this type of translation we are about to encounter. We may thus locate Cicero's translation of the *Timaeus* in his wider-reaching project of proving that his native language was capable of reproducing the words even of Plato himself.[29]

Cicero and the *Timaeus*

Why the Timaeus?

At *Fin.* 2.15 Cicero describes the *Timaeus* as an inaccessible text. The failure to grasp a text, he explains there, may be due to an author's intentional obscurity of expression, as

---

[26] Cf. his remark at *Opt. gen.* 13: 'I did not translate it in the manner of a mere translator, but in the manner of an orator (*nec converti ut interpres, sed ut orator*), with *interpres* apparently marking a literal style of translation. Cf. Jones 1959: 27.

[27] *Fin.* 1.6.

[28] *Fin.* 1.7: *quamquam si plane sic verterem Platonem aut Aristotelem ut verterunt nostri poetae fabulas, male credo mererer de meis civibus si ad eorum cognititionem divina illa ingenia transferrem. Sed id neque feci adhuc nec mihi tamen ne faciam interditum puto.* See also *Ac.* 1.9–10.

[29] For a more detailed analysis of Cicero's translation practice see Powell 1995: 292–7, Adams 2003: 459–68 and Seele, 1995: 53–7. I disagree with the conclusions drawn by Poncelet 1957, whose analysis of Cicero's translations from Platonic texts leads him to believe that Cicero was limited by a Latin language largely incapable of expressing abstract thought and, forced to resort to *variatio* by the poorly equipped Latin linguistic system, failed to develop a consistent technical philosophical

it is the case with Heraclitus' writings. Alternatively, such a failure may be caused by the obscurity not of the language (*verborum*) used, but of its subject matter (*rerum*), resulting in the fact that 'the narrative fails to be understood, as is the case in Plato's *Timaeus*'. Why did he choose to reproduce such a challenging text for his project of translating Plato?[30]

Cicero's reasonably literal translation of the dialogue presents a novelty when compared to his philosophical treatises whose contents, presumably based on philosophical manuals, are freely structured and phrased.[31] The announcement in the preface to the *De finibus* quoted above, along with the subject matter of the *Timaeus*, suggests a date of composition that falls within the period of 45–44 BCE, during which Cicero produced the majority of his philosophically themed writings.[32] Nevertheless, Cicero makes no mention of his translation in the preface to Book 2 of his *De divinatione* which provides a catalogue of his philosophical works.[33] This omission suggests that the text was not included among his publications. This did not hinder the translation from having a rather interesting afterlife. While Calcidius' translation was to become the main channel of the dialogue's transmission into the Middle Ages, Cicero's translation, as we will see in Chapter 5, was used by Augustine, and would eventually travel as far as the seventeenth century, where it found its way to the

---

vocabulary. Poncelet fails to take into account Cicero's deliberate use of literary and stylistic ornament. This feature in Cicero's approach to translation has been recognized and appreciated as an essentially 'artistic' achievement by Lambardi 1982, who evaluates Poncelet's conclusions on pp. 9–12.

[30] For the following, cf. Sedley 2013.

[31] Cf. Cicero's evaluation of his philosophical writings at *Ep. ad Att.* 12.52: 'They are copies and are require little effort. I merely supply the words, in which I abound' (*apographa sunt, minore labore fiunt; verba tantum adfero, quibus abundo*).

[32] For a chronological listing of his works, cf. Powell 1995: xiii–xvii. Sedley 2013: 189 suggests that the date of composition falls into the period from July to September 45 BCE. See further Lévy 2003: 96–8.

[33] Lévy 2003: 97–8 suggests that the translation is not listed in this preface because Cicero intended it to represent his final and crowning discussion of natural philosophy in which he was moving away from the Hellenistic philosophical systems discussed in his *Tusculanae disputationes*, *Academica*, *De natura deorum*, and *De divinatione*, and reverting to Plato and Aristotle. It will become clear in the course of the present chapter that I do not agree that Cicero was beginning to distance himself from the Academy – quite the contrary.

astronomer Johannes Kepler, who quotes Cicero's Latin translation of *Tim.* 30a in his *Mysterium cosmographicum* (1596).[34] Yet, given its absence from Cicero's inventory of publications in the *De divinatione*, two questions arise. Apart from his wish to produce a literal translation of Greek philosophy, what might have been the philosophical attraction of such a project that initially attracted Cicero's interest?[35] Further, what led him to abandon this project eventually?

With regard to the first question, some general features of his translation betray Cicero's intentions. The beginning (*Tim.* 27d6) and end (47b2) of the translation put the creation of the cosmic body and soul by a craftsman god at the centre of the ensuing text. The preface, accordingly, suggests that the chosen topic will be natural philosophy, but does not mention theology. What is more, from a methodological point of view, the preface links the ensuing discussion to that in the *Academica* and other exchanges with P. Nigidius Figulus: 'I have participated in a great deal of discussions *against the natural philosophers*, in the tradition and manner of Carneades: those that are recorded in the *Academica* and the ones I often had with P. Nigidius Figulus.'[36]

Before discussing the topic and method announced in the preface in greater detail, let us turn, for a moment, to the dramatis personae introduced by Cicero. Initially, we note that Cicero omits the dialogue's introductory discussion that identifies the Greek original's cast, and in which Critias offers the historical background to his account of Athens' prehistoric ancestors and the inhabitants of Atlantis, which is to

---

[34] '... as Cicero, in his book on the universe, quotes from Plato's *Timaeus*, it is not right that he who is best should make anything except what is most beautiful', *Mysterium cosmographicum* 92 (eds. von Dyck and Caspar 1937). Plasberg and Giomini read '[it is not lawful] ... for him who is best to make ...' (*[fas autem nec est nec umquam fuit] quicquiam nisi pulcherrimum facere ei qui esset optimus*). For his later work *Harmonice mundi* (1619) Kepler was using the original Greek text of *Tim.* 35a–36e, and quotes Proclus at the beginning of *Harmonice mundi* 4.

[35] Cf. Sedley 2013: 188–9, 193–6.

[36] *multa sunt a nobis et in Academicis conscripta contra physicos et saepe cum P. Nigidio Carneadeo more et modo disputata* (*pref.* 1).

succeed Timaeus' cosmological narrative. Cicero ignores the connection between an account of an ideal society, such as is promised by Critias, and Timaeus' account that provides the wider framework for such a society, an orderly cosmos. He transfers the Timaean creation account into the exclusive context of natural philosophy. What is more, Cicero introduces a thoroughly Roman set of interlocutors, illustrious figures of the Roman Republic: P. Nigidius Figulus is introduced as a 'passionate and assiduous researcher' of natural philosophy (*pref.* 1.1, 5). Polymath, former consul, and Roman of high standing, Nigidius was known for his adherence to Pythagorean teaching and had produced works on human physiology (*De nominum natura*) and meteorology (*De vento*). He took a particular interest in oracles and similar topics. His works *De augurio privato*, *De extis*, *De sphaera*, and *De deis* treat of subjects such as divination from entrails, astrology, and the divine.[37] A representative of the Neopythagorean movement seems an apt choice for a discussion on what would have been considered Plato's natural philosophy. At *De finibus* 5.87, we learn of Cicero's view according to which Plato travelled to the Pythagoreans of Locri, Echecrates, Timaios, and Acrion, so that he, 'once he had exhausted Socrates, might add to his [teaching] the Pythagorean doctrine and acquire knowledge also about the subjects Socrates had rejected'.[38]

Cicero introduces as a second interlocutor the Greek Cratippus,[39] who was a close acquaintance of his and had been entrusted with the education of Cicero's son. While Cratippus[40] is praised by Cicero as a most distinguished Peripatetic[41] whose

---

[37] On the figure of Nigidius and his works, see Della Casa 1962. Liuzzi 1983 presents and discusses the collected fragments. For a discussion of the Pythagorean movement in Cicero's day, see Petit 1988.

[38] ... *ut, cum Socratem expressisset, adiungeret Pythagoreorum disciplinam eaque quae Socrates repudiabat addisceret.* The view of the *Timaeus* as essentially Pythagorean in content was still reiterated by Taylor 1928.

[39] Given Cratippus' Greek identity, a novelty for Cicero's *philosophica*, Sedley 2013: 194–5 suggests that Cratippus' presence may have been merely symbolic, and intended to lend weight to a possible Peripatetic speaking part to be assumed by a Latin character.

[40] Cf. Sedley 2013: 195.

[41] See the preface to the translation: *Cratippus, Peripateticorum omnium quos ego audierim, meo iudicio facile princeps*; further, Cic. *Off.* 1.1, 3.5.

ethical doctrine he considered close to his own, no evidence points towards an interest on Cratippus' part in natural philosophy.[42] Nevertheless, Cicero's praise of Cratippus, specifically, as 'easily the most distinguished' (*facile princeps*) of all Peripatetics indicates that the Peripatetic stance will play a role in what ensues.

Are we to assume that Cicero had reserved a speaking part for himself? At this point, it is helpful to take into account the methodology announced in the preface. There, Cicero recalls prior discussions *Carneadeo more et modo*, 'in the tradition and manner of Carneades', with Nigidius on the subject of natural philosophy. The method of Carneades was that of a philosophical *disputatio in utramque partem*, the advancing of arguments upon a given topic from opposed points of view, a method Cicero adopts in his *Academica*, *De finibus*, *De natura deorum*, and *De divinatione*.[43] Taking into account the fact that the interlocutors identified thus far are representatives of rival philosophical systems – a Neopythagorean, likely to be aligned with Plato, a Peripatetic, and an Academic sceptic – it is reasonable to assume that Cicero envisaged the finished product of his treatment of Plato's dialogue as taking the form of a philosophical *disputatio*,[44] such as we find it in his other writings of the period. In fact, it may have been what Cicero had in mind when remarking, at the outset of the *De finibus*, that 'even if I were to produce a translation of Plato or Aristotle ... I believe

[42] At *Div.* 1.70–1, 113, Cicero lists Cratippus' approval of divination by dreams and episodes of ecstasy. The are few Peripatetics of the first century BCE explicitly mentioned by Cicero: Staseas of Naples (*Fin.* 5.8, 75; *De orat.* 1.103), who appears in a rhetorical context (cf. Flashar 1983 vol. 3: 592), and Ariston of Alexandria, of whom it is known that he, like Cratippus, had moved away from Antiochean Platonism towards the Peripatetics. No clear doxographical evidence on this figure exists, cf. Flashar 1983 vol. 3: 594–5. For the Peripatetic Strato, cf. n. 122.

[43] I shall have rather more to say below on Philo's contribution to the appropriation of this method for his sceptical Academy. A further method, adopted by Cicero in his *De fato* and the *Tusculan disputations*, is ascribed to Carneades, that of merely arguing 'against a thesis' advanced by a dogmatist. Cf. Cic. *Fin.* 2.1–2. At *Tusc.* 1.8, Cicero credits Socrates with this method. Cf. Brittain 2001: 337–8 for further discussion.

[44] Sedley 2013 suggests that likely candidates to have featured in a polemical response were Aristotle's *De caelo*, in which the createdness and everlastingness of the Timaean cosmos are criticized, and his fragmentary *De philosophia*.

I would render a service to my fellow citizens in bringing about their acquaintance with their divine genius'.[45] Alongside the Neopythagorean/Platonic and the Peripatetic positions, then, Cicero might have intended for himself a role along the radical sceptical lines familiar from the *Academica*, or he may have intended to add a shorter evaluation, along probabilist lines, to the views advanced, such as we find in the closing paragraph of the *De natura deorum*.

An alternative scenario is possible. Like Cicero's other philosophical treatises, his translation of the *Timaeus* betrays the influence of sceptical terminology,[46] an aspect of the text I shall discuss in detail in the subsequent section. Yet, unlike the other philosophically themed works, the translation maintains the monologue form of Timaeus' original speaking part. What we appear to have in the translation is a sceptical viewpoint on natural philosophy that appropriates the *Timaean* creation account on behalf of the Academy.

Let us spin out the scenario of a sceptical take on cosmology in greater detail. Cicero might have taken on the narrative himself, with Nigidius, as an authoritative natural philosopher, bearing witness. Alternatively, Nigidius might himself have taken on the part, with Cicero bearing witness as an authoritative voice of the sceptic Academy. Either way, in such a scenario, a sceptical outlook would oblige the speaker to present the contents of Timaeus' original as the 'most likely' account, from a probabilist viewpoint, thus eschewing a full doctrinal commitment to the cosmological views advanced.[47] It is this scenario to which I shall subscribe in the present chapter. More precisely, I shall adopt the view that Cicero himself would have been the most likely candidate to have taken on Timaeus' creation account, along with the assumption that he would have done so as a representative of probabilist scepticism. I shall

---

[45] *Fin.* 1.7, cf. n. 28.
[46] Stressed most recently by Sedley 2013: 202–5. Cf. also Fuhrer 1993, Glucker 1995, Peetz 2005.
[47] Cicero had emphatically rejected any doctrinal position on natural philosophy in his discussion *contra physicos* in the *Academica*.

adduce new and comprehensive evidence in support of such a scenario in the next section of this chapter.

Aside from the characters introduced in the preface, Nigidius, Cratippus, and Cicero himself, is it likely that Cicero may have intended to add other philosophical perspectives to his *disputatio*? The preface to his translation, unhelpfully, ends in a lacuna. Given the methodology of the *disputatio in utramque partem* adopted in his philosophical treatises, and the translation's chronological proximity to these works, we cannot rule out that Cicero intended Stoic and Epicurean perspectives to feature in the conversation alongside the ones identified above, thus resulting in a more expansive discussion such as we find in the *De natura deorum*, with a Peripatetic perspective added.

Let us spin out the possible implications of a *disputatio* between these various stances on the subject of cosmology, which lies at the centre of the translation. Alongside Cicero, appropriating the Timaean creation account along probabilist sceptic lines,[48] a Stoic representative would argue for a cosmos created by intelligent design, while a Peripatetic and an Epicurean character would defend an uncreated universe.[49] The view of the universe as teleologically structured would be supported, in turn, by a Stoic and a Peripatetic character, while opposed only by an Epicurean. What is more, the Peripatetic interlocutor would presumably agree on the future everlastingness of the cosmos. Against this, Stoic and Epicurean representatives would have maintained the view of a cosmos whose existence is temporary, either due to recurring *ekpurôsis* in the case of a Stoic, or through the random dissolution of atoms in the case of an Epicurean.

---

[48] To reiterate: in the scenario adopted in the present study, I shall maintain throughout that a sceptic, whether in the person of Cicero himself or of Nigidius, would portray the contents of Timaeus' original speaking part from a probabilist viewpoint. Thus, unlike the other participants of the discussion, the Academic sceptic would support specific doctrinal views discussed without, however, committing to them fully.

[49] The createdness of the universe as the possible subject matter for their debate is suggested by Sedley 2013: 195–9.

While theology is not part of the programme set out in the preface, a divinity in its specific role as a creator and providential force in the cosmos does feature in the Timaean creation narrative, and would have provided further room for disagreement with other interlocutors.[50] Aristotle rejected the Platonic assumption of a providential creator, considering the blueprint for the physical makeup of the cosmos to be a feature built into its very structure, with the immanent activity of nature, not the external impulses of craftsmanship, held responsible for cosmic order.[51] Furthermore, Aristotle's unmoved mover as the ultimate principle of movement in the cosmos maintains a merely indirect relation to the sublunary realm and is considered the direct principle of motion only of the heavenly bodies that produce their orderly effects upon the lower spheres.[52] With regard to a creative and providential role, Aristotle's central deity thus stands in sharp contrast to the Timaean demiurge.[53] This contrast is noticeable in Cicero's philosophical works, where Aristotelian theology is presented as opposing that associated with Plato by insisting upon a supreme divinity that neither creates the cosmos nor manifests any immediate providential care for human beings.[54] The Aristotelian divinity,

[50] In the preface to the *Nat. deor.* Cicero himself expresses his disgust at those who denied divine providence, a view that, he holds, would result in a *perturbatio vitae* and *magna confusio* (*Nat. deor.* 1.3).

[51] Cf. Ar. *Phil.* fr. 18, ed. Ross (= Philo, *Aet. mund.* 3.10–11).

[52] Ar. *Cael.* 2.6, 288a27–288b4; Diog. Laert. 5.32; Atticus fr. 3.56, 69; see also Happ 1968: 77–84. The role of Aristotle's unmoved mover is sometimes phrased in providential terms, cf. Moraux 1949: 33–4. The various viewpoints on the topic that were current in the Aristotelian tradition are discussed in Sharples 1982.

[53] The assumption of a providential god in Plato appears, aside from *Tim.* 41e2–3, for instance, at *Leg.* 10.901a–903a.

[54] Cf. Cic. *Nat. deor.* 1.33, a passage thought to bear witness to Aristotle's lost *De philosophia* (fr. 26, Ross): Velleius reports that in the third book of Aristotle's work, the latter 'confuses many things, dissenting from his master Plato' (*Aristoteles in tertio de philosophia libro multa turbat, a magistro suo Platone dissentiens*). The Epicurean Velleius (from whom, admittedly, we should expect no concern to grant Aristotle a fair portrayal) enumerates apparently confusing statements of Aristotle on the nature of the highest divinity, ascribing its role to intellect (*menti*) while elsewhere depicting it as the world itself (*mundum ipsum*) or as a separate being (*alium quendam*) in charge of regulating and safeguarding its motions by means of some kind of reverse rotation (*replicatione quadam mundi motum regat atque tueatur*). Finally, divinity is assigned to aether (*caeli ardorem*). The 'confusion' in Aristotle's statements has been accounted for by the fact that the use of the noun

of course, contrasts sharply also with the Stoics' creative and providential god that permeates the cosmos. Any notion of a creative agent who implemented its providential design upon the very fibre of the cosmos stands, moreover, in opposition to the far-removed Epicurean gods who are unconcerned by the random atomic collisions and disintegration that account for the repeated coming to be of a universe.

Thus far the potential philosophical attraction a philosophical *disputatio in utramque partem* on the subject of cosmology may have held for Cicero. The partial translation of the *Timaeus*, on this view, would have featured in a philosophical *disputatio* that, to judge from the preface, would have contrasted, at the very least, two different viewpoints on the subjects of cosmology and theology, that of an Academic sceptic representing the Timaean creation account as the most probable view, and that of a Peripatetic stance.

On to our second question. Why did Cicero not continue this literary project? Its subject matter, the creative act of a providential divinity, features also in Cicero's treatise on theology *De natura deorum*. Cicero is believed to have composed this treatise in close proximity to his *Timaeus* translation, and there are further hints that suggest a close connection between

theos and the adjective *theion* may have been inaccurate and blurred, deliberately or not, either in Cicero's source or in his Latin translation. Of interest to us is the fact that Velleius portrays Aristotle as 'dissenting' from Plato: the god is charged with 'the regulating and safeguarding of the motions of the world' with the help of a mysterious *replicatione quadam*. A possible manner of accounting for the original notion behind this expression is to understand it as describing the workings of the highest divinity who, while removed from the physical cosmos, is responsible for the movement of the heavens as their ultimate cause – in other words, the workings of a divine entity that may anticipate the characteristics attached to the unmoved mover we encounter in Aristotle's later works (Chroust 1975: 212–17 offers a discussion of the various interpretations of this expression). The aspect of providential care associated with the Aristotelian divinity is thus apparently limited to the safeguarding of heavenly motion by the highest divinity, described as a separate being, *alius quidam*. Regarding the *replicatio quaedam*, Chroust 1975: 206, 212–17, points to *Met.* 11.8.1074a2 and to the mention of a type of planetary rotation (*aneilixis*) in Plato's *Statesman* 270d and 286b. A possible emendation of <non> *dissentiens*, suggested in support of arguing for an alignment with Platonic theology, has been rejected by most recent studies. Cf. Chroust 1975: 208 with nn. 2–5; Furley 1989: 212–14.

Cicero and the *Timaeus*

both works. Consider Cicero's translation of *Tim.* 29c4–7 where Timaeus comments on the accuracy of his account:

Table 1. *Plato, Tim. 29c4–7*

29c4	**A:** ἐὰν οὖν, ὦ Σώκρατες, πολλὰ πολλῶν πέρι θεῶν καὶ τῆς τοῦ παντὸς γενέσεως, μὴ δυνατοὶ γιγνώμεθα πάντη πάντως αὐτοὺς ἑαυτοῖς ὁμολογουμένους λόγους καὶ ἀπηκριβωμένους ἀποδοῦναι, μὴ θαυμάσῃς·	**A:** Therefore, Socrates, if in our extensive discussions regarding many topics, the gods and the generation of the universe, we are unable to give accounts that are entirely and in every way self-consistent and perfectly exact, do not be surprised.

Table 2. *Cicero's translation of Plato, Tim. 29c4–7 (Cic., Tim. 3.8, 3–7 ed. Ax / Plasberg)*

29c4	**B:** *quocirca si forte de deorum natura ortuque mundi disserentes minus id quod avemus animo consequemur, ut tota dilucide et plane exornata oratio sibi constet et ex omni parte secum ipsa consentiat, haut sane erit mirum ...*	**B:** Therefore, if by chance, in discussing the nature of the gods and the coming to be of the universe, we achieve less than what we desire, namely that our speech be entirely lucid, full in detail, self-consistent, and coherent in every part, this will, admittedly, not be surprising.

Having set out the limited epistemological value of accounts pertaining to created objects, Timaeus declares in the original text that Socrates must not be surprised should his account be less than self-consistent and exact regarding many topics, the gods, and the generation of the universe (ἐὰν οὖν, ὦ Σώκρατες, πολλὰ πολλῶν πέρι, θεῶν καὶ τῆς τοῦ παντὸς γενέσεως ... μὴ θαυμάσῃς). Cicero paraphrases this statement in the following manner: 'discussing the nature of the gods and the coming to be of the universe ...' (*quocirca si forte de deorum natura ortuque mundi disserentes ...*). The small but significant addition of *deorum natura* may indicate that the nature of the gods, including that of the Timaean

53

demiurge, was a topic Cicero intended to accentuate also in the *disputatio* he had envisaged.[55] Given the thematic overlap between the *Timaeus* translation and the *De natura deorum*, let us take a closer look at the latter treatise. As his own literary *persona* there notes,[56] Cicero chose to omit a representative of the Peripatetic school in the *De natura deorum*, a dialogue that, unlike the *Timaeus* translation, did make it onto his list of publications in his *De divinatione*. Instead, the conversation covers the theological positions of the Stoics and the Epicureans, both of which are countered by the Academic Cotta. Accounting for this omission, Cotta reminds his interlocutors of the opinion held by Antiochus, who believed that Stoics and Peripatetics agreed with regard to the essence (*re*) of their doctrine while disagreeing in their terminology only.[57] This conflation of the Stoic and Peripatetic doctrinal stance is duly rejected by the Stoic Balbus, who, however, in order to stress the disagreement between the two schools, refers to an ethical matter: the distinction between *honesta* and *commoda*.[58]

Curiously, Cicero fails to address the rather more urgent issue, namely that Antiochus' harmonization of Stoic and Peripatetic perspectives is problematic, not least with regard to the aspects of cosmological and theological doctrine outlined above. While both parties would have agreed, to a certain extent, on the teleological structure of the cosmos, they would have parted ways on its origin and everlastingness, and on the assumption of a creative divinity.[59] In what follows, it is the Epicurean Velleius who launches a twofold onslaught against the

[55] See further Sedley 2013: 189–93, who points out that Cicero's translation of *Tim.* 33a–b, the description of the universe's spherical shape, is echoed closely at *Nat. deor.* 2.47, in the context of the Stoic Balbus' exposition of theological doctrine.
[56] *Nat. deor.* 1.16: 'If M. Piso were present, no philosophical school of standing would fail to be represented' (*M. enim Piso si adesset, nullius philosophiae, earum quidem quae in honore sunt, vacaret locus*).
[57] *Antiocho enim Stoici cum Peripateticis re concinere videntur verbis discrepare.*
[58] I.e. the distinction between what is truly virtuous and morally good, as opposed to what is merely 'advantageous' and bears no reference to virtue.
[59] On the difficult question concerning the doctrinal overlap of these schools in the field of natural philosophy, such as it is presented by Antiochus' mouthpiece Varro at *Ac.* 1.24–9, cf. Long 1974: 151–2, and Sedley 2012.

Platonic and the Stoic creative and providential divinities.[60] What was the reason for Cicero's apparent preference for the format of the *De natura deorum*, which excludes a Peripatetic perspective from the discussion? It is possible that, in a discussion concerning the origin, everlastingness, and teleological design of the universe, as well as the possibility of a creative agent, the framework of the *De natura deorum* presented a richer potential for singling out and disparaging Epicurean doctrine, the doctrine that stands out among the others by denying a created, everlasting, teleologically[61] structured cosmos, *as well as* the presence of a providential creator god. A Peripatetic, in turn, would have allowed for the universe's everlastingness and teleological structure. The Epicurean perspective would, on this account, have been in more urgent need of refutation.

Timaean Methodology

As we turn to Cicero's Timaean methodology, my aim is to provide evidence for the agenda I believe him to have followed in his *Timaeus* project: to present the Timaean creation account as the cosmological theory that would have been adopted by the sceptical Academy as the most probable position.

I will go about answering these questions in several steps. In the first part of this section, I illustrate how Cicero translated *Tim.* 29b2–d3, the passage in which Timaeus reflects upon his methodology as a narrator, by resorting to vocabulary characteristic of the investigative methodology associated with Philo's sceptical Academy. At the same time, I shall emphasize the extent to which Cicero stresses the rhetorical nature of the sceptical investigative method, an aspect of his Latin translation that has gone unnoticed thus far. Taking Cicero's

---

[60] Cf. the series of arguments presented by Velleius at *Nat. deor.* 1.18–24, cf. pp. 90–91. At *Nat. deor.* 1.54 he rejects the idea that the gods must be feared: 'For who would not fear a nosy and meddling god who foresees and thinks and observes everything, and who believes that everything is his business?' (*quis enim non timeat omnia providentem et cogitantem et animadvertentem et omnia ad se pertinere putantem curiosum et plenum negotii deum?*).

[61] A point made by Furley 1989: 201–4.

translation of this passage to be representative of his overall authorial approach, I shall argue that Timaeus' speaking part was most likely intended for Cicero himself. Finally, I shall argue that Cicero found in Timaeus' narrative at *Tim.* 29d7–30c1 an argumentative pattern that, with the help of some minor modifications of the Greek text, appeared rather like an example for the application of sceptical–rhetorical investigative method to a question of fundamental import, the inquiry after the reason that induced the demiurge to create the visible cosmos.

Tim. 29b2–d3: The Εἰκὼς Λόγος as a Sceptical–Rhetorical Investigation

Let us turn directly to Cicero's translation of a crucial passage in the dialogue, *Tim.* 29b2–d3:[62]

Table 3. *Plato, Tim. 29b2–d3*

29b2	**A§1:** μέγιστον δὴ παντὸς ἄρξασθαι κατὰ φύσιν ἀρχήν. ὧδε οὖν περί τε εἰκόνος καὶ περὶ τοῦ παραδείγματος	**A§1:** Now, in regard to every matter it is most important to begin at the natural beginning. Accordingly, in the case of a likeness and its model, we
5	αὐτῆς διοριστέον, ὡς ἄρα τοὺς λόγους, ὧνπέρ εἰσιν ἐξηγηταί, τούτων αὐτῶν καὶ συγγενεῖς ὄντας·	ought to determine that the accounts bear a kinship to the subject matters of which they serve as exegetes.
29b5	**A§2a:** τοῦ μὲν οὖν μονίμου	**A§2a:** Therefore, accounts that deal
10	καὶ βεβαίου καὶ μετὰ νοῦ καταφανοῦς μονίμους καὶ ἀμεταπτώτους – καθ᾽ ὅσον οἷόν τε καὶ ἀνελέγκτοις προσήκει λόγοις εἶναι καὶ	with what is abiding and firm and discernible by the aid of thought will be abiding and unshakeable; and to the extent that it is possible and fitting for statements to be irrefutable and
15	ἀνικήτοις, τούτου δεῖ μηδὲν ἐλλείπειν –	invincible, they must in no wise fall short thereof;
29c1	**A§2b:** τοὺς δὲ τοῦ πρὸς μὲν ἐκεῖνο ἀπεικασθέντος, ὄντος δὲ εἰκόνος, εἰκότας ἀνὰ λόγον	**A§2b:** whereas the accounts concerning that which has been fashioned in the likeness of that model, and which is
20	τε ἐκείνων ὄντας·	itself a likeness, ought to be fashioned in a like manner and possess likelihood;

[62] Parts of this section appear in a condensed and modified form in Hoenig 2013.

Table 3 (*continued*)

29c3 A§3: ὅτιπερ πρὸς γένεσιν οὐσία, τοῦτο πρὸς πίστιν ἀλήθεια.	**A§3:** for as being stands in relation to coming to be, so truth stands in relation to convincingness.
29c4 A§4: ἐὰν οὖν, ὦ Σώκρατες, 25 πολλὰ πολλῶν πέρι θεῶν καὶ τῆς τοῦ παντὸς γενέσεως, μὴ δυνατοὶ γιγνώμεθα πάντῃ πάντως αὐτοὺς ἑαυτοῖς ὁμολογουμένους λόγους καὶ 30 ἀπηκριβωμένους ἀποδοῦναι, μὴ θαυμάσῃς·	**A§4:** Therefore, Socrates, if in our extensive discussions regarding many topics, the gods and the generation of the universe, we are unable to provide accounts that are entirely and in every way self-consistent and perfectly exact, do not be surprised;
29c7 A§5: ἀλλ᾽ ἐὰν ἄρα μηδενὸς ἧττον παρεχώμεθα εἰκότας, ἀγαπᾶν χρή, μεμνημένους ὡς 35 ὁ λέγων ὑμεῖς τε οἱ κριταὶ φύσιν ἀνθρωπίνην ἔχομεν, περὶ τούτων τὸν εἰκότα μῦθον ἀπο – δεχομένους πρέπει τούτου μηδὲν ἔτι 40 πέρα ζητεῖν.	**A§5:** rather we should be content if we can produce accounts that are inferior to none in likelihood, remembering that both I who speak and you who judge are but human creatures, so that it becomes us to accept the likely story of these matters and forbear to search beyond it.[63]

Table 4. *Cicero's translation of Plato,* Tim. *29b2–d3*
(*Cic.* Tim. *2.7, 12–3.8, 10*)

29b2 B§1: *difficillimum autem est in omni inquisitione orationis exordium; de iis igitur quae diximus, haec sit prima* 5 *distinctio. omni orationi cum iis rebus de quibus explicat videtur esse cognatio.*	**B§1:** In every investigation the beginning of the speech is the most difficult part. Concerning the matters about which we have been conversing, let this be my first distinction: each speech appears to bear a kinship with the subject matter it sets out.
29b5 B§2a: *itaque cum de re stabili et inmutabili disputat oratio, talis* 10 *sit qualis illa: neque redargui neque convinci potest;*	**B§2a:** Therefore, if the speech discusses a subject matter that is steadfast and immutable, let the speech be like the subject matter: it can be neither refuted nor defeated.
	(*continued*)

63 Transl. Lamb, with modifications.

Table 4 (*continued*)

29c1 15	**B§2b:** *cum autem ingressa est imitata et efficta simulacra, bene agi putate si similitudinem veri consequatur:*	**B§2b:** Whereas, when the speech has entered upon subjects that are likenesses or copies, consider likelihood the best result that can be attained.
29c3	**B§3:** *quantum enim ad id quod ortum est aeternitas valet, tantum ad fidem veritas.*	**B§3:** For to the same degree as eternity impacts upon what has come to be, truth impacts upon faith.
29c4 20 25	**B§4:** *quocirca si forte de deorum natura ortuque mundi disserentes minus id quod avemus animo consequemur, ut tota dilucide et plane exornata oratio sibi constet et ex omni parte secum ipsa consentiat, haut sane erit mirum,*	**B§4:** Therefore, if by chance, in discussing the nature of the gods and the coming to be of the universe we achieve less than what we set our mind upon, namely that our speech be lucidly and intelligibly furnished and entirely self-coherent, congruent in every part, this will, admittedly, be of little surprise,
29c7 30	**B§5:** *… contentique esse debebitis, si probabilia dicentur, aequum est enim meminisse et me qui disseram hominem esse et vos qui iudicetis ut, si probabilia dicentur, ne quid ultra requiratis.*	**B§5:** … and you will have to be content if probabilities are stated. For it is advisable to remember that both I, who am speaking, and you, who are the judges, are human, so that you [ought to] inquire no further if probabilities are stated.

Cicero[64] in **B§1** explains that, in every investigation, the beginning of the *oratio* is the most difficult part. He disambiguates the Greek ('in regard to every matter', παντὸς, **A§1**, l. 1) by indicating that the subject of his discussion is an *oratio*, a 'speech' that forms a part of an 'inquiry', *inquisitio*. We thus expect from the ensuing statements a description of the type of *oratio* Cicero considers suitable for a particular investigation.

He continues by setting out the desired relation between subject matter and discourse: 'concerning the matters about which we have been conversing, let this be my first distinction. Each

---

[64] As indicated previously, I will assume throughout this section that Cicero intended the Timaean speaking part for himself. I will present my reasons for doing so in due course.

speech appears to bear a kinship with the subject matter it sets out' (*de iis igitur quae diximus, haec sit prima distinctio. omni orationi cum iis rebus de quibus explicat videtur esse cognatio*). It is possible that the addition of *prima* was prompted by the mention of a 'beginning of the speech' (*exordium orationis*, for ἀρχή, 'origin') immediately before. Cicero may have considered the present context to refer to the initial difficulty (*difficillimum exordium*, **B§1**, ll. 1–2) of finding a type of speech that is suited to a particular subject matter. The difficulty at the outset of a speech may thus lie in the initial distinction between the different types of subjects and in identifying an appropriate type of speech or argument.[65] This relation is illustrated more clearly in the ensuing statement **B§2b** where Cicero translates: 'when the speech has entered upon subjects that are likenesses or copies, consider likelihood [*similitudo veri*, corresponding here to the Greek εἰκότας λόγους] the best result that can be attained' (*cum autem ingressa est imitata et efficta simulacra, bene agi putate si similitudinem veri consequatur*). A look ahead reveals *similitudo veri* is not the only rendering Cicero provides for the all-important expression εἰκὼς λόγος/ μῦθος. In **B§5**, l. 28 we encounter the term *probabilia*. At *Tim.* 30b6, a passage that will be of importance to the ensuing section, the expression is rendered by *coniectura*, 'inference':

Table 5. *Plato*, Tim. *30b6–c1*

30b6 **A:** οὕτως οὖν δὴ κατὰ **λόγον** τὸν **εἰκότα** δεῖ λέγειν τόνδε τὸν κόσμον ζῷον ἔμψυχον ἔννουν τε τῇ ἀληθείᾳ διὰ τὴν τοῦ θεοῦ γενέσθαι πρόνοιαν.	**A:** In this manner, therefore, we must conclude in accordance with **the likely account** that this cosmos is a living creature possessing soul and intellect and that, truly, it has come to be on account of the god's providence.

---

[65] The addition of ***prima distinctio***, which has no counterpart in the Greek, may have been motivated also by Cicero's omission of Timaeus' preliminary statement ἔστιν οὖν δὴ κατ᾽ ἐμὴν δόξαν πρῶτον διαιρετέον τάδε at *Tim.* 27d5. In the Greek, this statement anticipates the ensuing distinction between τὸ ὄν and τὸ γιγνόμενον. Cicero's translation begins immediately after this sentence.

Table 6. *Cicero's translation of Plato, Tim. 30b6–c1 (Cic. Tim. 3.10, 11–4)*

30b6	**B:** *quam ob causam non est cunctandum profiteri (si modo investigari aliquid coniectura potest) hunc mundum animal esse idque intellegens et divina providentia constitutum.*	**B:** For this reason one ought not hesitate to declare (if it is in any way possible to inquire after anything **by inference**) that this world is a living creature that is intelligent and has been built with divine providence.

To appreciate Cicero's choice of these Latin terms, let us examine his use of them in greater detail. We frequently encounter both *veri simile* and *probabile*,[66] or their cognate forms, as renderings of the Greek technical terms *eikos* and *pithanon* in Cicero's rhetorical treatises. Both Greek terms appear in a rhetorical context already in Plato (*Phaedr.* 266e3; 272d8–e1) and are familiar also from Aristotelian rhetoric,[67] where *pithanon* appears in Aristotle's definition of the art of rhetoric as 'the faculty of observing the available means of persuasion [or: that which is persuasive] in reference to any particular subject'.[68] The *eikota*, in turn, belong to the so-called *entechnoi pisteis*, the technical modes of persuasion that fall under the *enthumêma*.[69] A somewhat similar, if not strictly consistent,[70] differentiation of terms is discernible in several of Cicero's rhetorical works. In his early *De inventione* 1.9, for instance, the *veri similia* are individual components of a rhetorical argument, whereas *probabile* denotes the argument's convincingness: ' "invention" is the inventing of matters that are true or truth-like and make for a convincing argument'

---

[66] Cf. Sedley 2013: 202–4.
[67] Cf. Peetz 2005: 119–21 n. 47. Glucker 1995, a most valuable source for my following discussion, cites amongst other evidence Aristotle, *Rhet.* 2.23 1400a8,12, but warns that his use of *pithanon* was at no time universally consistent (see esp. pp. 123–6).
[68] Ar. *Rhet.* 1.2 1355b25–6: ἔστω δὴ ἡ ῥητορικὴ δύναμις περὶ ἕκαστον τοῦ θεωρῆσαι τὸ ἐνδεχόμενον πιθανόν (transl. Freese).
[69] E.g. Ar. *Rhet.* 1.2.1357a31ff. An excellent discussion is Schweinfurth-Walla 1986.
[70] See Glucker 1995: 128–9. On Cicero's knowledge of Aristotle's rhetorical works, cf. Fortenbaugh and Steinmetz 1989: 39–60, whose analysis suggests that Cicero mostly accessed Aristotle's *Rhetoric* via intermediary sources, but that his direct knowledge of Aristotle improved in the course of his career.

(*inventio est excogitatio rerum verarum aut veri similium quae causam probabilem reddant*). *probabile*, moreover, is employed by Cicero to translate the Aristotelian *endoxon* at *Inv.* 1.44–9.[71] In his *Partitiones oratoriae* Cicero uses the term *fides* in a similar manner to denote the effect achieved by *veri similia*:

> With regard to likelihoods (*veri similia*), some of them convey their force-fulness by themselves, while others, even if they appear slight in them-selves, nonetheless have an impact when gathered together ... the highest convincingness (*maximam fidem*) is given to a likelihood (*similitudinem veri*) first by an example (*exemplum*) ...[72]

I shall return to Cicero's term *fides* in due course. We encounter the terms *probabile*, *veri simile*, and their cognates also in Cicero's philosophical writings, in the context of sceptical epistemology.[73] Both terms, without any apparent distinction, denote the outcome of the familiar sceptical investigative method, the *disputatio in utramque partem*.[74] It served to establish a viewpoint that was 'persuasive' or 'convincing', and that could serve as a guideline for the sceptical philosopher without requiring from him an ultimate commitment to cognitive certainty. This is made explicit at *Ac.* 2.32 where the Antiochean Lucullus criticizes the sceptics in the following manner: 'They claim that something is persuasive (*probabile*) and, so to speak,[75] truth-like (*veri simile*), and that they use this as a guideline in their conduct of life as well as in their investigations and discussions.'

Philo, his predecessors, and even Cicero himself have been credited with advancing the concept of the *pithanon*, translated by Cicero as *probabile* or *veri simile*, to serve as a criterion for decision-making, in a development from the Carneadean

---

[71] Noted also by Burnyeat 2009: 169.
[72] Cic. *Part. or.* 40. *Exemplum* translates Aristotle's *paradeigma*, a further possible component of rhetorical proof alongside *eikota*, *tekmêria*, and *sêmeia*. Cf. Ar. *Rhet.* 1.2 1357a31ff.; *An pr.* 70a2.
[73] Noted already by Baltes 1976–8: 39 n. 60, Aronadio 2008: 119–29, and pointed out by Sedley 2013: 202–5.
[74] *Ac.* 2.7–8. Cicero reports that this method was taught already by Aristotle as an exercise of rhetorical invention, cf. *Or.* 46; *De orat.* 3.80.
[75] Translating *quasi*. Fuhrer 1993 suggests that Cicero's use of *quasi* in this context indicates his awareness of the fact that *veri simile* was not part of the sceptics' epistemological vocabulary. Cf. p. 64.

pithanê phantasia.[76] Carneades had advanced the concept of the *pithanê phantasia*, the 'convincing impression' or 'persuasive impression', translated by Cicero as *probabilis visio* or *probabile visum*,[77] as a presumably dialectical[78] alternative to the Stoic criterion of truth, the *katalêptikê phantasia*, or 'cognitive impression'. It was Philo, according to Cicero's testimony,[79] who transferred the use of the *pithanon* from practical decision-making to intellectual discourse, and imparted to the concept a more positive value: what seemed persuasive, to Philo, might now be taken as evidence for the truth.[80]

Bearing in mind the fact that, in the field of rhetoric, Cicero usually, although not universally, uses *veri simile* for *eikos* whilst rendering *pithanon* as *probabile*, his apparently synonymous use of both Latin terms in his philosophical works to translate the Academic *pithanon* is noteworthy.[81] There is no evidence to suggest that Plato's specific application of the term *eikos*, originally a rhetorical term, to epistemological contexts, such as we encounter in the *Timaeus*, was maintained by his

---

[76] Cf. Couissin 1929: 55. Görler 1992 and Peetz 2005 esp. 116–18 credit Cicero, not Philo, with the innovation of the concept of the *probabile* (for *pithanon*) as a development of the Carneadean *pithanê phantasia*; cf. Glucker 1995: 133–5, cf. Görler 1994a: 876. Against this view, cf. Brittain 2016: 19 n. 13. Carneades' predecessor Arcesilaus is credited with turning the *eulogon*, a term taken from Stoic ethical theory and modelled after the *katorthôma*, as a criterion of action and decision-making (albeit with a polemical agenda). Cicero translates the *eulogon* likewise with *probabile* at *Fin.* 3.58. Cf. Sextus Empiricus, *M.* 7.158; see also Long and Sedley 1987 vol. 1: 456–7. The notion of persuasiveness is also apparent in Clitomachus' position, cf. *Ac.* 2.104.

[77] *Ac.* 2.33; 99; cf. Glucker, 1995: 117–18, 135.

[78] The Academic *pithanê phantasia* as an alternative criterion is thought to have been a response to the charge of *apraxia*, the inability to make decisions and to act on them, which, the Stoics argued, was a necessary consequence of a suspension of judgement (*epochê*) resulting from the sceptical denial of cognitive certainty. Cf. Plut. *Col.* 1122A; Sextus Empiricus *M.* 11.160–4; see further, Striker 1980: 63–9. Clitomachus, in Cicero's testimony (*Ac.* 2.78, 108; cf. *Fin.* 5.20), believed that his master, following his predecessor Arcesilaus, had designed the concept of the *pithanê phantasia* merely as a dialectical device tailored to rival the Stoic *katalêptikê phantasia* and thus advanced it as a point of reference in the evaluation of sense impressions. As such, it should not be understood to carry any epistemological significance, in the way it did for Philo, but to have taken the role merely of an *ad hominem* argument. This is supported by Augustine (*Contr. ac.* 3.41). Cf. also Brittain 2001: 14–18; Long and Sedley 1987 vol. 1: 459–60; Dal Pra 1975 vol. 1: 270–81; Couissin 1929: 241–76.

[79] Cf. Cic. *Ac.* 2.32; *Fin.* 2.36.

[80] Cf. Brittain 2001: 73–120.

[81] Further instances of an 'epistemological' use of *veri simile* are *Tusc.* 2.9 and *Fin.* 2.43.

school. Unlike *pithanon*, *eikos* does not appear to have been a part of the sceptic philosopher's epistemological vocabulary. It is possible, therefore, that *veri simile*, as an apparent synonym for *probabile*, was incorporated by Cicero into the vocabulary of sceptical epistemology, despite the fact that its usual Greek counterpart, *eikos*, did not belong to this field.

Was a *deliberate*, philosophically charged reinterpretation of the rhetorical *veri simile* as a synonym for *probabile*, translating the epistemological *pithanon*, original to Cicero?[82] Perhaps a conflation of the rhetorical *eikos*/*veri simile* and the epistemological *pithanon*/*probabile* had occurred previously, in the process of assimilation between rhetorical argument and philosophical investigation. This assimilation is credited to a large extent to Philo, who appropriated parts of the rhetorical curriculum and integrated these, with some modification, into that of the sceptical Academy.[83] The intrinsic relation between the two methodologies is made explicit in the well-known passage *De oratore* 3.107–9, where the orator Crassus explains how the *disputatio in utramque partem*, an exercise originally used in the field of rhetoric, had become a philosophical investigative method. Having characterized this exercise, more specifically,

[82] Görler 1992 argues that, based on his use of *probabile*, Cicero must be credited with the original, although 'accidental', development of contemporary Academic philosophy towards a more positive, constructive form of scepticism that had as its aim the *probabile* as a criterion for one's conduct of life. Görler believes further that, while initially using both *probabile* and *veri simile* to translate *pithanon*, Cicero began to consider the latter less suitable and therefore abandoned it gradually in favour of *probabile*. Glucker 1995 after an extensive review of Cicero's use of *probabile*, *veri simile*, and their cognate forms, concludes that Cicero used the terms inconsistently. Fuhrer 1993 esp. 113–14 holds that Cicero must accept the charge of incorrectly employing the rhetorical *veri simile* in an epistemological context. Peetz 2005, building on Görler, goes as far as crediting Cicero alone with advancing the newly devised concept of the *probabile* as an independent development of the Carneadean *pithanê phantasia* by combining in his *probabile* Aristotle's rhetorical *pithanon* with what he terms the 'metaphysical' *eikos* of Plato's *Timaeus*, translated as *veri simile*. I am hesitant to subscribe to such a positive evaluation of Cicero's philosophical ambitions, and think it more likely that Cicero's use of *veri simile* for *eikos*, if intentional, was prompted by his wish to stress the essentially rhetorical nature of sceptic investigative method by elevating it to a status equal to the *probabile*. Nevertheless, I owe to Peetz and the other contributions many illuminating insights.

[83] The most detailed study is Brittain 2001: 298–344. Brittain ascribes a considerable influence upon Philo's adopted rhetorical curriculum to his colleague Charmadas, cf. ibid. 319–28.

Cicero

as a method of constructing 'two-sided debates (*ancipites disputationes*) in which it was permitted to argue copiously both *pro* and *contra* (*in utramque partem*)', he explains further: 'This exercise is now considered peculiar to [the Academy and the Peripatetics] but in the old days it was the activity of the persons who were sought to provide arguments and material for speeches on all kinds of public affairs ...'.[84] In the subsequent paragraph, Crassus associates the use of rhetorical method with Philo, in particular.[85] I shall return to this passage shortly.

It is possible that Cicero, brought up on rhetoric and philosophy from a young age, might not have drawn a clear distinction between *pithanon/probabile* and *eikos/veri simile* as, respectively, a *purely* epistemological and a *purely* rhetorical concept. The mingling of rhetorical and epistemological expressions and nuances, likely practised by Philo's Academy, might have appeared to him natural as a consequence of the inherent affinities between the two methodologies.[86] It is evident, however, that he was acutely sensitive to subtle terminological differences. We recall his phrasing of Antiochus' critical portrayal of sceptical policy at *Ac.* 2.32: 'They claim that something is persuasive (*probabile*) and, so to speak (*quasi*), truthlike (*veri simile*), and that they use this as a guideline in their conduct of life as well as in their investigations and discussions.' Cicero's use of *quasi* qualifies the expression *veri simile* and indicates that it might not readily be understood as belonging to the same terminological field of application as *probabile*.[87]

What is more, Cicero plays on the concurrence of both rhetorical and epistemological undertones in the expression

---

[84] Regarding the development of the sceptical-rhetorical method, cf. Reinhardt 2000 esp. 533–9, and Brittain 2001: 298–345.
[85] '[The rhetoricians] hold on to that former type [of rhetorical argument], the one that is bound to dates, locations, and individual parties, and this itself is slipping through their fingers – for now, under Philo, who I hear is held in great esteem in the Academy, they learn and practise these cases, too' (*nam illud alterum genus, quod est temporibus, locis, reis definitum, obtinent atque id ipsum lacinia. nunc enim apud Philonem, quem in Academia vigere audio, etiam harum iam causarum cognitio exercitatioque celebrator*). Cf. also *Tusc.* 2.9.
[86] At *Or.* 11–12 Cicero describes his rhetorical expertise as a consequence of his philosophical training.
[87] Cf. Fuhrer 1993. On Cicero's (*ad*)*probare*, cf. Schweinfurth-Walla 1986: 30–46; Görler 1992: 162–5.

probabile at *Ac.* 2.104–5, where he accentuates the ambiguous meaning of (*ad*)*probare* in its Stoic epistemological sense of 'to approve an impression', as well as in its rhetorical meaning of 'to convince/persuade' (*probamus*, LS III: *probare aliquid alicui*, 'to convince someone of something') somebody of an argument. Only sense impressions that are unhindered (*ea quae nulla re impedirentur*) may be approved of. If the Academics cannot persuade (*probamus*) the Stoics of their tenets, these may, indeed, be false, but are certainly not detestable. The only difference between the Stoic and the sceptic is that the former speaks of something that is 'perceived' or 'cognized', whereas in the latter's opinion it only 'seems to do so' on the condition that it be 'persuasive' (*probabilia*).

Cicero possessed in-depth knowledge of both rhetorical and philosophical terminology, which undoubtedly increased further in the course of his project of creating a Latin philo-sophical vocabulary. Given that no evidence points to the use of the term *eikos* in Philo's vocabulary, it is possible to imagine that the use of *veri simile*, as a synonym for the epis-temological *pithanon/probabile*, may be original to Cicero, the former orator–politician, who was now advocating the merits of rhetorical expertise in the context of philosophical debate by elevating the merely rhetorical *veri simile* to a status equal to the rhetorical–epistemological *probabile*. On this account, the appearance of *eikos* in our *Timaeus* passage, where, in addition to its rhetorical meaning, *eikos* is given a distinct-ively epistemological significance by Plato himself, would have validated Cicero's agenda.

Let us return to Cicero's translation. In **B§2b**, ll. 14–5 (Table 4), the ambiguity of the Platonic εἰκότας (**A§2b**, l. 19, Table 3) is reproduced, with *similitudo veri* both admit-ting of a literal interpretation, thus describing the type of *oratio* in question as resulting in 'resemblance to the truth',[88] and as referring to the persuasive effect of a likely speech that is expressed by εἰκός in its rhetorical meaning. Cicero's

---

[88] The view of Krämer 1971, who recognizes in the present passage an 'Umdeutung' of Cicero's concept of *veri simile/pithanon*.

Cicero

wording here establishes a further link between his *oratio* and the sceptic investigative method he himself employed.

In A§3 (Table 3) Timaeus' analogy between the correlated dichotomous pair of γένεσις and οὐσία and its epistemological counterpart of πίστις and ἀλήθεια, translated by Cicero as *fides* and *veritas*, fits well with the sceptical-rhetorical slant we have detected so far in Cicero's translation of the methodology passage. We have seen above that Cicero uses *fides* as a technical term of rhetorical theory. At *Partitiones oratoriae* 40, we recall,[89] *fides* describes the convincing effect of the individual 'probabilities', *veri similia*, at the orator's disposal.[90] Significant for our ensuing discussion is, moreover, the fact that Cicero's definition of *fides* in the *Part. or.* occurs within his discussion of the *loci coniecturae*, commonplace methods of inference used for rhetorical invention. The *loci coniecturae* depend entirely on probabilities (as opposed to scientific proof): 'All inference takes place in the context of probabilities' (*in veri similibus ... posita est tota [coniectura], Part. or.* 34). With the help of the *loci coniecturae*, arguments are attained that possess *fides*.[91] I shall return to the method of *coniectura* below.

Significantly, *fides* is also used by Cicero to describe Stoic trust in impressions that are *probabilia*. It is important to note that Cicero here makes use of the term not in the sense of an inherent quality, the 'convincingness' or 'credibility' of somebody or something, but uses it to describe the reaction of the onlooker who bestows 'trust' upon somebody or something.[92]

---

[89] Cf. p. 61.

[90] 'The greatest degree of convincingness of a probability is achieved, firstly, by an example; next, by introducing a similar case ...' (*maximam autem fidem facit ad similitudinem veri primum exemplum, deinde introducta rei similitudo ...*). Cf. *Inv.* 1.25; *Part or.* 27; *Top.* 8. The possible influence of Aristotle's theory of enthymemes on Cicero's use of *veri simile* is discussed by Peetz 2005: 102. At *Top.* 98, *fides* refers to a part of a speech. A similar use of the term's Greek equivalent πίστις predates Aristotle's *Rhetoric*, cf. Wisse 1989: 88–104.

[91] Cf. *Part. or.* 33.

[92] Cicero associates this sense with *fides* (which he considers a derivative form of *fio*) at *Off.* 1.23: 'The foundation of justice is trustworthiness (*fides*), that is, the steadfastness and truth of words and agreements. For this reason ... let us follow the Stoics [i.e. Stoic practice] ... and believe that this is called "trustworthiness" (*fides*) because it [describes things] that come to be (*fiat*)' (*fundamentum iustitiae est fides, id est dictorum conventorumque constantia et veritas. ex quo ... audeamus imitari*

66

At *Ac.* 2.35–6, Lucullus censures the sceptic notion of *probabile* and *veri simile* in a passage that is worth quoting in full:

So what does this *probabile* of yours mean? For, if what each person encounters, and what, more or less at first sight, appears persuasive to them, is confirmed as certain, what could be more unreliable than that? Whereas, if they are going to profess themselves to follow an impression (*visum*) [only] after some circumspection and careful consideration, they can nevertheless still not get away with it, firstly because those impressions that have no difference from each other are, all of them, equally denied their trust (*fides*) …[93]

Lucullus mocks the sceptics' inability to lend *fides* to a particular impression (*visum*) even after scrupulous evaluation, given that, according to their tenets, true and false impressions can both appear the same due to the lack of a distinctive mark. Both *probabile* and *fides* are thus notions that come into play in the Academic–Stoic debate on the evaluation of sense presentations. While the Stoic assents to the *kataleptikê phantasia*,[94] the Carneadean sceptic, according to Lucullus' polemic, is unable to lend *fides* without contradicting his own epistemological precepts. *Fides* and its cognate forms are, of course, the equivalent of the Greek *pistis/pithanon*. In Cicero's translation, I take it to express the same degree of epistemological trustworthiness as is carried by his *probabile/ veri simile*. Where a Stoic 'assents to' and 'approves of' (usually rendered *adsentiri/adprobare* by Cicero) cataleptic impressions, the sceptic would presumably claim to bestow

---

Stoicos … credamusque quia fiat quod dictum est, appellatam fidem). Cf. Dyck 1996: 114–15. I refrain from even attempting to reproduce this etymological connection in English. Occasionally, *fides* is used with a somewhat difference sense in Cicero's rhetorical works, e.g. *Part. or.* 9, where it describes the effect of a speech produced in the audience, i.e. 'conviction': 'Conviction is an established opinion' (*fides est firma opinio*). Cf. a similar use at *Inv.* 1.25, and see Fraenkel 1916: 189.

[93] *quod est igitur istuc vestrum probabile? nam si quod cuique occurrit et primo quasi aspectu probabile videtur id confirmatur, quid eo levius; sin ex circumspectione aliqua et accurata consideratione quod visum sit id se dicent sequi, tamen exitum non habebunt, primum quia iis visis inter quae nihil interest aequaliter omnibus abrogatur fides.* Lucullus, moreover, uses the verb *confidere* in the same context in the remainder of his statement.

[94] Similarly, in this description of Zeno: 'he bestowed trust on the senses because, as I said earlier, an apprehension that had come about with the help of the senses appeared [to him] true and trustworthy' (*sensibus etiam fidem tribuebat, quod ut supra dixi comprehensio facta sensibus et vera esse illi et fidelis videbatur, Ac.* 1.42).

merely 'trust' (*pistis/fides*) in those impressions that are 'persuasive' (*pithana/probabilia, veri similia*). While Cicero's rendering *fides* B§3, l. 18 (Table 4), at first sight, appears straightforward, its appearance in close proximity to the preceding mention of *veri similitudo* and *probabilia* results in a heightened rhetorical–epistemological nuancing of the Latin text that, given Cicero's expertise in both oratory and philosophy, is unlikely to have been casual. As the convincing effect and inherent quality of those *orationes* which treat of sensible subject matter, *fides* may simply be taken to describe the result of the *veri similia* presented in Cicero's speech. His speech stands in relation to *veritas* as does his subject matter, the sensible cosmos, to the intelligible realm. At the same time, *fides* in its role as a technical term of Academic–Stoic epistemology, where it refers to trust, a degree of epistemological certainty that falls short of the Stoic notion of 'assent', in sense presentations, is associated by Cicero with the realm of becoming and change that is characterized as ultimately unreliable, a characterization to which the sceptic philosopher would presumably have subscribed.

In B§4 (Table 4) Cicero comments on the topic of his investigation: 'Therefore, if by chance, in discussing the nature of the gods and the coming to be of the universe ...' (*quocirca si forte de deorum natura ortuque mundi disserentes ...*). While Cicero remains relatively close to the Greek ('... [in our extensive discussions regarding many topics], the gods and the generation of the universe', πολλὰ πολλῶν πέρι θεῶν καὶ τῆς τοῦ παντὸς γενέσεως, A§4, ll. 25–6, Table 3), the slight modification achieved by the omission of 'regarding many topics' (πολλὰ πολλῶν πέρι), and his addition, in turn, of *natura*, not only results in a rendering immediately reminiscent of the title of Cicero's *De natura deorum*, composed in close proximity to his *Timaeus* translation,[95] but, moreover, identifies the nature of the gods as one of the subjects of his *oratio* in his *Timaeus* translation. In addition, the fact that the *De natura deorum* is

---

[95] Cf. Powell 1995: 280–1.

presented as a *disputatio in utramque partem*[96] lends support to the impression that Cicero had approached his *Timaeus* project with the same intention of expressing conflicting viewpoints on the topic of cosmology, with the additional variation of presenting his own position in Plato's very own words, albeit in a translation that represented these words with a good dose of Academic scepticism added. The envisaged result would have aligned Academic–rhetorical methodology with the master himself.[97] Cicero's speech would, on this interpretation, have provided a sceptical thesis on the topic of cosmology, considered to possess likelihood, *veri similitudo*, or probability.

In **B§5** (Table 4), Cicero explains that, within the framework of an *oratio* whose subject matter is located in the sensible realm, his listeners 'will have to be content if probabilities are given' (*contentique esse debebitis, si probabilia dicentur*). As discussed above, Cicero's habitual synonymous usage of *probabile* and *veri simile* as technical terms of rhetorical theory encourages the reader to add to the notion of epistemological trustworthiness that of rhetorical convincingness, and thus lends further substance to the view that he is aligning Plato's εἰκὼς λόγος with sceptical-rhetorical methodology.

Let us revisit Cicero's translation of *Tim.* 29b2–d3. He describes the process of adapting one's argumentative method to the type of investigation at hand from the beginning (*exordium*). This is the most crucial or difficult part of the speech since it is necessary to draw an initial distinction (*prima distinctio*) bearing on the type of subject matter to be discussed, and to find a corresponding type of *oratio*. In the ensuing statements Cicero deliberately emphasizes the similarities between sceptic and rhetorical methodology with the help of terminology that is characteristic of both areas of expertise.

[96] Cic. *Fat.* 1: 'The method I followed in those other books concerning the nature of the gods ... (*qui sunt de natura deorum ...*) was that of unfolding a continuous discourse both for and against [a given view] (*feci ut in utramque partem perpetua explicaretur oratio*), with the aim that each [reader] can more easily adopt the view that seems to him most probable (*quod cuique maxime probabile videretur*).'

[97] Cf. Cic. *Ac.* 1.46.

The *oratio* treating of subjects that are unstable and changing can attain no more than *similitudinem veri*. The person who has engaged in a speech of this kind therefore bases his investigation on *fides*, and his individual arguments can be no more than *probabilia*. We saw, moreover, how Cicero's indication that the subject of his inquiry (*inquisitio*) is the 'nature of the gods and the origin of the world' (*natura deorum* and the *ortus mundi*) establishes a link between the *Timaeus* translation and Cicero's *De natura deorum*, a dialogue which is structured as a *disputatio in utramque partem* and thus corresponds to the methodology practised in the sceptical Academy. The two key terms *probabile* and *similitudo veri* chosen to render Timaeus' εἰκὼς λόγος should be understood as programmatic of the type of *oratio* Cicero considers suitable for the contents of the Timaean creation account, and allow for the mention of *fides*, a seemingly straightforward equivalent to πίστις, to appear in a new light: as describing a degree of epistemological trustworthiness as well as that of rhetorical convincingness achieved by an *oratio*. The Platonic εἰκὼς λόγος, in Timaeus' methodological manifesto at *Tim.* 29b2–d3, is identified by Cicero with the method of sceptical-rhetorical investigation. Given his expertise in both rhetorical and philosophical method, I suggest that it is Cicero himself who, among the speakers identified in the preface, appears most qualified to undertake this kind of investigation. While the former consul Nigidius would likely have been schooled in rhetorical practice, there is no evidence that connects him to the sceptical cause. Instead, the methodology at the centre of Cicero's translation very much points to the method espoused by himself in his other philosophical treatises.

The translation thus has the tone of a cosmological account of the type that would have been advanced by Philo's Academy, a position that advances *probabilia*, probable viewpoints that could, in turn, be opposed by the other interlocutors Cicero may have envisaged for his *Timaeus* project. The fact that he had embarked on it suggests that the *Timaeus* had experienced during Philo's tenure renewed attention from various philosophical factions, whether Stoic or Antiochean, and was considered as representative of the Platonic heritage, in whichever way this heritage was portrayed. Cicero's translation of the dialogue may thus have been motivated by his desire to represent the text in explicitly sceptical terms, as an Academic take on natural philosophy that sketched out the most probable viewpoints concerning the creation of the universe. In producing a reasonably *literal* translation of the dialogue, Cicero would have been all the more convincing in claiming the master's allegiance for the sceptic cause.

In the present section, I have been arguing that Cicero's creation account contained viewpoints that would have been considered probable by the Academic sceptic. In what follows, I will argue that a specific passage in his translation, *Tim.* 29d7–30c1, demonstrates how, or with the help of which argumentative steps, the Academic sceptic might have arrived at such probable viewpoints.

Tim. 29d7–30c1: An Example of the Sceptical-Rhetorical Quaestio

Table 7. *Plato*, Tim. *29d7–30c1*

29d7 **A§1a:** Τί. λέγωμεν δὴ δι᾿ ἥντινα αἰτίαν γένεσιν καὶ τὸ πᾶν τόδε ὁ συνιστὰς συνέστησεν.	**A§1a:** Tim: Let us state the reason on account of which the builder built [the realm of] coming to be and this All.
29e1 **A§1b:** ἀγαθὸς ἦν, ἀγαθῷ δὲ 5 οὐδεὶς περὶ οὐδενὸς οὐδέποτε ἐγγίγνεται φθόνος· τούτου δ᾿ ἐκτὸς ὢν πάντα ὅτι μάλιστα ἐβουλήθη γενέσθαι παραπλήσια ἑαυτῷ.	**A§1b:** He was good, and in one who is good no grudge concerning anything will ever arise. Free from grudge, he wished for everything to come to be in likeness of himself as much as possible.
29e4 **A§1c:** ταύτην δὴ γενέσεως καὶ κόσμου μάλιστ᾿ ἄν τις ἀρχὴν κυριωτάτην παρ᾿ ἀνδρῶν φρονίμων ἀποδεχόμενος ὀρθότατα ἀποδέχοιτ᾿ ἄν.	**A§1c:** Whosoever accepts this as the most authoritative principle of coming to be and the cosmos, [obtained] from wise men, will do so most rightly.
...	...

(continued)

Cicero

Table 7 (continued)

30b6 15	**A§2:** οὕτως οὖν δὴ κατὰ λόγον τὸν εἰκότα δεῖ λέγειν τόνδε τὸν κόσμον ζῷον ἔμψυχον ἔννουν τε τῇ ἀληθείᾳ διὰ τὴν τοῦ θεοῦ γενέσθαι πρόνοιαν.	**A§2:** Thus, in accordance with the likely account, it must be stated that, truly, this cosmos has come to be a living creature possessing soul and intellect, on account of the providence of the god.

Table 8. *Cicero's translation of Plato,* Tim. *29d7–30c1 (Cic.* Tim. *3.9, 11–3.10, 14)*

29d7	**B§1a:** *quaeramus igitur causam* *quae impulerit eum qui haec* *machinatus sit ut originem rerum* *et molitionem novam quaereret.*	**B§1a:** Let us therefore seek the reason that impelled him who constructed [the All] to seek a beginning of things and a new effort.
29e1	**B§1b:** *probitate videlicet* *praestabat, probus autem invidet* *nemini; itaque omnia sui similia* *generavit.*	**B§1b:** he manifestly excelled in goodness; but one who is good begrudges nobody. Therefore, he created everything in likeness to himself.
29e4 10	**B§1c:** *haec nimirum gignendi* *mundi causa iustissima.*	**B§1c:** This is without doubt the most just reason for the coming to be of the world.
30b6 15	**B§2:** *quam ob causam non est* *cunctandum profiteri (si modo* *investigari aliquid coniectura* *potest) hunc mundum animal* *esse idque intellegens et divina* *providentia constitutum.*	**B§2:** For this reason one should not hesitate to declare (if it is at least possible to inquire after anything by inference) that this world is a living creature and, moreover, one that is intelligent and has been built with divine providence.

In **B§1a**, ll. 1–4 (Table 8), Cicero by means of his phrasing
quaeramus ... quaereret aligns his own 'seeking' with the
craftsman's 'seeking' to create this cosmos, thereby constructing
a *cognatio* between his *oratio* and its subject matter as postulated
earlier in the dialogue (*Tim.* 29b4–5). But Cicero's choice of
quaerere, which may be rendered, alternatively, as 'to ask', for
the Greek λέγειν (**A§1a**, l. 1) 'to say', has further implications.
The question at stake is the following: 'What was the reason

that impelled the creator to seek the beginning of the universe and a new construction?' In what follows, I shall argue that the Academic sceptic would have employed a specific argumentative method in order to establish a probable viewpoint on this question, and that the argumentative steps taken may have been similar to Cicero's translation of *Tim.* 29d7–30c1. This similarity, I suggest, further underlines Cicero's endeavour to portray the Timaean creation account along sceptical lines.

It is important to understand what exactly Cicero is announcing with his use of the term *quaerere*. The noun *quaestio* is one of his Latin renderings of the rhetorical *thesis*,[98] a specific type of question or proposition. In his early *De inventione* 1.8 Cicero describes the *quaestio* (corresponding to *thesis*) as a general type of question that is distinguished from a more particular type of controversy, the *causa* (*hupothesis*).[99] Cicero chides the presumed author of this rhetorical theory, Hermagoras, for wrongly assuming that the *thesis* would be used by the forensic orator rather than the philosopher, who was much better equipped for discussing abstract concerns.[100]

---

[98] At *De orat.* 3.109 Cicero translates *thesis* as *consultatio*, cf. *Top.* 86. For the following, the evidence presented by Brittain 2001: 334–45, Reinhardt 2000 and 2003 has been invaluable to me. Throm's *Die Thesis* (1932) remains a helpful account of the history and the development of the rhetorical *thesis*. See also Patillon-Bolognesi 1997: lxxxiii–xci.

[99] In later writings Cicero notes how closely related the two question types are, cf. *Part. or.* 61–2: 'A discussion [translating *consultatio*, a further rendering of *thesis*], however, is, as it were, a division of a cause and controversy [*causa*, *controversia*, both of which are renderings for *hupothesis*]. For what is limited contains an element that is unlimited, and all matters contained in the former have a reference nevertheless to the latter' (transl. Rackham). At *De orat.* 3.106 Crassus explains that the so-called *loci*, rhetorical devices aimed at supplying arguments, are applied to both the specific inquiry, *causa*, and to the inquiry *de universa re*; cf. *Top.* 79. It is their association with the general inquiry, according to Crassus, that has led to the label 'commonplaces', [*loci*] *communes*.

[100] 'Hermagoras, does not seem to be paying attention, nor to understand what he is announcing when he divides the subject matter covered by the orator into *hupothesis* and *thesis* ... for it appears to be great folly to assign to the orator, as if it were mere trivialities, the subject matter that we know is dealt with by the philosophers' outstanding ingenuity with great toil' (*Hermagoras quidem nec quid dicat attendere nec quid polliceatur intellegere videtur, qui oratoris materiam in causam et in quaestionem dividat ... nam quibus in rebus summa ingenia philosophorum plurimo cum labore consumpta intellegimus, eas sicut aliquas parvas res oratori attribuere magna amentia videtur*), cf. *De orat.* 2.65–8. It is unclear to what extent the method of *thesis* was, in fact, applied in the field of forensic oratory. Cf. Brittain 2001: 303 with n. 17 and 334 with n. 71.

At *De oratore* 3.111, a passage we encountered above, Cicero similarly distinguishes between rhetorical subject matters 'that are discussed in the city and forensic cases' (*quae in civitate et in forensi disceptatione versantur*, corresponding to the *hupothesis/ causa*), and, on the other hand, concerns of a more *general* type, the so-called *consultationes infinitae* (corresponding to the *thesis/quaestio*). His testimony in the *De oratore* makes it clear, moreover, that the rhetorical *thesis/quaestio* was associated with the sceptical *disputatio in utramque partem*. At *De orat.* 3.107 Crassus describes this methodology of Academics and Peripatetics as 'two-sided discussions, in which one may argue copiously on either side of the general type [of question]' (*ancipites disputationes, in quibus de universo genere*[101] *in utramque partem disseri copiose licet*). Once a *universa res*, corresponding to the *quaestio*, had been advanced, a *disputatio in utramque partem* of such a *quaestio* would follow.[102] At *De oratore* 3.110, Crassus suggests that the method of *thesis* was now associated with Philo, who had, at this point, appropriated also the method of *hupothesis*: '[The rhetoricians] hold on to that former type, the one that is bound to dates, locations, and individual parties, and this itself is slipping through their fingers – for now, under Philo, who I hear is held in great esteem in the Academy, they learn and practise these cases, too.' I suggest that the passage I have singled out for discussion, *Tim.* 29d7–30c1, would have accommodated, from Cicero's viewpoint, the argumentative steps associated with the *thesis* method such as it was taught in Philo's Academy.

It is helpful in this context to elaborate, first, on the details of the method the speaker applies when making use of the *quaestio*. Let us return to Crassus. His description, at *De orat.* 3.111–18,[103] of the *thesis* method includes a *divisio* of question types that may lie at the outset of two-sided discussions. He credits 'most learned men', *doctissimi homines* (3.117), with the

---

[101] Referring back to the *universa res* in the preceding chapter 106 of the work.
[102] See also the extensive discussion by Mansfeld 1990, who identifies parallel structures between Academic dialectic and Peripatetic rhetorical exercises.
[103] The methodological *divisio* is discussed in detail by Brittain 2001: 333–45, Reinhardt 2000: 538–9.

theory behind this *divisio* of question types. Given his mention
of Philo, in particular, as the person to have appropriated rhetorical technique for the Academy, it is reasonable to assume
Philo's influence behind this *divisio*.[104]

Once the topic under investigation had been identified as a
thesis or *quaestio infinita*, the next step was to build arguments
by certain means of invention. These *modi inventionis* are
defined as *coniectura* ('inference', a term we have already
encountered above), *definitio* ('definition'), and *consecutio*
('consequence'). It is in Cicero's translation of *Tim.* 30b6 that
we learn which *modus inventionis* is chosen to respond to the
quaestio posed at 29d7, to find 'the reason that impelled him
who constructed [the All] to seek a beginning of things and
a new effort'. In **B§2**, ll. 11–6 (Table 8), Cicero states: 'one
should not hesitate to declare (if it is at least possible to inquire
after anything **by inference**) that this world is a living creature and, moreover, one that is intelligent and has been built
with divine providence' (*non est cunctandum profiteri (si modo
investigari aliquid **coniectura** potest) hunc mundum animal esse
idque intellegens et divina providentia constitutum*). Cicero's use,
in his *Timaeus* translation, of *coniectura* as the third rendering
for the Platonic εἰκὼς λόγος is an indicator that the various
individual cosmological perspectives that are assembled in the
Timaean narrative, such as the *quaestio* at *Tim.* 29d7–30c1,
could qualify as sceptical-rhetorical *quaestiones de universo
genere*, 'of the general kind', that were answered with the help
of *coniectura*, 'inference', with the overall intention of arriving
at a convincing and probable answer.

To illustrate this point, let me set out in greater detail the
minute workings of the *modus coniecturae*. At *De oratore*
3.113–14, in Crassus' *divisio* of the *thesis* methodology, this

---

[104] For further arguments in favour of Philo's authorship of the method set out in
De orat. 3.118, cf. Brittain 2001: 339–42. It is Hermagoras who is credited with
a series of rhetorical *loci communes/loci inventionis* that served as the tools for
treating a *quaestio*, which was then appropriated as a general philosophical type of
inquiry, cf. Brittain 2001: 304–6. Reinhardt 2000: 542–44 illustrates the close relationship between the Aristotelian rhetorical *topoi* and the *divisio*, arguing that the
former may have been integrated into sceptical–rhetorical argumentative method
by Philo, an argument reiterated in greater detail in Reinhardt 2003, e.g. 14–17.

modus is associated, specifically, with the question type *quid sit in re*, which inquires into the essential properties of the subject in question. He next lists several possible questions that may fall under this type, concerning 1. *quid sit*, the existence of the object under investigation, 2. *quae sit origo*, the starting point or origin of the object/event in question; further, 3. *[quae sit] causa aut ratio*, the reason or motive that prompted an event or a state of affairs, and 4. *de immutatione*, the object's ability to undergo change.

We encounter the *thesis* division also in Cicero's *Part. or.* 64, where the *modus coniecturae* is associated with questions of the type *sit necne*, 'does [something] exist or not?'. This question type is, in turn, divided into further types, one of them asking 'how does something come about?', *quemadmodum quidque fiat.* On this latter type, Cicero elaborates: 'To this class belong all the inquiries in which the reasons and motives of things are unfolded; as, for instance, in metaphysics and natural science' (*cuius generis sunt omnes in quibus ut in obscuris naturalibusque quaestionibus causae rationesque rerum explicantur.* Transl. Rackham, with modifications), a statement that echoes question type 3: *[quae sit] causa aut ratio*? associated with the *modus coniecturae* in the thesis division at *De oratore* 3.114. Earlier in the *Part. or.*, while discussing the parts of a speech that are aimed at 'creating convincingness' (*ad fidem faciendam, Part. or.* 33), Cicero explains, further, that the specific *loci* of the *modus coniecturae* are associated, as in chapter 64, with questions concerning a subject's existence (*an sit necne*). The *loci coniecturae* are 'likelihoods' (*verisimilia*) or essential properties (*propria nota*) that apply to the subject under discussion (*Part. or.* 34).[105] 'Likelihoods', he explains, are defined as 'that which usually occurs in such and such a way' (*quod plerumque ita fiat*), while essential properties are 'what is never otherwise' (*quod numquam aliter fit*). In the subsequent chapter, *Part. or.* 35, Cicero elaborates on the kinds of *verisimilia* that may be

---

[105] Replying to his son's request 'now I ask about the *loci* of inference' (*nunc coniecturae locos quaero*), Cicero explains: 'Inference is based entirely on probabilities and on the essential characteristics of things' (*in verisimilibus et in propriis rerum notis posita est tota.* Transl. Rackham, with modifications).

obtained. The *verisimilia* are drawn from the 'parts or members of the account' (*ex partibus et quasi membris narrationis*), and found in persons, locations, times, actions, and events. In the case of persons, one might point to somebody's bodily or mental attributes. For likelihoods concerning a person's 'mind' (*animus*), one might consider men's dispositions in respect of virtues, vices, and other aspects (*quemadmodum affecti sint virtutibus, vitiis ...*). Summarizing these and many more types of likelihoods that may be discovered, Cicero describes in chapter 38 the manner in which one may build upon them in order to construct an argument based on inference: 'all parts of the material that has been supplied as a basis for the argument must be examined by mental review and an inference must be drawn from each with reference to the matter that will be under consideration' (*huius igitur materiae ad argumentum subiectae perlustrandae animo partes erunt omnes et ad id quod agetur ex singulis coniectura capienda*. Transl. Rackham, modified). Finally, in chapter 68, Cicero affirms that the method of discovery (*ratio inveniendi*) for *loci* that are used for the treatment of a thesis will be the same method as that which had been set out previously (*eamdem quae est exposita*), in his discussion leading up to chapter 38: 'all material intended to convince and to discover arguments is drawn from the same topics' (*ut ex eisdem locis ad fidem et ad inveniendum ducantur omnia*).

Finally, Cicero sheds yet more light on the *loci coniecturae* in his *Topics*. Defining *loci* as 'as it were, basic principles which can indicate and point the way to any argument' (*Top.* 25, transl. Reinhardt), and providing, in chapters 81–6, the *thesis* division already familiar from the *De oratore* III and the *Partitiones oratoriae*, he specifies in chapter 87 which *loci* are particularly suited to which type of question. The arguments that are best suited to questions associated with the *modus coniecturae* are those obtained from 'reasons, effects, and accompanying factors' (*quae ex causis, quae ex effectis, quae ex coniunctis*). The *loci* drawn from reasons, *ex causis*, had been discussed at length in chapters 58–65. In chapter 62, Cicero points, among many other types, to reasons that 'have an effect through an act of will, agitation of the mind, disposition, nature, skill, or chance' (*voluntate efficient aut perturbatione animi at habitu aut natura aut arte aut casu*, transl. Reinhardt). An example of a reason that has an effect through a person's 'disposition' (*habitus*), Cicero suggests, may be 'someone who gets angry easily and quickly' (*qui facile et cito irascatur*). Based on Cicero's descriptions, in the above works, of the *quaestio de universo genere*, the *modus coniecturae*, and the types of questions associated with this *modus*: questions intended to gather *loci communes* which are then employed for building an argument based on inference, I suggest that we can draw the following conclusions with regard to Cicero's translation of *Tim.* 29d7–30c1, 'Let us therefore seek (*quaeramus*) the reason that impelled him who constructed [the All] to seek a beginning of things and a new effort.' The *quaestio* found in this passage – what is the reason that impelled him who constructed the All to seek a beginning of things and a new effort? – is a question *de universo genere* that would be classified by Cicero as one of the question types associated with the *modus coniectura*. That Cicero had this *modus* in mind when translating the *Timaeus* appears even more likely if we consider that the views advanced in the account are based on *verisimilia*, 'likelihoods', which result in *fides*, 'convincingness' (cf. especially *Part. or.* 33–4, discussed above). Further, among the questions listed under the *modus coniecturae* at *De oratore* 3.114, the third question type listed, which asks for the 'reason or motive' (*causa et ratio*) that prompted an event or state of affairs, appears particularly to the point, given that *causa* appears in Cicero's translation of *Tim.* 29d7–30c1 which, in the original Greek, runs as follows: λέγωμεν δὴ δι' ἥντινα αἰτίαν [Cicero: *causam*] γένεσιν καὶ τὸ πᾶν τόδε ὁ συνιστὰς συνέστησεν, **A§1a**, ll. 1–3, Table 7). With regard to the argument that follows: 'He manifestly excelled in goodness; but one who is good begrudges nobody. Therefore, he created everything in likeness to himself' (*probitate videlicet praestabat, probus autem invidet nemini; itaque omnia sui similia generavit*, **B§1b**, ll. 5–8, Table 8), we can argue that the creator's goodness is a type of likelihood (*verisimile*) that is based on a person's mental attributes and disposition in respect of virtues, vices, and other aspects (*quemadmodum affecti sint* *virtutibus, vitiis* ...) as set out in *Part. or.* 35. Finally, in the context of the *loci causarum* listed in Cicero's *Topics*, the creator's goodness may be classed as one of those *causae* that 'have an effect through an act of will, agitation of the mind, disposition, nature, skill or chance' (*voluntate efficient aut perturbatione animi at habitu aut natura aut arte aut casu*, *Top.* 62, transl. Reinhardt). The particular effect of the creator's *habitus*, his goodness, was his creation of the orderly cosmos.

The creator's excellence, a characteristic trait of divinity likely to be accepted by his listeners, is pronounced by Cicero in **B§1c**, l. 10 (Table 8) the *causa iustissima* of the creation of the world, while no reference is made by him to the authority of tradition ('of wise men': παρ' ἀνδρῶν φρονίμων, **A§1c**, ll. 12–13, Table 7), an omission in line with the sceptical refusal to grant authority on a particular subject to representatives of any philosophical system.[106] Thus, while his paraphrase, at face value, appears to name the reason for the world's creation with rather more certainty than does Timaeus' carefully phrased statement, the attribute *iustissima* may suggest that the creator's goodness is pronounced the reason for the world's creation with the highest level of *justification* (*OLD* 5: *iustus*, 'justified', 'sound'), thus adding a forensic slant that remains in the background of the question *de universo genere*. The expression *causa iustissima* is elsewhere used by Cicero mostly in forensic contexts,[107] and perhaps best interpreted here as 'the most justified [i.e., by arguments]' reason for the creation of the universe. It is thus a suitable description of a 'verdict' that has been reached as inviting the highest degree of *fides*, achieved by the method of *coniectura* and thus built

---

[106] Lévy 2003: 99 suggests that Cicero's rendering *causa iustissima* and his omission of the reference to the 'wise men' dogmatizes Plato's thought, turning Plato's appeal to human authority into a proposition of absolute truth. In the light of the further evidence adduced in this present chapter for Cicero's sceptical position, I reject this position.

[107] *Leg.* 2.48: 'The heirs have the most legitimate reason, for there is nobody who is closer to assuming the position of a person who has passed away' (*heredum causa iustissima est; nulla est enim persona, quae ad vicem eius, qui e vita emigrarit, propius accedat*); *Pro P. Quinctio* 58: 'these numerous witnesses, all of whom had the most legitimate reason for being in the know, but none for lying ...' (*testes tot quibus omnibus **causa iustissima** est cur scire potuerint, nulla cur mentiantur* ...).

upon *verisimilia* in the absence of verifiable evidence. The forensic slant that is noticeable in Cicero's argumentation links up with a statement in an earlier passage of the translation:

Table 9. *Plato,* Tim. *29c7–d3*

29c7	A: ἀλλ' ἐὰν ἄρα μηδενὸς ἧττον παρεχώμεθα εἰκότας, ἀγαπᾶν χρή, μεμνημένους ὡς ὁ λέγων ἐγὼ ὑμεῖς τε οἱ κριταὶ φύσιν ἀνθρωπίνην ἔχομεν, ὥστε περὶ τούτων τὸν εἰκότα μῦθον ἀποδεχομένους πρέπει τούτου μηδὲν ἔτι πέρα ζητεῖν.	A: Rather, we should be content if we can provide accounts that are inferior to none in likelihood, remembering that both I who speak and you who judge are but human creatures, so that it becomes us to accept the likely account of these matters and forbear to search beyond it.
5		

Table 10. *Cicero's translation of Plato,* Tim. *29c7–d3 (Cic.* Tim. *3.8, 7–10)*

29c7	29c7 B: ... *contentique esse debebitis, si probabilia dicentur, aequum est enim meminisse et me qui disseram hominem esse et vos qui iudicetis ut, si probabilia dicentur, ne quid ultra requiratur.*	B: ... and you will have to be content if probabilities are stated. For it is advisable to remember that both I, who am speaking, and you, who are the judges, are human, so that you [ought to] inquire no further if probabilities are stated.
5		

As in the Greek, Cicero's listeners are the judges who preside over the discussion and who pass judgement on the argument advanced. Given the human nature of speaker and judges, the speaker Cicero, in his presentation of a sceptical-rhetorical *quaestio,* is able merely to achieve *probabilia,* while they are able to judge not what is the true reason or motive for the creation of the universe, but the *causa iustissima,* established by means of inference.[108]

---

[108] For a summary of the rhetorical device of *iudicatum,* cf. Ernesti, *Lexicon technologiae latinorum rhetoricae, ad loc.*: 'In a probable form of argument, a "judgement" is a matter that is proven through somebody's assent or authority or decision, or through other such factors' (*in probabili argumentatione, iudicatum*

On a final note, the omission from Cicero's text of the mention of 'truth' (τῇ ἀληθείᾳ, A§2, l. 15 in the original; Table 7) provides further evidence of the sceptical tone he imposes on the text. Cicero states not that 'in accordance with the likely account, it must be stated that, truly (τῇ ἀληθείᾳ), this cosmos has come to be a living creature possessing soul and intellect, on account of the providence of the god', but concludes 'for this reason one should not hesitate to declare (if it is at least possible to inquire after anything by inference) that this world is a living creature and, moreover, one that is intelligent and has been built with divine providence'.[109] His passing over the reference of τῇ ἀληθείᾳ is in line with a sceptical-rhetorical *quaestio* treated with the inferential method, and is in line also with the sceptical position Cicero so frequently stresses in his *Academica*. While the sceptic may accept probabilities as likenesses of the truth, he stops short of a full doctrinal commitment.[110] Any mention of the truth is omitted, not because there is no truth, but because an Academic presumably should not claim to have identified it.

With the help of certain terminological modifications in his translation (i.e. the use of *probabile*, *veri simile*, *quaerere*, and *coniectura*), Cicero was able to emphasize the rhetorical character of the Academy's methodological curriculum, which had helped render it an instrument that was well suited to philosophical investigation.[111] The viewpoints advanced in the Timaean creation account, I suggest, would have presented

dicitur res assensione aut auctoritate aut iudicii alicuius, aut aliquorum comprobata, with reference to Cic. *Inv.* 1.47: *omne autem – ut certas quasdam in partes tribuamus – probabile, quod sumitur ad argumentationem, aut signum est aut credibile aut iudicatum aut comparabile*).

109 Pointed out by Sedley 2013: 203.

110 '... we, who do not deny that something can be true, deny that it can be perceived. [Democritus] straightforwardly denies that anything is true' (... *nos, qui veri esse aliquid non negamus, percipi posse negamus; ille verum plane negat esse, Ac.* 2.73). Cf., further, ibid. 119: 'These doctrines may be true (see how I grant that something can be true) but I deny, nevertheless, that they can be apprehended' (*sint ista vera (vides enim iam me fateri aliquid esse veri), comprendi ea tamen et percipi nego*).

111 In this respect, Peetz's 2005 thesis that Cicero was keen to promote rhetorical methodology as 'applied philosophy' is justified. I do not agree, however, with his suggestion that Cicero advanced a newly devised epistemological concept of *probabile* as an alternative to the Stoic criterion, and the view that he claimed the leadership in the contemporary Latin philosophical debate.

themselves to Cicero, by their very nature, as concerns *de universo genere*, concerns that were discussed with the help of the *thesis* method such as it was taught in Philo's Academy. The framing of the individual viewpoints that compose the Timaean creation account as a whole, as the most convincing and probable conclusions of philosophical *quaestiones*, would have made for a cosmological viewpoint that was entirely in line with sceptical policy. A definite 'criterion of truth', *iudicium veritatis* – we note the legal connotations[112] – could not exist in the sensible world. Instead, the sceptic philosopher must form a *iudicium* based on *coniectura*, relying on *verisimilia* that can, at best, provide *fides*. The individual viewpoints advanced in the Timaean creation account, according to Cicero's portrayal, would have been those found to be most persuasive in intra-Academic discussions *in utramque partem*.[113] Naturally, such might in turn be the subject of a discussion *in utramque partem* with representatives of a dogmatic position, as in the scenario Cicero may well have envisaged for his *Timaeus* translation.

And yet – despite the sceptical potential that could be found in the *Timaeus*, the work's absence from Cicero's inventory of publications in the *De divinatione* indicates that the doctrinal considerations discussed above may eventually have outweighed the importance of methodological concerns. Cicero may have felt more comfortable with his established practice of merely arguing against viewpoints advanced, the scenario we find in his published treatises. This scenario, I suggest, may have given him more space and opportunity than a monological sceptical manifesto would have done for a direct, critical engagement with the various dogmatic positions advanced.

In the final part of the present chapter, therefore, I shall examine the cosmological positions advanced in Cicero's philosophical writings, and the contents of his *Timaeus* translation.

---

[112] Cic. *Ac.* 1.142: 'Plato, however, thought that each criterion of truth, and truth itself, was removed from opinions and from the senses. He thought that it belonged to thought and mind' (*Plato autem omne iudicium veritatis veritatemque ipsam abductam ab opinionibus et a sensibus cogitationis ipsius et mentis esse voluit*).

[113] Cf. the close relationship between the *quaestio* and the *disputatio in utramque partem* illustrated by Crassus at *De orat.* 3.107, discussed above.

In doing so, I will shed further light on the relationship between the published philosophical treatises and his translation, and on the interplay of the doctrinal perspectives he might have wished to set up against one another in this work. I shall single out two points of doctrinal contention that would likely have been at the centre of Cicero's Timaean *disputatio*, had it been completed: the universe's origin and its everlastingness.

Cicero and the Creation of the Cosmos: His Philosophical Treatises

In his *Tusculan disputations* 1.62–3 Cicero makes a passing note on the createdness of the cosmos in the context of a discussion centring around the subject of death. Associating the belief in an immortal soul with Plato, Cicero argues that there exists a kinship between human and divine intellect, in terms that are reminiscent of *Tim.* 47b–c:[114] 'we looked up to the heavenly bodies ... and the one who perceived in his soul their orbits and all of their movements taught us that his soul is similar to that of the one who built the stars in the heavens'.[115] He adds a more explicit reference to the *Timaeus* by giving an original twist to the argument from design. Just as the

---

[114] *Tim.* 47b2–c4: 'This, I say, is the greatest benefit of vision ... But let it be affirmed by us that this is the cause of vision, that the god invented and bestowed upon us vision, that we might perceive the revolutions of reason in the heavens, and that we might make use of them for the revolutions of our own reasoning, since they are akin to the former ... and that, by learning and participating in thoughts that are by nature correct, by imitating those revolutions of the god that never vary, we might lend stability to the varying revolutions in ourselves' (λέγω δὴ τοῦτο ὀμμάτων μέγιστον ἀγαθόν· ... ἀλλὰ τούτου λεγέσθω παρ' ἡμῶν αὕτη ἐπὶ ταῦτα αἰτία, θεὸν ἡμῖν ἀνευρεῖν δωρήσασθαί τε ὄψιν, ἵνα τὰς ἐν οὐρανῷ τοῦ νοῦ κατιδόντες περιόδους χρησαίμεθα ἐπὶ τὰς περιφορὰς τὰς τῆς παρ' ἡμῖν διανοήσεως, συγγενεῖς ἐκείναις οὔσας ... ἐκμαθόντες δὲ καὶ λογισμῶν κατὰ φύσιν ὀρθότητος μετασχόντες, μιμούμενοι τὰς τοῦ θεοῦ πάντως ἀπλανεῖς οὔσας, τὰς ἐν ἡμῖν πεπλανημένας καταστησαίμεθα).

[115] *astra suspeximus ... quorum conversiones omnisque motus qui animo vidit, is docuit similem animum suum eius esse qui ea fabricatus esset in caelo.* Lévy 2003: 105 believes that, by suggesting that the demiurge has an *animus*, and by linking the *deus* to Archimedes' *divinum ingenium*, Cicero implies that the relation between the demiurge and humans is comparable to that between the Stoics' human and universal *logos*. Lévy's overall thesis is that Cicero was unable, in his *Timaeus* translation, to move beyond the terminology and concepts of Stoic physics. I agree with Lévy that Cicero's translation is couched in the terms of Hellenistic philosophy.

ingenious Archimedes built his sphere replicating our world, the divine intellect constructed (*fabricatus esset*) the Timaean cosmos: 'for when Archimedes arranged the motions of the moon, the sun, and of the five planets in his replica sphere he brought about the same as Plato's god who built the world in the *Timaeus*'. Neither product could have come about without divine intellect, whether on a cosmic or on a human scale.[116]

Incorporated into his argument against the fear of death is Cicero's assumption of a god who created the universe (*mundum aedificavit Platonis deus*), in which planetary motion 'cannot come about without god' (*fieri sine deo non potest*). His analogy in the passage builds upon the Timaean narrative taken at face value: Archimedes built his *facsimile* of the universe in imitation of the visible cosmos that had been constructed by the Platonic divine intellect, enabled to do so by the power of his own immortal intellect that is akin to the divine mind.

It is worth pointing out that, while Cicero here is relying on a literal reading of this element in the Timaean narrative, he stops short, in his analogy, of equally declaring Archimedes' intellect to be, as it were, a created *facsimile* of the world soul, in the manner the human intellect is described in the *Timaeus*, the dialogue he cites in support of his broader argument. Nothing in this passage suggests that Cicero was aware of the tensions arising from the assumption of a created cosmos *and* soul in Timaeus' narrative, and the argumentative line he is pursuing in the *Tusculans*. Quite the contrary. At *Tusc.* 1.32 Cicero explicitly distinguishes Plato's belief in an immortal soul from that of the Stoic Panaetius, who insisted on the soul's perishability, based on his creed that whatever has come to be is perishable: 'Should we believe Panaetius on that point on which he disagreed with his authority Plato?

[116] *Tusc.* 1.63: 'Archimedes fixed the movements of the moon, sun, and the five planets on a globe, just like Plato's god who constructed the world in the *Timaeus* ... if this cannot come to pass in our world without the god, neither could Archimedes have been able to reproduce these same motions without divine ingenuity, not even on a globe' (*Archimedes lunae solis quinque errantium motus in sphaeram inligavit, effecit idem quod ille, qui in Timaeo mundum aedificavit, Platonis deus ... quod si in hoc mundo fieri sine deo non potest, ne in sphaera quidem eosdem motus Archimedes sine divino ingenio potuisset imitari*).

Plato, whom on all occasions he calls "divine", "most sage", "most holy", "the Homer of philosophers": Panaetius did not approve of this single tenet of Plato's concerning the immortality of the soul. For Panaetius believed – nobody denies it – that whatever has been created is perishable; he believes that souls are born ...'.[117]

No mention in this context of the Timaean tenet of a soul that is *natus*. It is, of course, not hard to imagine why Cicero would have chosen to suppress an allusion to a created soul in the present context, where any such complications in his presentation of the Platonic view would certainly have been counterproductive with regard to the main objective of his argument, proving the soul's immortality. Thus, while we note that Cicero is relying in his present argument on a created universe, we must acknowledge that it would be an ill-suited occasion to enter upon the inherent difficulties of the Timaean portrayal of a created but immortal soul.[118]

Elsewhere in the same dialogue the Timaean demiurge appears in connection with the Aristotelian divinity. Crediting Plato with the belief that all physical bodies in the universe have come to be, *nata sunt*, Cicero distinguishes this view from Aristotle's, which postulates the eternal existence of the physical cosmos: 'these have always existed' (*[haec] semper fuerunt*).[119] While Cicero's argument is not ultimately aimed at proving the createdness of the cosmos but, rather, at inferring the existence of a divine power that oversees and safeguards its expanse,[120] his language is reminiscent of the Timaean portrayal of divine

---

[117] *credamus igitur Panaetio a Platone suo dissentienti? quem enim omnibus locis divinum, quem sapientissimum, quem sanctissimum, quem Homerum philosophorum appellat, huius hanc unam sententiam de inmortalitate animorum non probat. volt enim, quod nemo negat, quicquid natum sit interire ...*

[118] Admittedly, proponents of a temporal reading such as Plutarch did not consider the description of soul's creation in the *Timaeus* to be in conflict with other passages in Plato that describe an ungenerated soul. Cf. Plut. *Procr. an.* 1003a, 1013c, f; cf. *Is. et Os.* 370f.

[119] *Tusc.* 1.70; cf also Baltes 1976: 28–9.

[120] Cicero is adapting the argument from design: just as we are able to infer from the wondrous workings of the universe the existence of a divinity, we can infer also from the mental processes of the human soul its effects: 'thus it is also with the human mind. Even though you may not see it, just as you do not see god,

activity. Following the rhetorical question 'can we doubt that anybody oversees [the cosmos]?' (*possumusne dubitare quin iis praesit aliquis*), Cicero offers as a further identification of the *aliquis*: either, in the case of Plato, an *effector*, somebody who has built or brought about the orderly cosmos, or, in the case of Aristotle, a *moderator* who governs but has not created the eternal universe.

More precisely, Cicero describes the deities as either a 'creator', *effector*, or 'the one who directs such a great work and task', *moderator tanti operis et muneris*, with the latter addition being reminiscent of his portrayal of the Timaean demiurge who labours in his endeavour to construct the cosmos. At *Tim.* 28a6 ὁ δημιουργός is translated *is qui aliquod munus efficere molitur*, 'he who labours to accomplish some task'. At 28c5ff. 'builder of this entire work', *fabricator huius tanti operis*, rehders 'the one who frames', ὁ τεκταινόμενος, while 'new labour/ laborious undertaking', *molitionem novam*, at 29a7 represents 'the All', τὸ πᾶν. It is true that in the specific context of *Tusc.* 1.70 it is the government of the universe rather than its construction that is portrayed as a strenuous task, but this comes as no surprise: any mention of a strenuous *creation* of the All would be manifestly inconsistent with the Aristotelian assumption of an uncreated universe. Rather, it is in Cicero's interest here to deemphasize the divergences between the two divinities so as to bolster his argument for the need of *some* divine authority to administer the great machinery of the cosmos (his ultimate purpose is to argue from a divine power who has authority over the cosmos to the human soul, similarly in charge of the human body due to its kinship with the divine). Thus, while the expression *tanti operis et muneris* is somewhat unhappy in combination with the Aristotelian *moderator* who is detached and disengaged from effort, the immediate context of Cicero's

nevertheless, just as you recognize god from his works, in the same manner you recognize the mind's divine power from your memory of things, by discovery and the swiftness of movement and all the beauty of virtue' (*sic mentem hominis, quamvis eam non videas, ut deum non vides, tamen, ut deum adgnoscis ex operibus eius, sic ex memoria rerum et inventione et celeritate motus omnique pulchritudine virtutis vim divinam mentis adgnoscito, Tusc.* 1.70).

argument requires a degree of rapprochement between the Aristotelian god and the Platonic divinity, both of whom Cicero wishes to associate with an authoritative role. As in the previous passage of his *Tusculans*, Cicero's views on the createdness of the cosmos, whilst woven into the context of his particular line of argument, endorse an actual creation of the cosmos by the Platonic god.

In other contexts, we encounter a similar use of language, this time put by Cicero to the contrary effect of criticizing Platonic and Stoic cosmology. We shall find here that Plato is explicitly associated with a temporal creation. Showcasing the doctrinal disagreements between the rival philosophical systems at *Ac.* 2.118ff., Cicero initially informs us that 'Plato believed that the world was created by god to be everlasting, from matter that contained everything within itself' (*Plato ex materia in se omnia recipiente mundum factum esse censet a deo sempiternum*). He criticizes the tenet of a universe that has come to be by alluding to the Aristotelian denial[121] that a 'new design', *novum consilium*, could have come about that had been responsible for the world's coming to be: 'along will come ... Aristotle who says that [the Stoic sage] is foolish. For the world never began to exist since there was no beginning,

---

[121] In the context of his criticism of the Timaean cosmology in his *De caelo* 1.10 Aristotle argues for the destructibility of *all* things generated, a property established and confirmed by experience as the common attribute of such objects (ὅσα ἐπὶ πολλῶν ἢ πάντων ὁρῶμεν ὑπάρχοντα, 279b19). Destructibility, moreover, requires mutability which, in turn, depends upon some cause (τι αἴτιον, b23) that is able to bring about change within any given object at any given time. These properties cannot be reconciled with eternal objects incapable of undergoing change (279b22–33). Even if there had existed a causative agent responsible for bringing about the change that must have effected the coming to be of the universe, no reason can be sufficient to explain why this change had not taken place at an earlier point (279b23f: ἔσται γάρ τι αἴτιον, ὃ εἰ ὑπῆρχε πρότερον, δυνατὸν ἂν ἦν ἄλλως ἔχειν τὸ ἀδύνατον ἄλλως ἔχειν). This last line of reasoning ties in with further objections against a created universe that, according to Effe 1970: 23–31, may have featured in the third book of Aristotle's now fragmentary *De philosophia*. The view that god is 'unchanging' is incompatible with the assumption that any change within the creator god's mind, in Cicero's words, a *novum concilium*, had been required to initiate its creation. A further, related objection is that such a change in mindset and activity on the part of the creator must necessarily have followed a period of inactivity and idleness – yet again an untenable position. Cf. the discussion by Sorabji 1983: 232–52, esp. 232–8.

prompted by a new design [on the part of a divinity], of such a magnificent work (*veniet ... Aristoteles qui illum desipere dicat; neque enim ortum esse umquam mundum quod nulla fuerit* **novo consilio** *inito tam praeclari operis inceptio*). Cicero continues to present Aristotle's objections, declaring the cosmos to be uncreated since it is constructed in such a robust manner throughout that no [divine] power could have undertaken such a labour as would have been necessary to bring about its generation (*ita* [*est*] *undique aptu*[*s*] *ut* **nulla vis tantos queat motus mutationemque moliri**). Let me summarize briefly. Aristotle argues against the possibility of a change of mind on the part of the divinity supposedly responsible for the coming to be of the cosmos. This argument stands in close connection with the denial of the view that any exertion by the divinity could have been sufficient to bring about the creation of the All.[122]

We encounter what must be an instance of the same polemical strand in Cicero's *De natura deorum* where the notion of a divinity that is toiling and exerting itself, and appears to undergo a change of activity, is put to Epicurean use in terms that echo the previously cited passage in an astonishing manner. At *Nat. deor.* 1.18–24, the Epicurean Velleius presents a polemical survey of the Timaean creation account, which he transforms by picking up and sharpening Timaeus' metaphors

---

[122] A further parallel is *Ac.* 2.121, where the discussion turns to the Peripatetic Strato. Cicero describes Strato as having rejected any divine authorship in the coming to be of the cosmos: 'he denies that he is in need of the gods' help for creating the world' (*negat opera deorum se uti ad fabricandum mundum*), freeing the god from such great duty (*deum opere magno liberat*, fr. 32, 33, edition of Wehrli, vol. 5; cf. Baltes 1976: 24 n. 1.) At *Ac.* 1.33, Strato is reported to have diverged considerably from his Peripatetic schooling in the field of natural philosophy to which he had dedicated himself in particular: 'he had commited himself entirely to the inquiry into nature, and in this very field he then categorically disagreed with them' ([*totum*] *se ad investigationem naturae contulisset, in ea ipsa plurimum dissedit a suis*). Strato's digression was his assumption of a coming to be of the universe by natural causes; cf. *Ac.* 2.121: 'he taught that all things that exist have been made by nature ... and that whatever exists or comes to be is or has come to be on account of weights and motions' (*quaecumque sint docet omnia effecta esset natura ... quidquid aut sit aut fiat naturalibus fieri aut factum esse docet ponderibus et motibus*). Such a viewpoint brings him within a short distance of the entirely mechanistic viewpoint of atomism, a fact duly picked up by Cicero's ensuing mention of Democritus. It is thus not surprising to find Strato arguing in terms similar to those of the Epicurean Velleius, to whom we are about to turn.

of construction, into a manufacturing scheme on a universal
scale: 'what mental vision could your master Plato use to
behold a building site of such a great product ...? What kind
of labour was this, what were his tools, who were his assistants
in such a great task?' (*quibus enim oculis animi intueri potuit
vester Plato fabricam illam **tanti operis** ...? **quae molitio,** quae
ferramenta ... qui ministri **tanti muneris** fuerunt*, 1.19)? The language put into the mouth of Velleius is here strikingly similar
to Cicero's description of the creation process in the passages
of the *Tusculans*, and to his reference to Aristotle's criticism of
Stoic cosmology in the *Academica* cited previously. It reflects
the polemic against a Platonic and Stoic[123] creator god who
was actively involved in the coming to be of the cosmos (and
indirectly, through the world soul, in its maintenance, cf. Ar.
Cael. 2.1 284a27–35).

Velleius' aim is to expose the weaknesses of Platonic and
Stoic theology, which he accuses of pulling out of its hat a
divine cause (*cum explicare argumenti exitum non potestis
confugitis ad deum*) whose appearance on the scene is deemed
necessary (*quod quia ... natura efficere sine aliqua mente possit
non videtis Nat. deor.* 1.53) not only for the creation of the
cosmos, a process Epicureans conceived to come about in
a non-rational, non-teleological, and mechanistic manner,
but also for its everlastingness, a point equally contended by
Epicureans: '[Plato] not only taught that the world had a beginning but also that it was made practically "by hand", yet he
said that it would be everlasting' (*qui non modo natum mundum*

[123] Cf. *Nat. deor.* 2.133 where the Stoic Balbus anticipates polemic against an overly
industrious divinity: 'here somebody may ask, for whose sake did the laborious
undertaking of such enormous deeds occur?' (*hic quaeret quispiam cuiusnam causa
tantarum rerum **molitio** facta sit?*). Bénatouïl 2009: 23–45 evaluates the extent of
the Stoic god's industriousness and shows that Stoic divine activity is described
as toilsome mostly in polemical contexts by rival philosophical systems. Balbus
at *Nat. deor.* 2.59 makes the point that divine activity is not to be conceived of
as labour or toil in the case of human activity (*nec ... quae agant molientium cum
labore operoso ac molesto*), a notion criticized by Cotta at 3.92. Bénatouïl also
discusses the influence of Peripatetic theology on Chrysippus who, like Cicero's
Balbus, appears to conceive of a certain dualistic notion of divine activity (36).
Passive divine activity is at work in the sky and on the earth, whereas its main field
of activity is the region of aether.

introduxerit sed etiam manu paene factum, is eum dixerit fore sempiternum, 1.20).[124] The issue of the everlastingness of the world aside, Velleius directs his mockery of a creative principle by which the world is supposedly *manu paene factum* with equal force also against Stoic *pronoia*, or the 'old fortune teller', *anus fatidica* (1.18), responsible for the construction of the Stoic cosmos: 'I ask [what were] the assistants, the engines, the arrangement and the organization of this entire project?' (*requiro … ministros machinas omnem **totius operis** dissignationem atque apparatum*, 1.20).

Velleius next moves to the crucial matter of the universe's createdness, in what appears to be the only context in Cicero's philosophical treatises that specifically addresses the difficulties inherent in the assumption of a temporal creation. We re-encounter some already familiar points of criticism. Velleius addresses the problematic assumption of a divine agent who appears to have been idle prior to its creative activities, a criticism yet again directed at the Timaean demiurge and the Stoic *providentia*: 'I ask both of them why the creators of the world suddenly woke up after sleeping for countless ages' (*ab utroque autem sciscitor cur mundi aedificatores repente exstiterint, innumerabilia saecla dormierint*, Nat. deor. 1.21).[125] Velleius exploits a further argument against a created universe in his refutation of Platonic and Stoic theology, bringing up the question of 'why did the god begin creating then and not sooner?' which we encounter already in Aristotle's *De caelo* 1.10.279b21–3 and *Phys.* 8.1.251a17–20.[126] Moreover,

---

[124] Cf. *Nat. deor.* 1.20: 'Do you believe that a man has, so to say, even had a first taste of physics, the study of nature, if he believes that what has come to be can be eternal? What is this compound that is indissoluble, and what is it that has a beginning, but no end?' (*hunc censes primis ut dicitur labris gustasse physiologiam id est naturae rationem, qui quicquam quod ortum sit putet aeternum esse posse? quae est enim coagmentatio non dissolubilis, aut quid est cuius principium aliquod sit nihil sit extremum?*).

[125] Cf. Sedley 2013: 198–9.

[126] This argument is made explicit also by Lucretius: 'what was new that, after such a long time, could have incited those who, before, had remained still, to desire to change their previous existence? (*quidve novi potuit tanto post ante quietos inlicere ut cuperent vitam mutare priorem, Lucr.* 5.168–70). For a discussion of Epicurean arguments and counterarguments, see Sedley 2007: 139–55.

he implicitly criticizes the fact that the creative agents would have had to undergo a change of mind in order to suddenly (*repente*) set themselves to constructing the universe after a period of inactivity, an argumentative line that echoes the unlikely occurrence of a *novum consilium* on behalf of a divine agent, a criticism ascribed by Cicero to Aristotle at *Ac.* 2.119.

By considering the role of the Timaean and Stoic creative agents prior to the creation process, Velleius' subsequent train of thought cuts into the problematic notion of a 'time before time' (1.21). Even if there existed no universe, it does not follow that there existed no period before its coming to be (*non enim si mundus nullus erat saecla non errant*); thus, there must have been a 'time before time'.[127] Velleius describes such a period preceding the creation of the universe during which the creative agents were apparently inactive:

> I am not speaking of the ages that are made up from a number of days and nights in their yearly successions. For I acknowledge that these could not have existed without the revolutions of the heavens. There was, however, some kind of eternity, from infinite times, that could not be measured by any temporal divisions but that could, nevertheless, be understood in terms of 'extension'. For it is out of the question that there had ever been a time in which there was no time.

Velleius distinguishes between pre-cosmic time and time that had come to be simultaneously with the celestial bodies whose rotations and circular motions determine and record the temporal units familiar to us – the same line of argument picked up by Plutarch, Atticus, and other supporters of a temporal creation.

Finally, let us return to the *Academica*. At *Ac.* 2.120, Cicero adopts a line of attack similar to that of Velleius in advancing against the Stoic creationist account the sceptic disclaimer of certain knowledge in the context of cosmology. He mocks the elaborate detail with which the Stoic creative agent has constructed the universe: 'you claim that [the All] could not have been built in such a refined and intricate manner without divine resource?' (*negatis haec tam polite tamque subtiliter effici potuisse sine divina aliqua sollertia?*). His rejection, in general,

---

[127] Cf. Ar. *Met.* 11.6 1071b6ff., cf. *Phys.* 8.1 251b10–27.

of divine involvement in the creation process and of a teleo-logically structured cosmos[128] should be considered within its immediate context, a textbook exposition of the sceptic viewpoint and the simultaneous refutation of his Antiochean counterpart Lucullus. Cicero's line of argument here, there-fore, has a different aim than do the sentiments expressed, for instance, in the above-cited passage of *Tusc.* 1.62–3.[129] At the same time, it is Cicero's very commitment to the sceptic prin-ciple of adopting the viewpoint that appears *probabile* that renders less baffling his varying verdicts on any particular issue of concern. This becomes apparent in the conclusion of his discussion with Lucullus. Regarding the question whether the universe has been constructed by a divine agent, as according to the Stoics (and Platonists), or has come about without such an intelligent driving force but, instead, by natural and mech-anical processes,[130] Cicero professes that 'sometimes this view seems more probable, sometimes the other view' (*modo hoc modo illud probabilius videtur, Ac.* 1.121).

We draw from the evidence of Cicero's philosophical works the following conclusions. Firstly, in the context of cosmological polemical debate, Cicero, often through representatives of rival philosophical systems, attributed to Plato the belief in a created universe, and he shows awareness of the doctrinal consequences of this viewpoint. Secondly, we find evidence of a number of arguments against Platonic creationism which, frequently used in close connection with each other, appear also in other contexts that reject a created universe. Assuming a sceptic position at *Ac.* 2.119, Cicero himself uses criticism he attributes to Aristotle as a shield against Stoic cosmological theory. Similar arguments are put into the mouth of the Epicurean Velleius, and are perhaps also associated with individual thinkers such as the Peripatetic Strato. Cicero's philosophical treatises thus bear witness to a polemical cluster of criticisms that appear to have been closely

---

[128] *Ac.* 2.126: 'I do not believe even that this world was built by divine resolve' (*ne exaedificatum quidem hunc mundum divino consilio existimo*).

[129] And, for that matter, his own conclusion at the end of *Nat. deor.* 3.95: 'To me, Balbus' discourse appeared to be closer to likelihood' (*mihi Balbi [disputatio] ad veritatis similitudinem videretur esse propensior*).

[130] The view Cicero attributes to Strato.

connected: the motif of a creator who was toiling to bring about the cosmos, the question 'why did the creator not create sooner?', and the contentious assumption of a 'new design', *novum consilium*, on the part of the supposedly immutable divine creator.[131] The impression arises from our present analysis that Cicero made use of the same battery of arguments also in several of his other treatises, albeit in varying contexts and with varying emphasis on individual aspects. Divergences between Plato and other philosophical systems are at times accentuated, at times downplayed, as appropriate to the immediate argumentative context. With such considerations in mind, let us turn to the Ciceronian *Timaeus* and see to what effect Cicero employs these arguments in his Latin translation.

Cicero and the Creation of the Cosmos: Evidence from Cicero's Timaeus Translation

Previously we imagined what form Cicero's completed discussion *Carneadeo more* between himself and his counterparts might have taken. In this final section of the present chapter, I shall illustrate that the most noticeable points of contention to be emphasized in Cicero's translation are, indeed, the question concerning the universe's createdness and everlastingness. These points of contention are emphasized in Cicero's narrative in a manner that would have offered any potential interlocutors the opportunity to counter with a polemical response. To stress once more, I shall assume, throughout this final section of the present chapter, that Cicero would have advanced specific viewpoints, in line with Philonian policy, as merely probable, without suggesting any doctrinal commitment on his part. His agenda thus differs from the one he appears to pursue elsewhere, where, according to the specific context, Plato is sometimes associated with a dogmatic perspective. Let us begin with Cicero's rendering of the crucial passage *Tim.* 28b2–c2:

---

[131] This connected strand of arguments has been identified by Effe 1970: 23–31 as originating from Aristotle's lost work *De philosophia*. Velleius' anti-creationist arguments are connected by Effe to Lucr. 5.156–234 and Aetius 1.7.4–9 (= *Dox. Graec.* pp. 299–301).

Cicero

Table 11. *Plato, Tim. 28b2–c2*

28b2	**A§1:** ὁ δὴ πᾶς οὐρανὸς ... σκεπτέον δ' οὖν περὶ αὐτοῦ πρῶτον, ὅπερ ὑπόκειται περὶ παντὸς ἐν ἀρχῇ δεῖν σκοπεῖν,	**A§1:** The entire heaven: ... concerning it we must consider first the underlying principle that must be considered at the beginning of every
5	πότερον ἦν ἀεί, γενέσεως ἀρχὴν ἔχων οὐδεμίαν, ἢ γέγονεν, ἀπ' ἀρχῆς τινος ἀρξάμενος.	matter: whether it has always been, having no beginning of coming to be, or whether it has come to be, having begun from some beginning.
28b7	**A§2:** γέγονεν· ὁρατὸς γὰρ	**A§2:** It has come to be, for it is
10	ἁπτός τέ ἐστιν καὶ σῶμα ἔχων, πάντα δὲ τὰ τοιαῦτα αἰσθητά, τὰ δ' αἰσθητά, δόξῃ περιληπτὰ μετ' αἰσθήσεως, γιγνόμενα καὶ γεννητὰ ἐφάνη. τῷ δ' αὖ	visible and tangible because it also has a body, but all objects of such a kind are perceptible. Perceptible objects are grasped by opinion with the aid of sense perception. They
15	γενομένῳ φαμὲν ὑπ' αἰτίου τινὸς ἀνάγκην εἶναι γενέσθαι.	come to be, as we found, and are generated. Concerning that which has come to be, in turn, we said that they necessarily have come to be by the agency of some cause.

Table 12. *Cicero's translation of Plato, Tim. 28b2–c2 (Cic. Tim. 2.4, 3–2.6, 13)*

28b2	**B§1:** *omne igitur caelum ... de quo id primum consideremus quod principio est in omni quaestione considerandum,*	**B§1:** The entire heaven ... concerning it, let us consider first that which is to be considered first in every inquiry: whether it has
5	*semperne fuerit nullo generatus ortu, an ortus sit ab aliquo temporis principatu.*	always been and was not generated from a beginning, or if it has begun from some beginning in time.
28b7	**B§2:** *ortus est, quandoquidem cernitur et tangitur et est*	**B§2:** It has begun, since it is seen and touched and is corporeal on
10	*undique corporatus, omnia autem talia sensum movent, sensusque moventia quae sunt, eadem in opinatione consident, quae ortum habere gignique*	each side. All such objects, however, affect the senses, and that which affects the senses is also located in opinion. We said that such objects have a beginning and come to be,
15	*diximus, nihil autem gigni posse sine causis.*	but that nothing can come to be without any causes.

94

Cicero's translation of πότερον ἦν ἀεί, γενέσεως ἀρχὴν ἔχων οὐδεμίαν, ἢ γέγονεν, ἀπ᾽ ἀρχῆς τινος ἀρξάμενος. γέγονεν (**A§1** l. 5–**A§2**, l. 9), 'whether it has always been, having no beginning of coming to be, or whether it has come to be, having begun from some beginning. It has come to be', bears witness to the controversy surrounding the createdness of the Timaean cosmos. Timaeus inquires whether the universe has any starting point of generation or not, that is, whether it has come to be or has always existed. The answer is given promptly: γέγονεν – in Cicero's words, *ortus est* (**B§2**, l. 8). Cicero deals with the contentious terms ἀρχή and γέγονεν in the following manner. His addition of *temporis* (**B§2**, l. 7) at once removes the ambiguity in Plato's text and points explicitly to a *temporal* creation of the world: 'whether it has always been and was not generated from a beginning, or if it has begun from some beginning **in time**' (*semperne fuerit nullo generatus ortu, an ortus sit ab aliquo temporis principatu*, **B§1**, ll. 5–7).[132] Compared with the Greek ἀρχή whose meaning 'starting point' or 'first principle' does not necessarily convey temporality, Cicero's *temporis principatu* forestalls any interpretation other than a temporal meaning, as must equally be assumed for the subsequent *ortus est* which translates the notorious γέγονεν. Just as the Greek γέγονεν appears to do, Cicero's *ortus est* identifies the coming to be of the cosmos as a past event.

Let us return to a passage discussed in an earlier context (cf. Tables 7, 8) where a chronological series of events is further emphasized by Cicero.

In our familiar passage *Tim.* 29d7–e1, Cicero paraphrases Timaeus' statement λέγωμεν δὴ δι᾽ ἥντινα αἰτίαν γένεσιν καὶ τὸ

Cf. Sedley 2013: 197–9, and see the discussion by Baltes 1976: 28–9. Cicero presents an alternative rendering for ἀρχή at *Tusc.* 1.54 where, in an exposition of Plato's *Phaedrus*, the soul is described as an *origo*, principle, without beginning (*principium*). His choice of *principatus temporis* in the present instance thus appears all the more deliberate.

πᾶν τόδε ὁ συνιστὰς συνέστησεν in the following manner: 'Let us therefore seek after the reason that impelled him who constructed [the All] to seek a beginning of things (*originem rerum* for γένεσιν: "coming to be") and a new effort (*molitionem novam* for τὸ πᾶν: "the All").' Cicero's *molitio* (**B**, l. 4, Table 8) is reminiscent of the Epicurean mock portrayal of the Stoic[133] and Platonic divinity at *Nat. deor.* 1.19: 'what mental vision could your master Plato use to behold a building site of such a great product ...? What kind of labour was this, what were his tools ... who were his assistants in such a great task?' (*quibus enim oculis animi intueri potuit vester Plato fabricam **illam tanti operis** ... quae **molitio** quae ferramenta ... qui ministri tanti muneris fuerunt* ...), as well as of further instances of anti-Platonic or anti-Stoic polemic we have encountered elsewhere in Cicero's writings, e.g. at *Ac.* 2.119, ascribed by Cicero to Aristotle. It appears that Cicero reinforced this nuance in the present context so as to expose such points of contention as would have been most likely to invite an attack by anti-creationist counterparts. Thus, a Peripatetic would have argued in favour of a divinity who, unlike the Timaean creator, had no hand in the coming to be (naturally, given the eternity of the Aristotelian cosmos) of the All.

What is more, Cicero's addition of *nova* reinforces the chronological dimension of the creation process by insinuating that the coming to be of the universe marked a new undertaking carried out by the divinity. This addition to the Greek reflects, yet again in close connection with the emphasis on a laborious involvement (*molitio*) of the divine creator in the construction process, the criticism of a change of mind experienced by the divine intellect that prompted the creation of the universe. As previously, it may have been Cicero's aim to draw attention to such aspects of Timaean creationism as would have provoked opposition. In this context, let me point to a final passage in Cicero's translation, *Tim.* 29b1–2, that is relevant to our present context:

---

[133] We recall that the same emphasis is reiterated by the Stoic Balbus *in support of* an active creative principle at *Nat. deor.* 2.133: 'here somebody may ask, for whose sake did the laborious undertaking of such enormous deeds occur?' (*hic quaeret quispiam cuiusnam causa tantarum rerum **molitio** facta sit?*).

Table 13. *Plato,* Tim. *29b1–2*

29b1	A: τούτων δὲ ὑπαρχόντων αὖ πᾶσα ἀνάγκη τόνδε τὸν κόσμον εἰκόνα τινός εἶναι.	A: Based on these assumptions it is necessary, in turn, that this cosmos is a copy of something.

Table 14. *Cicero's translation of Plato,* Tim. *29b1–2* *(Cic.* Tim. *2.7, 10–11)*

29b1	B: *efficitur ut sit necesse hunc, quem cernimus, mundum simulacrum aeternum esse alicuius aeterni.*	B: It turns out that this cosmos we behold is of necessity an eternal copy of something eternal.

Timaeus states that, on the condition that his previous explanations be granted, our world is 'of necessity a copy of something', πᾶσα ἀνάγκη τόνδε τὸν κόσμον εἰκόνα τινός εἶναι. One would expect, given the previous distinction between model and copy, a somewhat clearer definition by Timaeus than is implied by the declaration that the universe, a thing created, is a copy of just 'something', τινός. The present context would naturally suggest the addition of, perhaps, 'of something eternal'. This is, in fact, what we observe in Cicero, but it is not the only modification we encounter in his text. He renders *necesse* [*est*] *hunc, quem cernimus, mundum* **simulacrum aeternum** *esse alicuius aeterni*, 'an eternal copy of something eternal', which, at face value, is an incorrect interpretation of the original on his part. While Timaeus would certainly ascribe to the intelligible model the possession of eternal being, he has been intent on showing that the generated model is bound to coming to be and perishing and does not partake of eternity. Initially, Cicero's addition of *aeterni* to *alicuius*, which assigns eternal being to the intelligible model, is in line with this position. From a literary point of view, it reaffirms his general tendency to increase syntactical balance in his translation of those passages that, in the Greek, exhibit brevity. The addition of *aeterni* may also have been motivated by the anticipation of an attribute in the Greek, as I have suggested above. On

97

the other hand, Cicero's ascription of the attribute *aeternum* also to the *simulacrum* is confusing. Excluding *ex hypothesi* any textual interpolations, it is possible that Cicero had in mind the remainder of Timaeus' narrative, in particular *Tim.* 41a7–b2,[134] a passage which reveals that the universe, despite being subject to perishing, is granted everlastingness due to the grace of its maker. In other words, by adding a second *aeternum*, Cicero could have alluded to the universe's *future* everlastingness, a view that would have provoked disagreement among potential Epicurean and Stoic interlocutors.

A further motivation for Cicero's addition of *aeternum* may have been what appears to be an erroneous identification, on his part, of the intelligible model not as a generic form, but as the specific Form of Eternity,[135] as a copy of which the universe would acquire future sempiternal existence. Consider his translation of *Tim.* 29a2–b2:

[134] 'What has come to be through my hands cannot become undone, save by my own will. While all that has been bound together can be undone, only one who is evil would wish for something that is finely put together and in good condition to be undone.'

[135] I am grateful to David Sedley for this suggestion. Baltes 1976: 30 argues that the second *aeternum* must be erroneous even if it had been added by Cicero with a view to *Tim.* 41a7 since the All's everlastingness would have been of a different kind from the model's natural eternity. Nigidius appears to have taken a keen interest in eradicating erroneous lexical meanings in his grammatical works (cf. for instance fr. 1, ed. Swoboda, where Nigidius discusses the difference between sempiternal and perpetual existence: 'sempiternity belongs to immortal things, perpetuity to mortal things. For perpetuity is in our nature ... perpetuity is infinite ...' (*sempiternum inmortalium rerum, perpetuum mortalium est; perpetuitas enim in nostra natura est ... sempiternitas infinita est ...*)). Such precision is, however, not apparent in Cicero, who throughout his writings tends to use *aeternus* and *sempiternus* and their cognate forms without any notable distinction (e.g. *Div.* 1.125, on the Stoic *heimarmenê*: 'this is sempiternal truth, which flows from all eternity' (*ea est ex omni aeternitate fluens veritas sempiterna*). The term one might have expected him to attribute to the cosmos is *perpetuus*, given that *perpetuitas* is used by Cicero in his rendering of *Tim.* 41b4–6, where the perpetual existence of the god's creation (i.e. the lesser gods and, by inference, the world soul and the visible cosmos) is distinguished from an immortal existence: 'my resolve, which is a greater bond for your perpetual existence' (*consilium meum quod maius est vinculum ad perpetuitatem vestram*). Nevertheless, it appears that he is not consistent in his use of this term either. At *Nat. deor.* 1.40, Velleius reports Chrysippus to have identified Jupiter with the 'power of the perpetual and eternal law' ([*vis*] *legis perpetuae et aeternae*), as well as with the 'sempiternal truth of the future' ([*sempiterna*] *rerum futurarum verita*[*s*]). This accumulation of adjectives by the Epicurean Velleius may, however, be polemically motivated in order to mock the plurality of names and functions attributed to the Stoic divine principle. A precise distinction, if ever such had been drawn by Cicero, between the various terms is unsurprisingly missing in this context.

Table 15. *Plato, Tim. 29a2–b2*

29a2	**A§1:** εἰ μὲν δὴ καλός ἐστιν ὅδε ὁ κόσμος ὅ τε δημιουργὸς ἀγαθός, δῆλον ὡς πρὸς τὸ ἀίδιον ἔβλεπεν· εἰ δὲ ὃ μηδ᾿ εἰπεῖν τινι θέμις, πρὸς	**A§1:** If, then, this cosmos is beautiful and the demiurge good, it is clear that he was looking towards the eternal [model].
5	γεγονός.	If not, which is not lawful for anyone to say, he was looking towards a created [model].
29a4	**A§2:** παντὶ δὴ σαφὲς ὅτι πρὸς τὸ ἀίδιον· ὁ μὲν γὰρ κάλλιστος τῶν γεγονότων, ὁ δ᾿ ἄριστος τῶν αἰτίων.	**A§2:** Indeed, it is clear to everybody that he was looking towards the eternal [model]: for the cosmos is the most beautiful of all things created, and [the demiurge] is the best of all causes.
29a6	**A§3:** οὕτω δὴ γεγενημένος πρὸς τὸ λόγῳ καὶ φρονήσει περιληπτὸν καὶ κατὰ ταὐτὰ ἔχον δεδημιούργηται.	**A§3:** Having been generated in this way, it has been fashioned after that which is grasped by reason and thought and is self-same.
29b1 15	**A§4:** τούτων δὲ ὑπαρχόντων αὖ πᾶσα ἀνάγκη τόνδε τὸν κόσμον εἰκόνα τινὸς εἶναι.	**A§4:** Again, if these assumptions apply, it is entirely necessary that this cosmos is the image of something.

Table 16. *Cicero's translation of Plato, Tim. 29a2–b2* (*Cic. Tim. 2.6, 1–2.7, 11*)

29a2	**B§1:** *atqui si pulcher est hic mundus et si probus eius artifex, profecto speciem aeternitatis imitari maluit; sin secus, quod ne*	**B§1:** But if this cosmos is beautiful and its craftsman good, he certainly preferred to copy the form of eternity; if not (and even
5	*dictu quidem fas est, generatum exemplum est pro aeterno secutus.*	to say so would be impious), he followed the generated model instead of the eternal.
29a4 10	**B§2:** *non igitur dubium quin aeternitatem maluerit exsequi, quandoquidem neque mundo quicquam pulchrius neque eius aedificatore praestantius.*	**B§2:** Thus, there is no doubt that he preferred to follow eternity, since, indeed, there is neither anything more beautiful than the cosmos nor more formidable than the creator.

(*continued*)

Table 16 (*continued*)

29a6 15	B§3: *sic ergo generatus ad id est* *effectus quod ratione sapientiaque* *comprehenditur atque aeternitate* *inmutabili continetur.*	B§3: Thus, then, [the cosmos] has been created with a view to that which is grasped by reason and wisdom and which is held fast by immutable eternity.
29b1 20	B§4: *ex quo efficitur ut sit* *necesse hunc, quem cernimus,* *mundum simulacrum aeternum* *esse alicuius aeterni.*	B§4: From this it is concluded, of necessity, that this cosmos which we perceive is an eternal image of something eternal.

τὸ ἀίδιον is described in **B§1** as the *species aeternitatis*, the Form of Eternity, (l. 3). Thereafter, it becomes the *aeternum* [*exemplum*] (ll. 6–7), with *exemplum* itself disappearing in an ellipsis. In **B§2** Cicero translates 'thus, there is no doubt that he preferred to follow eternity (*aeternitatem*, cf. τὸ ἀίδιον)'. In **B§3** it is, again, merely *aeternitas*, presumably as the quality proper of the *species* referred to, which is imitated by the demiurge for his creation.[136] Translating [τὸ] κατὰ ταὐτὰ ἔχον, Cicero's *quod aeternitate immutabile continetur* picks up the element of unchangeability as well as that of eternal being, which he describes as being 'held fast by' eternity. The impression arises that Cicero imagined the demiurge to be looking towards the Form of Eternity, specifically.[137]

Cicero's noticeable focus on the attribute of eternity supports the assumption that the topic of cosmic everlastingness was a crucial interpretative aspect on Cicero's mind in the set-up of his translation. In an intended polemical setting, his translation would have accentuated the everlastingness of a *created* cosmos, a property he assigned to it as an instantiation of the intelligible Form of Eternity. In this context, Cicero may have associated Timaeus' statement that the cosmos is a 'copy of

---

[136] In Plato, 'F-ness' likewise can equal 'the F itself'.

[137] In this context, Cicero's rendering *quantum enim ad id quod ortum est aeternitas valet*, 'for to the same degree as eternity impacts upon what has come to be', for ὅτιπερ πρὸς γένεσιν οὐσία, 'for as being stands in relation to coming to be' at *Tim.* 29c3 may express a relation in which the Form of Eternity, in virtue of its paradigmatic function, has an impact upon, or determines, the nature of its copy, time. Cf. 262–4.

something' (εἰκόνα τινὸς) with the notion of a 'moving image of eternity', as cosmic temporality is described at *Tim.* 37d5 (εἰκὼ δ᾽ ἐπενόει κινητόν τινα αἰῶνος ποιῆσαι). On this view, of course, he failed to mark in his terminology the ontological difference between eternity and sempiternity. An alternative explanation may have been the wish to draw attention to the superficial agreement that would presumably have existed between Nigidius and Cratippus regarding the everlastingness of the universe, all the while presenting an opportunity for a Peripatic interlocutor to attack the possibility of everlasting existence as an attribute of generated objects, regardless of the will of any divine power within the cosmos.

Conclusion

Cicero's Latin translation of the *Timaeus*, like his philosophical treatises, manifests specific evidence of the doctrinal controversies that had been attached to the Timaean creation account already in the preceding centuries. Problematic elements such as the ambivalent meaning of the Greek term ἀρχή, duly disambiguated by Cicero in favour of a temporal interpretation, as well as the notion of a *novum consilium* on the part of the creative agent are reflected in the translation. The comparison between the manner in which Cicero integrates these dogmatic differences into his translation of the Timaean monologue, and the treatment he affords them in his other philosophical treatises, supports the overall conclusion that the latter framework, in which Cicero or another representative of the sceptical Academy would have responded critically to opposing views, gave Cicero more leeway to illustrate in detail the individual doctrines and the subtle polemic between opposing parties.

CHAPTER 3

APULEIUS

Preliminaries: Rhetoric, Philosophy, and the Second Sophistic

With Apuleius we enter into the second century of our era. Apuleius communicates his interpretation of Platonic philosophy through a variety of literary genres. Among them we find gracefully crafted declamations such as the *Apology*, his defence speech against the charge of practising magic, and the *Florida*, a collection of epideictic orations. In his *De deo Socratis* Apuleius uses the Socratic guardian spirit, the *daimonion*, as a springboard for a philosophical lecture, delivered in highly ornamental style, of a complex system of demonology. Of a rather more sober style is his compendium on Platonic physics and ethics, the *De Platone et eius dogmate*.[1]

---

[1] In his recent contribution *A New Work by Apuleius: The Lost Third Book of the De Platone* (2016) Justin A. Stover argues that the *Compendiosa expositio* (*exp.*), a previously unknown Latin work appearing in a thirteenth-century manuscript discovered by Raymond Klibansky, was authored by Apuleius and intended by him as the third volume of the *DPD*. Stover presents the *exp.*'s *editio princeps*, to which he has added a lucid English translation and a commentary. In the manuscript, the *exp.* is grouped with the *Asclepius*, the Latin translation of Plato's *Timaeus* by Calcidius, the *DDS*, the *DPD*, and the *De mundo*. The work presents a selective summary of Plato's *Republic*, *Menexenus*, *Apology*, *Crito*, *Phaedo*, a short self-referential passage discussing the *divisio librorum* (*exp.* §14), and further summaries of Plato's *Laws*, *Epinomis*, *Letters*, *Parmenides*, *Sophist*, *Statesman*, *Timaeus*, and *Critias*. According to Stover, the *exp.* was intended as a discussion *de libris*, an index of Platonic *loci* that provided the working notes and were used by Apuleius 'as a handy guide on the dialogues in composing his own synthetic overview of Plato's teaching' (34) in the *DPD* 1 and 2. The evidence gained from Stover's lexical and stylistic analyses makes a compelling case of Apuleian authorship. Nevertheless, the extent to which the *exp.* and the *DPD* vary in their treatment of certain dogmata and, on occasion, in their use of terminology, raises questions about the *exp.*'s overall usefulness for the composition of *DPD* 1 and 2. I, therefore, hesitate to commit to the view that the work's date of composition coincides with that of the *DPD*, or that Apuleius composed it with the intended purpose of integrating it into his Platonic exegesis in the *DPD*. Cf. Hoenig 2018b. It had been assumed previously by some (e.g. Beaujeu 1973: vii–viii) that another work, the introductory treatise

The *De mundo*,[2] a loose translation of a pseudo-Aristotelian treatise, offers a cosmological theory that combines Aristotelian, Platonic, and Stoic elements. Aside from Apuleius' *rhetorica* and *philosophica*, there is, of course, the comic novel *Metamorphoses*. Switching between linguistic registers and social milieux, the narrative tells of young Lucius' transformation into an ass, followed by his apparent salvation by the goddess Isis, after many episodes of violence and vulgarity that are recounted with affectionate detail.[3]

Apuleius is often characterized as a 'man of his time', i.e. as a writer and orator entrenched in the cultural setting of the Second Sophistic.[4] Prone to literary embellishment and displays of learnedness, Apuleius certainly bears the hallmarks of this era. What is more, the intellectual milieu of Apuleius' second century CE is sometimes characterized by a domineering focus on, and veneration for, the past.[5] On the literary plane, this would result in an output of an often imitatory nature, fostered by a rhetorical curriculum designed primarily to encourage not original thought but the preservation and transmission, in ornamental yet intellectually simplified form, of material from the Classical age. Apuleius' skill as an orator and writer, it is assumed, had been forged by such contemporary ideals, catering to an audience that valued polished expression more highly than originality and substance.[6]

Peri hermeneias on the subject of logic, was intended to supply the announced third volume of Apuleius' *DPD*, a view that is now discredited.

2 Previously doubted by Redfors 1960 on account of stylistic and linguistic reasons, the authenticity of this work has convincingly been reaffirmed by Regen 1971, Beaujeu 1973: xi–xxviii. A general discussion of the authenticity of the Apuleian works is given by Hijmans 1987: 408–15; Moreschini 2015: 203–4.

3 The chronology of Apuleius' works is difficult. It has been assumed that the distinct, rather sober, literary style used in the *DPD* and the *De mundo* points to a date of composition prior to the stylistically elaborate *DDS*, *Apology*, *Florida*, and *Metamorphoses*. However, the addressee of some of these treatises appears to be Apuleius' son Faustinus, which appears to discredit the assumption that Apuleius composed them during his youthful stay in Athens. For further conjectures, see Beaujeu 1973: xii–viii; Dillon 1996: e.g. 232, 310.

4 See, for instance, Tatum 1979: 105–10; Helm 1955 vol. 1: 86–8; Beaujeu 1973: 58.

5 Notably so by Sandy 1977.

6 Sandy 1977: especially chapter 2.

On the philosophical plane, similarly, second-century Platonism is sometimes[7] characterized as having been reduced to the schematized recasting of doctrines, usually with the syncretic gloss of Stoic and Peripatetic elements. Active philosophical investigation appeared to have come to a standstill.[8] Among the works classified as Apuleius' *philosophica* proper, the *DPD* has duly been perceived as a bullet-point systematization of what had come to be regarded as standard Platonic doctrine, streamlined and repackaged for popular consumption.[9] At times, this work has been denied much intrinsic value aside from its role as a patchwork display of earlier philosophical source material.[10] The rather more ornate tone of the *DDS*, in turn, has been perceived as leaning towards oratorical performance to such an extent as to provoke the suggestion that its author's interest in matters philosophical may be explained in part by its benefit to the repertoire of the consummate orator.[11]

The premise of portraying Apuleius as an orator with a merely ornamental interest in Platonic philosophy prevents us from detecting his intelligent use of Platonic themes in the various literary settings he creates. At the same time, while mining Apuleius' *philosophica* in the name of Quellenforschung has delivered most valuable insights for the historian of philosophy, it has not brought us sufficiently close to 'Apuleius the philosopher', a complex and creative writer whose

[7] Dillon 1996: e.g. 230 (on Plutarch), 232, 270 (on the author of the *Anonymous Commentary on the Theaetetus*); cf. the verdict of Gersh 1986 vol. 2: 200.

[8] An often-cited early warning against this development is given by Seneca in his *Epistle* 108, where he cautions against the dangers of 'drifting off into the philologist's or the scholar's terrain' while practising philosophy (*ne et ipse ... in philologum aut grammaticum delabar*). To find the appropriate approach to philosophy, 'we should not reach for archaic or contrived expressions, nor for over-the-top tropes and figures of speech' (*non ut verba prisca aut ficta captemus et translationes inprobas figurasque dicendi*, 108.35), or else 'what had been philosophy [is] turned into philology (*quae philosophia fuit facta philologia est*, 108, 23).

[9] E.g. Sandy 1997: 182.

[10] Dillon 1996: 311.

[11] Dillon 1996: 306–7. In the case of Apuleius' philosophical works, Sandy accounts for his focus on the 'sophistic and artistic performance qualities' (183) of these writings with the view that they are derivative in nature and partly constructed for oral performance in front of a live audience.

philosophical project stretches from his *DPD*, *DDS*, and *De mundo* to the *Florida*, the *Apology*, and the *Metamorphoses*.[12] In this context, welcome recent contributions to Apuleian scholarship have been Richard Fletcher's *Apuleius' Platonism* (2014) and Claudio Moreschini's *Apuleius and the Metamorphoses of Platonism* (2015), which encourage a more comprehensive approach to Apuleius' philosophical project, a project in which the manner of communication of philosophical material, and the context in which it is presented, are intrinsic to its very content.

'Doing philosophy' for Apuleius, I will illustrate in the present chapter, is the cross-genre infusion of his works with his religious–dogmatic interpretation of Platonism. His sensibility for style and linguistic register allowed him to adjust philosophical subject matter to individual contexts and audiences,[13] and should be understood as a crucial instrument in the author's philosophical toolbox. Thus injecting Plato's thought into his entire literary output, Apuleius aimed at portraying himself as a consummate Platonist interpreter while drawing his listeners towards his philosophical project. It is this undertaking, I shall argue, that Apuleius identifies with philosophical activity and, more specifically, with dialectic, the 'true rhetoric'.[14]

My strategy to examine Apuleius' interpretation of Platonic cosmology in the context of his wider philosophical project consists of several steps. In the section 'Apuleius' Plato and Platonism', I initially place our author in the context of the Platonism contemporary with him and survey his portrayal of Plato. As a part of this section, I shed further light on Apuleius' way of 'doing philosophy' along the lines I have set out above.

---

[12] It has been acknowledged that Apuleius' interpretation of Platonic doctrine surfaces across the spectrum of his various literary works. Cf. Sandy 1997: 187, who adduces Regen's 1971 graphical representation of philosophical elements throughout the Apuleian corpus. Against Moreschini 1966, Hijman 1987: 397 considers Apuleius' philosophical enterprise intrinsically linked to his religiosity.

[13] A point argued by Fletcher 2014: 173–261, especially 226–61.

[14] Apul. *DPD* 2.8; Plato, *Phaedr.* 258d4–5, 277b–c. In his discussion with Phaedrus Socrates identifies the dialectician or 'noble' and 'true' rhetorician as able to convey his expertise by adapting his speech to audience and occasion in the most suitable manner. Cf. Moreschini 2015: 49–57, 147–85.

Turning next to Apuleius' relationship with the *Timaeus*, I examine Apuleius' Timaean methodology and show that his dogmatic interpretation of Timaeus' creation account claims authority through its appeal to 'faith', *fides*. In what appears to be, prima facie, a rather startling reinterpretation of the original text, the *fides* of the Timaean creation account turns out to be the chief validation of Plato's doctrine. The final part of the present chapter studies Apuleius' treatment of specific doctrinal themes arising in the *Timaeus*, such as his interpretation of the 'createdness' that is at play in Plato's dialogue, and his complex theological doctrine that allows him to construct a relationship between a transcendent divinity and the material sphere with the help of a network of divine providential powers. Of particular interest for the final part of the present chapter will be the relation between Apuleius' *DPD* and his *De mundo*, his translation of the Ps.-Aristotelian treatise *Peri kosmou* on cosmology and theology.[15] I will discuss at length the manner in which Apuleius negotiates a doctrinal stance that aligns Platonic and Aristotelian material. While, unlike Cicero, Apuleius does not offer us a theoretical discussion of his translation policy, I will also point to various passages in the *De mundo* in which Apuleius modifies the underlying Greek text in such a way as to align it with the exegesis we encounter in his *DPD* and his *DDS*, in particular.

Apuleius' Plato and Platonism

Platonism in the Second Century CE: Dogmatism and Religion

By the early centuries of our common era the Platonic school had changed its course.[16] With Antiochus of Ascalon in the first century BCE Platonists had begun to distance themselves from the Academy's previous sceptical turn and to lean

---

[15] The work is thought to have been composed between the first and second century CE, cf. the discussion by Furley 1965: 337–41. Further useful discussions on this work remain Strohm 1952, Festugière 1949 vol. 2: 460–518.
[16] Dörrie/ Baltes 1993: 121; Glucker 1978: 342–4.

towards a dogmatic perspective.[17] Where doctrinal coherence could not be obtained from Plato's writings alone, the incorporation of Stoic and Peripatetic elements helped define an increasingly coherent and orthodox Platonic doctrine. If we choose to accuse the Platonic tradition of the time of unoriginality, we should take into account the circumstances that went along with the adoption of a steady doctrinal line. Intellectual curiosity and active philosophical investigation in the form of dialectical argument had not miraculously come to a halt. Rather, the motivation to modify or develop one's philosophical position was mitigated by the perception that 'the truth' had already been revealed in Plato's works.[18] What it needed was clarification, structure, and dissemination, not further modification.[19]

Beginning in the first century CE the Platonic curriculum reflected this effort to systematize the master's doctrines and took on the shape of a study programme whose foundation, ethics, was followed by physics and finally theology or metaphysics.[20] A learner's advance along this spectrum was sometimes perceived as resembling the initiation process into the Eleusinian mysteries. Such an association of philosophical wisdom with cult initiation may have been inspired by Socrates' use of subject-specific terminology in the *Symposium* and the *Phaedrus*.[21] It may have been encouraged further by

---

[17] For Antiochus' philosophical development and its impact on the Platonic tradition, cf. Sedley 2012, Dillon 1996: 52–106. There remained individual proponents of a sceptic conviction such as Favorinus, who features in Gellius' *Attic nights*.

[18] Cf. Hadot 2002: 152–3. Even the second-century Middle Platonist Numenius of Apamea, who polemicized that there had never existed true unity among Plato's successors and followers, credits Plato's doctrine with inherent accuracy and coherence. Cf. Numenius fragments 24–8 (ed. Des Places).

[19] Cf. the thoughts of Hadot 2002: 148–9.

[20] Cf. Hadot 1982: 441. The order of reading varied, as reported by Diogenes Laertius 3.62. In chapter 5 of his *Introductio in Platonem* Albinus explains that the order in which the dialogues were read could depend on very particular circumstances, such as the intellect and the age of the student, his motivation, and the time frame available to him.

[21] Diotima at *Symp.* 209e–212a describes the student's ascent from particular instances of beauty to the knowledge of the essence of beauty, the highest level of philosophical advancement and 'ultimate secret', by using terminology associated with the Mysteries, i.e. μυέω; τὰ δὲ τέλεα καὶ ἐποπτικά (210a1); τὸ τέλος (211b); τὸ … ἐπὶ τὰ ἐρωτικὰ ἰέναι ἢ ὑπ' ἄλλου ἄγεσθαι (211b–c); see also *Phaedr.* 250e1–2; *Phd.* 69c.

the exposure of philosophical writers to the oriental revelatory cults that had begun to spread throughout the empire of the early centuries.[22] Plutarch, one of the chief witnesses to such influences in the late first century CE, explains that Plato and Aristotle themselves had established the study of 'epoptical', i.e. theological, subject matter, to follow upon physics.[23] The term 'epoptical' is borrowed from the vocabulary of the Mysteries (used in a philosophical context by Socrates' Diotima in the *Symposium*), where it described the highest level of an initiate's spiritual progress. The use of mystery cult imagery is a feature we encounter also in other authors of the early centuries, such as Theon of Smyrna and Origen.[24] In an intellectual climate that saw the absorption of foreign rituals and practices, often secretive and restrictive as far as access was concerned, it is perhaps not surprising that accusations of magical practice against those engaged in philosophical activity could have arisen and thrived, as in Apuleius' own case.

Divine Plato and Apuleius the High-Priest

As in the case of the revelatory cults with which second-century philosophical activity was associated, the Platonism of the time centred on a divine figure by whom the 'truth' had been revealed. Apuleius was certainly not the first to bestow upon Plato the epithet 'divine'; nevertheless, the detailed record of the master's divine lineage in the 'bibliography' at the outset of the *DPD* has invited comparison with hagiographic literature.[25]

---

[22] Beaujeu 1973: xxxii.
[23] 'Plato and Aristotle call this part of philosophy "epoptical", since those who have left behind opinable and mixed things, and others of that sort, with the help of reason leap towards that first, simple and immaterial [principle] and once they have reached entirely its pure truth, they believe them to have reached, as it were, the highest hold of philosophy' (Πλάτων καὶ Ἀριστοτέλης ἐποπτικὸν τοῦτο τὸ μέρος τῆς φιλοσοφίας καλοῦσιν, ὡς οἱ τὰ δοξαστὰ καὶ μικτὰ καὶ παντοδαπὰ ταῦτα παραμειψάμενοι τῷ λόγῳ πρὸς τὸ πρῶτον ἐκεῖνο καὶ ἁπλοῦν καὶ ἄυλον ἐξάλλονται, καὶ θιγόντες ὅλως τῆς περὶ αὐτὸ καθαρᾶς ἀληθείας οἷον ἐν τελετῇ τέλος ἔχειν φιλοσοφίας νομίζουσι, *Is. et Os.* 382d7–e2). Cf. Ross, Aristotle fr. 15, on the ἐποπτής, i.e. 'the one who has seen'. For Calcidius' use of the term, cf. p. 176.
[24] Cf. Theon of Smyrna *Rer. math.* 14 (ed. Petrucci) esp. 14,19–16,1. Cf. Baltes and Dörrie 1996: 228–31 and Hadot 1982: 436; 439; ibid. 2002: 154; Beaujeu 1973: 55.
[25] Cf. Beaujeu 1973: 249, and cf. Hijmans 1987: 434. Cf. also Moreschini 2015: 192–7.

In the very first paragraph, Plato's father Ariston is identified as a descendant of the god Neptune, his mother Perictione as a relation of Solon, a most venerable, if not quite celestial, in-law. But Apuleius is happy to repeat speculation about a lineage of an even finer pedigree: 'There are some who believe Plato sprung from an even nobler birth [i.e. nobler than being a descendant, merely, of Neptune], when Apollo in [human] disguise lay with Perictione' (*DPD* I.I, 181).[26] Apuleius' Socrates, in turn, recounts his vision of a cygnet – the swan being traditionally associated with Apollo – that ascended into the air from the altar of Cupid in the Academy. Once in flight, the bird delighted the ears of gods and men with his melodious song, *canore musico*.[27] Upon meeting the boy Plato, Socrates took this 'cygnet of Cupid's Academy' into his tutelage.[28] While these mythical elements in Plato's bibliography are certainly not exclusive to Apuleius,[29] their sheer accumulation at the outset of his compendium emphasizes Plato's divine status and thus validates the ensuing doctrine.

Once revealed by the divine source, dogmatic creed relies on messengers, teachers, or other mediators for its dissemination. It is precisely the role of such an intermediary that Apuleius constructs for himself: he is the mediator between the divine philosopher and his audience.[30] Apuleius bases his authority for

---

[26] This assumption is fuelled by the coinciding of Plato's birthday with that of Apollo and his sister Diana, cf. Apul. *DPD* I.I, 181: 'on the day on which it is said that Latona gave birth to Apollo and Diana on Delos' (*die qua apud Delum Latona fertur Apollinem Dianamque peperisse*).

[27] Literally: 'stroked' the ears: *mulcentem*. Incidentally, this brings to mind another well-known preface of Apuleius' that talks about the 'stroking of ears'. The mysterious speaker of the very first sentence in Apuleius' *Metamorphoses* promises the reader that he will 'stroke his willing ears with charming whispers' (*at ego tibi ... auresque tuas benivolas lepido susurro permulceam*). Cf. p. 116.

[28] *DPD* I.I, 183: 'When he had caught sight of him, and seen his innermost potential in his outward appearance, he said: "This here, friends, was Cupid's cygnet in the Academy"' (*quem ubi adspexit ille ingeniumque intimum de exterior conspicatus est facie: 'hic ille erat, amici', inquit, 'de Academia Cupidinis cygnus'*).

[29] See, for instance, Diog. Laert. 3.1–2, 5, who credits Speusippus with this account (cf. Moreschini 1966: 27). Apuleius himself points to Speusippus' testimony at *DPD* 1.2, 183. But see also Alcinous' *Didaskalikos*, which begins *in medias res* without appealing to such mythical details.

[30] Fletcher takes Apuleius' role as a mediator further and argues that the author associates his work as Plato's interpreter with the mediating efforts of the *daimôn*,

Apuleius

such an office on his standing as a *sacerdos*, a priest of various religious cults.[31] In his appeals to his sacerdotal authority the conflation between philosophical and religious activity is at its most obvious. Thus at *Apol.* 41 Apuleius merges the role of a natural philosopher with the religious office of the *augur* and *haruspex*, sealing the validity of his argument by referring to Aristotle:

> Should it be permissible for any soothsayer to lay open the livers [of victims] but not permissible for the philosopher to interpret them, one who knows he is an augur[32] of all animal victims, one who knows that he is the high-priest of every god? Is this what you accuse me of, the same [ability] myself and Maximus admire in Aristotle? Unless you ban his writings from the libraries and snatch them away from the hands of the learned, you cannot accuse me.[33]

Apuleius is the *sacerdos* 'of all gods', an office he legitimately holds due to his philosophical expertise.[34] While this line of argument, cited from Apuleius' defence against charges of magical practice, serves the immediate purpose of explaining

an intermediary between the human and divine spheres, thereby integrating Apuleius' philosophical method with one of the core doctrines of his Platonic creed. Cf. Fletcher 2014: 100–72.
[31] Cf. Apul. *Apol.* 55: 'In Greece I participated in many initiations to sacred rites. I carefully preserve certain paraphernalia and tokens of these sacred rites, entrusted to me by the priests. I am saying nothing that is unusual or unheard of. Those of you here, for instance, who are inititates of Father Liber alone: you know what you conceal hidden at your house and worship in private, removed from all who are uninitiated. I, however, as I mentioned, have studied many sacred doctrines, numerous rites and various ceremonial customs, because of my zeal for the truth and my duty towards the gods' (*sacrorum pleraque initia in Graecia participavi. eorum quaedam signa et monumenta tradita mihi a sacerdotibus sedulo conservo. nihil insolitum, nihil incognitum dico. vel unius Liberi patris mystae qui adestis, scitis quid domi conditum celetis et absque omnibus profanis tacite veneremini. at ego, ut dixi, multiiuga sacra et plurimos ritus et varias cerimonias studio veri et officio erga deos didici*). Cf. Moreschini 2015: 39–42.
[32] Note the distinction Apuleius draws between the *hariolus*, the *haruspex*, and the *sacerdos*. It appears that *hariolus* is a disparaging term that expresses a lack of legitimacy or expertise, while the authority of the *haruspex* and the *sacerdos*, according to Apuleius' interpretation, is validated by his philosophical expertise. Cf. Cic. *Div.* 1.132, who (in turn drawing on Ennius) lumps together *superstitiosi vates* and *inpudentes harioli*.
[33] *an hariolis licet iocinera rimari, philosopho contemplari non licebit, qui se sciat omnium animalium haruspicem, omnium deum sacerdotem? hoc in me accusas, quod ego et Maximus in Aristotele miramur?*
[34] Apuleius underlines his philosophical expertise by frequent references to the doctrines he ascribes not only to Plato but also to other members of the philosophical tradition such as Pythagoras, Zeno, and Aristotle, to name but a few. For detailed references, see Hijmans 1987: 416–18 with notes 85–8.

his actions (in the present example: the examination of fish!)[35] in the face of his accusers, it reaffirms the privileged relation 'by office' that he professes to maintain with the divine realm. Similar associations of religious authority with philosophical expertise appear in other contexts. At *DDS* 3, 122, for instance, the crowd of commoners is the target of a fierce invective, their lack of philosophical learning identified with irreverence:

The crowd of those who are unlearned, uninitiated in philosophy: [a crowd] devoid of purity, deprived of truthful reason, wanting in piety, incapable of [accessing] the truth, slights the gods either by fastidious worship or insolent scorn ...[36]

What is more, in the protrepic conclusion of the *DDS*, after discussing the nature of Socrates' demon, Apuleius stresses the importance of 'worshipping one's [own] demon', which is nothing other than the 'solemn obligation to practise philosophy'.[37] Finally, a telling addition that appears in Apuleius' translation *De mundo* explains that human soul[38] grants to a limited amount of mortals, such as prophets (*prophetae*) the ability to direct their mental gaze beyond the confines of the mortal sphere. These prophets 'filled with the grandeur of the gods, announce to the others what they alone, grace to the privilege [bestowed upon them] by the gods, are able to see'.[39] In the Greek *Peri kosmou*, it is human soul itself that is 'making its prophecy to humans' (τοῖς ἀνθρώποις προφητεύουσα, 391a) without the need for *prophetae*. Apuleius appears to be promoting his own authority as a *sacerdos* who enjoys privileged access to the divine.[40]

[35] Cf. Fletcher 2014: 213–5; Moreschini 2015: 32–4.
[36] *profana philosophiae turba imperitorum, vana sanctitudinis, priva verae rationis, inops religionis, impos veritatis, scrupulosissimo cultu, insolentissimo spretu deos neglegit ...*
[37] *DDS* 22.170: *daemonis cultum qui cultus non aliud quam philosophiae sacramentum est.*
[38] At *DDS* 15, the (virtuous) human soul is, in fact, listed as a type of immortal *daimôn*, albeit of the lowest, incarnate type.
[39] *De mundo*, pref.: *[anima] aliis etiam eius scientiam tradidit, veluti prophetae quidam deorum maiestate conpleti effantur ceteris, quae divino beneficio soli vident.* Beaujeu, *comm. ad loc.* notes that the term *propheta*, which does not occur before Apuleius, appears e.g. at *DPD* 1.3, 186, where it refers to Egyptian priests whose apprentice Plato became on his travels.
[40] Cf. n. 31.

To worship the divine is of paramount importance to Apuleius' philosophical activity. Access to philosophical wisdom, however, is limited to those who stand in a close relation with the higher realm,[41] be it a blood relation – as in Plato's case – or a relation 'by office' – as in Apuleius' case.

'Doing Philosophy': Apuleian Cross-Genre Dialectic

Aside from Apuleius' privileged access to matters divine, a further indispensable qualification for the office of the Platonic *sacerdos* and mediator is the ability to communicate his revelatory knowledge in a suitable manner. I will now examine in greater detail our author's concept of dialectic or 'true rhetoric'.[42]

For Apuleius, the intellectual value of the subject matter determines the quality required for the delivery of the speech. The philosopher's rhetoric is distinguished from forensic rhetoric due to the nature of its contents. Thus, at *DPD* 2.8, 231 the discipline of philosophical rhetoric is identified as the 'observer of what is good' (*contemplatrix bonorum*). Its subject matter is far removed from the everyday trivialities dealt with by the public orator. Apuleius clearly has in mind the type of dialectic familiar from Plato's *Gorgias* when he describes this type of rhetoric as 'firmly attached to what is just' (*iusti tenax*) and a suitable method for one who wishes to be considered a political leader (*apta et conveniens cum secta eius qui politicus vult videri*), i.e. the future philosopher kings. Philosophical rhetoric is differentiated from public rhetoric also by its ability to convey knowledge. The 'false' type of rhetoric is described as the art of flattery (*adulandi scientia*), capable merely of expressing likelihoods (*captatrix verisimilium*), a method devoid of rational cohesion (*usus nulla ratione collectus*). Such empty, albeit aesthetically pleasing, word-mongery is a mere shadow of the 'true rhetoric' that is based on and conveys

---

[41] Cf. e.g. Apul. *Apol.* 12: 'the lofty and divine Platonic doctrines, familiar only to a few select and entirely unknown to all non-initiates'.

[42] Cf. Fletcher 2014: 173–261, especially 173–98.

knowledge. It is able to 'persuade [only] without teaching' (δύναμιν τοῦ πείθειν ἄνευ τοῦ διδάσκειν).[43]

Apuleius associates dialectic with the sage man[44] who not only surpasses others by the excellence of his intellect (*ingenio praestet*) but who, at the same time, is experienced in passing on his knowledge through constructive actions and advice. He is endowed with self-restraint, endurance, and all learning (*omnibusque doctrinis*) afforded to him by his knowledge of things and his ability to converse eloquently (*ex rerum scientia eloquentiaque*).[45] The sage thus combines *scientia* and *eloquentia*, with both allowing him to access 'all learning', a combined set of skills that allows for maximum educational success.[46]

The overall Apuleian concept of philosophical rhetoric, according to this description, will have few surprises for the reader familiar with those of Plato's dialogues that address the subject of rhetoric.[47] Significant for our purpose of understanding Apuleius' philosophical project, however, is the fact that the author relies specifically on the combination of philosophical expertise and rhetorical skill for constructing his own role as a consummate Platonic interpreter. With his philosophical expertise vouched for thanks to his initiation into Platonic doctrine, his literary and rhetorical versatility ensures a successful communication of his knowledge.

In the course of his *Apology*, for instance, Apuleius finds plenty of opportunities to showcase his Platonic expertise. At

[43] As noted by Beaujeu 1973: 292, this is an inexact quotation of Plato, *Gorgias* 454e.
[44] While the perfect sage is certainly a central element of Stoic ethics (noted by Moreschini 1966: 92–8), the ensuing description of the sage man who has been geared from boyhood (*a pueris*) towards public leadership is most reminiscent of the young men undergoing a philosophical education in the *Republic* (cf. *Rep.* 7.535–7), as suggested also by Beaujeu; cf. Socrates' description of the philosophical nature of future guardians at *Rep.* 6.485a–491e.
[45] Apul. *DPD* 2.20, 247–8.
[46] Cf. *DDS* 17.158 for Apuleius' portrayal of Nestor as the *orator* whose wisdom (*prudentia*), in combination with the *dulcedo* of his words, is able to hold in check the belligerent Greek warriors at Troy. Cf. Hijmans 1987: 426.
[47] See, for instance, Plato's *Phaedo* 89c–91c; *Phaedr.* 269b, and *Gorgias* 463–464e. See also Beaujeu 1973: *comm. ad loc.*, who suggests Apuleius is borrowing specific expressions from these dialogues for his characterization of the two types of rhetoric.

the same time, his rhetorical skill allows him to tailor the level of his exposition to the proficiency of his listeners – this, too, being a requisite for the Platonic interpreter. Recall Socrates' request that the dialectician match his conversation not only to the nature of his subject matter but, moreover, to the condition of the various souls on the receiving end (*Phaedr.* 264c–d). Thus at *Apol.* 48–51[48] Apuleius' knowledge of Platonic (Timaean) anatomy allows him to counter the charge of 'bewitching' (*incantare*) his wife-to-be in order to gain greater influence upon her and her possessions. Apuleius accounts for an apparently suspicious physical examination of Pudentilla at his own hands with his intention to diagnose whether or not she suffered from epilepsy. He portrays himself as sufficiently qualified to carry out such an examination thanks to his medical expertise acquired from Plato's *Timaeus*,[49] parts of which (*Tim.* 69c–70e; 82a–e; 84c–85b) he references at length. Further validating his authority in the matter, he points to the fact that he had been motivated to examine Pudentilla by a physician proper (*petitu medici*). With Apuleius' expert knowledge sufficiently attested, his rhetorical versatility allows him to address his speech to a jury made up of non-philosophers in a manner suitably matched to the level of their expertise, that is: strongly simplified.[50] This Apuleius himself points out to the acting judge, proconsul Claudius Maximus. Professing himself anxious not to 'bore' Maximus with his rather elementary exposition, he recruits his judge as his intellectual ally[51] against

---

[48] Cf. Fletcher 2014: 198–226 for a broader analysis of Apuleius' Platonic method in his defence speech.

[49] Apul. *Apol.* 49: 'In his magnificent work *Timaeus*, the philosopher Plato laboriously creates our entire universe (*universum mundum molitur* – perhaps a nod to Cicero's translation, cf. pp. 86, 89, 96? Unfortunately, the passage of the *Timaeus* which Apuleius references in the subsequent passage is *Tim.* 81e–86a, a part of the dialogue for which no translation by Cicero has reached us) with a sort of divine eloquence. Following his expert discussion of the tripartite human soul, and his concise explanation of the reason why divine providence shaped all our limbs, he sets out three types of causes [responsible for] all diseases …'.

[50] This passage is usefully set out against the relevant parts of the *Timaeus* by Hijmans 1987: 418–21.

[51] Cf. Hijmans 1987: 430. Claudius Maximus is, however, described as the *Stoic* teacher of Emperor Marcus Aurelius in the *Historia Augusta* 1.3.

the remaining jurors – uninitiated into Platonic wisdom – at whom the ensuing lecture is directed.[52] On an intellectual par with Apuleius, Claudius Maximus is able, for all his boredom, to appreciate the succinctness of the defendant's exposition:

> You, Maximus, recognize Plato's doctrine. I have set it out as clearly as I could in the present circumstances.[53]

Relying on his twofold set of skills, his Platonic expertise and his rhetorical ability, Apuleius makes use of his philosophical methodology by transforming his court case into a vehicle for practising 'noble', philosophically anchored rhetoric. Elsewhere Apuleius, versatile mediator of philosophical wisdom, declares himself capable of communicating in whatever literary form is required. At *Apol.* 12f. he recounts the different literary genres, attempted likewise by philosophers of the past, through which he communicates his expertise.[54] Like Empedocles, Apuleius has composed lyric; he has written poetry[55] and dialogues like Plato, hymns like Socrates. Such

[52] Cf. *Apol.* 51: 'In talking about these matters, I have been referring to the discussions of esteemed philosophers, and have been careful to name their relevant books. I have decided to avoid any mention of physicians or poets, so that my accusers may cease to be astounded by philosophers who have learned about the origins and the treatments of diseases as part of their studies.'

[53] *Apol.* 51. Shortly after, he attests to his familiarity with the scientific tradition by pointing to the medical expertise of Aristotle and Theophrastus to support his argument: 'Aristotle, indeed, recorded in his *Problemata* that in patients whose epilepsy begins on the right-hand side of their body, their condition is more difficult to treat. It would tiresome if I were to report the opinion also of Theophrastus on this illness ...'. Cf. Fletcher 2014: 212–18 for a more detailed interpretation of Apuleius' manipulation of Maximus and his audience in relation to the passage quoted.

[54] Apul. *Flor.* 20: 'Empedocles recited poems, Plato wrote dialogues, Socrates hymns, Epicharmus comedies, Xenophon histories, Crates satires. All of these, your Apuleius has mastered, and he reveres the nine Muses with equal zeal ...' *(canit enim Empedocles carmina, Plato dialogos, Socrates hymnos, Epicharmus modos, Xenophon historias, Xencorates satiras: Apuleius vester haec omnia novemque Musas pari studio colit ...).*

[55] Cf. *Apol.* 12–13, where Apuleius proves capable of writing poetry, just like his master Plato. Just as Plato's compositions do, those by Apuleius concern the subject of love. However, far from forging smutty rhymes of vulgar passions, Plato was concerned with heavenly love. Once again displaying his expertise in Platonic doctrine, Apuleius implies that those uninitiated (*profani*) in the 'lofty divine Platonic dogmas' (*alta illa et divina Platonica*) are unable to recognize the difference between the Venus of the common crowd (*vulgaria*) and celestial (*caeles*) Venus, the Ἀφροδίτη οὐράνια familiar from Plato's *Symposium*. If Apuleius' accusers cannot condone verse writing in Plato's case, despite its noble subject matter, Apuleius will gladly

comprehensive literary expertise validates his authority as a successful conveyor of philosophical knowledge.[56] Apuleius' *eloquentia* is not merely the cosmetic shell of a specific subject matter, but the very tool by which speech is attuned to the setting. As with Cicero, it is rhetorical method that, albeit in a rather different manner, is shown to be the crucial instrument that allows Apuleius to develop his own brand of Platonism.

Stressing once more the privileged relationship he maintains with Plato, Apuleius emphasizes rhetoric as an essential feature also of his master's status as the ideal philosopher. Plato's *Timaeus*, for instance, is recounted with 'divine eloquence' (*caelesti quadam facundia*), and it is no coincidence that Plato's enchanting 'swan song' appears at the very outset of the *DPD*, Apuleius' exposition of Platonic doctrine. Rather, its appearance there carries a programmatic function. Plato, the model exemplar of the 'noble rhetorician'/dialectician, is able to reveal and communicate his divine knowledge owing to his rhetorical skill, 'stroking the ears of gods and men alike with his melodious song' (*canore musico auditus hominum deorumque mulcen[s]*).[57] At *DDS* 6, 132, while illustrating the need for communication between the human and divine spheres, Apuleius validates his viewpoint by portraying himself as his master's very own mouthpiece. Divine Plato's doctrine on divine–human communication is, at this very instant, itself being disseminated by his priest Apuleius: *responderit enim Plato pro sententia sua mea voce*.[58] At the same time, he proves himself as a skilled, actual translator who renders philosophical wisdom accessible to his audience by supplying the suitable Latin terminology needed for the classification of the various types of demons.[59]

---

share his master's guilt (*ego me facile patiar in huiuscemodi versibus culpari cum Platone*).

[56] Barra 1963: 8–10. Barra puts Apuleius' bibliography of Plato in relation to the author's own bibliography.
[57] Cf. n. 27.
[58] Cf. Fletcher 2014: 31–99 and 152–3.
[59] Cf. Apuleius' insistence on providing Latin terminology at *DDS* 15, 150. See also Fletcher 2014: 162.

Modern readers may be left unimpressed by Apuleius' concept of philosophical rhetoric even as an attempt to reproduce the sort of philosophical discourse Socrates defined as the 'true type of rhetoric' (*Phaedr.* 270c1–2). In the case of our sample passage above one might argue, somewhat unkindly, that Apuleius' appeal to the juror Claudius Maximus' intellectual merit, issued alongside his simplified exposition of Platonic doctrine for a non-Platonic audience, is not so much an example of Apuleius' sensitivity for the varying levels of expertise he was facing. On the contrary, it appears to be a rather fine specimen of the *adulandi scientia* so strongly condemned at *DPD* 2.8, 231. On some occasions, Apuleius' philosophical *persona* may thus seem like a sophisticated construct rather than a genuine philosophical outlook. Nevertheless, we should acknowledge that Apuleius the Platonist, thanks to his privileged access to divine wisdom and his immense communicative abilities, most likely felt as justified in his approach to Plato as many scholars of Platonism today are confident in their belief that dissecting Plato's elegantly flowing prose into complex strings of propositions, conveyed with the convenient brevity of logical formulae, will bring us closer to the essence of Plato's philosophy.[60]

Apuleius and the *Timaeus*

The Timaeus *in the Early Centuries* CE

During the early centuries CE, the *Timaeus* continued to play a central role in the development of Platonic doctrine and fuelled the interest of thinkers across the philosophical and theological spectrum. Outside Platonist circles, it attracted the attention of the first-century Jewish scholar Philo of Alexandria, who was among the first in line to establish a firm exegetical connection between the Timaean cosmology and the Christian creation story recounted in the book of Genesis.[61] Within Platonist

---

[60] See Gallop 2003: 313–14.
[61] After Philo, a further Jewish exegete whose work connected the Timaean creation story with Genesis was the second-century Jewish Alexandrian Aristobulus. For

Apuleius

circles the Timaean creation account, presented in continuous flow safe from elenctic scrutiny, recommended itself as an exposition of Platonic dogma covering mathematics and logic, physics and theology, and offered a solid grounding for the construction of an increasingly fixed Platonic syllabus.

The development of Platonism during these early centuries has been associated, until not too long ago, with two different 'schools', with the term 'school' intended to capture a shared exegetical stance between their various representatives. Alongside the 'School of Athens' linked to the authors Plutarch, Taurus, and Atticus, the so-called 'School of Gaius', constructed around Alcinous and Apuleius, has been considered an important strand of second-century Platonism. Credited with the theory of the 'School of Gaius' is Sinko, whose thesis of a substantial doctrinal overlap between Alcinous and Apuleius was followed by Theiler and Moreschini.[62] Sinko's thesis leant on the erroneous identification of Alcinous as Albinus, and on the assumption that Albinus' Platonist teacher Gaius also counted Apuleius among his students.[63] Very little is known about the shadowy figure of Gaius, whose legacy appears to be confined to the works of his student(s),[64] and Sinko's conclusions regarding the extent of exegetical parallels between

---

a discussion of specific Timaean elements in Philo's exegesis, see Runia 1986 and 2003.

[62] Theiler 1964, Moreschini 1966.

[63] Sinko based his theory on his comparison between Apuleius' *DPD* and the *Didaskalikos* in his *De Apulei et Albini doctrinae adumbratione* (1905). Beaujeu 1973: 56 thinks it likely that a student of Gaius', not the latter himself, was Apuleius' teacher. Along with the 'School of Gaius' theory, the similarities between Apuleius' *DPD* and Alcinous' *Didaskalikos* have been explained, moreover, by their possible common source Arius Didymus. Such a thesis, first proposed by Diels *Dox. Graec.* 76–7, is supported amongst other by Theiler 1964, Moreschini 1966, and Beaujeu 1973: 57. Dillon 1997: 269 accepts Arius Didymus as a source for Alcinous. Cf. Gersh 1986 vol. 1: 226 for further references on various scholarly positions in this matter. A third document associated with Gaius' influence is the anonymous commentary on Plato's *Theaetetus*. See Dillon 1997: 270–1 on the possible identity of this anonymous author and Alcinous, and *contra* Dillon, see Sedley and Bastianini 1995: 251–3. Cf. further Moreschini 2015: 15–18.

[64] Gaius is assumed to have been active in Alexandria or Asia Minor. There are no extant works by this author even though several lost volumes attributed to Alcinous and entitled *Notes of Gaius' lectures* seem to suggest that Gaius wrote his own works. Cf. Dillon 1997: 267 and on the 'School of Gaius' in general, 266–340. See also Gersh 1986 vol. 1: 222–3.

118

Alcinous' *Didaskalikos* and Apuleius' *DPD* has since been challenged. Against Sinko Dillon, to name but one sceptic, has brought into view the Platonists Calvenus Taurus and Sextus of Chaeroneia as potential tutors of Apuleius.[65] But regardless of the extent of the mutual influences between Apuleius and the other Platonic writers of the early centuries,[66] it is clear that the *Timaeus* is a constant and dominant exegetical frame of reference.

Plutarch, the central figure of second-century Platonism in Athens, continued the dogmatic, syncretizing course on which the school had set. For this interpreter, a priest of the cult of Apollo at Delphi, the cosmological doctrine of the *Timaeus* provided the backdrop to a strongly dualistic interpretation of Platonism that comprised the notions of a good and an evil world soul. Most notably, Plutarch and Atticus are known as proponents of a temporal reading of the Timaean creation.[67] Plutarch has been linked also with Apuleius, whether from a doctrinal philosophical perspective or based on their shared interest in the goddess Isis expressed in Plutarch's *De Iside et Osiride* and in Book 11 of Apuleius' *Metamorphoses*.[68]

In the compendium *Didaskalikos* by Alcinous, whose Platonism, as discussed above, has been linked, most likely incorrectly, with Apuleius via the figure of the Platonist Gaius, the influence of the *Timaeus* is most perspicuous in the discussion of the first principles, matter, ideas, and god, and in the theory of a first and second divine intellect. The second instance of this divine entity, according to Alcinous, is to be identified with the Timaean demiurge. The dialogue is the

<hr>

[65] Dillon 1996: 308–11. On possible parallels between Apuleius' and Taurus' works, see Gersh 1986 vol. 1: 222. Before Dillon, Baltes 1976: 100 with n. 88 had questioned the similarity in content of Alcinous' and Apuleius' writings. Further sceptical voices include Loenen 1956 and Portogalli 1963: 227–41.

[66] I will comment on possible doctrinal parallels between Apuleius and other Platonists in the final part of the present chapter, as appropriate.

[67] See p. 28 and cf. Procl. *In Plat. Tim.* 2.276.31–277.7; further, Philop. *Aet. mund.* 211.11ff., 519.22–5.

[68] Apuleius' protagonist Lucius claims to be a descendent of Plutarch at *Met.* 1.2. For a cautious interpretation of this connection, see Van der Stockt 2011; cf. Moreschini 2015: 143–4.

dominating influence also on Alcinous' exposition of Platonic physics in chapters 12–22; further, in his discussion of demons, of the sublunary world, and human psychology.[69] The second century, moreover, saw the composition of a collection of texts that proved seminal in the development of a more religious form of Platonism that, in turn, would find its climax in the work of the Neoplatonist thinkers of the fifth and sixth centuries. These verses, the *Chaldean Oracles*, reinterpreted Platonism with a tinge of mystery and magic,[70] their revelatory content taking its origin to a large extent in the cosmological theory provided by the *Timaeus*.

Thus far only some approaches to Plato's *Timaeus* that are contemporary[71] with Apuleius. As we explore the latter's own Platonic exegesis we will encounter in it parallels, both faint and firm, to the writings of these and other authors.

Apuleius' Timaean Methodology

I will postpone until the final part of this chapter the examination proper of specific doctrinal elements in Apuleius' exegesis that have their origin in the Timaean cosmology. We find such elements in the *DPD*, where the *Timaeus* is echoed in Apuleius' reference to the cosmological ἀρχαί, god, matter, and idea (cf. *Tim.* 48–51). The dialogue underlies Apuleius' distinction between the two ontological οὐσίαι at *DPD* 1.6 (cf. *Tim.* 37bc) and his theory of the basic make-up of our physical world (cf. *Tim.* 52–6). Timaean psychology (cf. *Tim.* 34–7) provides the background for Apuleius' discussion of the world soul (*DPD* 1.9), while the address to the subordinate gods by the demiurge and Timaeus' theory on the origin of the gods of popular religion

---

[69] Alcinous may have written a commentary on the *Timaeus*, cf. Tertullian, *De anima* 28–9.

[70] The oracles are ascribed to the two Julians, father and son, of whom the latter, Julian the 'theurgist', is assumed to have put them into verse. An examination of Timaean material in the Chaldean Oracles is Brisson 2003.

[71] In the case of the *Didaskalikos*, the second-century date is favoured by Dillon 1993: xii–xiii and Donini 1994: 5057–8. Sedley 1996: 300–1 with n. 2 is less confident and suggests that a first-century date is possible.

(*Tim.* 40–1), along with *Symp.* 202e–203a,[72] inspire Apuleius'
theory of demons (*DPD* 1.10–12; *DDS*) and the interrelations
between fate, divine providence, and free will (*DPD* 1.11–13).

Before I address some of these items in Apuleius' exegesis,
let us determine the character of his methodology as an interpreter of the Timaean creation account. To do so, we turn
to his interpretation of our familiar passage *Tim.* 29b2–d3,
where Plato's narrator reflects on his own methodology. At
Tim. 29b2–d3 and on other occasions throughout the dialogue, we recall, Timaeus discusses the character and scope
of his creation account, describing it as an εἰκὼς λόγος or
εἰκὼς μῦθος, a 'likely account'.[73] Timaeus' reflections on his
own methodology as narrator recommend themselves to the
investigation also of Apuleius' methodology by presenting
him with the opportunity to display his own approach to
the discourse. Given his second-century background, we are
likely to find a dogmatic interpretation of the cosmological
theory revealed by Plato, and may expect our author to expli-
cate the master's word in a manner that eliminates controversial, ambiguous, or doubtful elements. A further possible
feature we may expect from Apuleius is a devout, affirmative
tone in his exegesis that emphasizes the authority of Plato's
divine revelation.

We encounter our passage *Tim.* 29b2–d3 at Apul. *DPD* 1.6
where we find that it has been fused with *Tim.* 27d5–28a4.
Timaeus' analogy between the ontological status of a given
subject matter and the epistemological status of its description is thus directly linked with the initial delineation of his
account's dualistic metaphysical frame. We recall that Cicero's
interpretation of this passage revealed a sceptical view of
discussions pertaining to the physical realm, with trustworthiness or convincingness (*fides*) being the highest possible degree
of certainty to be obtained. Apuleius has no time for such
qualms. Let us compare his loose, simplified paraphrase of the
two Timaean passages with the original text:

---

[72] Cf. also *Rep.* 620d8–e1.
[73] Cf. pp. 18–21 for the range of possible interpretations of this expression.

Table 17. *Plato*, Tim. *27d5–28a4* + Tim. *29b2–d3*

1   **A§1:** ἔστιν οὖν δὴ κατ' ἐμὴν
δόξαν πρῶτον διαιρετέον τάδε·
τί τὸ ὂν ἀεί, γένεσιν δὲ οὐκ
ἔχον, καὶ τί τὸ γιγνόμενον
5   μὲν ἀεί, ὂν δὲ οὐδέποτε; τὸ
μὲν δὴ νοήσει μετὰ λόγου
περιληπτόν, ἀεὶ κατὰ ταὐτὰ
ὄν, τὸ δ' αὖ δόξῃ μετ'
αἰσθήσεως ἀλόγου δοξαστόν,
10   γιγνόμενον καὶ ἀπολλύμενον
ὄντως δὲ οὐδέποτε ὄν.

Plato, *Tim.* 29b2–d3

A§2: μέγιστον δὴ παντὸς
ἄρξασθαι κατὰ φύσιν ἀρχήν.
ὧδε οὖν περί τε εἰκόνος καὶ
15   περὶ τοῦ παραδείγματος αὐτῆς
διοριστέον, ὡς ἄρα λόγους,
ὧνπέρ εἰσιν ἐξηγηταί, τούτων
αὐτῶν καὶ συγγενεῖς ὄντας.
A§3: τοῦ μὲν οὖν μονίμου
20   καὶ βεβαίου καὶ μετὰ νοῦ
καταφανοῦς μονίμους καὶ
ἀμεταπτώτους – καθ' ὅσον
οἷόν τε καὶ ἀνελέγκτοις
προσήκει λόγοις εἶναι καὶ
25   ἀνικήτοις, τούτου δεῖ μηδὲν
ἐλλείπειν –
A§4: τοὺς δὲ τοῦ πρὸς μὲν
ἐκεῖνο ἀπεικασθέντος, ὄντος
δὲ εἰκόνος, εἰκότας ἀνὰ λόγον
30   τε ἐκείνων ὄντας· ὅτιπερ πρὸς
γένεσιν οὐσία, τοῦτο πρὸς
πίστιν ἀλήθεια.

A§5: ἐὰν οὖν, ὦ Σώκρατες,
πολλὰ πολλῶν πέρι θεῶν καὶ
35   τῆς τοῦ παντὸς γενέσεως, μὴ
δυνατοὶ γιγνώμεθα πάντη
πάντως αὐτοὺς ἑαυτοῖς
ὁμολογουμένους λόγους καὶ
ἀπηκριβωμένους ἀποδοῦναι,
40   μὴ θαυμάσῃς.

A§1: In my opinion, we first have to
make the following distinction: what
is that which always is and has no
coming to be, and what is that which
is always coming to be, but never is?
The former is grasped by intellect with
the help of reason and is always self-
same. The latter is opined by opinion
with the help of unreasoning sense
perception, comes to be and perishes,
and never truly is.

A§2: Now, in regard to every matter
it is most important to begin at the
natural beginning. Accordingly, in the
case of a likeness and its model, we
ought to determine that the accounts
given will be akin to the objects of
which they serve as exegetes;
A§3: therefore, accounts that deal
with what is abiding and firm and
discernible by the aid of thought will
be abiding and unshakeable; and to
the extent that it is possible and fitting
for statements to be irrefutable and
invincible, they must in no wise fall
short thereof;
A§4: whereas the accounts concerning
that which has been fashioned in
the likeness of that model, and
which is itself a likeness, ought to
be fashioned in a like manner and
possess likelihood; for as being stands
in relation to coming to be, so truth
stands in relation to belief.

A§5: Therefore, Socrates, if in our
extensive discussions regarding many
topics, the gods and the generation of
the universe, we are unable to provide
accounts that are entirely and in every
way self-consistent and perfectly exact,
do not be surprised;

Table 17 *(continued)*

A§6: ἀλλ' ἐὰν ἄρα μηδενὸς ἧττον παρεχώμεθα εἰκότας, ἀγαπᾶν χρή, μεμνημένους ὡς ὁ λέγων ἐγὼ ὑμεῖς τε οἱ κριταὶ 45 φύσιν ἀνθρωπίνην ἔχομεν, ὥστε περὶ τούτων τὸν εἰκότα μῦθον ἀποδεχομένους πρέπει τούτου μηδὲν πέρα ζητεῖν.	A§6: rather we should be content if we can produce accounts that are inferior to none in likelihood, remembering that both I who speak and you who judge are but human creatures, so that it becomes us to accept the likely story of these matters and forbear to search beyond it.[74]

Apuleius fuses the two passages in a much-simplified manner:

Table 18. *Apuleius, DPD 1.6, 192–4*

1 B§1: *οὐσίας, quas essentias dicimus, duas esse ait* B§2: *per quas cuncta gignantur mundusque ipse;* 5 *quarum una cogitatione sola concipitur, altera sensibus subici potest. sed illa quae mentis oculis comprehenditur semper et eodem modo et sui par ac similis* 10 *invenitur, ut quae vere sit; at enim altera opinione sensibili et irrationabili aestimanda est, quam nasci et interire ait.* B§3: *et sicut superior vere esse* 15 *memoratur, hanc non esse vere possumus dicere. Et primae quidem substantiae vel essentiae primum deum esse et mentem formasque rerum et animam;* 20 *secundae substantiae omnia quae*	B§1: [Plato] says there are two οὐσίαι – we use the term 'essences' – B§2: from which everything, even the world itself, comes to be. One of them is grasped by thought alone, the other can be subjected to the senses. Now, the one that is comprehended by the eyes of the intellect is always found to be in the same condition and self-same, like one that has true being. The other one, in turn, is to be appraised by opinion, itself irrational and bound up with sense perception. This [essence], he explains, is generated and perishes. B§3: And just as the former is said to have true being, we can affirm that the latter does not have true being. [He explains, further, that] the first god, intellect,[75] the [intelligible] forms [of things] and [human] soul [all belong to] the first substance or essence. To *(continued)*

---

[74] Transl. Lamb, with modifications.
[75] At *DPD* 1.9, 199 *anima* is used to describe both human and cosmic soul; the *anima caelestis*, however, is referred to also as *mens*: 'but that one, the source of all souls, the heavenly soul ... the essence of this soul is constructed out of numbers and

Table 18 (continued)

informantur quaeque gignuntur et quae ab substantiae superioris exemplo originem ducunt, quae mutari et converti possunt, 25 *labentia et ad instar fluminum profuga.*	the second substance belong all objects that are endowed with form, are generated and draw their origin from the pattern of the former substance. These objects are mutable and prone to change; they fluctuate and wander aimlessly, just like streams.
B§4: *adhuc illa, quam dixi, intellegendi substantia quoniam constanti nititur robore, etiam* 30 *quae de ea disputantur, ratione stabili et fide plena sunt; at eius, quae veluti umbra et imago est superioris, rationes quoque et verba, quae de ea disputantur,* 35 *inconstanti sunt disciplina.*	**B§4:** Now as for the substance of reasoning I have mentioned, seeing that it relies on invariable firmness, [accounts] that treat thereof are also of sound reasoning and entirely trustworthy. Accounts and statements concerning [the other substance] however, the one that is just like a shadow and a likeness of the former [substance], are the result of uncertain teaching.

Apuleius' decision to fuse the two passages has likely been prompted by the key expression οὐσία which appears in both contexts of the original. We shall find that his interpretation of this term sets the tone for the exegesis he offers of the two

harmonic proportions' (*sed illam, fontem animarum omnium, caelestem animam ... substantiam **mentis huius** numeris et modis confici*). Apuleius at *exp.* 32.17 uses *anima mundi* in his summary of the *Timaeus*. It has been suggested that Apuleius is distinguishing here between a first god and second-level divinity corresponding to the demiurge (cf. Dillon 1996: 313). Such a distinction is not maintained consistently in Apuleius' portrayal of the divinity elsewhere (it does, however, appear to feature at *DPD* 2.1, 220), which suggests to me that Apuleius did not have a full-fledged notion of the relationship between a first and a second god. Cf. Moreschini 2015: 225–9, who identifies Apuleius' first god with *mens* = intellect. As noted by Gersh 1986: 271, Apuleius' hierarchy, in placing god and intellect before the ideas, diverges from the standard doctrine of the three principles god, matter, and idea. See also Gersh 1986: 252–3; Petrucci 2018: 91–6. Finamore 2006: 35–8 suggests that the mention of *mens*, along with similarly ambiguous descriptions of the highest god in Apuleius' works, expresses Apuleius' view of a transcendent divinity who is 'immanent in the world through his intermediaries' (38), but *mens* does not reappear in the context of Apuleius' descriptions of god's role in the cosmos or of the intermediaries and their assigned tasks. Finamore concludes that Apuleius 'distinguished the Demiurge' s mind from god himself' in order to 'differentiate two features of god: the philosophical concept of god as pure intellect and the religious concept of god as savior' (40). Such a differentiation between a philosophical and a religious aspect of the divinity, in my view, feels somewhat unnatural in the context of Apuleius' religious Platonism.

passages combined. It is thus necessary first that we take a detour and examine his version of *Tim.* 27d5–28a4 before we can turn to his interpretation of the εἰκὼς λόγος at *Tim.* 29b2–d3. The ontological categories τὸ ὄν and τὸ γιγνόμενον in **A§1**, ll. 3–4, distinguished in Timaeus' cautiously phrased[76] lead-up to his creation account, are characterized by Apuleius in **B§1**, l. 1 and **B§3**, l. 17, as 'substances', *essentiae* and *substantiae*, that comprise the Timaean metaphysical frame. In other words, these two Latin renderings serve to describe both the ontological class assigned to the physical realm, τὸ γιγνόμενον, and the ontological class assigned to the intelligible realm, οὐσία/τὸ ὄν. The rendering *substantia* is sometimes used with material connotations by Apuleius. At *DPD* 1.17, 215, for instance, he describes corporeal objects that are made out of three *substantiae*, i.e. three combinations of various bodily materials.[77] At *De mundo* 24 *substantia* serves as a rendering for the Aristotelian ὕλη.[78] An identification of the Aristotelian ὕλη with the Platonic receptacle or χώρα, 'space', not with the Timaean concept of οὐσία, is common in Middle Platonic writers,[79]

---

[76] The Greek text in **A§1** (starting from line 3) is syntactically ambiguous. One possibility, the standard interpretation of the passage, is to read the section running from τὸ μὲν δὴ νοήσει to ὄντως δὲ οὐδέποτε ὄν as the direct reply to the demand for a definition of being and becoming immediately before, τί τὸ ὄν … τί τὸ γιγνόμενον. According to this interpretation of the passage, of the two objects 'that which always is' is described as 'grasped by intellect with the help of reason and is always self-same' while 'that which becomes' is described as 'is opined by opinion with the help of unreasoning sense perception, comes to be and perishes, and never truly is'. A further, possible interpretation is to read τὸ μὲν δὴ νοήσει … and τὸ δ' αὖ δόξῃ … not as replies to τί τὸ ὄν and τί τὸ γιγνόμενον, but as continuing the question: 'What is that which always is … and what is that which becomes …: The [former] is grasped by intellect … the other one by opinion …'.

[77] *At cum totius corporis tres dicat esse substantias, primam vult videri ex igni et aqua et ceteris elementis, aliam ex consimilibus partibus viscerum, ossiculorum, cruoris et ceterorum, tertiam de discrepantibus diversisque membris, id est capite, utero et articulis disparibus.*

[78] Apul. *Mund.* 24, 343: *hanc opinionem vates secuti profiteri ausi sunt, omnia Iove plena esse, cuius praesentiam non iam cogitatio sola, sed oculi et aures et sensibilis substantia conprehendit;* ibid. 24, 336: *sic totius mundi substantiam, initiorum inter se inparium conventu[s], pari nec discordante consensu, natura veluti musicam temperavit.* Cf. Moreschini 2015: 253.

[79] Ultimately going back to Aristotle, *Phys.* 4.220 9b11–12 and *Cael.* 3.8 306b17, the identification of ὕλη and χώρα is found also in Alcinous, *Didask.* 8; Plutarch, *Procr. an.* 1014b; Calcidius, *Comm. in Tim.* chapter 306. By the time of Calcidius,

but we do find the term *substantia* used to refer to the divine nature in Augustine and Boethius.[80] Apuleius appears to use the term *substantia* as a generic expression, much like its literal Greek equivalent, ὑπόστασις, to describe a type of 'existence', possessed by both the intelligible and the corporeal realm.

His further explanation, at **B§2**, that the intelligible substance *cogitatione sola concipitur* 'is grasped by thought alone', merges the roles of intellect and thought (distinct in the Greek), which in this context may have been motivated by a wish to reserve the notion of νοῦς, rendered *mens* by Apuleius, for the highest god (*DPD* 2.1, 220).

In **B§3** Apuleius explains that the primary *substantia*, corresponding to the realm of being (τὸ ὄν), is associated with the highest god, the cosmic soul, and the forms. The second *substantia*, associated with the realm of coming to be (τὸ γιγνόμενον), is associated with objects that are generated and trace their origin to the model of the primary substance. These mirror images are mutable, they fluctuate and wander aimlessly, just like streams (*labentia et ad instar fluminum profuga*, ll. 25–26).[81]

In **B§4** Apuleius takes on the methodology passage 'proper'. According to his interpretation, accounts treating of subject matter that is associated with the primary *substantia* – itself relying on invariable firmness (*constanti nititur robore*) – are of sound reasoning and entirely trustworthy (*ratione stabili et fide plena sunt*). In turn, accounts and words that describe what pertains to the secondary *substantia* – a mere shadow and likeness of the former – are the result of uncertain teaching (*inconstanti sunt disciplina*).

Fides in **B§4**, l. 31 is the straightforward equivalent to the Greek πίστις which, in its original context,[82] describes the degree of reliability exhibited by descriptions of the physical

---

it had carried over into the Latin term *silva*. Cf. van Winden 1959: 31; Beaujeu 1973: 255–8.

[80] Calcidius (see p. 171, n. 46), also uses the term *substantia* to refer to the divine nature.

[81] We find the same image in Seneca, *Epist.* 58.22 and in the *Didaskalikos*, 1.2, 2.2.

[82] In the context of *Tim.* 29 (**§A4**, Table 17), we recall, it is to be taken as denoting 'convincingness', as opposed to something that is *bestowed upon* the sensible realm by the onlooker: 'trust', 'faith'. Cf. p. 66 n. 92.

world, the trustworthiness, convincingness that is assigned to descriptions that are 'likely' (εἰκότες, **A§4**, l. 29, see Table 17). Apuleius' term *fides*, likewise, describes the epistemological status of accounts or arguments. Astonishingly, however, he associates *fides* with descriptions of the *intelligible* realm, descriptions Timaeus had originally characterized (regardless of our ability to access them) as epistemologically *certain* (see Table 17: **A§3**, 'abiding', 'firm', 'irrefutable', 'invincible') because they contain the truth. In Apuleius' version, accounts concerning the highest god, and cosmic and human soul, at first sight exhibit epistemological *convincingness* which, according to this interpretation, appears to be the highest degree of cognitive reliability that can be achieved.

We may take for granted, based on the general nature of his philosophical output, that Apuleius wished to eradicate any possible controversial or ambiguous elements from his dogmatic Platonism. I think it unlikely, moreover, that Apuleius remembered his *Timaeus* incorrectly or translated the passage wrongly. Granted, it is difficult to determine if Apuleius had direct access to Plato's dialogue, given his independence as a translator that allowed him to integrate his philosophical agenda into his translations or adaptations in the Greek, as illustrated by the frequent additions, cuts, and modifications he makes to his sources.[83] Nevertheless, given the example of our passage *DPD* 1.6, 192–4 above, as well as his rather self-assured report of Timaean anatomical theory as applied in his *Apologia*, we may be confident that Apuleius, a skilled translator at that, showed more than a superficial familiarity with the dialogue. It thus appears that the term *fides* as a rendering of πίστις had by Apuleius' time lost the epistemological connotations it carried in the original dialogue, where it describes a degree of epistemological reliability, as an inherent quality of accounts. In Apuleius' translation of the above passage, *fides*[84] does describe an account's inherent

---

[83] I will discuss further examples of Apuleius' translation practice as I turn to the *De mundo* in the subsequent sections. Apuleius also produced at least partial translations of Plato's *Phaedo* and *Republic*, cf. Moreschini 2015: 16.

[84] Cf. Fraenkel 1916: 198–90.

degree of reliability, but appears to assume the role of 'certainty' associated with the *veritas* in Plato's metaphysical doctrine. I think it possible that the term, for Apuleius, would have been a natural, perhaps instinctive, choice in line with his religious philosophical outlook.

In turn, the term *fides* in the sense of 'faith' or 'trust' that is bestowed upon a philosophical doctrine occurs elsewhere in Apuleius' writings. In a rather transparent validation of his own standing as an Isiac priest as well as a Platonic interpreter Apuleius argues at *DDS* 14, 148 that the exotic identities given outside the Roman world to the various types of demons should not diminish one's belief in them. As the structure of the universe, and with it the same hierarchy of divine beings he has elicited from Plato's writings, is the same for all inhabitants of this world, foreign belief systems should be granted *fides*:

We should have faith (*fides*) *also* in the various rituals of [foreign] religions, and in their manifold sacrificial rites ...[85]

Apuleius' demonology, just as other elements of Platonic doctrine (*sententia, DDS* 16, 155, cf. ibid. 6, 132) he sets out in his writings, possesses 'trustworthiness' and thus is deserving of 'trust' or 'faith' even in foreign religious rituals. A further example occurs at *Apol.* 51, a passage we recall from our previous discussion, where *fides* is bestowed upon Platonic doctrine in the same manner as it is bestowed upon religious practices in the above passage from his *DDS*. Apuleius at *Apol.* 51 confirms his faith in the Timaean theory on the causes of bodily diseases:

[85] ... *etiam religionum diversis observationibus et sacrorum variis suppliciis fides impertienda est* ... With regard to the content of this statement, note the similiar sentiment expressed by his protagonist Lucius in the *Metamorphoses* who, at the close of his narrative, implores the goddess Isis: 'Queen of Heaven, whether [you reveal yourself] as bountiful Ceres ... or as heavenly Venus ... or as Diana, sister of Apollo ... or as terrifying Proserpine herself ... by whatever name, with whatever ceremony and under whatever aspect [of your godhead] we should invoke you: make an end to my desperate toils ...' (Apul. *Met.* 11.2).

I have faith in [Plato's teaching] that the cause of the divine disease is the overflow of pestilent fluid into the head.[86]

Returning to **B§4**, l. 31 (see Table 18) of Apuleius' paraphrase above, the term *fides*, moreover, implicitly credits with trustworthiness his own theological discussions presented in the *DPD*, the *DDS*, and the *De mundo*, all of which are concerned in part with subject matter associated with the first *substantia*. According to *DPD* 1.6, 194, these discussions 'rely on invariable firmness', exhibit 'sound reasoning', and are 'entirely trustworthy' (*fide plena*) – an important statement to make for Apuleius, the messenger of Plato's divine wisdom.

Let us turn to the close of Apuleius' version of the methodology passage. According to his explanation, accounts that pertain to the physical world are not reliable but, instead, are the result of uncertain teaching, *inconstanti disciplina* (see Table 18: **B§4**, l. 35). Apuleius' choice of expression is perhaps symptomatic of how entrenched the dogmatic philosophical stance had become in his contemporary intellectual milieu. Even in the case of objects that, according to Timaeus' account, are cognitively unreliable due to their kinship with the physical world, their representation in word or letter still presents a 'teaching', a *disciplina*.[87] The careful, investigative tone set by Plato's narrator Timaeus in the passages examined above, where it is λόγοι (see Table 17: **A§3** and **A§4** 'accounts' rather than 'teachings') that are described as εἰκότες, has vanished in Apuleius' interpretation.

---

[86] *Cui ego fidem arbitratus causam divini morbi esse, cum illa pestis in caput redundavit ...*

[87] The term *disciplina* is used almost invariably by Apuleius to describe material, whether written or spoken, that has been transmitted via instructive teaching. See, for instance, Apul. *DPD* 1.3, 186: 'After Socrates had left the mortal sphere, [Plato] was seeking [a subject] from which he might profit, and devoted himself to Pythagorean teaching ' (*sed posteaquam Socrates homines reliquit,* [Plato] *quaesivit unde proficeret et ad Pythagorae disciplinam se contulit*); at *Flor.* 7, philosophy is 'the august teaching of good speech and the good life' (*disciplinam regalem tam ad bene dicendum quam ad bene vivendum*).

The Creation of the Cosmos

In the final sections of this chapter I will examine Apuleius' responses to some of the central interpretative concerns that emerge in Plato's *Timaeus*, beginning with the createdness of the cosmos.

Apuleius states his position concerning the createdness of the universe at *DPD* 1.8, 196–8:

Table 19. *Apuleius, DPD 1.8, 196–8*

I	*mundumque omnem ex omni aqua totoque igni et aeris universitate cunctaque terra esse factum ... et hunc quidem mundum nunc sine*	[Plato says that] the world as a whole has been made up from the entirety of water, fire, air and earth ... And on one occasion he
5	*initio esse dicit, alias originem habere natumque esse: nullum autem eius exordium atque initium esse ideo quod semper fuerit; nativum vero videri, quod ex his*	states that this world is without beginning, but elsewhere that it has an origin and is created. [But he states that] there is no origin and beginning because
10	*rebus substantia eius et natura constet, quae nascendi sortitae sunt qualitatem. hinc et tangitur et videtur sensibusque corporeis est obvius. sed quo ei nascendi causam*	it has always been, [but that the world merely] appears to have been created because its substance and nature is made up from elements that have
15	*deus praestitit, ideo inmortali perseverantia est semper futurus.*	been assigned the attribute of undergoing generation. For this reason, [the world] is tangible, visible and accessible to the sense organs of our body. Nevertheless, since god[88] furnishes the cause of its creation, for that reason it is destined to be forever, with immortal perpetuity.

This piece of Apuleian exegesis is remarkable in that it draws together different contexts of Plato's *Timaeus*, opposing viewpoints concerning the dialogue's interpretation,[89] and two unrelated

---

[88] Cf. *Tim.* 41b, taken up by Seneca, *Ep.* 58.28; Plut. *De E. ap. Delph.* 393–4.
[89] Cf. the criticism levelled at Apuleius by Moreschini 1964: 32, and the broader discussion at Moreschini 2015: 265–79.

arguments in support of Apuleius' preferred doctrinal position. The initial description of the world's elementary make-up (ll. 1–3) provides the foundation of his stance on the createdness of the world, as will become clear shortly. The reference to the various elements captures Timaeus' discussion at *Tim.* 32c, and thereby anchors Apuleius' exegetical stance in the original text from the outset. The author next (ll. 3–6) makes reference to the interpretative controversy regarding the world's createdness by noting that Plato himself appeared to have issued contradictory statements on this matter.[90] While the *Timaeus* is clearly the point of reference for "Plato's" statement (*dicit*, l. 5) that the world was created, Apuleius, aside from other source material, may have had in mind passages such as *Phaedr.* 245c6–e2 when ascribing to Plato also the view that the world was uncreated.[91]

What follows is a disambiguation of Plato's stance. The world is uncreated, has always been (*semper fuerit*) and, therefore, can have no origin or beginning. Apuleius makes use of a familiar argument against a temporal creation of the world, which we have encountered previously in Taurus. The world may *seem* to have been created since it is of the same *genus* as its elements which, in turn, themselves are subject to generation and destruction.[92] The world itself, however, has no beginning. It would appear that Apuleius has fulfilled the requirements for a Platonic interpreter: he has presented an apparent exegetical dilemma that is to be solved with the

---

[90] We find a similar commentary in Alcinous, *Didask.* 14.3.

[91] 'Every soul is immortal, for that which is always in motion is immortal. But that which sets something else in motion, and that which is set in motion by something else, when it ceases to move, it ceases to live. Only that which is self-moving, since it does not leave itself, never ceases its motion, but it is the source and beginning of motion also for everything else that is in motion. A beginning is uncreated. For it is necessary that everything that comes to be does so from a beginning, but this beginning is not generated from anything. For if the beginning itself were created from something else, it would no longer be the beginning' (ψυχὴ πᾶσα ἀθάνατος.
τὸ γὰρ ἀεικίνητον ἀθάνατον· τὸ δ' ἄλλο κινοῦν καὶ ὑπ' ἄλλου κινούμενον, παῦλαν ἔχον κινήσεως, παῦλαν ἔχει ζωῆς. μόνον δὴ τὸ αὐτὸ κινοῦν, ἅτε οὐκ ἀπολεῖπον ἑαυτό, οὔποτε λήγει κινούμενον, ἀλλὰ καὶ τοῖς ἄλλοις ὅσα κινεῖται τοῦτο πηγὴ καὶ ἀρχὴ κινήσεως. ἀρχὴ δὲ ἀγένητον. ἐξ ἀρχῆς γὰρ ἀνάγκη πᾶν τὸ γιγνόμενον γίγνεσθαι, αὐτὴν δὲ μηδ' ἐξ ἑνός· εἰ γὰρ ἔκ του ἀρχὴ γίγνοιτο, οὐκ ἂν ἔτι ἀρχὴ γίγνοιτο).

[92] This is Taurus' first interpretation of the term γενητός. Cf. pp. 27–8. Cf. Dillon 1996: 242–4, Moreschini 2015: 278–9.

help of his own exegetical expertise. He next chooses a particular viewpoint (no temporal creation has occurred) and
explains that the createdness at play in the *Timaeus* is not
that of the world itself, but that of its elemental components.
It is with this notion of createdness in mind that Apuleius'
statements elsewhere are to be understood.[93] In the remainder
of our passage, however, we find that Apuleius adds a further
layer to his interpretation: since god furnishes the cause of
the coming to be (*nascendi*, that is: of the coming to be of
its elemental materials), the world is granted perpetual existence. He thus advances two arguments, one arguing for a non-
temporal type of createdness (the world is of the same *genus* as
its components); the other arguing for the world's everlasting
existence (the world was created by the god).[94] While one might
consider the world's everlastingness as being entailed already
by the fact that it was not itself created, i.e. in a temporal sense,
but merely of the same *genus* as its components, which are
subject to coming to be, Apuleius appears anxious not to leave
any room for doubt on the matter and explains, in addition,
that its everlastingness is owing to its ontological dependence
upon the god. The thesis of an uncreated, everlasting universe is reiterated also in his translation of the *De mundo*. The
overall Aristotelian dogmatic framework of this treatise poses
no hindrance to his Platonic exegesis. Instead, with the help
of several modifications in his translation, Apuleius injects
Platonizing elements into this framework that allow him to
align its contents with Plato, thereby recruiting Aristotle as
a follower and representative of Platonic cosmology and theology. Thus, at *De mundo* 1, 290 Apuleius explains that an
artifex is responsible for the world's rotation around its own
axis, whereas the Greek original ascribes this movement to
the earth's being balanced between the two opposing poles
that hold it in place. No reference to divine agency is made

---

[93] For instance, the description of the central divinity as *genitor* and *deus artifex* who
shapes (*conformat*) matter at *DPD* 1.5, 191 Cf. *aedificator mundi* (*DPD* 1.7, 194),
fabricator deo (ibid. 1.8, 198; 1.9, 199; 1.10, 201).

[94] Cf. Aristotle's criticism at *Cael*. 1.10, 279b12–13; 280a28–30. A similar argument
for the world's everlasting existence is found in Seneca *Ep*. 58.28.

(*Kosm.* 391b19–25). *De mundo* 24, 342, in turn, explains that god, according to an old doctrine (*vetus opinio*), is held to be the *auctor originis*, 'founder' of the origin of things, where the Greek source states that 'all things are from the divine and have been framed by the divine' (ἐκ θεοῦ πάντα καὶ διὰ θεὸν συνέστηκεν, *Kosm.* 397b14–15). With, admittedly, subtle effect, the Latin disambiguates the Greek phrasing, which leaves undetermined whether θεοῦ is masculine or neuter and omits a direct reference to an 'origin'.

Nevertheless, soon after, the Greek author himself adopts a syncretistic phrasing by referring to the god who is the 'father of all things that have been brought about in whatever manner throughout the cosmos' (γενέτωρ τῶν ὁπωσδήποτε κατὰ τόνδε τὸν κόσμον συντελουμένων ὁ θεός). Apuleius retains the notion of a father, but turns him into the 'father of all those who are born and created for the sake of completing the cosmos' (*genitor omnium qui ad conplendum mundum nati factique sunt*), in a deliberate modification of the text that allows for a reference to the divine hierarchy of subordinate divinities Apuleius himself establishes in the universe at *DPD* 1.11–12 and throughout the *DDS*.[95] The assumption of a creative divine father is immediately brought in line with that of an uncreated universe at *De mundo* 24, 343: '[This is not to suggest] that he has furnished this world with his own hands, through physical labour' (*non tamen ut corporei laboris officio orbem istum manibus suis instruxerit*). 'Instead, with the help of some untiring providence, he touches even what is located far away, and encompasses even what is separated by a great distance' (*sed qui quadam infatigabili providentia* [*providentia* renders the Greek δύναμις, cf., pp. 157–8] *et procul posita cuncta contingit et maximis intervallis disiuncta conplectitur*). The contrast between a one-off creation and the continuous providential activity bestowed upon the world by the god is emphasized by Apuleius' choice of the perfect tense for the

---

[95] The passive participle συντελουμένων, 'the things that have been brought about', is transferred by Apuleius into the gerund *conplendum* '(the) bringing about (of)', while additional divine players come into play by the addition of *qui nati factique sunt*, 'those that have been born and created (for the sake of bringing about the cosmos)'. Cf. Regen 1971: 46–51; Finamore 2006: 34.

scenario of a creation at a certain moment in time (*instruxerit*), which is duly rejected, and of the present tense (*contingit*) to describe the uninterrupted nature of divine power.

Without clarifying what precise notion of toil-free creation is at play, the text focuses, instead, on the god's toil-free care and continued maintenance of the cosmos. Nevertheless, Apuleius manages to insert what may well be a Platonizing nuance with his reference to the divine *providentia* at *Mund.* 24, 343 that ensures the cosmos' preservation, an aspect of divine power that presents one of Apuleius' most prominent exegetical lines in his *DPD* and the *DDS*, as discussed in the subsequent section. The notion of continuing 'perseverance' (*perseverantia*) of the world's structure is, in turn, emphasized also in Apuleius' exegesis at the conclusion of *DPD* 1.8, 198, quoted above (Table 19, l. 16).

Apuleius' cosmology in both the *DPD* and the *De mundo* at times reflects the different contexts, placing emphasis either on standard 'Platonic' (an elaborate definition of the 'createdness' at play in Plato's cosmology) or 'Aristotelian' (emphasis of the world's continued existence; de-emphasizing of the notion of 'createdness') lines of argument. This strategy becomes apparent when comparing *DPD* 1.8, 198, our passage cited above, with *De mundo* 21. While Apuleius in the former passage, as we saw, integrates the topic of the world's elemental make-up in a discussion of the type of createdness at work in the Platonic cosmos, *De mundo* 21, 336 makes reference to this topic in order to stress the world's *perpetual existence*: 'The agreement between the elements has resulted in a harmonious union (*concordiam*) between them, but it is the equal distribution of their qualities that has rendered possible the continuity of their mutual bond (*perseverantiam amicitiae*) ... harmonious union has resulted in the beauty and everlastingness (*aeternitatem*) of the world that generates all things.'[96] In this context, it is the harmonious concord between the elements, specifically, that ensures the

---

[96] *principiorum igitur consensus sibi concordiam peperit, perseverantiam vero amicitiae inter se elementis dedit specierum ipsarum aequa partitio ... <concordiam> omni[a]parentis mundi amoenitatem aeternitatemque repperisse.*

world's everlasting existence. Nevertheless, despite such subtle differences in emphasis, we note that Apuleius' doctrinal stance in both works, overall, appears consistent in advancing the thesis of an uncreated universe that owes its everlasting, persevering existence to the care of the central divinity.

A Note on Time

This may be a good moment to clear up a perceived oddity in Apuleius' Timaean exegesis. A concern that is immediately tied up with the createdness of the world is the createdness also of time. Given Apuleius' assumption of an uncreated world, we may expect a corresponding exegetical stance on this related issue. Apuleius at *DPD* 1.10, 201 reports Timaeus' well-known description of time as an image of eternity[97] without, however, mentioning Timaeus' all-important sentence that time came to be along with the heavens at *Tim.* 38b6–c3. His emphasis, instead, is on the relation between time and eternity.

[Plato says that] time is an image of eternity (*aevi*) since time is moveable; the nature of eternity (*perennitatis*), however, is fixed and immovable. Time can progress towards eternity, it can come to an end within [eternity's] extent and cease,[98] should the divine craftsman of our world so decree.

---

[97] Cf. also Cal. *Comm. in Tim.* chapter 105; Plut. *Plat. quaest.* 1007c, d.

[98] *tempus vero aevi esse imaginem, si quidem tempus movetur, perennitatis fixa et inmota natura est; et ire in eam tempus, et in eius magnitudinem finiri ac dissolvi posse, si quando hoc decreverit fabricator mundi deus.* Beaujeu interprets this sentence to say that time can, *potentially*, progress perpetually and emphasizes its dependence upon the demiurge rather than reading it as a straightforward affirmation of time's perpetual course. Hijmans, correctly in my mind, reaffirms the latter portrayal of time by pointing to *De mundo* 1, 22; *DDS* 2; *DPD* 1.10–12. I would add *De mundo* 37, 370, where the god Kronos, the divine personification of time, is described as 'beginningless from the outset, without limit until the end', *incoeptu[m] ab origine, interminu[s] ad finem* (translating διήκων ἐξ αἰῶνος ἀτερμονος εἰς ἕτερον αἰῶνα, 'reaching from one limitless age to another'). At *DPD* 1.12, 206 the highest divinity is reported to have elevated to the everlastingness of time (*ad aevitatem temporis*) those mortals who, even though destined to die, surpass other living creatures in their wisdom. Cf. *DPD* 2.20, 248, where the sage man is 'everlasting in some sort of manner' (*quodammodo intemporal[is]*).

On the lexical plane, we note that Apuleius uses the terms *aevum* and *perennitas* as apparently interchangeable synonyms to denote 'eternity'.[99] From an exegetical point of view the passage is a selective summary of *Tim.* 37d[100] and as such is standard Platonist fare.[101]

A difficulty has been perceived in the remainder of the passage in which the author sets out the role played by the heavenly bodies in the measuring of time. While Timaeus had explained the temporal divisions as resulting from and fixed by the periodic movements of the heavenly bodies, Apuleius' exegesis may appear to turn this perspective on its head. It is our perception of the various temporal extensions that, in turn, allows us to measure the duration of the cosmic revolutions. The passage in question is *DPD* 1.10, 201, which we find in Table 20, p. 137.

The first statement of this passage, 'The time frame of our world's revolution is understood also with the help of the extensions of time', does not of necessity indicate the priority of temporal extensions over cosmic movement. The fact that these temporal extensions help us perceive the intervals of our world's movement does not imply that they existed prior to this movement, or that they prompted it. Apuleius may simply be describing the close relation between time and cosmic movement, as originally claimed by Timaeus. Nevertheless, it has been noted by Hijmans that in the subsequent statement, *solis quippe et lunae globum hoc agere*, either temporal extension or cosmic movement is credited with priority depending

---

[99] Recall, however, that Plato's own terminology in this passage draws no clear distinction between the ongoing, perpetual nature of time and the eternity, describing both as αἰώνιος.

[100] *Tim.* 37d: 'The nature of the living being [i.e. of the intelligible paradigm] happened to be eternal, but it was not possible to bestow this quality upon the generated living being [i.e. the cosmos] unqualifiedly. [The demiurge] thus intended to create it as a kind of moving image of eternity and, thus establishing order in the heavens, he created it as an everlasting image that proceeded according to number, all the while eternity remained as one. This image we call time' (ἡ μὲν οὖν τοῦ ζῴου φύσις ἐτύγχανεν οὖσα αἰώνιος, καὶ τοῦτο μὲν δὴ τῷ γεννητῷ παντελῶς προσάπτειν οὐκ ἦν δυνατόν· εἰκὼ δ' ἐπενόει κινητόν τινα αἰῶνος ποιῆσαι, καὶ διακοσμῶν ἅμα οὐρανὸν ποιεῖ μένοντος αἰῶνος ἐν ἑνὶ κατ' ἀριθμὸν ἰοῦσαν αἰώνιον εἰκόνα, τοῦτον ὃν δὴ χρόνον ὠνομάκαμεν).

[101] Apuleius may also have in mind *Tim.* 38b6 where time and eternity might be 'dissolved together if their dissolution should ever come about', cf. *Tim.* 41a–b. Cf. also *Didask.* 15.2; Moreschini 2015: 286–8.

Table 20. *Apuleius,* DPD *1.10, 201*

1 [*dicit*] *eiusdem temporis spatiis mensuras mundanae conversionis intellegi. solis quippe et lunae globum hoc* 5 *agere, ceterasque stellas, quas nos non recte erroneas et vagas dicimus ... ceterum ille rerum ordinator moras progressusque constituit, ut ne modico quidem* 10 *errori locus esset.*	[He says that] the time frame of our world's revolution is understood also with the help of the extensions of this same time. In fact, [Plato says that] the spherical motions[102] of the sun and the moon prompt this [i.e. our understanding of the temporal extensions], and also the other cosmic bodies we incorrectly describe as wandering planets[103] ... Moreover, the divine architect has determined the intervals of their stationary and mobile phases so that there be no room even for the slightest error.

on whether *globum*[104] or *hoc* is the subject. If the former serves as the subject, time is described to be the result of cosmic movement after all; if *hoc*, the relationship is inverted.[105] Yet this latter interpretation would require an unlikely use of Latin on the part of our author. With *hoc* as the subject, the translation 'This [i.e. our understanding of the extensions of time] *initiates* the revolutions of sun and moon' would require Apuleius' *agere* to take on a meaning that differs from the other occurrences of this term in similar contexts. Within the cosmological contexts of the *DPD* and the *De mundo* Apuleius uses *agere* to describe one particular *physical body* that 'sets in motion' or 'drives on' something else.[106] Thus considering *globum* to be the subject,

---

[102] Reading 'spherical motion' for *globus*. Cf. *DPD* 1.11, 203: '[he says that] of all the spherical motions in the heavens ... the best one is that which is believed to travel along an unerring course' (*globorum vero caelestium ... omnium supremum esse eum qui inerrabili meatu censetur*); *De mundo* 2, 292: 'the wandering stars, which are given varying spherical motions, adhere to an, as it were, disorderly order' (*errant[es stellae] ... adfixae diversis globis inordinatum, ut sic dixerim, ordinem servant*).

[103] Cf. Plato, *Leg.* 7.822aff.; Cic. *Nat. deor.* 2.20, 51.

[104] In the case of both *globum* and *hoc*, the accusative is due either to the statement's indirect speech, or due to its role as the direct object.

[105] Hijmans 1987: 449.

[106] Cf. *De mundo* 1, 290, where heaven in its entirety sets the starry constellations into movement: *caelum ... agens choros stellarum*; at *DPD* 1.9, 199, in turn, the cosmic soul is the *agitatrix* of other bodies.

I take Apuleius' passage to reflect the relation between temporal extensions and cosmic revolutions as set out originally by Timaeus. The fact that, according to Apuleius' subsequent portrayal, the time frames of the individual cosmic revolutions have been determined by the demiurge (*ille rerum ordinator moras progressusque constituit ...*), again, does not imply of necessity that these temporal extensions existed *before* the cosmic movements began. Moreover, the priority of cosmic revolution over temporal extensions is reaffirmed in clear terms in the remainder of this chapter of Apuleius' *DPD*:

> It was only once these heavenly constellations had begun to blaze in their shining splendour that the measuring of time could commence. [The ability] to observe this measurement will end if, one day, this heavenly concert of old were to come to a halt ... The months come to an end whenever the moon, having traversed its circular course, returns to its former position. The span of a year is complete whenever the sun has lit upon the four seasons and taken its place in its original constellation.[107]

The individual temporal extensions are clearly identified by Apuleius as the immediate result of the movements undergone by the cosmic bodies.[108] A similar stance appears at *De mundo* 22, 338: 'As the sun, the moon and the other resplendent stars travel along their regular course, the duration of their intervals thus safeguarded and free from random disruptions, the temporal extensions are determined and, in turn, set out on [their journey] ... the months are made up by the course of days and nights, the months fill the years and the years build up to a succession of centuries.'[109]

---

[107] *DPD* 1.10, 201–2: *nec prius quam signa haec luce siderea ardere coeperunt, iniri potuerunt temporum numeri, perituramque esse observationem conputationis huius, si hic olim chorus antiquus steterit ... mensesque effici, cum luna, circuli sui conpleto curriculo, ad eundem locum, a quo discesserit, revertatur; anni vero spatia concludi, cum sol quadrinas temporum contigerit vices et ad idem signum fuerit invectus.* The entire passage is inspired by *Tim.* 39b, 47a. Cf. Moreschini 1966: 53, and 2015: 287, who points to parallels in Stoic doctrine, expressed by Balbus at Cic. *Nat. deor.* 2.19–21.

[108] See also *DDS* 1, 116–17 where the moon is described as the *diei opifex ... mensem ... aestimans.*

[109] *euntibus sole atque luna ceteraque luce siderea per easdem vias, custoditis temporum vicibus nec ullius erroris interiectione confusis, diguntur tempora et rursus incipiunt ... dierum etiam noctiumque curriculis ordiuntur menses, menses texunt annos, anni*

Theology: Introducing the Summus Deus

In the above passage *DPD* 1.8, 196–8 (Table 19) Apuleius does not associate the Timaean demiurge with a literally creative role, but portrays him as an external cause for the existence of the cosmos.[110] My aim in the present section is to explore further the nature of this divinity such as it is presented in the various contexts of his Platonic and Platonizing exegesis. I shall focus, moreover, on the manner in which Apuleius presents the relationship between this transcendent god and the material cosmos. In this latter context, the two most prominent features of Apuleius' Platonism, his doctrines on demons and on divine providence,[111] will be of central importance.

Let us begin with the *DPD*. Throughout this work Apuleius ensures that the supreme divinity, even if mentioned only cursorily, remains a recurring point of reference in his expositions of Platonic metaphysics, physics, and ethics.[112] Aside from the god's appearance in our above passage *DPD* 1.6, 192–4 (Table 18), where he is associated with the *prima substantia* or the intelligible realm, Apuleius had previously, at *DPD* 1.5, 190, pointed to his role as one of three metaphysical principles, alongside matter and ideas.[113] The god is, subsequently, described with an impressive array of characteristics:

---

seriem conficiunt saeculorum. The phrase *digeruntur tempora et rursus incipiunt* suggests to Hijmans 1987: 450 that 'time both precedes and is the result of the movements of the cosmic system'. I assume this is due to *rursus incipiunt* read as 'they set out again', which is at odds with the immediately preceding notion of the temporal extensions being determined by the heavenly movements, without having existed before. This problem is resolved if *rursus incipiunt* is taken not to indicate that the temporal extensions 'begin their journey *yet again*', but that 'the temporal extensions, *in turn* [i.e. following the cosmic movements that determine their dimension] set out on their journey'.

[110] There the god is described as the world's *causa nascendi* (l. 14).

[111] E.g. Beaujeu 1983, Krafft 1979, Mortley 1972, Portogalli 1963.

[112] At the outset of *DPD* 2.1, 219, Apuleius turns to the subject of ethics, professing his wish to teach his addressee Faustinus the precepts of how to live a happy life (*ut scias quibus ad beatam vitam perveniri rationibus possit*). In the ensuing classification of goods, the highest god and divine intellect, νοῦς, are identified as the highest goods within the cosmos. The identification of god with the highest good is likely inspired by Socrates' intelligible Form of the Good, introduced at *Rep.* 7.517b, and see *Leg.* 1.631c; Diog. Laert. 3.90.

[113] The doctrine of three metaphysical principles, a standard exegetical item in Middle Platonic writers, is ultimately drawn from *Tim.* 48–51. Cf. Plutarch,

[Plato] believes this concerning the god, that he is incorporeal. He says that [god] is one, without limit, the creator and enforcer of all things, blessed and beneficent, the best, in need of nothing, himself bestowing everything. [Plato] declares that he is preeminent, ineffable and cannot be named, and he says himself that [the god] is invisible and unsubdued.[114]

An analysis by Hijmans has shown the careful design of Apuleius' description, in which seven 'positive' characteristics (*unus, genitor rerumque omnium extstructor, beatus, beatificus, optimus, ipse conferens cuncta, caelestis*) are balanced by seven 'negative' ones (*incorporeus, nihil indigens,* ἀπερίμετρος, ἀόρατος, ἀδάμαστος, *indictus, innominabilis*).[115] What is more, Hijmans's comparison of the god's characterization in the *DPD* with that in Apuleius' *Apology, DDS*, and *De mundo* indicates that, despite a certain overlap, no one passage corresponds directly to another, which underlines the assumption that Apuleius carefully tailored his portrayal of the highest god to the individual works.

Before turning to the specific context of these works, we note that Apuleius' use of Greek terms in the list of descriptors at *DPD* 1.5, from the perspective of the Latin reader, might reinforce the impression of authenticity of Apuleius' theological exegesis. This impression is reinforced in the ensuing statement by a familiar warning that ties the divinity of *DPD* 1.5, 190 to the figure of Timaean demiurge discussed at *Tim.* 28c: '[the god's] nature is difficult to find and, once it is found, it cannot be disclosed to the many. These are Plato's words: "θεὸν εὑρεῖν τε ἔργον εὑρόντα τε εἰς πολλοὺς ἐκφέρειν ἀδύνατον".'[116]

Quaest. convivales 720a–b, Alc. *Didask.* 8–10, Cal. *Comm. in Tim.*, chapter 307, John Philoponus *Aet. mund.* 165,4; cf. Aet. *Plac.* 1.3.21. See also Beaujeu's extensive commentary ad loc. Sharples 1995 discusses diverging counts of Platonic principles in ancient sources.
[114] *haec de deo sentit, quod sit incorporeus. is unus, ait,* ἀπερίμετρος, *genitor rerumque omnium extortor, beatus et beatificus, optimus, nihil indigens, ipse conferens cuncta. quem quidem caelestem pronuntiat, indictum, innominabilem et, ut ait ipse,* ἀόρατον, ἀδάμαστον ...
[115] See Hijmans 1987: 436–9; further Moreschini 1978: 70ff., and van den Broek 1982.
[116] *[dei] naturam invenire difficile est, si non inventa sit, in multos eam enuntiari non posse. Platonis haec verba sunt* ... To compare, Timaeus' original statement at 28c is τὸν μὲν οὖν ποιητὴν καὶ πατέρα τοῦδε τοῦ παντὸς εὑρεῖν τε ἔργον καὶ εὑρόντα εἰς πάντας ἀδύνατον λέγειν. Cf. Moreschini 2015: 221.

It has been noted that Apuleius' Greek *vorlage* reads πολλούς, 'many', instead of Timaeus' πάντας, 'all', but the effect of this modification appears minimal.[117] What is more, 'maker and father of this All' (ποιητὴν καὶ πατέρα τοῦδε τοῦ παντὸς) has been replaced simply by θεός, for which Apuleius renders 'the nature of god', [*deī*] *natura*. It is possible that Apuleius who, at *DPD* 1.5, has not yet clarified his view on the type of creation he associates with the god, at this point wished to downplay the idea of an actual 'father' of the cosmos.[118] In turn, the insertion of *natura*, the 'nature' of the god, may serve to clarify that, according to Apuleius' interpretation, the difficulty is not so much to discover the impact of a divinity in the world. The presence and impact of a god upon the cosmos, presumably, would not have been in doubt in Apuleius' religious environment.[119] What could *not* be known, except perhaps to a select few who, like Apuleius, were initiated into philosophical wisdom, was the precise 'nature' of this divinity. And it is, in fact, the nature of the highest god that Apuleius has just been explaining to his readers with the help of the above list of qualifications.

A rather more cautious echo of the same passage, *Tim.* 28c,[120] introduces the *summus deus* at *DDS* 3, 124–5. At the outset of

---

[117] Mortley 1972: 584–90, and more recently Moreschini 2015: 42, believe that the reference to the πολλοί is rather more derogative than the Greek wording since it may be taken to refer to those uninititated in Platonic wisdom. Stover 2016: 80 cleverly suggests that Apuleius' incorrect quotation from the Greek, which is exclusive to the *DPD*, is in fact a back translation of the preceding Latin at *DPD* 1.5, *cuius naturam invenire difficile est, si inventa sit, in multos eam enuntiari non posse*. Unfortunately, the corresponding treatment of *Tim.* 28c in the *exp.* (§32.8) is corrupt: *ipse deum difficile <...> posse narrari*.

[118] Shortly after in the same chapter the god is described as the *genitor rerum*, 'creator of things', perhaps a more subtle notion than that of a *pater*. The latter term is used at *DPD* 1.11, 204, after Apuleius has clarified the type of createdness associated with the god, on which his interpretation of the dialogue leans.

[119] Indicated also by the abundance of names and titles given to the creator god. The 'many-namedness' of the highest god is discussed at *Mund.* 24 and 37, and compare also p. 128 n. 85; Moreschini 2015: 232.

[120] Alongside *Tim.* 28c, a further passage that contributed to the idea of god's ineffability, and that is likely on Apuleius' mind in the present passage, is *Ep.* 7.341c. The author appears to be referring to the divine, intelligible realm: 'This [subject] can in no way be put into words, like others, but from intensive engagement and association with the subject itself, suddenly, just as light is kindled by a spark of fire, it

Apuleius

his lecture on Platonic demonology, Apuleius restricts his subject matter to those divine beings who are subordinate to the highest god:

> As concerns their father, the lord and founder of all things, who is bound by no obligation, active or passive, and who is unhampered by reciprocal duty, why should I even begin to talk about him, when Plato, who was gifted with divine eloquence and whose discourse could match the immortal gods, often announced that this divinity alone, in his unimaginable and ineffable profusion of majesty, cannot be captured even remotely by any kind of discourse, on account of the poverty of human speech ... I shall therefore not discuss this topic, for which neither I, not even Plato himself, have at our disposal any words grand enough for its magnitude, and, facing a subject matter that goes far beyond my mediocre ability, I shall announce my retreat and finally recall my discourse down from the heavens to the earth.[121]

Apuleius points to the authority of Plato to justify his omission of the highest divinity from his discussion. Such a reinforcement is well advised, since his audience might have expected him to cover the topic of the highest god, considering the specific relationship between him and the subordinate gods at the centre of the lecture. Plato's authority, drawn from *Tim.* 28c, is thus effectively used to set the boundaries for the particular context of the *DDS*, in which the discussion of the highest god has no place, while the reference to Socrates, an echo of Cicero's *Tusc.* 5.10, may indicate that the divinities discussed will not exceed the rank of Socrates' own *daimonion*.[122]

comes to be in the soul and then feeds on itself' (ῥητὸν γὰρ οὐδαμῶς ἐστιν ὡς ἄλλα μαθήματα, ἀλλ᾽ ἐκ πολλῆς συνουσίας γιγνομένης περὶ τὸ πρᾶγμα αὐτὸ καὶ τοῦ συζῆν ἐξαίφνης, οἷον ἀπὸ πυρὸς πηδήσαντος ἐξαφθὲν φῶς, ἐν τῇ ψυχῇ γενόμενον αὐτὸ ἑαυτὸ ἤδη τρέφει).

[121] *quorum parentem, qui omnium rerum dominator atque auctor est, solutum ab omnibus nexibus patiendi aliquid gerendive, nulla vice ad alicuius rei munia obstrictum, cur e[r]go nunc dicere exordiar, cum Plato caelesti facundia praeditus, aequiperabilia diis immortalibus disserens, frequentissime praedicet hunc solum maiestatis incredibili quadam nimietate et ineffabili non posse penuria sermonis humani quavis oratione vel modice comprehendi ... missum igitur hunc locum faciam, in quo non mihi tantum, sed ne Platoni quidem meo quiverunt ulla verba pro amplitudine rei suppetere, ac iam rebus mediocritatem meam longe superantibus receptui canam tandemque orationem de caelo in terram devocabo.*

[122] The echo of Cicero's description, in which Socrates is associated with ethics as opposed to physics and metaphysics, moreover, indicates that Apuleius' lecture on demons will carry a strongly ethical message, which comes to the fore in his

142

In Apuleius' *De mundo* 24, 341–2, in turn, we find yet another introduction of the highest god. Apuleius, for the most part, follows his Greek source closely but makes several interesting modifications to the text:

> It remains for me to speak about the master of the cosmos, which is the central[123] topic of my discourse. It would certainly be incomplete unless, in our reflections about the cosmos, we also discuss [the god], even if we do so with less detail, but in whatever manner we can. It is certainly not better to remain silent concerning this master, as that man believes, but instead, it is preferable to address the topic, even if it is done inadequately.[124]

The reference to 'that man' (*ille*) here is not, I believe, a reference to Plato, but instead a verbal echo of Sallust, *Jugurtha* 19.2: 'Concerning Carthage, I believe, it is better to remain silent than to speak inadequately.'[125] I doubt that it would have been Apuleius' intention, even when operating within a (Ps.-)Aristotelian framework, to refer to Plato with the somewhat depreciatory reference 'that man'. This becomes even less likely if we consider that Apuleius' overall strategy, in the *De mundo* as elsewhere, is to integrate Aristotelian with Platonic doctrine instead of pitting one against the other. Apuleius is happy to follow his Greek source in including the subject of the highest god in his discussion from the outset.[126] Unlike the *DDS*, this work does not impose any restrictions as regards the precise level of

---

appeal to the audience to worship their own demon, the virtuous soul, with the help of philosophy. Cf. the analysis of Apuleius' agenda by Fletcher 2014: 144–72, esp. 156–7.

[123] Apuleius takes κεφαλαιωδῶς to mean 'as the central point' as opposed to 'summarily', more likely the meaning of the Greek text, given its author's expression ὡς εἰς τυπώδη 'in the form of an outline' only little later at 397b. Given the central role of theology in Apuleius' own thought, it is no surprise that Apuleius (wilfully?) would have understood the Greek term in such a manner. Cf. Fletcher 2014: 140 n. 74 and Beaujeu ad loc.

[124] *restat, quod caput est sermonis huius, ut super mundi rectore verba faciamus. indigens quippe orationis huius videbatur ratio, nisi de mundo reputantes, etsi minus curiose, at quoquo modo possemus, <de deo> diceremus. de rectore quippe omnium non, ut ait ille, silere melius est, sed vel parum dicere.*

[125] *Contra* Fletcher 2014: 140; noted by Beaujeu, *comm. ad loc.*

[126] *Kosm.* 391b: '"cosmos" means the orderly arrangement of all things that is safeguarded by and through god' (λέγεται ... κόσμος ἡ τῶν ὅλων τάξις τε καὶ διακόσμησις ὑπὸ θεοῦ τε καὶ διὰ θεὸν φυλαττομένη).

divinity to be discussed. Apuleius' reference to 'that man', then, is more likely one of his numerous Romanizing features that are incorporated into his translation to increase its accessibility to a Roman audience. While a metaphysical discussion of the highest god is out of place in the *DDS*, whose message is an appeal to the audience to improve their personal δαίμων through philosophical learning and virtuous action, it is entirely at home in the *De mundo*. At the same time, however, Apuleius' phrasing in the latter work, which qualifies his treatment of this metaphysical subject matter as 'in whatever manner we can' (*quoquo modo possumus*, compare the Greek 'in the manner of an outline', ὡς εἰς τυπώδη μάθησιν, *Kosm.* 397b), along with the addition of *vel parum*, 'even inadequately', injects into the text an appropriate level of humility on the part of the author, who is aware of his limitations. *Parum*, in particular, differs from the rather methodological, programmatic tone of ὡς εἰς τυπώδη μάθησιν, 'in the manner of an outline', emphasizing, instead, the notion of inadequacy on the part of the author.

Apuleius carefully adjusts his discussion of the highest god to the various contexts in which it appears. While the textbook *DPD* provides a list of presumably standard characteristics associated with the highest god without further analysis, the *DDS*, in which Apuleius imparts to his demonology a thoroughly ethical message, avoids a substantial discussion of the highest god, justifying such a programme by echoing Timaeus' cautious remarks at *Tim.* 28c in the form of a dramatic profession of the god's elusive sublimity. Finally, the rather programmatic tone used in the introduction of the *summus deus* in the Ps.-Aristotelian *vorlage* to Apuleius' *De mundo* 24 is given a slightly more reverential character, first by stressing the discussion of the highest god as central to the work[127] and, secondly,

---

[127] Cf. p. 143 n. 123.

by pointing to the author's inadequacy to address such a sublime subject matter.

Theology: The Summus Deus and the Cosmos

Having been introduced to Apuleius' highest divinity in the various contexts of his philosophical writings, let us examine the god's relation to the Apuleian cosmos. At *DPD* 1.5, 190 we encountered the following epithets that stress the god's creative agency: the god is described as the 'creator and producer of all things' (*genitor rerumque omnium extractor*),[128] who 'himself bestows everything' (*ipse conferens cuncta*). In the subsequent passages, we recall, Apuleius describes the god as the 'divine craftsman' who 'lends form to matter' (*deus artifex conformat materiam*, 1.5, 191), as 'divine builder' and 'artificer' of the world' (*aedificator mundi deus*, 1.7, 194; *fabricator deus* (ibid. 1.8, 198; 1.9, 199; 1.10, 201). He holds the conjoint roles of the 'father and architect of this divine world' (*pater* and *architectus huius divini orbis* at *DPD* 1.11, 204). At *DDS* 3, 124 he is described in similar terms as the 'father, lord, creator of all things' (*paren*[s], *dominator*, *auctor omnium rerum*). In the very first chapter of the *De mundo*, in turn, the world is identified as an orderly arrangement adorned through the favour of god (*ornata ordinatio dei munere*), while the divinity himself is described as an artificer (*artifex*). This array of creative, 'hands-on' labels for the god throughout his works, we found, must be aligned with Apuleius' view of an uncreated cosmos, expressed at *DPD* 1.8, 196–8, where the author clarifies that the transcendent divinity is the ontologically distinct cause responsible for the coming to be ([*mundo*] *nascendi causam deus praestitit*) of the orderly universe.[129] Such a view is confirmed by Apuleius' use of the terms 'incorporeal' (*DPD* 1.5, 190) and

---

[128] Accepting the emendation by Oudentorp *extractor* to *exstructor*, as the majority of modern editors.
[129] This would correspond to the fourth possibile interpretation of γενητός by Taurus, cf. pp. 27–8.

'supramundane' (1.11, 204),[130] descriptions that exclude an involvement with the material sphere.

Accordingly, Apuleius at *De mundo* 30, 357–8 follows the Greek source[131] in offering a striking analogy that illustrates the notion of a transcendent divinity acting as an impulse responsible for the world's orderly functioning. Like a leader commanding an army to advance into battle, the highest god 'orders' the parts of the cosmic machinery to engage in their individual movements:

When the king and father of all things, whom only the thoughts of our soul's eye can see, orders his entire machinery, joined together and bound by his laws in a circular motion, bright and resplendent with starlight, in its countless different constellations, now manifest, now concealed – when he orders all this to set itself in motion from a single origin, as I said previously, we are allowed to think that this [enterprise] is similar to a military operation. For, when the trumpet has sounded its war signal, the soldiers are fired up by the sound. One girds his sword, another picks up his shield, this one puts on his breast plate, the other one puts a helmet on his head or greaves over his legs, puts the reins on his horse and harnesses them in pairs. At once, everyone takes up his own task: the foot soldiers prepare for battle, the centurions attend to the battle ranks, the cavalry leads on the flanks, the others carry out their assigned tasks, all the while this great army obeys the command of a single leader, whom they have appointed as commander, and with whom lies the supreme power of all things. Mortal and immortal affairs are governed in the same way, when, under one governing agent, everything eagerly takes on the duty of its own work, and a hidden power takes charge, invisible only to eyes illuminated by the keen sight of the intellect.[132]

---

[130] Cf. Alc. *Didask.* 28.3.8. The term picks up ὑπερουράνιος at *Phaedr.* 247c, cf. Moreschini 2015: 223–5, Finamore 2006: 35.

[131] The Greek author was likely inspired by Aristotle's discussion, at *Met.* Lambda 11.10, 1075a11–18, cf. 1075b24–6, of the manner in which the supreme good exists in the universe, either as a separate element, or more immediately as the orderly arrangement pervading the universe. Aristotle, making use of the same military imagery we find in Apuleius' Greek source, likens the relationship between the good and the universe to the asymmetrical relationship between a general and his army. The general provides a causal impulse for the battle array (ἐκείνη [ἡ τάξις] διὰ τοῦτόν ἐστιν, 1075a11) and thus, to an extent, participates in the state of affairs, but remains separated from the individuals over whom he commands.

[132] *cum igitur rex omnium et pater, quem tantummodo animae oculis nostrae cogitationes vident, machinam omnem iugiter per circuitum suis legibus terminatam, claram et sideribus relucentem speciesque innumeras modo propalam, saepe contectas, ab uno, ut supra dixi, principio agitari iubet, simile istuc esse bellicis rebus hinc liceat*

While it is possible to understand the reference to a single moment at which the heavenly apparatus is set in motion as referring to a creation of the orderly world at a certain moment in time (cf. Apuleius' *ab uno principio*, 'from one beginning', translating the Greek ἐκ μιᾶς ἀρχῆς), the context in which this analogy appears suggests rather that it serves to reinforce the solitary authority ('the command of a single leader', *unius ducis imperio*, rendering ὑφ' ἕνα σημάντορα; further, 'one governing agent', *uno moderamine*, for ὑπὸ μιᾶς ῥοπῆς) of the transcendent divinity over the complex and multipartite cosmic machinery of which it is not a part itself.[133] This effect is strengthened by further analogies, translated at *De mundo* 35, 365, that liken the god's role within the cosmos to that of the *gubernator* of a trireme, the *rector* of a carriage, and the *praecentor* of a choir.

An interesting amplification of the Greek text in Apuleius' translation occurs at the beginning of the above quoted passage, where the entirety of the heavenly apparatus is 'joined together and bounded by his laws in a circular motion' (*machinam omnem iugiter per circuitum suis legibus terminatam*), where the Greek author merely states that, upon a sign by the god (σημήνῃ, *Kosm.* 399a31–2) 'every [natural kind] is moved in continuing, spherical motions and within its own particular limits' (κινεῖται πᾶσα [φύσις] ἐνδελεχῶς ἐν κύκλοις καὶ πέρασιν ἰδίοις, ibid. 32–3), without any reference to a divine 'law'. Only later, at *Kosm.* 400b13–401a12[134] (Apuleius' *De mundo*

arbitrari. nam cum tuba bellicum cecinit, milites clangore incensi alius accingitur gladio, alius clipeum capit, ille lorica se induit, hic galea caput vel crura ocreis involvit et equum temperat frenis et iugales ad concordiam copulat; et protinus unusquisque conpetens capessit officium: velites excursionem adornant, ordinibus principes curant, equites cornibus praesunt, ceteri negotia quae nacti sunt agitant cum interea unius ducis imperio tantus exercitus paret, quem praefecerit, penes quem est summa rerum. non aliter divinarum et humanarum rerum status regitur, quando uno moderamine contenta omnia pensum sui operis agnoscunt curatque omnibus occulta vis, nullis oculis obvia, nisi quibus mens aciem suae lucis intendit.

[133] See the analysis by Betegh and Gregoric 2014 of the numerous analogies in the Greek text. Concerning the battle analogy, the authors stress the distance of the auditory trumpet signal, sounded from outside the battle ranks: 'The army alarm, the sound of the trumpet, is a purely auditory signal, whereas the trumpeter remains invisible for the majority of troops' (581–2).

[134] 'Just as, for instance, the law of the city, remaining fixed in the souls of those who abide by it, regulates everything in the state ... we must suppose that it is the same

35–6),[135] does the Greek text offer a further analogy in which the power of the transcendent divinity over the cosmos is likened to the power of law over a city. Once issued, it remains the single point of reference for the structure and governance of the city down to the smallest affair. The point in this later context is the idea that the highest divinity, unlike any of the commanding roles to which it has been likened previously, is in no way burdened by his power. Just like the law that regulates the city without the need for physical presence or exertion, the god himself remains *immobilis* while, at the same time, everything within the universe unfolds and takes his course in accordance with his will. Apuleius explicitly inserts this notion of divine law also into the cosmological context of the above passage, which focuses on the role of the highest god as an external impulse to the workings of the cosmos, rather than on the continuous penetration of the cosmos by his power.

Theology: Providence and Demons

The significance of the relationship, stressed by Apuleius' amplification of the Greek text in the above-cited passage *De mundo* 30, 357–8, between divine law and the heavenly bodies becomes clearer as we turn to the two most salient, closely intertwined features of Apuleius' theology, his doctrine of divine providence

in the greater city, that is, the cosmos. For the god to us is a well-balanced law, admitting neither amendment nor change, but is better, I believe, and more secure than the laws that are engraved in tables. Under the guidance of god, unchanging and harmonious, the entire heavens and earth are regulated, dispersed across all natures through their proper seeds, into plants and living ceatures, according to their genus and species' (ὥσπερ ἀμέλει καὶ ὁ τῆς πόλεως νόμος ἀκίνητος ὢν ἐν ταῖς τῶν χρωμένων ψυχαῖς πάντα οἰκονομεῖ τὰ κατὰ τὴν πολιτείαν ... οὕτως ὑποληπτέον καὶ ἐπὶ τῆς μείζονος πόλεως, λέγω δὲ τοῦ κόσμου· νόμος γὰρ ἡμῖν ἰσοκλινὴς ὁ θεός, οὐδεμίαν ἐπιδεχόμενος διόρθωσιν ἢ μετάθεσιν, κρείττων δέ, οἶμαι, καὶ βεβαιότερος ἐν ταῖς κύρβεσιν ἀναγεγραμμένων. ἡγουμένου δὲ ἀκινήτως αὐτοῦ καὶ ἐμμελῶς ὁ σύμπας οἰκονομεῖται διάκοσμος οὐρανοῦ καὶ γῆς, μεμερισμένος κατὰ τὰς φύσεις πάσας διὰ τῶν οἰκείων σπερμάτων εἴς τε φυτὰ καὶ ζῷα κατὰ γένη τε καὶ εἴδη).

[135] *De mundo* 36, 369: 'That law, intent on preserving balance, in need of neither improvement nor change, is god. This is, in fact, how the universe is governed, as its helmsman watches over and attends to everything, himself unchanged. This power is spread out, contained within seeds, and distributed throughout the essential nature of all things, and through the species and genera. Finally, the essential nature of all living creatures: wild or tame, winged, on land or in the water comes

and his doctrine of demons.[136] The metaphysical structure in the Apuleian cosmos ensures the detailed providential administration down to the smallest part of the universe through a hierarchy of divine executive agents, each assigned to its particular sphere of responsibility.[137] At *DPD* 1.11, 204 Apuleius clarifies that '[Plato] names three kinds of gods': the first kind is the highest divinity discussed above; second are the heavenly bodies and certain other divine powers (*numina*),[138] all of whom are referred to as *caelicolae*, 'inhabitants of the heavens'. The lowest divine class is that of the *medioximi*, 'intermediaries', located, both geographically and in terms of potency, on an

into existence, is nourished and, in turn, perishes in observance of the divine ordinances' (*lex illa vergens ad aequitatis tenorem sit deus nulla indigens correctione mutabili. quippe sic et mundi universitas regitur, dum speculatur ad omnia rector eius atque immutabiliter incumbit spargiturque vis illa seminibus inclusa per naturas omnium speciesque et genera digesta ... tandem omnium animalium agrestium et cicurum, pinnatarum et pedestrium et aquatilium natura gignitur, nutritur, absumitur parens caelestibus institutis*). It is through *semina*, seeds, that the providential divinity, identified as divine law, extends its power throughout the cosmos and thereby generates the living creatures. The notion of *semina* is not picked up in Apuleius' other philosophical works. It appears to be an amalgam of Stoic and Aristotelian physics provided by the author of Apuleius' Greek *vorlage*. Cf. pp. 182, 247–9 with n. 107.

[136] On Apuleius' doctrine of demons, see also Dragona-Monachou 1994, and the contributions by Bernard 1994, Habermehl 1996, and Regen 1999, 2000; Moreschini 2015: 117–45.

[137] The providential metaphysical hierarchy is mirrored in the microcosmos that is the human body: *DPD* 1.6, 228–9 mentions the familiar Platonic division of the soul whose rational part is the leader, *dux*, and whose passionate part is the servant, *servatrix*. Likewise, the bodily members assist and serve the head and carry it aloft like a master and ruler through whose providential care they are safe from danger. 'The other body parts are subservient to the head ... they carry it on a lofty position, like a master and ruler and, in return, are protected from dangers by [the head's] providence' (*cetera enim membra ancillari et subservire capiti ... vectare etiam sublime positum ut dominum atque rectorem providentiaque eius a periculis vindicari, DPD* 1.13, 208). The internal organs are equally set out as part of a hierarchical system. The structures we find in Apuleius' description of the human body and soul emphasize that humans are a microcosmic version of the detailed providential hierarchy at play in the cosmos. Everything is set up as an interconnected system, with each part being assigned its specific function and duty. In a nutshell, Apuleius expands the hierarchical structure familiar from the *Republic* to the human body.

[138] Presumably corresponding to the invisible gods discussed at *DDS* 2, 119–21. Alongside the monad and dyad, Xenocrates had ascribed divinity to the sky, the 'fiery stars' (identified with the Olympian gods), and to other invisible demons in the sublunary sphere (Aet. *Plac.* 1.7, 30 = fr. 213 IP). A threefold division of divine beings, all charged with various providential functions, appears also in Ps.-Plut. 572f–574a. Cf. Moreschini 2015: 233–7.

intermediate level between the divine and human spheres.[139] It is the *medioximi* that correspond to the 'demons', whose nature Apuleius explores in much greater detail in the *De deo Socratis* where, at *DDS* 13, 48, we find the definition of demons as animals in kind, rational in thought, with a soul susceptible to passions, a body made from air, and possessing immortal endurance (*genere animalia, ingenio rationabilia, animo passiva, corpore aeria, tempore aeterna*).[140]

Apuleius' demonology provides the material platform for his doctrine of providence. The significance of divine providence, ultimately anchored at *Tim.* 30b–c,[141] increased with the

[139] 'He names three kinds of gods. The first is the one and only highest god, who is supramundane, incorporeal, whom we have shown earlier to be the father and builder of this divine world. The other kind is that of the stars and other divine powers whom we call "heaven dwellers". The third kind belongs to those whom our Roman ancestors called "intermediate gods", inferior to the highest gods in terms of condition, habitat, and power, yet certainly superior to humans by nature' (*deorum trinas nuncupat species, quarum est prima unus et solus summus ille, ultramundanus, incorporeus, quem patrem et architectum huius divini orbis superius ostendimus; aliud genus est quale astra habent ceteraque numina, quos caelicolas nominamus; tertium habent, quos medioximos Romani veteres appellant, quod est sui ratione, sed et loco et potestate diis summis sunt minores, natura hominum profecto maiores*). I take it that both the stars (*genus quale astra habent*) and the other divine powers (*cetera numina*) are included under the label *caelicolae*.

[140] Echoing Xenocrates, cf. F 145, F147 IP 2012 (= fr. 225, 227 IP 1982). Cf. n. 138 above. For the considerable influence of Xenocrates' concept of demons on the later Platonic tradition, cf. Timotin 2012, esp. 86–161; Dillon 2003: 123–30. The demons' possession of immortality, a characteristic shared with the gods, and of a passionate soul, shared with humans, is ultimately inspired by *Tim.* 31b4–32c4 where Timaeus makes reference to geometrical proportion in the context of the four material elements that make up the cosmos. Between any two extremes, the most effective bond for achieving true unity is that which is able to assimilate itself to the two extremes it unites (ὃς ἂν αὐτόν καὶ τὰ συνδούμενα ὅτι μάλιστα ἓν ποιῇ, 31c2–3), with the help of proportion (ἀναλογία): 'Whenever the middle term of three numbers ... between any two of them is such that what the first term is to it, it is to the last, and, conversely, what the last term is to the middle term, it is to the first, then, since the middle term turns out to be both first and last, and the last and the first likewise both turn out to be middle terms, they will all of necessity turn out to have the same relationship to each other, and, given this, will be unified' (transl. Zeyl.) (*Tim.* 31c4–32a7: ὁπόταν γὰρ ἀριθμῶν τριῶν ... ὧντινων οὖν ᾖ τὸ μέσον, ὅτιπερ τὸ πρῶτον πρὸς αὐτό, τοῦτο αὐτὸ πρὸς τὸ ἔσχατον, καὶ πάλιν αὖθις, ὅτι τὸ ἔσχατον πρὸς τὸ μέσον, τὸ μέσον πρὸς τὸ πρῶτον, τότε τὸ μέσον μὲν πρῶτον καὶ ἔσχατον γιγνόμενον, τὸ δ᾽ ἔσχατον καὶ τὸ πρῶτον αὖ μέσα ἀμφότερα, πάνθ᾽ οὕτως ἐξ ἀνάγκης τὰ αὐτὰ εἶναι συμβήσεται, τὰ αὐτὰ δὲ γενόμενα ἀλλήλοις ἓν πάντα ἔσται).

[141] 'There, the cosmos, according to the likely account, is described as having come to be as an ensouled, rational creature through divine providence' (οὕτως οὖν δὴ κατὰ λόγον τὸν εἰκότα δεῖ λέγειν τόνδε τὸν κόσμον ζῷον ἔμψυχον ἔννουν τε τῇ ἀληθείᾳ διὰ

Middle Platonic effort to align a transcendent divinity with the supervision of the material cosmos without allowing for a pollution of the divine nature with the corporeal, an effort we re-encounter also in Calcidius.[142] In Apuleius, accordingly, the highest god in this metaphysical structure issues his 'divine thought' (*divina sententia*),[143] identified by Apuleius with 'providence' (*providentia*) at *DPD* 1.12, 205, and defined, further, as the 'preserver of the wellbeing of that for the sake of which it has assumed such a task' (*conservatricem prosperitatis eius cuius causa tale suscepit officium*). The providential *sententia* of the 'most eminent of all gods' (*exsuperantissimus deorum omnium*) is then translated, it appears, into a divine law (*divina lex*) defined, more specifically, as 'fate' (*fatum*),[144] 'through which god's inevitable thoughts and plans are fulfilled' (*per quod inevitabiles cogitationes dei atque incepta conplentur*). Further, god's primary providence, it appears, is enacted by the divine dwellers of heaven whom he has stationed through all parts of the universe to ensure its safekeeping and its beauty (*deos caelicolas ordinavit quos ad tutelam et decus per omnia mundi membra dispersit*).

While still in the context of the transcendent first sphere and the secondary divine sphere, Apuleius at this point at *DPD* 1.12, 205–6 stresses that the god's providential outreach stretches as far as the human sphere. 'By establishing his laws [i.e. through fate], he assigns to the other gods the task of managing and safeguarding the day-to-day business of those matters that remain.'[145]

τὴν τοῦ θεοῦ γενέσθαι πρόνοιαν). For a general discussion of Apuleius' providence, cf. Regen 1971: 83–91.

[142] Cf. my discussion below, pp. 196–201.

[143] Cf. Ps.-Plut. *Fat.* 572F6, where the primary providence is described as god's νόησις and βούλησις.

[144] The definition of fate as 'divine law', developed first by Stoic and appropriated with enthusiasm by Middle Platonic authors, ultimately derives from *Tim.* 41e2, where the demiurge is reported to explain the 'laws of fate' to the newly created souls. Cf. e.g. Alc. *Didask.* 16.2, 5; Nemes. 38,109,18; Ps.-Plut. 568d6. See Calcidius' critical reference to the views of Chrysippus and Cleanthes at 380, 140, 29–31.

[145] ... *fundatisque legibus reliquarum dispositionem ac tutelam rerum quas cotidie fieri necesse est, diis ceteris tradidit*. Apuleius' description of a lower providential sphere, and the various tasks assigned to the divine agents, resembles Ps.-Plut. *Fat.* 573D–574A. Sharples 2003 offers Apuleius' *DPD*, Nemesius' *De natura*

Despite the highest god's providential reach, a suitable distance to the mortal sphere must be retained. Thus the *caelicolae*[146] are charged with the preservation of the divine ordinances, and thereby pass on the god's *sententia* or first providence to the lower spheres. To mark the distance from the source of providential ordinances to those affected, the *prima providentia* translates, in the material cosmos, into a *secunda providentia* which is preserved by the *caelicolae*: 'Having received the providence[147] from this source, the gods hold on to the secondary providence with such zeal that everything, even the heavenly display for mortals, maintains the immutable condition of the paternal government.'[148]

This description, in particular of the *secunda providentia*, has invited criticism. Instead of what appears to be a somewhat trivial reference to the orderly heavens,[149] he might have provided a definition of the sort he provided for the *prima providentia*, explained by him as the highest god's providential *sententia* or 'thought' and as the 'preserver of the well-being of that for the sake of which it has assumed such a task'. Interpretations that draw from Apuleius' description

---

hominis, and Ps.-Plutarch's *De fato* as the springboard to a historical examination of the origins of the doctrine of a tripartite providence, but also pays attention to the treatment of this doctrine by Alexander of Aphrodisias.

[146] Interestingly, we perceive an echo of the anti-creationist contention against a *novum consilium* (cf. pp. 187–8) in the context not of the highest divinity in the cosmos, but of the *caelicolae*, the dwellers of heaven, as set out in *DDS* 12, 146–7: 'how could one appear to have been perfect, who changes from a prior state to a more correct one, especially since nobody engages in anything new of his own accord unless he was dissatisfied with his former condition? Such a change in design cannot follow unless what preceded it was inferior' (*porro autem qui potest videri perfectus fuisse, qui a priore statu ad alium rectiorem statum migrat, cum praesertim nemo sponte capessat nova, nisi quem paenituit priorum? non potest enim subsequi illa mutata ratio sine praecedentium infirmatione*).

[147] Rejecting, with Krafft 1979: 157 n. 20 the emendation *provinciam*, 'office', 'duty', suggested by Thomas and Beaujeu. The repetition of the word *providentia* underlines the fact that two different providential forces are at play.

[148] *unde susceptam providentiam dii secundae providentiae ita naviter retinent ut omnia etiam quae caelitus mortalibus exibentur inmutabilem ordinationis paternae statum teneant.*

[149] Beaujeu 1973 *comm. ad loc.*: 'quelques lignes banales sur la belle ordonnance de l'univers'.

of the *secunda providentia* a more substantial role for the secondary gods have duly been offered. Most notably Peter Krafft interprets *quae caelitus mortalibus exibentur*, 'the heavenly display for mortals' (lit. 'what is displayed in the heavens for mortals'), along the lines of 'that which is *granted* (Krafft: 'gewährt') to mortals in the heavenly sphere', thereby lending more substance to the task fulfilled by the *caelicolae* than their spherical movements would otherwise suggest.[150] I shall return to this point shortly.

In addition to the criticism attracted by the seemingly unsatisfactory definition of the secondary providence, Apuleius' apparent failure to adequately describe the 'third providence' that follws the *secunda providentia* at *DPD* I.12, 206 has been seen as problematic. There, he explains that the lowest-ranking kind of divinity, the *daemones* – Apuleius provides as the Roman equivalent the *genii* or *lares* – are the appointed assistants to the *caelicolae* and serve as custodians and interpreters of human–divine relations. Unlike the doctrines advanced by other authors commonly cited in this context, most notably Ps.-Plutarch *De fato* 573A,[151] 3–6 and Nemesius *De natura hominis* 43,126, 8–12,[152] no attempt is made at *DPD* I.12 to define the role ascribed to the lowest divinities as a *tertia providentia*.

Both 'problems' in Apuleius' exegesis disappear, I suggest, upon closer examination of the relationship he establishes between providence and fate, such as it is set out at *DPD* I.12,

---

[150] Krafft 1979, esp. 157.
[151] This work distinguishes three 'providences' specifically, starting out with the hypostasis below a mysterious 'first god'. The primary providence is in charge of ordering the intelligible realm, the secondary one is 'that of the second gods who move through the heaven' (δευτέρων θεῶν τῶν κατ' οὐρανὸν ἰόντων, 573a). The third is the 'providence and forethought of the demons that oversee human affairs' (πρόνοιά τε καὶ προμήθεια τῶν ὅσοι περὶ γῆν δαίμονες). Cf. Dillon 1996: 324–5.
[152] τῆς δὲ διεξαγωγῆς καὶ τοῦ τέλους τῶν πρακτῶν καὶ τῆς τάξεως τῶν κατὰ τὸν βίον τῶν τε φυσικῶν καὶ τῶν ὑλικῶν τε καὶ ὀργανικῶν καλουμένων ἀγαθῶν καὶ τῶν τούτοις ἀντικειμένων τὴν τρίτην εἶναι πρόνοιαν Πλάτων ἀποφαίνεται, προΐστασθαι δὲ ταύτης τινὰς τεταγμένους δαίμονας περὶ τὴν γῆν φύλακας τῶν ἀνθρωπίνων πράξεων ('Plato declares that the third type of providence is over the conduct and end of actions and the ordering of goods in living, which are called natural and material and instrumental and their opposites. He says that certain appointed spirits around

205. The definition of the primary providence as the 'preserver of the wellbeing of that for the sake of which it has assumed such a task' (*conservatricem prosperitatis eius cuius causa tale suscepit officium*) is immediately followed by the statement that 'the divine law is fate, through which the inevitable reasonings and designs of the god are fulfilled' (*divinam legem esse fatum, per quod inevitabiles cogitationes dei atque incepta conplentur*). I believe that this statement *is*, in fact, Apuleius' definition of secondary providence which, in the form of fate, is the executive power wielded by the heavenly bodies upon the cosmic environment. The divine *sententia* that constitutes the first *providentia* is translated, in the cosmic field, into the secondary providence as the spherical motions of the heavenly bodies that regulate, safeguard, and beautify the lower spheres.[153] This executive function is stressed once again in the immediately following statement: 'what is accomplished by fate must appear to have been issued by providence' (*quod fato terminatur debet providentia susceptum videri*, *DPD* 1.12, 205). On this view, we can spare Apuleius the reproach of yielding the place for a much-needed definition of the second providence to a philosophically void description of the heavenly order. There is no need either to suppose, with Krafft,[154] that it would have been the role of heavenly bodies to 'grant' anything to humans. Their task, such as it is set out by Apuleius at *DPD* 1.12, i.e. the enactment of the god's primary providence in the form of fate, within the cosmic sphere, is complete.

With regard to the perceived need for a 'third' providence, to be executed by the demons, I suggest that we turn to *DPD* 1.11, 204, the passage that immediately precedes Apuleius' introduction of the hierarchical order of divinities and his discussion

the earth oversee this providence and are guardians of human actions', transl. Sharples and Van der Eijk 2008).

[153] Cf. the previous statement, *DPD* 1.12, 205, '[the highest god] orders the divine dwellers of heaven whom he has stationed through all parts of the universe to ensure its safekeeping and its beauty' (*deos caelicolas ordinavit quos ad tutelam et decus per omnia mundi membra dispersit*).

[154] Cf. p. 153 with n. 150.

154

of providence. There, four[155] types of living beings inhabiting the material cosmos are distinguished in accordance with their habitat, which is, in turn, determined by its elemental make-up. Apuleius lists a *species* 'of fiery nature' (*ex natura ignis*), among them the sun, moon, and stars. The second type of living being is composed of air (*ex aeria qualitate*), a third species composed of water and earth, which, described as the *genus mortale*, is divided again into a species that lives 'in the earth' (*terrenum*, for the Greek ἔγγειον; plants and other types of vegetation) and one that lives 'upon the earth' (*terrestre*, for the Greek ἐπίγειον; humans and animals).[156]

This diairesis illustrates an important point: the *caelicolae*, the 'fiery race', along with the other species listed, participate in the material habitat which is our universe, being set apart merely by their different elemental nature. Within the environment of the material cosmos, providence takes on the form of fate, as illustrated above. As a consequence, we no longer need to search in vain for Apuleius' reference to a 'third providence' associated with the demons. God's providence is passed on to the material sphere, received by the *caelicolae* and, ultimately,

---

[155] Apuleius' quadripartite diairesis in the present context, where it appears against the backdrop of an essentially dualistic framework, is noted by Timotin 2012: 113–15. Timotin also points to Varro *apud* Augustine, *Civ.* 7.6: '[Varro] adds that the world is divided into two parts, the heaven and the earth. The heaven is divided again into aether and air, the earth into water and firm ground. Out of these, aether is the highest, air is second, water is third, and earth is the lowest. And he says that all four parts are full of living creatures, immortal ones in the aether and the air, mortal ones in the water and on the earth' (*adiungit mundum dividi in duas partes, caelum et terram; et caelum bifariam, in aethera et aera; terram vero in aquam et humum; e quibus summum esse aethera, secundum aera, tertiam aquam, infimum terram, quas omnes partes quattuor animarum esse plenas, in aethere et aere inmortalium, in aqua et terra mortalium*). Nevertheless, Timotin still maintains the theory of a tripartite division of providential forces in Apuleius (ibid. 118–20).

[156] A classification of living creatures according to their elemental habitat, i.e. the association of an ontological hierarchy with a hierarchy of material elements, also appears in the *Epinomis* 984e, but see already the distinction of the four living kinds at *Tim.* 39e–40a (cf. Timotin 2012: 114–15). The *Epinomis*, however, includes aether as an additional, fifth element, a view we find also in Calcidius, cf. pp. 203–4 with n. 134. Xenocrates (142 IP 2012 = F 222 IP 1982 = Plut. *Def. orac.* 12, 416c–d) distinguishes between the gods, an intermediary race, and humans and associates with each a particular triangular shape, echoing *Tim.* 53c–54d. Cf. Moreschini 2015: 121 with n. 13. On the division of Timaeus' four living beings, cf. Regen 1971: 59 n. 206; Gersh 1986: 227–37.

passed to demons, who fulfil their appointed tasks, and who share a material habitat.[157] No switch from a 'second' to a third' providential level is necessary here, while the distinction between primary and secondary providence *was* required, previously, in order to indicate the ontological difference between the transcendent divinity and the *caelicolae*. On this view, the secondary providence, identified with fate, applies to the *caelicolae* and, by succession, to the demons whose specific task, in turn, is that of mediating between the higher and lower elemental races.[158] The perceived lack of a third providence, I believe, stems from the fact that the notion of providence has been linked with the tripartite diairesis of divine beings, without taking into account the first, quadripartite diairesis in which both the *caelicolae* and the lower demons are shown to operate within *the same* ontological sphere, the material cosmos.[159] The tasks Apuleius assigns to the lowest class in the divine hierarchy, the demons, are merely derivative and entailed by the executive role of the *caelicolae*. They are assumed to be the 'servants of the gods, and guardians and interpreters for men' (*ministros deorum arbitrantur custodesque hominum et interpretes*, DPD 1.12, 206).

Returning, finally, to our battlefield analogy in the *De mundo* 30, 357–8 (cf. p. 146–8), Apuleius' modified statement '[he] orders his entire machinery, joined together and bound

---

[157] Note that Apuleius, *DDS* 6, 132–7, 137, does not mention the term *providentia* in his detailed description of the demons' mediatory role between the divine and mortal spheres.

[158] Such a dualistic frame for the workings of providence is not at work in Ps.-Plutarch and Nemesius, who follow a tripartite division of providence for the managing of the intelligible and sensible spheres. The dualistic ontological framework that, as I have argued, may have led Apuleius to assume a dualistic providential hierarchy that subsumes fate under the secondary providence, comes closer to Calcidius who, however, associates the executive function of fate with the world soul. Cf. pp. 197–201.

[159] Krafft 1979: 161–3 explains the omission of a *tertia providentia* by Apuleius by the fact that the providential aspect of the specific duty associated with the demons is weakened and no longer deserves the label of an independent providence. Krafft suggests that the emphasis on their role as 'guardians' (φύλακες) in the Greek sources is much reduced by Apuleius, who describes them primarily as messengers and interpreters. Against a weakened providential role associated with the demons, cf. Moreschini 2015: 284–5.

by his laws in a circular motion, bright and resplendent with starlight, in its countless different constellations' thus injects into the Aristotelian framework a hint at Apuleius' own demonology, which provides the infrastructure necessary for disseminating the highest god's providence throughout the cosmos.

Other passages in the *De mundo* betray the influence of Apuleius' providential demonology. At *Kosm.* 397b16–20 the Greek author censures the ancient thinkers who believed that god's essence could be understood with the help of sense perception: 'Some of the ancients were persuaded to say that all things are full of gods, all that appear to us with the help of our eyes, hearing and all other senses. They may have established an account that befits the divine *power* (δύναμει), but not the god's *essence* (οὐσίᾳ). For the god truly is the preserver and creator of all things that, in whatever manner, are brought about throughout the cosmos.'[160]

The god's power (δύναμις), which exerts a perceptible influence throughout the material cosmos and is itself likely a conglomerate of Aristotelian and Stoic doctrine, occurs on numerous occasions in the Greek work. Apuleius' rendering in the present context is the unsurprising *potestas*, but this term will become more interesting in due course. More importantly, Apuleius' rendering for the Greek 'all things that, in whatever manner, are brought about throughout the cosmos' is 'all those (*omnium*) that are born and created for the sake of making the cosmos complete' (*qui ad conplendum mundum nati factique sunt*, De mundo 24, 343). The Greek neuter plural πάντα is changed to the masculine plural *qui*, and it is no longer the πάντα that 'are brought about, in whatever manner', but the masculine agents that are 'born and made', specifically 'for the sake of completing the cosmos'. Apuleius has found a place

---

[160] διὸ καὶ τῶν παλαιῶν εἰπεῖν τινες προήχθησαν ὅτι πάντα ταῦτά ἐστι θεῶν πλέα τὰ καὶ δι' ὀφθαλμῶν ἰνδαλλόμενα ἡμῖν καὶ δι' ἀκοῆς καὶ πάσης αἰσθήσεως, τῇ μὲν θείᾳ δυνάμει πρέποντα καταβαλλόμενοι λόγον, οὐ μὴν τῇ γε οὐσίᾳ. σωτὴρ μὲν γὰρ ὄντως ἁπάντων ἐστὶ καὶ γενέτωρ τῶν ὁπωσδήποτε κατὰ τόνδε τὸν κόσμον συντελουμένων ὁ θεός.

and role for his various demonic agents in the Aristotelian cosmos.[161]

Similarly, at *Kosm.* 398b6–10, the Greek author explains that it would be inappropriate for the highest god, even more so than for a king as mighty as Xerxes, to see personally to the various administrative tasks in his vast kingdom. Rather, it is more fitting for him that his power (δύναμις) should reach throughout the cosmos, thus putting the sun and moon into motion and all the heavenly bodies on their spherical courses. The highest god himself would thus be less directly responsible for the safeguarding of those upon the earth. Apuleius, in turn, reports that the highest god distributes his 'powers' throughout all parts of the world and the universe, his powers being the sun, moon, and the entire heavenly sphere (*[potestates] quae sint penes solem ac lunam cunctumque caelum*). It is their responsibility (*horum cura*) to manage the well-being of all terrestrial creatures. While we have already encountered *potestas*, in the singular, as a relatively straightforward rendering of δύναμις, the use of the plural form and the reference to the heavenly bodies put Apuleius' *caelicolae* in full sight on the cosmic stage.

Conclusion

Apuleius' interpretation of central Timaean themes, such as the εἰκὼς λόγος at *Tim.* 29b2–d3 at *DPD* 1.6, his view of an uncreated cosmos at *DPD* 1.8, his portrayal of the Timaean demiurge, and his system of demonic providential forces as described in the various contexts of his writings, increases in both coherency and originality once we subject it to a thorough context-based analysis. The author adjusts and tailors his Platonism carefully to the particular authorial agenda, genre, and audience of his works. This strategy is entirely in line with Apuleius' concept of 'philosophical rhetoric', a skill he has mastered thoroughly and with the help of which he is able to align himself with Plato and his divine eloquence. What

---

[161] Cf. Beaujeu *comm. ad loc.*; Regen 1971: 17–21, 33–83.

is more, in the context of Apuleius' translation of the Greek text *Peri kosmou*, we find that Apuleius' agenda of translation is diametrically opposed to that of Cicero. The latter, we saw above, with the help of textual modifications reinforced the varying doctrinal positions concerning the creation of the cosmos and its central divinity, with a view to accentuating contentious elements in the context of a philosophical *disputatio*. Apuleius, in contrast, true to the dogmatic vein of his Middle Platonic environment, is interested in stressing Platonic and Aristotelian harmony.

CHAPTER 4

CALCIDIUS

Preliminaries: Calcidius' Identity

Calcidius' identity remains a mystery.[1] His work, a partial translation of Plato's *Timaeus* that is accompanied by an extensive commentary, is dedicated to a certain Osius. Manuscripts of the eleventh to thirteenth centuries[2] identify Osius as a bishop in fourth-century Cordoba who was not only an associate of Constantine's court but, moreover, one of the principal authorities at the Christian councils of Nicaea (325 BCE) and Sardica (343 BCE). If this illustrious figure is, in fact, Calcidius' Osius, our author's work would have to be placed in the first half of the fourth century. This dating has proved popular,[3] yet, among several other problematic factors, it is difficult to reconcile it with the fact that Calcidius' vocabulary and literary style would fit more comfortably into the final decades of the same century.[4] A later date has been suggested by Waszink and Jensen (1962) and more recently Bakhouche (2011). Waszink conjectures that Osius may have been a Christian affiliated with the court at Milan in the late fourth century; Bakhouche identifies several other potential candidates.[5] The most extensive list of potential addressees is given by Magee (2016),[6] who identifies at least five Osii,

---

[1] The following chapter presents a modified and expanded version of subjects discussed in Hoenig 2013, 2014. The spelling 'Chalcidius', while favoured by the majority of early editions of Calcidius' work, has been rejected by Waszink and Jensen 1962: xvii and 1972: 236, based on an evaluation of the manuscript evidence. For the following, see also Waszink and Jensen 1962: ix–xvii, and Bakhouche 2011: 7–13.

[2] For a discussion of the manuscript evidence, see Bakhouche 2011: 68–75.

[3] For instance, Wrobel 1876, Switalski 1902, van Winden 1959, Dillon 1996, and, most recently, Reydams-Schils 2010.

[4] Cf. Bakhouche 2011: 30–4; Waszink and Jensen 1962: xiv–xiv.

[5] Bakhouche 2011: 10–1.

[6] Magee 2016: viii–xi.

but hesitates to make a commitment to any. Ultimately, the attempt to pinpoint for Calcidius a precise date of composition within the fourth-century bracket remains speculative.

Several clues concerning Calcidius' broader intellectual outlook are found in his commentary. Aside from his advanced proficiency in philosophical exegesis and a familiarity with elements of Scripture, he makes references to Homer,[7] Hesiod,[8] and Euripides,[9] transforms Greek poetry into Latin hexameters, and, at least in the letter of dedication to his patron and the preface to the commentary,[10] shows a concern for reasonably elegant diction. A closer look at Calcidius' vocabulary and syntax, nevertheless, leads to the impression that he was a native speaker of Greek,[11] and that his Latin phrasing was likely shaped by underlying Greek idioms and by what appear to be instances of incorrect Greek–Latin translation. A Greek identity for our author would certainly account for the, at times, disconcerting Latin syntax that awaits his readers, and for the rather more important fact that Calcidius' sources, as will become clear in the course of the present chapter, appear to have been exclusively Greek.

Placing Calcidius and his dedicatee in the early fourth century, along with the assumption that their relationship was one between bishop and (arch)deacon, has lent credence to the belief that Calcidius was a Christian.[12] This view, it would appear, is further substantiated by Calcidius' appeal to Scripture in several contexts of his commentary. The extensive scholarly discussion prompted by these passages has

[7] For instance, Cal. *Comm. in Tim.* ch. 93, p. 326, l. 17, 183, 415, 14–19. All citations of Calcidius are according to Bakhouche 2011.
[8] Cal. *Comm. in Tim.* 123, 360, 14–15; 134, 370, 28–371, 2. See further Bertolini 1990.
[9] An appeal to Osius' taste: it appears from the dedicatory letter that Osius had enjoyed a traditional liberal education (ibid. p. 132, ll. 8–9) and held command over the Greek language. Calcidius' flattering assertion that Osius had not only been playing with the idea of producing a translation himself, but would have been able to complete the task with far more ease ('even though you could have done this more easily and more skilfully', *quamquam ipse hoc cum facilius tum commodius facere posses*, 132, 11–12) may be distorted by hyperbole.
[10] Calcidius opens with a reference to Isocrates' *Ad Demonicum.*
[11] Magee 2016: 14–16, with further evidence of Greek interference in Calcidius' Latin.
[12] Switalski 1902, Steinheimer 1912, Waszink and Jensen 1962: xi; Baltes 1976 vol. I: 172–84.

not, in my opinion, produced decisive proof for our author's Christian identity. I have argued elsewhere that the expression and phrasing chosen by Calcidius in certain parts of his commentary betray no concern for the significant Christological developments that were of primary concern to the Council of Nicaea in 325 BCE, an event that witnessed the official articulation of the Nicene Creed.[13] The fact that Osius of Cordoba was one of the key players in bringing about the articulation of the consubstantiality of Christ with the Father renders problematic the assumption that Calcidius would have adopted any diction or vocabulary that could be perceived as opposing what must have been Osius' official stance.[14] Regardless of whether or not Calcidius' Osius is to be identified with Osius of Cordoba, we may still assume that an author identifying himself as a Christian would take into account the new developments of his chosen creed and, if not implement them explicitly, at least not counteract them in his treatment of Platonic theology. I suggest we may fare more comfortably in positing, based on a survey of Calcidius' references to Scripture, that Osius was versed in Christian dogma,[15] while it may suffice in the case of Calcidius himself to think of an author who betrays a basic familiarity with biblical literature, not uncommon for learned writers of his time, and who is comfortable to accommodate nuances of Christian doctrine in his exegesis where appropriate, as a gesture to his patron's faith.

[13] Hoenig 2014: 93–6.
[14] The Nicene Creed explicitly identifies the Son as *genitus, non factus*. Calcidius uses *genitus* in his description of the created world at 119, 356, 11, which would place the material world on an equal ontological level with Christ.
[15] Cf. the reference to the star that signalled the arrival of Christ on earth, a 'more sacred and venerable story' than Homer's *Iliad* (alluded to earlier in the same chapter, 126, 364, 5). 'With these things', Calcidius claims, Osius is 'much better acquainted than others' (ll. 11–12). See also Calcidius' statement on the vocabulary of his demonology at 133, 370, 12: '[we] should [not] be alarmed by this term [*daemones*], given indiscriminately to good and to evil demons, since the name "angels" does not alarm us, even though some angels are servants of god (those who are, are called "saints"), but others are attendants of the hostile force, **as you are well aware** (*ut optime nosti*)'.

Calcidius' Plato and Platonism

A large part of Calcidius' exegesis pertinent to the present discussion appears to me Middle Platonic in character, but the hypothesis of a predominantly Porphyrian influence on Calcidius has proven popular. Drawing clear lines between Middle and Neoplatonic doctrine, often arduous in itself, becomes even more difficult in that Calcidius rarely identifies any sources by name, and in that he was likely drawing from several individual sources for topical discussions, integrated in his commentary, on fate, demons, dreams, and matter, all of which venture far beyond the contents of the original dialogue. Various exegetical features in Calcidius have been aligned with Theon of Smyrna, who is assumed to have drawn, like Calcidius, on the second-century Peripatetic Adrastus;[16] further, Porphyry,[17] Alcinous' *Didaskalikos*, Ps.-Plutarch, Origen of Alexandria, and the Neopythagorean Numenius. Dillon is most outspoken against too strong a Porphyrian character in Calcidius' work,[18] while Reydams-Schils has emphasized Calcidius' authorial independence from Porphyry.[19] Bakhouche, without discounting Porphyry's impact altogether, points to material in Calcidius that would set him apart from the Neoplatonist, whose enthusiasm for the introductory conversation of the *Timaeus*, including the historical account of Atlantis, is

---

[16] Petrucci 2012: 514–21, esp. 517–18 examines the parallels between Theon and Calcidius vis-à-vis Adrastus, drawing attention to a number of differences between Theon and Calcidius in the context of their discussions of the geometrical proportion. Bakhouche 2011: 36–7 believes Calcidius was drawing from Theon rather than Adrastus. Waszink 1964: 68 had attributed chapters 8–19, 32–42, 44–50, 92–100, 108–12, 114–18 to Adrastus.

[17] See Waszink 1972: 240–2, and 1962: xc–cii, xcv, cv. Gersh 1986 vol. 2: 431–2 and 445–51 with n. 119, considers Calcidius' discussion on the transmigration of souls and the disorderly motion in the receptacle as Porphyrian and as representative of Calcidius' exegesis.

[18] Dillon 1996: 407–8. His focus is on Calcidius' characterization of matter and the triadic hierarchy of the divine in chapter 176. Van Winden had initially pointed to Numenius, Alcinous, and Adrastus but abandoned this view in a later edition (1965) in favour of Waszink's Porphyrian hypothesis. Den Boeft 1970 and 1977 concludes that Calcidius' discussions on fate and on demons are non-Porphyrian.

[19] Reydams-Schils 2007a: 311–14. Reydams-Schils suggests Calcidius may have confused the Christian Origen with the philosopher Origen (second to third century BCE).

not shared by Calcidius.[20] Finally, Runia (1993) has identified notable exegetical parallels between Calcidius and Philo of Alexandria's *De opificio mundi*, and suggests that Philo's influence may have reached Calcidius directly, or via Origen, Numenius, or Porphyry. The overall impression arises that Calcidius was drawing from a running commentary on Plato's dialogue, as well as from shorter, thematical treatises by various sources.[21]

Calcidius the Translator

Translation as a Commissioned Work

Calcidius does not comment extensively on his translation practice. The remarks we find scattered through his letter of dedication to Osius, the commentary, and, of course, the translation itself are the principal sources among the scarce material at our disposal regarding his methods and intentions as a translator. While studies that have focused on the philosophical aspects of Calcidius' work offer comments in passing about his literary style or his choice of individual expressions, there exist few examinations whose focus is directed exclusively upon his translation practice.[22] This is astonishing, not least because we find in Calcidius' translation a tendency to rephrase Plato's text in a manner that reveals a most interesting relationship with his exegesis in the commentary.

Osius' assignment had apparently comprised a translation of the *Timaeus* only, a task that, to Calcidius' knowledge, had not been attempted before: *op[us] intemptat[um] ad hoc tempus*, a view corroborated by the fact that we find no substantial parallels with Cicero's translation in Calcidius'

---

[20] Bakhouche 2011: 34–41.
[21] Bakhouche 2011: 29–30.
[22] Most recently, Bakhouche 2011: 107–20 has offered an analysis of Calcidius' grammar, style, and lexicon, set out against a number of passages taken from Cicero's text, in the introduction to her French edition of his work. Moreover, despite his main focus on Cicero, Puelma 1980 offers a number of insightful conclusions on Calcidius' translation practice.

work.[23] Calcidius' letter indicates that his dedicatee had planned to 'borrow' Plato's work from a Greek audience for Roman readers,[24] a sentiment in line with the linguistic development that had been taking place from the early centuries CE onwards. Greek proficiency in the Roman West had been on the decline since approximately the late second century, and Osius' commission falls into a period that saw a rising demand for Latin versions of Greek literature. Encouraged by the end of Christian persecution following the Edict of Milan in 312 CE, scholars of Christian faith increasingly participated in the theological and philosophical discussions of non-Christian authors,[25] eager to explore their adopted doctrine by way of an active engagement with the omnipresent non-Christian philosophical literature. The *Timaeus* attracted particular interest since the Platonic creation account and the assumption of a benevolent creator lent themselves well to a scholarly assertion of the Christian faith.

Translation and Commentary

Calcidius' assignment was to facilitate access to the dialogue's doctrine for a Roman readership. In the preface to the commentary he notes that any criticism[26] concerning the dialogue's difficulty is owing to the fact that Timaeus' account requires a familiarity with different types of technical jargon that are used by Timaeus[27] but are inaccessible to the

---

[23] *Contra* Ratkowitsch 1996.

[24] 'You had conceived in your mind the hope ... of seeing a work left unattempted until this time, and had decided that Latium should borrow it from Greece' (*conceperas animo ... spem proventuri operis intemptati ad hoc tempus eiusque usum a Graecis Latio statueras mutuandum*). Cal. *Ep. ad Os.* p. 133, ll. 8–11.

[25] Assuming a Christian identity for Osius. See also Waszink 1986: 53–4.

[26] Cal. *Comm. in Tim.* 1, 204, 1–3: 'Plato's *Timaeus* was held to be a difficult work to understand even by the ancients. But this was not because of weakness arising from the obscurity of its language – for what is more straightforward than Plato?' (*Timaeus Platonis et a veteribus difficilis habitus atque existimatus est ad intellegendum, non ex imbecillitate sermonis obscuritate nata – quid enim illo viro promptius?*).

[27] Ibid. 2, 204, 18–21: 'It was necessary to resort to all the subject-specific remedies of the various disciplines, to arithmetic, astronomy, geometry, and music,

layperson.[28] A Latin version of the dialogue, therefore, calls for an additional commentary that explains its contents in simplified terms: 'having approached the first parts of Plato's *Timaeus* ... I have not only translated [the text] (*transtuli*) but have, moreover, composed a commentary on the same parts, in the belief that a copy (*simulacrum*) of an obscure subject matter (*reconditae rei*) without the unfolding of an interpretation (*sine interpretationis explanatione*) would be rather more obscure than the model (*exemplo*) itself'.[29] Plato's Greek text, the *exemplum*, is illuminated not only by a translation, its *simulacrum,* but, moreover, by the commentary or 'the unfolding of an interpretation', *explanatio interpretationis*. As has been pointed out,[30] Calcidius creates a 'kinship' between his subject matter and his own exegetical project by likening the Greek original to the Platonic intelligible *exempla* or forms,

in order that the individual topics might be explained through related and cognate methods' (*cunctis certarum disciplinarum artificialibus remediis occurrendum erat, arithmeticis astronomicis geometricis musicis, quo singulae res domesticis et consanguineis rationibus explicarentur*). Calcidius in the preface deplores the fact that the technical and subject-specific passages of the *Timaeus* have been commented on by his own predecessors in an equally obscure and technical jargon, and thus remained inaccessible to those unversed in the particular sciences. Instead of granting to the unlearned audience access to the information provided in the dialogue, the explanations provided by other interpreters were equally obscure, by being aimed at 'those who are accustomed to using and applying all knowledge of this kind. While they should have communicated to others the considerable light of their knowledge, with detestable restraint caused by pitiable jealousy, they kept for themselves and did not communicate the stream of great beauty' (3, 206, 4–7: *qui in omnium fuerant huius modi scientiarum usu atque exercitatione versati; quos cum oporteret tantam scientiae claritudinem communicare cum ceteris, infelicis invidiae detestabili restrictione largae beatitudinis fusionem incommunicabilem penes se retinuerunt*). The fervour with which Calcidius criticizes those who wish to keep their knowledge under lock and key, and his own intention of remedying this deplorable situation by providing an interpretation of the dialogue that is accessible to the multitude, could be described as an ambition to open the doors to those still 'uninitiated' in the sciences and to render possible their ascent to Platonic doctrine. On this view, it is possible that Calcidius' understanding of his role as a commentator and a guide towards knowledge motivated him, in his translation of *Tim.* 28c3–5, to omit the reference to the πάντες, 'all people', who are unable to share in this wisdom. See below, p. 195 with n. 104.

[28] Ibid. 1, 204, 3–5.

[29] Ibid. *Ep. ad Os.* 133, 19–135, 2; discussed also by Dutton 2003: 189, and Reydams-Schils 2007a: 305.

[30] E.g. Dutton 2003: 189; Reydams-Schils 2007a: 305.

his translation to the forms' sensible *simulacra*.[31] As a consequence, his 'unfolding of an interpretation', the commentary, takes on the role of a go-between that elucidates for the reader the relation between the Greek and Latin texts.[32] A further, crucial point to take away is that Plato's text, the *exemplum*, is associated by Calcidius with a constant, steadfast, and irrefutable λόγος in a striking validation of Platonic doctrine (cf. *Tim* 29b2–c2).

Calcidius' methodology as a Platonic interpreter is thus a two-way project: on the one hand, he integrates from his translation into his commentary passages that guide the structure of his discussion; on the other, he modifies his Greek original text with the help of additions, omissions, and paraphrases intended to interpret, clarify, and disambiguate it even as he is translating.[33] As concerns the formal aspects of Calcidius' commentary, its structure corresponds by and large to that we encounter in other Latin philosophical commentaries of a similar date, as, for instance, in Macrobius' work on Cicero's *somnium Scipionis*.[34] Both commentaries follow, more or less consistently, a sequence that is outlined in their *prooemia*.[35]

---

[31] A 'kinship' that is demanded by Timaeus himself at *Tim*. 29b2, see e.g. A§1 (Table 21).

[32] This sentiment is repeated in the commentary (4, 206, 9–12) where Calcidius explains in similar terms: 'Not content with a translation alone, I reasoned that the translated image of an obscure and intransparent archetype, without an interpretation, would carry the same, or an even greater defect of obscurity' (*sola translatione contentus non fui ratus obscuri minimeque illustris exempli simulacrum sine interpretatione translatum in eiusdem aut etiam maioris obscuritatis vitio futurum*). Cf. also Dutton 2003: 189; cf. the conclusions drawn by Reydams-Schils 2007a: 313, who stresses the contrast between Calcidius' assertive authorial identity and the habit commonly displayed by Neoplatonic commentators of pledging allegiance to their masters and predecessors within the Platonist tradition.

[33] For further detail, cf. Bakhouche 2011: 27–30, 'Les rapport de la traduction au commentaire', who lists the citations of Plato's text (or rather, of Calcidius' translation thereof) in the commentary and discusses the space Calcidius dedicates to the various topics.

[34] Macrobius is thought to have written after 410 CE; an accurate dating and identification of his person remains difficult. Cf. Flamant 1977: 151–2. The extent of a mutual influence between Calcidius and Macrobius is uncertain. While Flamant recognizes numerous parallels, dogmatic and structural, between the two works, Waszink 1972: 238 assumes that both were simply drawing on a contemporary pool of exegetical vocabulary.

[35] Termed the 'prolegomena-scheme', as discussed in Reydams-Schils 2007a: 304. The same pattern, according to Reydams-Schils, is recognizable also in the prefaces to

Initially, Calcidius determines the genre of the ensuing treatise,[36] the particular circumstances of its composition[37] and
any characters concerned.[38] Furthermore, the commentator's
aim is revealed[39] and the order of the impending discussion
disclosed.[40] What follows is a lemmatic treatment of the source
text, with various focal points arranged and extended at the
writer's liberty. The paragraphs chosen for discussion may
be paraphrased in simplified language, with attention given
to particular sentences, expressions, or individual terms of
interest,[41] while specific topics can be discussed in the form of
a short treatise.[42]

Calcidius and the *Timaeus*

Calcidius' Timaean Methodology: The Εἰκὼς Λόγος *as a* Mediocris Explanatio

Calcidius' commentary provides an explanatory account,
ratio, a programmatic term that appears already in the preface

---

Christian exegetical works, for instance in Origen's *Cant. cant.* For a comprehensive
study of the methodologies in the ancient commentary tradition, cf. I. Hadot 1991,
Mansfeld 1994.

[36] In Calcidius' case, an account of natural science: 'Since, then, the subject of this
book is the constitution of the universe and an explanatory account of all things
embraced by the world is provided' (*in hoc porro libro cum de statu agatur universae
rei omniumque eorum quae mundus complectitur causa et ratio praestetur*, 2, 204,
14–15).

[37] The commentary is described as an addition to the translation of the *Timaeus*
commissioned by Osius, cf. ibid. 4, 206.

[38] Plato is mentioned in the very first sentence of Calcidius' preface. The context of
the dialogue as a discussion between Timaeus, Socrates, and the other characters is
mentioned at ibid. 6, 208–9.

[39] Explained by Calcidius in chapters 1 and 4. The commentary is an explanatory
account intended to elucidate the *obscuritas* of the dialogue caused by the specialist
language used by Plato.

[40] Ibid. 7, 208–10. Flamant 1977: 150–2 who, taking the example of Proclus' commentary on the *Timaeus*, describes this as the standard procedure displayed by
both grammatical and philosophical commentaries. The specific characteristic of a
grammatical commentary lies in the discussion proper of the given text, where short
phrases or individual words are discussed in contrast to the predominantly longer
passages chosen for discussion in philosophical texts.

[41] E.g. Calcidius' explanations concerning the astronomical vocabulary of *Tim.*
36a–d.

[42] As, for instance, in Calcidius' extensive discussions on fate, demons, and on
matter.

to the work: for Plato's dialogue, which treats of the status of the universe and all that is embraced within the cosmos, 'let an explanatory account be provided', *causa et ratio praestetur*.[43] To gain a better understanding of Calcidius' own perception of his role as an exegete, let us turn to his rendering of the methodological passage at *Tim.* 29b2–d3. This passage of his *Timaeus* translation, I shall argue, betrays his own reflections on his methodology as a commentator on and translator of Plato:

Table 21. *Plato*, Tim. *29b2–d3*

29b2	**A§1:** μέγιστον δὴ παντὸς ἄρξασθαι κατὰ φύσιν ἀρχήν. ὧδε οὖν περί τε εἰκόνος καὶ περὶ τοῦ παραδείγματος	**A§1:** Now, in regard to every matter it is most important to begin at the natural beginning. Accordingly, in the case of a likeness and its
5	αὐτῆς διοριστέον, ὡς ἄρα τοὺς λόγους, ὧνπέρ εἰσιν ἐξηγηταί, τούτων αὐτῶν καὶ συγγενεῖς ὄντας·	model, we ought to determine that the accounts bear a kinship to the subject matters of which they serve as exegetes.
29b5 10	**A§2a:** τοῦ μὲν οὖν μονίμου καὶ βεβαίου καὶ μετὰ νοῦ καταφανοῦς μονίμους καὶ ἀμεταπτώτους – καθ᾽ ὅσον οἷόν τε καὶ ἀνελέγκτοις προσήκει λόγοις εἶναι καὶ ἀνικήτοις,	**A§2a:** Therefore, accounts that deal with what is abiding and firm and discernible by the aid of thought will be abiding and unshakeable; and to the extent that it is possible and fitting for statements to be
15	τούτου δεῖ μηδὲν ἐλλείπειν –	irrefutable and invincible, they must in no wise fall short thereof;
29c1	**A§2b:** τοὺς δὲ τοῦ πρὸς μὲν ἐκεῖνο ἀπεικασθέντος, ὄντος δὲ εἰκόνος, εἰκότας ἀνὰ λόγον τε ἐκείνων ὄντας·	**A§2b:** whereas the accounts concerning that which has been fashioned in the likeness of that model, and which is itself a likeness, ought to be fashioned in a like manner and possess likelihood;

(*continued*)

---

[43] Cal. *Comm. in Tim.* 2, 204, 15–16. Somfai 2004: 204–20 interprets Calcidius' *ratio*, to which she attaches a programmatic significance, as a mathematical analogy. *Ratio* as an originally mathematical concept is described by her as the leading thread throughout Calcidius' commentary and applied by him to the structure and the contents of the work. Initially, Plato's mathematical analogy is set out with the help of diagrams; this concept is then transferred to his exegesis.

Table 21 (continued)

29c3	A§3: ὅτιπερ πρὸς γένεσιν οὐσία, τοῦτο πρὸς πίστιν ἀλήθεια.	A§3: for as being stands in relation to coming to be, so truth stands in relation to convincingness.
29c4 25 30	A§4: ἐὰν οὖν, ὦ Σώκρατες, πολλὰ πολλῶν πέρι θεῶν καὶ τῆς τοῦ παντὸς γενέσεως, μὴ δυνατοὶ γιγνώμεθα πάντῃ πάντως αὐτοὺς ἑαυτοῖς ὁμολογουμένους λόγους καὶ ἀπηκριβωμένους ἀποδοῦναι, μὴ θαυμάσῃς·	A§4: Therefore, Socrates, if in our extensive discussions regarding many topics, the gods and the generation of the universe, we are unable to provide accounts that are entirely and in every way self-consistent and perfectly exact, do not be surprised;
29c7 35	A§5: ἀλλ' ἐὰν ἄρα μηδενὸς ἧττον παρεχώμεθα εἰκότας, ἀγαπᾶν χρή, μεμνημένους ὡς ὁ λέγων ἐγὼ ὑμεῖς τε οἱ κριταὶ φύσιν ἀνθρωπίνην ἔχομεν, ὥστε περὶ τούτων τὸν εἰκότα μῦθον ἀπο – δεχομένους πρέπει τούτου μηδὲν ἔτι πέρα ζητεῖν.	A§5: rather we should be content if we can produce accounts that are inferior to none in likelihood, remembering that both I who speak and you who judge are but human creatures, so that it becomes us to accept the likely story of these matters and forbear to search beyond it.[44]

Table 22. Calcidius' translation (156, 19–158, 4) of Plato, Tim. 29b2–d3[45]

29b2 5	B§1: et quoniam rationem originis explicare non est facile factu, distinguendae sunt imaginis exemplique naturae. causae quae cur unaquaeque res sit ostendunt, earundem rerum consanguineae sunt.	B§1: Since it is not easy to set out the account of the origin [of the cosmos], we must distinguish between the nature of a copy and of a model. The reasons that show why each particular thing exists are akin to those things.
29b5 10	B§2a: ita constantis quidem generis stabilisque naturae intellectui prudentiaeque perspicuae rei causa et ratio constans perspicuaque et inexpugnabilis reperitur,	B§2a: Thus, the explanatory account of an object that is of a constant kind and stable nature and transparent to intellect and wisdom, is [itself] found to be constant, transparent, and irrefutable.

[44] Transl. Lamb, with modifications.
[45] 156, 19–158, 4.

Table 22 (*continued*)

29c1	**B§2b:** *at vero eius quae ad similitudinem constantis perpetuaeque rei facta est ratio, utpote imaginis imaginaria simulacrumque*	**B§2b:** But an account that is made in similarity to an object that is constant and eternal, since it is then an imitative account of an image and thus a copy of [the other type of]
20	*rationis, perfunctoriam similitudinem mutuatur.*	account, borrows mere perfunctory likeness.
29c3	**B§3:** *quantoque est melior essentia[46] generatione, tanto fama et opinionis incerto*	**B§3:** For to the same degree as being is better than generation, so the truth is better than rumour and the
25	*praestantior veritas.*	uncertainty of opinion.
29c4	**B§4:** *quare praedico iam nunc, Socrate: si, dum de natura universae rei disputatur,*	**B§4:** Thus, Socrates, I should now like to warn you: do not be surprised, in our discussion of the nature of the universe, if I should render accounts
30	*minime inconcussas inexpugnabilesque rationes afferre valuerim, ne miremini,*	that are of little steadfastness and reliability,

(*continued*)

---

[46] *essentia* is used in Calcidius' translation and commentary in alternation with *substantia*, without a difference in meaning, e.g. 'for an essence is something's substance' (*nam essentia quidem alicuius rei substantia est*, 325, 548, 27–8). Similarly, *substanti*[a] *sive, ut Cicero dicit, essenti*[a] (27, 234, 20–1) – cf. Sen. *Ep.* 58.6: [on *essentia*]: 'Cicero is my authority for this word' (*Ciceronem auctorem huius verbi habeo*). Calcidius uses these terms for the Greek οὐσία in the context of everlasting being as opposed to created time, with the exception of *Tim.* 37e5, where ἡ αἴδιος οὐσία is rendered *aevum*, but is subsequently paraphrased, in an inserted addition, as a *solitaria natura*, lacking the parts that are years, months, and days. These examples show that Calcidius employed *substantia* and *essentia* in the sense of *natura*, i.e. 'the essential nature of a thing', which links the analogy in **B§3** to his distinction between the *naturae* of model and copy in **B§1**. In the present context, *essentia* describes a constant and stable type of nature, which is contrasted with *generatio*, a 'partial' kind of existence. See also his description of Plato's characterization of the receptacle at 321, 316, 20f.: *naturam vero substantiam eius significat.* Cf. Moreschini 2003: 699. For Apuleius' use of the term *substantia*, cf. pp. 125–6.

Calcidius

Table 22 (*continued*)

29c7	**B§5:** *quin potius illud*	**B§5:** but, instead, pay attention
	intuere, si nihilo minus quam	to this, namely if I shall render
35	*quivis alius⁴⁷ consentaneas*	assumptions that are no less suitable
	assertiones afferam;	than those of another; for we
	memento enim tam me qui	must bear in mind that I, who am
	loquor quam vos qui iudicatis	speaking, and you, who are judging,
	homines fore atque in rebus	are human, and that, regarding
40	*ita sublimibus mediocrem*	objects of such sublimity, a mediocre
	explanationem magni	explanation [or perhaps: 'a mediocre
	cuiusdam esse onus laboris.	manner of setting out'] is [already]
		a burden that requires some great
		effort.

While Timaeus speaks of a method for '*every* matter' (παντός, A§1, l. 1), Calcidius describes his inquiry as 'the account of the origin' (*rationem originis*, **B§1**, ll. 1–2), seemingly implying the origin 'of the cosmos', which is the subject of the preceding sentence in the narrative, with παντός taken as the genitive of τὸ πᾶν, 'the All'. On this view, the ontological distinction between *exemplum* and *simulacrum* in this loose paraphrase of the Greek would apply to the subject matter at hand only, the sensible and the intelligible objects whose *natura* (**B§1**, l. 54) must be distinguished. Calcidius was perhaps encouraged in his focus on the *natura* of the model and the copy by the

⁴⁷ Calcidius' interpretation is an alternative to that chosen by Cicero and the majority of commentators, e.g. Bury 1960, Cornford 1937. H.D.P. Lee in his edition of the dialogue (1965) and Zeyl 2000 *ad loc*. Cf. *Tim.* 48d1–3: 'Holding on to what we said at the beginning, the authority of the likely account, I shall attempt to give an account that is no less likely than any other' (τὸ δὲ κατ' ἀρχὰς ῥηθὲν διαφυλάττων, τὴν τῶν εἰκότων λόγων δύναμιν, πειράσομαι μηδενὸς ἧττον εἰκότα ... λέγειν). In our present passage Calcidius understands ἐὰν ἄρα μηδενὸς ἧττον παρεχώμεθα εἰκότας not to say 'if we produce likelihoods inferior to nothing else', but takes μηδενός as masculine instead of neuter and connects μηδενὸς ἧττον not with the εἰκότας but with the predicate παρεχώμεθα, rendering *si nihilo minus quam quivis alius consentaneas assertiones afferam*: 'if I shall render assumptions that are no less suitable than those of another'. This interpretation has recently been argued for by Burnyeat 2009: 172, with n. 13 (following Taylor and Johansen), who considers a personal μηδενός to be in line with the emphasis Timaeus lays on his and his listeners' human nature in his subsequent statement (Burnyeat refers to Parmenides, fr. 8.60–1). I would add, in favour of the more common interpretation 'inferior (in their likelihood) to nothing else', that this reading may be intended to correspond, and to form a contrast to, μηδὲν ἔτι πέρα, 'nothing further beyond', at the close of the statement.

172

Greek κατὰ φύσιν (**A§1**, l. 1), which he may have thought to refer to the φύσις of model and copy respectively, in the sense of 'according to their ontological status'.

At this point, we recall that Calcidius previously, in his letter to Osius, identified the *exemplum* as Plato's Greek text, the *simulacrum* as his own translation. Between these, the unfolding of his commentary or exegesis, *explanatio interpretationis*, was to serve as the bridge which made possible a transition from the *simulacrum* to the *exemplum*. That the *explanatio interpretationis* is foremost in his mind also in the present passage becomes evident from his rendering of Timaeus' λόγοι (to be supplied from **A§1**, ll. 5–8, διοριστέον, ὡς ἄρα τοὺς **λόγους** ὧνπέρ εἰσιν ἐξηγηταί τούτων αὐτῶν καὶ συγγενεῖς ὄντας) with *causa et ratio* (**B§2a**, l. 12), an expression echoing Calcidius' definition of his commentary in the preface to the work: 'In this work, since it treats of the constitution (*status*) of the universe and of all things the cosmos comprises, let an explanatory account be provided (*causa et ratio praestetur*).'[48] It is his *commentary* that is referred to also in our methodology passage. At **B§2a**, l. 9, the suitable type of *causa et ratio*, or exegesis, must be chosen in accordance with the subject matter in question, and we recall that previously, in **B§1**, ll. 1–2, a *ratio originis*, an account of the origin of a particular *res*, in our case of the cosmos, must be unfolded or explained (*explicare*). As previously in this letter to Osius, Calcidius merges his roles as an exegete and narrator also in the present context.

At **B§2b** an 'account that is given regarding an object/subject matter made in likeness of a constant and eternal *res*' (*eius quae ad similitudinem constantis perpetuaeque rei facta est ratio*, **B§2b** ll. 15–8), and that is thus 'portraying an image' – in Calcidius' case, the *simulacrum* that is his translation, a copy of the *exemplum* that is Plato's dialogue – obtains a fleeting likeness,[49] *perfunctoriam similitudinem* (**B§2b**, ll. 20–1), an

---

[48] Cal. *Comm. in Tim.* 2, 204, 15.
[49] *perfunctorius* occurs in Calcidius in the senses of 'cursory', 'fleeting' (330, 556, 19), 'superficial' (in contrast to 'thorough', 142, 378, 25), and 'uncertain' (249, 478, 23).

Calcidius

expression that here renders εἰκότας λόγους and to which I shall return shortly.

At **B§5**, ll. 39–42, Calcidius evaluates his *explanatio* in relation to 'matters of great sublimity',[50] the latter expression rendering περὶ τούτων (**A§5**, l. 36) which refers back to πολλὰ πολλῶν πέρι, θεῶν καὶ τῆς τοῦ παντὸς γενέσεως (**A§4**, ll. 24–5), 'many topics, the gods and the generation of the universe', as the subject matter of Timaeus' account. The attribute *sublimis*, in the remainder of Calcidius' work, invariably and unsurprisingly, describes characters or objects of divine nature.[51] An example occurs in chapter 127, in the context of *Tim.* 40d7f., where Timaeus asserts that 'to discover and declare the origin of the other, subordinate divinities, is a task that lies beyond us'.[52] Calcidius interprets this statement by explaining that the sanctity and sublimity of the subject matter cannot be adequately addressed in the context of his present discussion of natural philosophy and requires, instead, an *inquisitio epoptica*:

[He says so not because] this exposition is unfitting for philosophers – whom else would it suit more? – but because the examination of this subject is the task of a reflection of prime and surpassing rank, [and such an examination is described as] *epoptica*. It is considerably more august than physics and therefore does not seem to be appropriate to us who are now treating the physical nature of things...[53]

It appears that an adequate discussion of the *res sublimes* Calcidius refers to at **B§5**, ll. 39–40, would be a discussion that is *epoptica*, to be separated from his discussion of physics. In order to appreciate his reasoning, it is necessary to elaborate further

The adjective appears in the works of fourth-century Christian writers, particularly Ambrosius.

[50] Calcidius omits the mention of the gods in **B§4**, cf. **A§4**, l. 24, likely with the intention of smoothing over the portrayal of a multitude of gods he may have considered problematic in view of Osius' Christian affiliations.

[51] E.g. Calcidius' paraphrase of *Phaedr.* 246e4–247a1 at the beginning of chapter 178 in his commentary, which describes Zeus as the *dux sublimis* heading the succession of divinities.

[52] περὶ δὲ τῶν ἄλλων δαιμόνων εἰπεῖν καὶ γνῶναι τὴν γένεσιν μεῖζον ἢ καθ' ἡμᾶς ...

[53] Cal. *Comm. in Tim.* 127, 364, 13–18: *dicit ... non quo disputatio haec a philosophis aliena sit – quibus enim aliis magis competat? sed quod inquisitio istius rei primariae supervectaeque contemplationis sit, quae appellatur epoptica, altior aliquanto quam physica, proptereaque nobis, qui de rerum natura nunc disputamus, nequaquam conveniens esse videatur.*

174

on the distinctions between the various sub-disciplines of philosophy and their position in the later Platonic curriculum. The philosophical disciplines had by Calcidius' time been organized into systematized strands of philosophical thinking. The Middle Platonists established a variation of the familiar division of philosophy into the three disciplines ethics, physics, and logic.[54] Picking up Aristotle's classification of subject matter, practical philosophy, i.e. ethics, was distinguished from the theoretical fields of theology, physics, and mathematics. As a result of this we find in some philosophical writers a separation of theology, the study of the divine, from physics as the study of the phenomena in the physical world only, with both disciplines considered two distinct subdivisions of theoretical philosophy.[55] Calcidius, accordingly, identifies physics as a part of theoretical philosophy but clearly distinguishes it from theology.[56]

We saw already in the context of Apuleius that a student's final stages of intellectual progress were likened to the initiation rites familiar from the Eleusinian mysteries.[57] It is theology

[54] The hierarchical ordering of the three disciplines varies. Xenocrates is credited by Sextus (*M.* 7.16 = fr. 1 IP 2012 = Test. 1 IP 1982) with the systematic division of philosophy into physics, ethics, and logic. Later philosophers such as Antiochus (cf. Cic. *Ac.* 1.19) and Apuleius (*DPD* 1.3) ascribe this classification to Plato himself. See also Plato, *Plt.* 258d4–6: ἆρ' οὖν οὐκ ἀριθμητικὴ μὲν καί τινες ἕτεραι ταύτῃ συγγενεῖς τέχναι ψιλαὶ τῶν πράξεών εἰσι, τὸ δὲ γνῶναι παρέσχοντο μόνον. Cf. P. Hadot 1995: 63–4; Dillon 1993: 57–8, 86. See further Ar. *Met.* 6.1,1026a18–20. Aristotle, however, places mathematics higher than physics, whereas Alcinous and Calcidius place mathematics at the lowest position.

[55] Cf. p. 107 above with n. 20. A thorough exposition of the various types of divisions of philosophical disciplines is P. Hadot 1982.

[56] *Comm. in Tim.* 264, 492, 24–5: 'it [i.e. *consideratio* or theoretical philosophy, as opposed to practical philosophy, *actus*, ibid. l. 20) is thus divided into three kinds: theology, the inquiry into nature, and the study of how to apply reason' (*dividitur porro haec trifariam, in theologiam et item naturae sciscitationem praestandaeque etiam rationis scientiam*). Reydams-Schils 2007a: esp. 314–19 suggests dividing Calcidius' work into three parts, mathematics (chapters 8–118), physics (119–267), and theology (268–355). This division corresponds to the didactic arrangement of the Platonist curriculum, in which the ascent to theology begins with mathematics, physics taking the intermediate position. The *Timaeus*, moreover, is considered by Calcidius as treating of a *iustitia naturalis*, as opposed to justice *in rebus humanis* that is established in the *Republic*, which is presented as the prequel to the *Timaeus* (described in chapter 6 of the commentary). See also Reydams-Schils 2002: 194.

[57] Cf. p. 107 n. 21; Bakhouche 2011: 729–30 with n. 51; Hadot 1982: 436. To my knowledge, Calcidius is the only Latin writer to have used the term *epoptica*, transliterated from the Greek.

that is assigned the specific type of investigation termed the *disputatio epoptica*, as encountered previously. The difference between accounts dealing with physics, on the one hand, and theology on the other, is explained further in the commentary at 272, 502, 1–3, where the *disputatio naturalis* is described as an 'image that shifts to some degree and is restricted to the kind of reliability associated with verisimilitude' (*ut imago nutans aliquatenus et in veri simili quadam stabilitate contenta*), whereas the *epoptical* discussion 'flows out from the source of the purest knowledge of things' (*ex sincerissimae rerum scientiae fonte manat*).

From this we can draw several inferences for the present context of **B§5**. Calcidius' rendering *mediocris explanatio* (Table 22, ll. 40–1) for Timaeus' εἰκὼς μῦθος (Table 21, **A§5**, ll. 36–7) qualifies his treatment of this part[58] of the *Timaeus* as 'intermediate', most likely in view of the subordinate status of physics in relation to the subject of theology. What is more, the *mediocris explanatio* links up to Calcidius' previous rendering of εἰκότας λόγους at *Tim.* 29c2 (**A§2b**, l. 18), where *perfunctoria similitudo* (**B§2b**, ll. 20–1) is described as the result of such accounts as treat of 'copies'. His discussion of natural philosophy, a *disputatio naturalis*, which discusses the image that is the physical world (cf. *imaginaria*[59] [*ratio*] in **B§2b**, ll. 19–20), can achieve the reliability of likelihood (*veri similis stabilitas*, 272, 502, 2–3) only. In contrast to a *disputatio epoptica*, which reveals true knowledge, it is a mere *mediocris explanatio* that possesses fleeting similarity to the former type of account.

Calcidius associates the λόγοι or types of exposition distinguished by Timaeus with the various types of exegesis

---

[58] In turn, a heavy emphasis on mathematics and its subdisciplines arithmetics, geometry, music, and astronomy is visible at the outset of his commentary. Calcidius considers these disciplines to serve a preparatory function. Cf. Somfai 2003: 130–1.

[59] Calcidius elaborates on ἐκεῖνο at **A§2b**, l. 17, whose meaning in the Greek is not explicit, filling in *constan[s] perpetu[a]que re[s]. imaginis* seems to capture ὄντος δὲ εἰκόνος. The attribute *perfunctoria* reinforces the effect achieved by the expression *similitudo*. While the Greek implies that accounts of what is unstable and subject to change are likenesses of those accounts treating of stable and constant matters, Calcidius reasons that the likenesses contained by the former are not only mere likenesses but, moreover, *superficial* and *perfunctory* likenesses.

that set out the different philosophical disciplines or fields of inquiry. More precisely, he interprets Timaeus' concern to locate the discussion of the universe's creation on a different epistemological plane from that of a λόγος concerning the intelligible sphere, as a concern to distinguish those contexts in his commentary that deal with natural philosophy, covered by a *disputatio naturalis*, from others treating of metaphysics, to be covered in a *disputatio epoptica*.[60] Calcidius' interpretation of *Tim*. 29b2–d3 thus incorporates the systematizing methodology of later Platonists into the dialogue itself, thereby incidentally claiming Plato's authority for the structuring of the later Platonic curriculum. Overall, the fact that we encounter in Calcidius' translation an episode of self-reflection upon the scope and character of his task as a commentator shows the intrinsic connection between his identity as a translator, on the one hand, and his identity as a commentator, on the other.

The Creation of the Cosmos

I will approach Calcidius' views on the creation of the universe in several steps. Initially, I return to the specific role of natural philosophy as a part of the Platonic curriculum, a subject I have touched upon already in the preceding section. I then give a cursory account of exegetical viewpoints in other authors who show a similarity with Calcidius' position, before examining those chapters and passages in his commentary that are relevant to our understanding of his exegetical stance. Finally, turning to his translation of the dialogue proper, I discuss the manner in which Calcidius' philosophical mindset and his views on the creation of the universe are reflected in his Latin version of the text.

We saw previously that the Platonist tradition considered natural philosophy a discipline that was separate from theology. We saw, moreover, that Calcidius associated with

---

[60] These would presumably have included Calcidius' discussion of the *intellegibilis deus*, which he had apparently envisaged, as suggested by the proposed outline Calcidius offers in chapter 7 of his commentary (7, 210, 5).

both fields of inquiry a specific genre of discussion. Physics was dealt with in a *disputatio naturalis*, while a *disputatio epoptica* was reserved for theological matters. Calcidius, we recall, represents Timaeus' εἰκὼς λόγος, in the context of the methodology passage *Tim.* 29b2–d3, first and foremost as a *disputatio naturalis*, while himself branching out in his commentary to deal also with matters pertaining to theology, such as the cosmological ἀρχαί. In associating the *Timaeus* (and other dialogues) with a specific discipline of the Platonic curriculum, Calcidius ascribes to Plato a pedagogical agenda that is reflected in the systematic progress towards theology. At 272, 500, 35–502, 2 in his commentary, for instance, he credits Plato with the intentional separation of physics and thereby accounts for the fact that the narrator does not, in the context of his exposition on the origin of the four elements (*Tim.* 48c2–4), discuss their paradigmatic forms since such a discussion would touch upon intelligible form (as the original principle(s) of the universe),[61] something we see Plato doing in his *Parmenides*, for instance. Calcidius explains that the reason why Plato does not discuss these matters at present was not an intention to avoid the effort (*declinandi laborem*) this would require, but his intention 'not to add a discussion that is unsuitable to the account upon which we have entered. For this [present one] is a *disputatio naturalis*, the other type a *disputatio epoptica*.'

Calcidius shows himself aware of the particular role the *Timaeus* is given within the Platonism of his time. In his commentary, he alludes to a programmatic order of disciplines, associated with specific dialogues of Plato, that encourages and makes possible the student's progress towards wisdom. The *Timaeus* is explained by him as the sequel to the *Republic* inasmuch as the latter establishes 'justice that concerns human affairs' (*quae versaretur in rebus humanis*) and is therefore a

---

[61] Ibid. 272, 500, 30–4: 'at this point he does not ask ... if there is a single archetypal form that is common to all things that exist, or if there are countless ones ... or if the same thing is both one and many, as he teaches in the *Parmenides*' (*unane sit archetypa species eorum quae sunt communis omnium, an innumerabiles ... an vero idem unum partier et multa sint, ut docet in Parmenide*).

contemplatio positivae[62] *iustitiae*, while the former is an 'investigation into natural justice and equity', *naturalis iustitiae
atque aequitatis* [*contemplatio*].[63] While the *Republic* offers an
examination of political and ethical content, the next level on
the ascending ladder of a Platonist's expertise was to appreciate a higher form of justice pertaining not to the immediate human political environment, but to the kind of justice
current among the divine races in the city or state shared by
all, so to speak, of this sensible world ([*iustitia*] *qua divinum
genus*[64] *adversum se utitur in mundi huius sensilis veluti quadam
communi urbe ac re publica*).[65] Calcidius' commentary is a
witness to the progress from ethics to physics and theology, a
development he associates with the *Republic*, the *Timaeus*, and
the *Parmenides*.[66] As we turn to the views Calcidius expresses
on the topic of creation in his commentary, we will find that
he ascribes to Plato himself the idea of an ascending hierarchy
of disciplines that corresponds to the various stages within a
student's intellectual development.[67] Crucially, the fact that
Calcidius perceived in Plato's writings a concern to accommodate varying levels of expertise will be of significance as we
turn to examine his interpretation of Plato's views regarding
the createdness of the cosmos.

Against the backdrop of the continuous expansion of
Christian doctrine, this very topic remained of central import-
ance in the fourth- to fifth-century melting pot of Middle/
Neoplatonist, Christian, and Jewish intellectual thought
that Calcidius undoubtedly witnessed.[68] We saw earlier that
Apuleius was comfortable to use 'creative' terminology while

---

[62] I remain perplexed by Calcidius' use of the term *positiva* in the present context. It appears to describe justice in a political setting.
[63] 6, 206, 29–208, 3.
[64] Calcidius refers here to the demons who dwell in the various spheres of the physical cosmos and are thus subject of a *disputatio naturalis*.
[65] Cal. *Comm. in Tim.* 6, 208, 7–9.
[66] Cf. Reydams-Schils 2007a esp. 314–19.
[67] The ascribing to Plato of pedagogical considerations in the context of a student's intellectual development may have been inspired by passages such as Plato's *Rep.* 521c1–8. Cf. P. Hadot 1982: 435–6.
[68] It should be remembered that creation in the Judaeo-Christian tradition usually involved the idea of a creator god who created also the matter from which he formed the All, in other words, a *creatio ex nihilo*. See, however, Sorabji 1983: 194–5.

following, overall, a non-temporal reading of the dialogue. Similarly, in the Middle Platonic work *Didaskalikos*, the author's language[69] initially appears to describe a temporal creation. At 14.3, 1–4, however, he clarifies: 'When [Plato] says that the world is generated (γενητόν), one must not understand him to assert that there ever was a time when the world did not exist; but rather that the world is always in a state of coming to be, and reveals a more primordial cause of its own existence.'[70] He thus provides the temporal narrative of Timaeus' creation account before advising the reader to decode it in non-temporal terms. His interpretation can be aligned with the third and fourth possible meanings of the term γενητός advanced by Taurus: (3) something that is γενητός is something that is eternally subjected to the process of coming to be and change; and (4) something γενητός is something whose existence is dependent on something external.[71]

We encounter a Neoplatonic perspective in the work of Macrobius, writing in the fifth century. Addressing the issue in his *Commentarii in somnium Scipionis*, Macrobius presents a stance according to which the creator god – with any aspect of temporality being rejected – is the 'maker' of the world which has always existed (*conditore quidem deo, sed non ex tempore*).[72] An important influence on Macrobius' position, in turn, was Porphyry. In his *Sententia* 14, Porphyry, intending to render compatible the ideas of createdness and imperishability, distinguishes two different meanings of γενέσθαι: (1) 'to be dependent on a cause' and (2) 'to be composed from various parts'.[73]

---

[69] With clear reference to the *Timaeus*, 12.1, 8–10: 'It is necessary that also the most beautiful structure, the cosmos, has been built by the god' (ἀναγκαῖον καὶ τὸ κάλλιστον κατασκεύασμα τὸν κόσμον ὑπὸ τοῦ θεοῦ δεδημιουργῆσθαι). Cf. 12.2, 1; 12.2, 8–13.
[70] Transl. Dillon 1993 with minor modifications.
[71] Cf. pp. 27–8 and see Dillon 1993 *comm. ad loc.*
[72] *Somn. Scip.* 2.10, 9; for further parallels between Macrobius and Calcidius, cf. Waszink and Jensen 1962: xxxvii; cf. further Galonnier 2009: 197.
[73] 'Corporeal things come to be in two [different] ways. They come to be as [things] dependent upon a cause that brings them forth, and as compounds' (τὰ μὲν οὖν

Returning to Calcidius himself, we find him addressing the creation of the cosmos in chapter 23 of his commentary, where he explains Plato's programmatic design of the dialogue. In order to make sound a view that goes against the common beliefs of men (*ut huic quod est praeter opinionem hominum medeatur*), namely that the cosmos, despite having been created (*factum*) and thus being liable to destruction, cannot be undone (*indissolubilem*), Plato offers an array of arguments: 'he explains by whom [the world] was created, out of which [components] it is made, with reference to what pattern it has been built, for what reason, and to what extent it persists through eternity' (*dicit a quo factus sit, ex quibus constet, ad quod exemplum institutus, qua de causa, quatenus aeternitati propagatus*, 23, 230, 4–6). We note the didactic design Calcidius perceives in Plato's dialogue. Since the latter advances the position that the cosmos is imperishable despite its createdness, two characteristics held by many to be incompatible, he issues a battery of arguments to facilitate their understanding.[74]

Regarding the question 'by whom [the world] was created' (*a quo factus sit*), Calcidius explains that a thing's origin determines whether it is perishable or everlasting. Three possible origins are named: things are created by god, by nature, and by humans imitating nature. Those created by nature have a temporal beginning and are subject to a temporal and perishable existence (as are, by inference, those created by humans, an option Calcidius drops in the remainder of his discussion) since the coming to be of nature and of time are the same and simultaneous (*quorum omnium ortus in tempore; par enim et aequaevum natale naturae ac temporis*).[75] Unlike in the case of nature's creations, the origin and beginning of god's works

---

σώματα διχῶς γενητὰ καὶ ὡς ἀπ᾽ αἰτίας ἠρτημένα τῆς παραγούσης καὶ ὡς σύνθετα). See Galonnier 2009: 194–5 and see also Brisson's commentary in vol. 2 of his 2005 edition of Porphyry's *Sententiae*, 422–6 (cf. 1.312–15). Cf. Aristotle's criticism at *Cael.* 1.10, 279b12–13; 280a28–30.

[74] Cf. Baltes 1976: 176–7.

[75] Cal. *Comm. in Tim.* 23, 230, 10–11, 74, 5; Philop. *Aet. mund.* 26; cf *Tim.* 37d5–7, 38b6.

cannot be grasped. There is no certain indication of a time from which his works may have originated (*dei operum origo et initium incomprehensibile; nulla est enim certa nota, nullum indicium temporis ex quo esse coeperunt*).[76] All there is, at best, is a 'cause' (cf. *Tim.* 29d7, αἰτία) that explains their existence; a cause that, just as seeds (*semina*)[77] are the foundations (*fundamenta*) of things created by nature, is the foundation of things created by god. This cause, however, while manifest (*perspicu[a]*) to divine providence, is barely fathomable [by us] (*haec* [causa] *ipsa vix intellegitur*).[78] In other words, the *semina* are the foundations for the coming to be of all physical objects, while specific 'causal impulses', *causae*, are the foundation of works created by god, as opposed to works created by nature. Calcidius is concerned to show that there is, as it were, an intelligible equivalent to the seeds that appear in the natural world, the intelligible *causa*, an ontological impulse responsible for the existence of divine creations.

Since god is before the construction of time (the latter being a *simulacrum* of eternity) and throughout eternity (*ante institutionem temporis et per aevum*), the causes of his works, accordingly, are 'prior (*antiquiores*) to time' and, as god is throughout eternity, so are the causes of his works. As a consequence (*quod sequitur*), Calcidius infers, god's *creation* is likewise non-temporal (*quicquid a deo fit temporarium non sit*),[79] and since it is not subject to the laws of time (*nulla temporis lege teneatur*), it remains unaffected by age, illness, and death. Its origin is 'causative', not temporal: *origo ... eius causativa*

[76] Cal. *Comm. in Tim.* 23, 230, 13–15. Cf. also Aug. *Conf.* 11.30.
[77] Apuleius at *De mundo* 36 makes reference to *semina* (translating σπέρματα) that will bring about various types of vegetation, an analogy to god's power working indirectly and from afar. Cf. p. 148 n. 135, and see also pp. 247–9.
[78] Cal. *Comm. in Tim.* 23, 230, 15–16. This statement may be the reason why Calcidius fails to address the question *qua de causa* the cosmos was created, whilst addressing 'by whom it is made' (*a quo factus sit*, ch. 23), 'what it consists of' (*ex quibus constet*, 24), 'after which model it has been built' (*ad quod exemplum institutus*, 25), and 'how far it is propagated to eternity' (*quatenus aeternitati propagatus*, 25), also addressed in chapter 28, where the universe's everlastingness is presented as a consequence of its being created by a god who is 'before the creation of time and throughout eternity' (*ante institutionem temporis et per aevum*).
[79] Cf. Galonnier 2009: 203.

est, non temporaria. In other words, the origin of our universe, a work of god, must be understood in terms of causal dependence. Despite its corporeal nature, the sensible cosmos possesses everlastingness since it was made by god (*sic mundus sensilis, licet et corporeus, a deo tamen factus atque institutus, aeternus est*). With regard to the specific aspect of temporality, Calcidius, in the present chapter, has established that the universe does not participate in a temporal framework. The terms 'created' (*factus est*/γέγονεν) and 'origin' (*origo*/ἀρχή) are clearly interpreted in a non-temporal manner.

In chapter 25 of the commentary,[80] Calcidius – still concerned with elucidating Plato's reasoning in support of the universe's combined characteristics of createdness and everlastingness – identifies the model 'according to which the cosmos has been created' (*ad quod exemplum institutus*) and explains how, despite having been created, the world persists through eternity (*quatenus*[81] *aeternitati propagatus*). Identifying as a crucial characteristic of the model its 'immutable everlastingness' (*immutabilis perennita*[s]), Calcidius explains further: since the cosmos is fashioned after a model that is 'everlasting' (*ad similitudinem ... exempli sempiterni*) it must itself 'possess what resembles perpetual existence' (*habere similitudinem perpetuitatis*). Further, since perpetuity exists in eternity (*perpetuitas in aevo*), the intelligible cosmos exists through eternity (*intelligibilis mundus per aevum*); the sensible cosmos persists through time (*per tempora*). It is characteristic

---

[80] The chapter is closely modelled after *Tim.* 37, a passage of the dialogue to which I shall turn in due course. I omit the discussion of *ex quibus constet*, a further explanation Plato offers, according to Calcidius, in support of the universe's everlastingness. In chapter 24 of the commentary, Calcidius explains how the various cold and hot elements that make up the world's body are contained within it in their entirety, thereby leaving no traces outside the cosmos that could potentially harm it (*quae quia omnia corpora partim frigida partim calida sunt, nulla importuna frigoris calorisve extrinsecus accessione moveant aegritudinem mundo; igitur extra necessitatem incommodi positus **aeternus est**,* 24, 230, 32–232, 2). Cf. Baltes 1976: 174.

[81] Calcidius uses *quatenus* in his translation as an equivalent for either πῶς (21d7) or ἢ (27d2). Accordingly, in the commentary the predominant sense is 'how' or 'to what extent' (e.g. 28, 234, 32: *quatenus ergo bimembris est natura*, 59, 274, 9–10: *quatenus igitur est mundi forma teres et globosa*). The term never appears in Calcidius in a temporal sense ('how long').

183

Calcidius

of time to progress (*temporis proprium progredi*); to remain and to persevere in its own being is characteristic of eternity (*aevi propria mansio*[82] *semperque in idem perseveratio*). Time consists of parts, the days, nights, months, and years; eternity is without parts. The aspects of time (*temporis species*) are the past, the present, and the future, while the essence of eternity is uniform (*aevi substantia uniformis*) and unitarily and perpetually present (*solo perpetuoque praesenti*).[83] The intelligible cosmos always 'is', its image always has been, is, and will be (*semper fuit est erit*).[84]

A note on Calcidius' vocabulary: throughout chapter 25, he associates with the 'intelligible world' (*intellegibilis mundus*) the terms *sempiternus*, *perennitas*,[85] and *perpetuitas*; with the created universe, in turn, *aeternitas*. Overall in his commentary, however, Calcidius is inconsistent in his application of these terms to things uncreated and imperishable, things created and perishable, and objects that are created yet imperishable, such as the world soul, the universe, the lesser divinities, and human souls. *Sempiternus* is applied to the intelligible model (339, 564, 31) and to human souls (201, 430, 7–8), *perennitas* at 201, 430, 12 appears to be associated, in contrast to its application to the intelligible model in chapter 25, with things subjected to temporality; moreover, it is contrasted with immortal existence.[86] *Perpetuitas* and its cognates are linked to *aevum*, eternity (101, 336, 1–2) and human souls (187, 418, 2; 225, 454, 27). *Aeternitas* and its cognates, on the other hand, describe the created universe also at 150, 384, 25, as well as the human soul's movement (225, 454, 19). *Aeternus* is, however, applied

[82] Regarding *mansio*, see *Didask.* 14.6, 4–6: 'he created time as the interval of the motion of the world, as an image of eternity, which is the measure of the stability of the eternal world' (transl. Dillon) (τὸν χρόνον ἐποίησε τῆς κινήσεως τοῦ κόσμου διάστημα, ὡς ἂν εἰκόνα τοῦ αἰῶνος, ὅς ἐστι μέτρον τοῦ αἰωνίου κόσμου τῆς μονῆς). Cf. Bakhouche 2011 *comm. ad loc.*
[83] Cf. *Tim.* 37e1–6.
[84] Cal. *Comm. in Tim.* 25, 232, 10–19.
[85] See also Apuleius, *DPD* 1.10, 201: 'the nature of eternity is fixed and without motion' (*perennitatis fixa et immota natura est*).
[86] '... [his providence] propagated immortality to divine and eternal beings, but sempiternity to those with a temporal existence' (*divinis quidem et aeternis immortalitatem propagans, temporariis vero perennitatem*).

184

to the divine intellect at 176, 408, 26: 'god's intellect is eternal, therefore god's intellect is the eternal act of understanding' (*est mens dei aeterna: est igitur mens dei intellegendi aeternus actus*). At 330, 556, 9, moreover, god's intellect is identified with the Platonic *idea* and given the same description, *aeternus*. The only tentative conclusion one might draw from all this is that, with the exception of *perennitas* at 201, 430, 12, where it is connected with things that are *temporaria* and thus presumably perishable, all terms serve to evoke an object's everlastingness and imperishability, regardless of its ontological status.

Let us return for a moment to chapter 25. Initially, Calcidius' explicit linking of the created universe with temporal exist-ence (*per tempora*) sits oddly with chapter 23 which, as shown above, concludes that the sensible cosmos, being a work of god, is *not* temporal (*quicquid a deo fit temporarium non sit*, 23, 230, 22–3). How can we account for this apparent contra-diction in Calcidius' exegesis?[87] One possible clue is given in the continuation of the statement just cited: 'whatever comes to be through the making of god is non-temporal, and that which is non-temporal is not bound by any law of time' (*quicquid a deo fit temporarium non sit, **quod temporarium non sit, nulla temporis lege teneatur***). It is possible that the meaning of *temporarium* in chapter 23 expresses an object's suscepti-bility to the specific conditions of a temporal existence that arise in a physical body: change, deterioration, and destruc-tion. These do *not* apply to objects created by the demiurge. His creation may exist *per tempora*; it is, however, not 'tem-poral' (*temporarium*), but *aeternum, sempiternum*, and *per-petuum*, all of which are terms that, as we have seen, denote 'everlasting' without a necessary attachment to the intelligible sphere. Admittedly, to refer to the deity's creation as *aeternum*

---

[87] Calcidius' contradictory phrasing is the focus of Galonnier 2009, who concludes that there appears to be a missing step in the exegetical content of chapters 23–5. He suggests that a position such as that of Augustine, who propounds a 'double creation' – one that was atemporal and of intelligible matter and another, temporal one, of the physical universe (cf. Chapter 5) – would make sense of Calcidius' statements. While Galonnier offers many helpful insights, it seems to me unnecessary to trouble Augustine in order to account for Calcidius' train of thought.

and 'non-temporal' (*non temporaria*) while, at the same time, describing it as existing 'through time' (*per tempora*), does little to further Calcidius' aim of elucidating the *obscuritas* of Platonic doctrine. Nevertheless, the classification, which eventually emerges from Calcidius' exegesis, of the cosmos as an object that is 'created' (*factum*) and '[exists] through time' (*per tempora*), but is *aeternum* (in the basic sense of 'everlasting'), captures, more or less, the familiar interpretation of the Timaean universe as created, yet everlasting and imperishable (cf. Ar. *Cael.* 1.10, 279b12–13; 280a28–30). With this in mind, let us turn to the corresponding passage in the Latin translation.

At *Tim.* 37d–38c, Timaeus famously depicts the creation of the universe as coinciding with that of time. Following the creation of the world soul, the demiurge intended to make his creation yet more closely resemble, as far as he was able to, its intelligible model. More specifically, with the model possessing eternal existence (τυγχάνει ζῷον ἀίδιον ὄν, 37d1), he sought to reproduce this property, as far as he was able to, also in the universe (καὶ τόδε τὸ πᾶν οὕτως εἰς δύναμιν ἐπεχείρησε τοιοῦτον ἀποτελεῖν). Calcidius renders: 'just as the divine model (*haec*)[88] was immortal and everlasting (*immortalis et sempiterna*, translating ἀίδιον), he likewise constructed the sensible world to be an immortal animal' (*sic mundum quoque sensibilem animal immortale constituit*, 168, 12–14 [*immortale* rendering τοιοῦτον). The omission of *sempiternum*, previously attached

[88] The statement in Greek, starting from *Tim.* 37c6, reads 'when the father, after generating it, perceived that it was moving and alive, come to be as a thing of joy to the other gods, he rejoiced and, in his delight, intended to make it resemble the paradigm even more. Accordingly, then, since the model is an eternal living being …' (ὡς δὲ κινηθὲν αὐτὸ [i.e. the sensible universe, cf. Cornford 1937: 97 n. 2] καὶ ζῶν ἐνόησεν τῶν ἀιδίων θεῶν γεγονὸς ἄγαλμα ὁ γεννήσας πατήρ, ἠγάσθη τε καὶ εὐφρανθεὶς ἔτι δὴ μᾶλλον ὅμοιον πρὸς τὸ παράδειγμα ἐπενόησεν ἀπεργάσασθαι. καθάπερ οὖν αὐτὸ τυγχάνει ζῷον ἀίδιον ὄν …). I take Calcidius' *haec* to refer to the *immortalis divinitas* (168 ll. 10–11), which seems to be his rendering for τῶν ἀιδίων θεῶν, by which, apparently, he means the intelligible model. ἄγαλμα is interpreted by Calcidius as denoting 'statue', 'likeness', rather than the frequently chosen rendering 'a thing of joy', 'a delight', or 'shrine for the eternal gods'. Cf. e.g. Cornford 1937 *ad loc.*, but see Brisson 2001: 'Or, quand le père qui l'avait engendré constata que ce monde, qui est une représentation des dieux éternels …'. Calcidius thus identifies the ἄγαλμα with the *simulacrum*, the sensible universe.

186

to the model, as a characteristic also of the sensible world may suggest that Calcidius wished to illustrate the different types of immortality attached to the intelligible paradigm, which is by nature ἀΐδιον, and the copy, which turns out to be 'immortal', or everlasting, owing to the creator's will only. We should bear in mind, however, that his inconsistent use of *sempiternus* in the commentary, where the term describes the everlasting yet created human souls (e.g. 201, 430, 7–8), recommends caution. Overall, the Latin statement ascribes 'immortality' to both model and copy, and a differentiation between the two appears to be de-emphasized by Calcidius' omission of εἰς δύναμιν. The same impression, however, does not arise in the subsequent statement.

At 37d3, Timaeus explains that the god's intentions were limited by the fact that the property of eternal existence (ἡ ... φύσις ἐτύγχανεν οὖσα αἰώνιος)[89] could not be fully attached to the copy he had generated (τοῦτο μὲν δὴ τῷ γεννητῷ παντελῶς προσάπτειν οὐκ ἦν δυνατόν). Calcidius paraphrases: 'The animal, however – the one that contained all other animals [i.e. the intelligible paradigm] – is on a par, in its nature, with eternity' (*sed animal quidem, id quod est generale*[90] *animal, natura aevo exaequatur*). Given its attachment to the paradigm, the subsequent association of eternity, in turn, also with the *product* that has been created and has come to be, is unsuitable (*unde facto nativoque operi cum aevo societas congruere*

---

[89] Note Plato's use of both ἀΐδιος and αἰώνιος to describe the intelligible model; αἰώνιος is attached, moreover, to time at *Tim.* 37d7. Cf. Cornford 1937: 98 n. 1.

[90] Bakhouche 2003: 11 with n. 7 points to *TLL* col. 1776 for *generale* as denoting *ad nativitatem pertinens*. This solution, however, runs into difficulties in the very next sentence: *unde facto nativoque operi cum aevo societas congruere minime videbatur*, where no sense can be made of *unde*, as Bakhouche readily admits (n. 8). I suggest that *generale* refers to the 'generic' model that contains in itself all other animals, with *generale* signifying the antonym of *speciale* (cf. *Tim.* 30c4–8, where μέρος is described as something that is *speciale*). The same viewpoint is expressed clearly, for instance, in William of Conches' commentary on Calcidius' work: '*id animal quod est generale', id est archetipus mundus, quia omnia ex eo generantur* (*Glos. sup. Plat.* 1.94, 39), which is noted in Bakhouche 2011 *comm. ad loc.* According to this interpretation, the ensuing statement – 'for this reason (*unde*), the association with eternity of the product that has been created and has come to be appeared unsuitable' – expresses the *consequence* resulting from (*unde*) the association of *aevum* with the paradigm, the fact that this type of everlastingness cannot likewise be attached to the *simulacrum*.

minime videbatur, 168, 14–15). It seems Calcidius did not have at his disposal a suitable equivalent to reproduce in a single adjective the etymological link between αἰών and αἰώνιος, thus resorting to the paraphrase 'is on a par, in its nature, with eternity', *natura aevo exaequari*.[91]

Instead, Timaeus continues, the demiurge contrived to produce 'some moving image of eternity' (εἰκὼ δ' ἐπενόει κινητόν τινα αἰῶνος ποιῆσαι, 37d5). Thus, when setting up the ordered heaven, he produced an everlasting image of unchanging, self-same eternity, an image that progressed according to number (καὶ διακοσμῶν ἅμα οὐρανὸν ποιεῖ μένοντος αἰῶνος ἐν ἑνὶ κατ' ἀριθμὸν ἰοῦσαν αἰώνιον εἰκόνα). This image, we call by the name of 'time' (τοῦτον ὃν δὴ χρόνον ὠνομάκαμεν). The Latin runs as follows: 'For this reason, the god attached to the construction built by him a moving image of it that proceeds according to number and is called "time"' (*quapropter imaginem eius mobilem numeroque serpentem factae a se machinae* [presumably corresponding to οὐρανὸν] *deus sociabat eam quae tempus dicitur*, 168, 16–17). It appears that Calcidius reads the phrase μένοντος αἰῶνος ἐν ἑνί as a genitive absolute: '[an image that proceeds according to number and is called time], with eternity remaining unharmed and per-severing in unity' ([... *eam quae tempus dicitur*], *aevo intacto et in singularitate perseverante*, 168, 17–18), instead of taking it as the genitive object of εἰκόνα, '[a picture] of immutable and selfsame eternity'.[92] αἰώνιον, this time attached by Timaeus to the εἰκών instead of the model, is thus omitted by Calcidius, possibly also for the purpose of minimizing the impression that both animals partake of the same type of everlastingness, which is, indeed, the impression given by the Greek.

Timaeus continues at 38b6: 'time has come to be with the heaven (μετ' οὐρανοῦ γέγονεν), in order that, having come to be simultaneously, they would also dissolve simultaneously'. Moreover, time was generated according to the pattern of eternal nature (κατὰ τὸ παράδειγμα τῆς διαιωνίας φύσεως, 38b8), in order that it be as similar to it as possible. While the

<hr/>

[91] Calcidius employs the same rendering for τῆς διαιωνίας ... φύσεως at 39e1–2.
[92] Cf. Bakhouche 2003: 10–12.

model exists throughout all eternity (πάντα αἰῶνά ἐστιν ὄν), its image exists throughout all time (διὰ τέλους τὸν ἅπαντα χρόνον), having come to be, being in the present, and set to be in the future (γεγονώς τε καὶ ὢν καὶ ἐσόμενος).

Calcidius translates: 'Time is coeval (*aequaevum*) with heaven (*caelo*), in order that, having come to be simultaneously (*una orta*), they would be dissolved simultaneously.' He continues at 38b7: 'Likewise, [time is coeval with heaven] in order that both worlds [i.e. intelligible and sensible] correspond to the pattern of everlasting existence [i.e. to the specific type of ever-lasting existence that is suitable for them]. The model, indeed, is always existent in all eternity, and this sensible world, its image, of such a kind as to have been and to be in the future, throughout all time' (*simul ut aevitatis exemplo similis esset uterque mundus, archetypus quippe omni aevo semper existens est, hic sensibilis imagoque eius est qui per omne tempus fuerit, quippe et futurus sit*, 168, 29–170, 1).[93]

κατὰ τὸ παράδειγμα τῆς διαιωνίας φύσεως, 'according to the pattern of the eternal nature', is captured by *ut aevitatis exemplo*[94] *similis esset uterque mundus*, 'in order that both worlds [i.e. intelligible and sensible] correspond to the pattern of everlasting exist-ence'. *Aevitas*,[95] a thing's 'everlasting existence', may refer to both types of everlastingness, the eternity of the intelligible cosmos and the sempiternity of the sensible cosmos. Rather than setting out, like the Greek, the correlation between the intelligible model and its sensible copy, Calcidius' text correlates both model and

---

[93] Note that Calcidius omits ὢν at 38c3, possibly with a view to 37e5–38a2: 'for we say that it "was", "is", and "will be", while in truth "is" alone befits here, while "was" and "will be" are suitably used for the coming to be that moves in time' (λέγομεν γὰρ δὴ ὡς ἦν ἔστιν τε καὶ ἔσται, τῇ δὲ τὸ ἔστιν μόνον κατὰ τὸν ἀληθῆ λόγον προσήκει, τὸ δὲ ἦν τό τ' ἔσται περὶ τὴν ἐν χρόνῳ γένεσιν ἰοῦσαν πρέπει λέγεσθαι), which he renders more or less faithfully. See, however, his statement in chapter 25 where he declares that the intelligible cosmos always 'is', its image always has been, *is*, and will be: *semper fuit est erit* (25, 232, 19).

[94] As in the Greek, *exemplum* here does not refer to the intelligible model – distinguished by Calcidius with the help of an alternative term, *archetypus* – but signifies the 'pattern' or 'model' of the respective types of everlasting existence.

[95] The term appears also in Apuleius, *DPD.* 1.12: *sed natura etiam mortales eos, qui praestarent sapientia ceteris terrenis animantibus, ad aevitatem temporis edidit* ... ('to the everlastingness of time', *LS* 11A).

copy (*uterque mundus*) to their respective kinds of everlastingness, one existing *omni aevo*, the other *per omne tempus*.

Thus far, Calcidius' translation has emphasized the fact that both model and copy partake of two different kinds of everlasting existence. With regard to the temporal aspect of the world's creation, Calcidius follows the Greek in depicting it as coinciding with the creation of time, contrary to his exegesis in the commentary which explains the origin of the god's work in terms of an ontological, as opposed to temporal, relation. Let us finally turn to his translation of *Tim.* 28b4–7 and see whether such impressions can be confirmed:

Table 23. *Plato,* Tim. *28b4–7*

A: σκεπτέον… πότερον ἦν ἀεί [ὁ κόσμος], γενέσεως ἀρχὴν ἔχων οὐδεμίαν, ἢ γέγονεν, ἀπ' ἀρχῆς τινος ἀρξάμενος.	A: it must be considered … whether [the world] always was, having no starting point of generation, or whether it has come to be, having begun from some starting point.

Table 24. *Calcidius' translation (156, 3–4) of Plato,* Tim. *28b4–7*

B: *mundus fueritne semper citra exordium temporis an sit originem sortitus ex tempore considerandum.*	B: It must be considered whether the world has existed always, without the beginning of time, or whether it has been assigned an origin starting out with time.

Timaeus inquires 'whether [the universe] always was, having no starting point of generation, or whether it has come to be, having begun from some starting point'. As we turn to the Latin translation, we notice that Calcidius, like Cicero, incorporates into his text the aspect of temporality. His protagonist inquires not whether the world 'has existed always, having no starting point of generation, or whether it has come to be, having begun from some starting point'. Instead, he asks whether the world has 'existed always, without (*citra*² OLD

5: "without something coming about"[96] or *OLD* 7: "without reference to"[97]) the beginning of time, or whether it has been assigned an origin starting out with time'.[98]

In answer to his preceding question, Timaeus responds at *Tim.* 28b7–c2:

Table 25. *Plato, Tim. 28b7–c2*

A: γέγονεν· ὁρατὸς γὰρ ἁπτός τέ ἐστιν καὶ σῶμα ἔχων, πάντα δὲ τὰ τοιαῦτα αἰσθητά, τὰ δ᾽ αἰσθητά, δόξῃ περιληπτὰ μετ᾽ αἰσθήσεως, γιγνόμενα καὶ γεννητὰ ἐφάνη.	A: It has come to be, for it is visible and tangible and has a body. But all objects of such a kind are perceptible. Perceptible objects are grasped by opinion with the aid of sense perception. They come to be, as we found, and are generated.

In place of this, the answer Calcidius provides is somewhat obscure:

Table 26. *Calcidius' translation (156, 4–7) of Plato, Tim. 28b7–c2*

B: *factus est, utpote corporeus et qui videatur atque tangatur, cuncta siquidem huius modi sensilis corporeaeque naturae, sensilia porro ea quae opinio sensu aliquo commota praesumit eaque omnia facta sunt habentque ex aliqua generatione substantiam.*	B: It has been created, inasmuch it is corporeal and of such a kind that can be seen and touched, and since all objects of this kind are of a sensible and corporeal nature, those things are sensible which opinion, stirred by some sensory faculty, apprehends, and all these objects have been created and acquire their existence from some generation.

---

[96] This is presumably the sense in which Calcidius uses the term *citra* in his translation of *Tim.* 33a, where he describes how the demiurge composed the physical universe as *unum perfectum ex perfectis omnibus citra senium dissolutionemque* (162, 12), with *citra* denoting 'without old age or weakening/disintegration (of its parts) coming about' (translating the Greek ἀγήρων καὶ ἄνοσον).

[97] Presumably the sense in which Calcidius uses the term in his commentary at 158, 392, 21: 'chance comes about without reference to human intentions' (*casus vero citra propositum hominis fit*). Apart from its appearance here, and its occurrence at *Tim.* 33a (see previous note), this is the only other instance in which the term *citra* is used by Calcidius.

[98] *ex tempore* is to be understood not in its adverbial function, 'instantaneously' or 'in the spur of the moment', but as 'going out from/with time'. We encounter the same phrase in Augustine, see p. 229, and Macrobius, see p. 180.

The initial emphasis on temporality (*citra exordium temporis, origo ex tempore*) is perplexing in view of Calcidius' statements in the commentary, where, we recall, he attaches a causative meaning to ἀρχή, 'origin' (*origo causativa, non temporaria*), thus defining the world's creation in non-temporal terms. Moreover, despite the fact that Calcidius explicitly frames the question concerning the creation of the world under the aspect of temporality, his reply, 'it has come to be', *factus est*, does not pick up this notion, addressing apparently only the ontological status of the cosmos. In view of the focus on temporality in the translation that results from Calcidius' alterations of the Greek, and, moreover, the fact that he follows the Greek text in describing the creation of the world, at *Tim.* 37–8, as coinciding with that of time, we may assume that he considered *factus est* to convey the meaning of a creation *ex tempore*, while considering the alternative of a world that 'has always been', *fuerit semper*, to exclude the possibility that a creation had taken place. Overall, it appears that it was Calcidius' intention to lend further emphasis in his translation to the language of temporality conveyed by the Greek, without adapting his version to the subsequent portrayal of a non-temporal creation in his commentary.

Calcidius' motivation for adopting this strategy is laid out in chapter 26 of the commentary. In the context of a discussion of the world soul, he explains that the *Timaeus* is the only work in which Plato contrives types of generation for things eternal (*aeternarum rerum genituras comminisci*, 26, 232, 25). This, Calcidius believes, Plato does in order to prevent readers from thinking, upon hearing of the existence of things that partake of no temporal[99] origin such as the universe and soul (*si audiant homines esse quaedam quae fuerint ex origine nata numquam*), that the pre-eminence of the highest god might [for this reason] be diminished (*principatui summi dei derogari*

[99] I am basing my rendering 'temporal' on the subsequent use by Calcidius of *numquam*, which suggests a temporal dimension.

putent).[100] Those people, Calcidius explains, are unaware of
the great difference between speaking of the origin of eternal
things and, on the other hand, of the origin of things that are
perishable (*longe aliter dici originem rerum aeternarum et item
caducarum*).

He explains, further, that a creative cause (*auctoritas*) and
origin (*origo*) in the case of mortal objects *precedes* the coming
to be of 'others' who succeed them. The origin and principle
(*arx*) of things divine and eternal, on the other hand, must
be understood not as temporal priority but as the pre-eminence of worth (*non in anticipatione temporis sed dignitatis
eminentia*). Calcidius emphasizes once again Plato's purpose
of guiding his audience with didactic concern as he sets out
his doctrine: it would be difficult to convince people that god is
the *auctor* of this world unless he has, just like, as it were, some
builder, constructed it with his hands and the exertion of his
body (*nisi eum tamquam opifex aliquis manibus ceterorumque
artuum molitione construxerit*).[101]

Calcidius thus accounts for Plato's description of the creation of everlasting objects in temporal terms by crediting him
with an essentially pedagogical agenda. It is out of consideration for his audience's belief in god's pre-eminence and dignity
that Plato resorts to a temporal framework, all the more since
the intellectual capacity of his readers might be stretched when
imagining anything other than an actual 'construction' of the
cosmos.[102] It appears that we find in Calcidius an interpretation of Plato's *Timaeus* as an account composed *didaskalias
charin*, 'for the sake of instruction'. For the dialogue's student the causal relations at work between the demiurge and

---

[100] We find the same argument in chapter 6 of Philoponus' *Aet. mund.* (187, 1–15, ed.
Rabe) who ascribes this view to Taurus.

[101] Cal. *Comm. in Tim.* 26, 232, 26–234, 9. We discover here echoes of Velleius'
polemic at *Nat. deor.* 1.19, cf. pp. 88–9, that are put by Calcidius to an astonishing
use: while the Epicurean mocks the detailed description of craftsmanship in
the *Timaeus*, the likening of the creation process to a monumental building site
appears to be exactly what Calcidius assumes Plato's readers to be in need of.

[102] Cf. Baltes 1976: 179. The same conclusion is drawn by Reydams-Schils 2007a, and
1999: 223 n. 43, where Calcidius' temporal language in chapter 23 is understood as
a metaphorical expression for the causality of the creation process.

his creations must be expressed in terms that are more readily accessible to him, in other words, in the language of temporality he employs in his translation.

Theology: Introducing the Summus Deus

Given Calcidius' view of an uncreated cosmos, what remains to be examined is the precise nature and role he assigns to the Timaean demiurge in his translation and commentary, and the solution Calcidius advances for reconciling a central transcendent divinity with the assumption of a providentially structured material cosmos. Like Apuleius, Calcidius introduces a network of demonic powers and diverging levels of providence. Nevertheless, while both authors exhibit a number of shared exegetical strands in these thematic contexts, we will find that such parallels are put to a rather different use in their resulting interpretations.

Let us begin with the introduction proper of the demiurge. In Timaeus' creation account the identity of the demiurge is addressed at *Tim.* 28c3–5:

Table 27. *Plato,* Tim. *28c3–5*

A: τὸν μὲν οὖν ποιητὴν καὶ πατέρα τοῦδε τοῦ παντὸς εὑρεῖν τε ἔργον καὶ εὑρόντα εἰς πάντας ἀδύνατον λέγειν·	**A:** It is a [difficult] task to find the maker and father of this universe and, once he is found, it is impossible to declare [his identity] to all.

Calcidius' translation expresses a somewhat different sentiment:

Table 28. *Calcidius' translation (156, 8–9) of Plato,* Tim. *28c3–5*

B: *igitur opificem genitoremque universitatis tam invenire difficile quam inventum impossibile digne profari.*	**B:** As difficult as it is to find the maker and creator of the universe, it is impossible to proclaim him in a worthy manner, once he is found.

Calcidius stresses the hopelessness of declaring the identity
of the demiurge in a manner that becomes his worth (*digne
profari*). He does not mention the audience of this declaration,
the 'all' (πάντες), of Plato's *Timaeus*, nor does he point to their
unworthiness of receiving such sublime knowledge, which may
suggest that he wished to affirm their claim to participate therein.
Calcidius' reticence to address the subject of the god, once
again, may be determined by the immediate context of his
statement. We recall that he had expressed a similar attitude
in his commentary in reference to *Tim.* 40d6–7,[103] in the context of his discussion on the nature of the gods associated with
the traditional pantheon: 'As for the other δαίμονες, to discover and speak of their origin is beyond our abilities' (περὶ δὲ
τῶν ἄλλων δαιμόνων εἰπεῖν καὶ γνῶναι τὴν γένεσιν μεῖζον ἢ καθ'
ἡμᾶς). Calcidius, we recall, had interpreted Timaeus' words by
explaining that the sublimity of the subject matter surpasses
the context of his present discussion of natural philosophy
and requires, instead, an *inquisitio epoptica*: '[He says so not
because] this exposition is unfitting for philosophers – whom
else would it suit more? – but because the examination of this
subject is the task of a reflection of prime and surpassing rank,
[and such an examination is described as] *epoptica*. It is considerably more august than physics and therefore does not seem to
be appropriate to us who are now treating the physical nature
of things …'. It is possible, therefore, that Calcidius understood
Timaeus' words to express his reticence in addressing the identity
of the god in the context of his *disputatio naturalis*, rather than
reading Timaeus' cautionary words as a negative assessment,
either of human ability to suitably express the god's identity, or
of the audience's ability to grasp such explanations.[104]

---

[103] Cf. pp. 174–5.
[104] In Boethius' *De consolatione* 5 pr. 6, 1, Philosophia announces that it is time to consider what is the nature or condition of the divine substance (*divinae substantiae
status*) – 'as far as it is lawful to do so' (*quantum fas est*, cf. also 4 pr. 6, 54: 'Nor
is it lawful (*fas*) that humans grasp with their intellect and set out in words all the
contrivances (*machinas*) of the divine work') – a cautionary remark reminiscent of
Tim. 28c3–5: 'It is a [difficult] task to find the maker and father of this All and, once
he is found, it is impossible to declare [his identity] to all' (τὸν μὲν οὖν ποιητὴν καὶ
πατέρα τοῦδε τοῦ παντὸς εὑρεῖν τε ἔργον καὶ εὑρόντα εἰς πάντας ἀδύνατον λέγειν).
A phrasing similar to Philosophia's present remark occurs in Cicero's translation of

Theology: The Summus Deus, Providence, and Fate

What, then, does Calcidius tell us about the identity of the demiurge? It appears from the proposed outline[105] Calcidius offers in chapter 7 of his commentary that he intended, in what he envisaged to be the twenty-seventh *liber*, to offer a discussion about theology under the heading *de deo intellegibili* (7, 210, 5), once his patron's approval had been secured.[106] Since we do not possess a discussion that corresponds to this part of Calcidius' proposed table of contents, we must turn to other parts of his commentary to find out if we can catch a glimpse of the *deus intellegibilis*. We find that he appears at the margins of a number of contexts throughout the commentary.

The highest god in Calcidius' universe appears in chapter 176 where the author sketches out the effects of divine providence and fate down to the human sphere. As in the case of Apuleius, providence is linked to a hierarchy of divine entities.[107] The details of Calcidius' hierarchical order, however, result in a

---

Tim. 28c3–5: 'it is difficult to find that, as it were, father of this universe, and it would be unlawful (*nefas*) to declare him to the crowd' (*atque illum quidem quasi parentem huius universitatis invenire difficile, et cum iam invenerit indicare in vulgus nefas*). In contrast to Plato's ἀδύνατον λέγειν, 'it is impossible to say/name', which may suggest primarily that it is epistemologically impossible to assign a name and identity to the demiurge in terms which are accessible and comprehensible to all, Cicero describes it as 'unlawful', *nefas*, to reveal the divine nature to the popular masses. Religious practice is thus portrayed as a private and elitist business. Despite the fact that the language is somewhat similar, it appears that the limitiations of *fas*, in Philosophia's case, are those of human cognitive abilities along with a sense of propriety, rather than the notion of religious exclusivity. See also Apuleius the high-priest who, it appears, has no such qualms and who retains the notion of an uninitiated multitude (Apuleius' vorlage appears to have read πολλούς instead of πάντας, cf. p. 141 above, with n. 117).

[105] Calcidius provides the *ordinationes* and *species* of twenty-seven *libri*, of which the last one is titled De intellegibili deo. His commentary cuts off after the thirteenth book, *de silva*. Waszink and Jensen 1962: xviii and van Winden 1959: 12–14 suggest that this is in fact the division of the dialogue itself, possibly based upon a current Middle Platonic practice, and not of Calcidius' commentary.

[106] Cal. *Ep. ad Os.* 134, 5.

[107] Waszink 1962: xl and *comm. ad loc.* believes Numenius was the most important source of Calcidius' striking combination of a metaphysical hierarchy and the doctrine on providence and fate; Theiler thinks of Porphyry and Ammonius. Den Boeft 1970: 85–98 believes that Plotinus and Numenius, via the works of Porphyry, inspired Calcidius, but also stresses the strong parallels in Ps.-Plutarch's *De fato* for the first parts of Calcidius' discussion on fate. Bakhouche, *comm. ad loc.*, provides an extensive review of possible source material.

rather different cosmic scenario. Instead of a highest god and various demonic executive agents in charge of disseminating the god's providential will, we find a trio of hypostases. The universe is contained and ruled, in the first instance, by the highest god, who is the highest good,[108] beyond all substance and all nature, and superior to opinion and intellect (*cuncta quae sunt et ipsum mundum contineri principaliter quidem a summo deo qui est summum bonum ultra omnem substantiam omnemque naturam*,[109] *aestimatione intellectuque melior*, 176, 408, 14–16). The highest god is complete perfection and requires no company (*plenae perfectionis et nullius societatis indiguus*).[110] At this point, however, Calcidius chooses not to elaborate any further upon the highest metaphysical hypostasis 'concerning which it would take too far to explain more' (*de quo plura dici nunc exorbitare est*, 176, 408, 16–18).[111] This time, however, Calcidius is not prevented from doing so by the fact that he is still merely dealing with physics, a subject that is certainly exceeded by the metaphysical content of the present chapter of the commentary. Instead, his reticence is likely due to the fact that the god is mentioned in the wider context of a discussion that focuses, specifically, on fate, defined by him as 'divine law' (*divina lex*, 176, 408, 12). This discussion had started as far back as chapter 142, where Calcidius had embarked on this topic prompted by *Tim.* 41e2, our familiar passage in Plato's dialogue in which the demiurge is reported to explain the 'laws of fate' to the newly created souls. In order to fully appreciate the metaphysical context into which Calcidius places the highest god in chapter 176, it is necessary to turn to the earlier development of his doctrine of providence.

---

[108] Cf. Apul. *DPD* 2.1, 220.
[109] On Calcidius' synonymous use of *substantia*, *natura*, and *essentia*, cf. n. 46. See also van Winden 1959: 220–1.
[110] Den Boeft 1970: 89–90 sees in *nullius societatis indiguus* a reference to the Neoplatonic One in support of this view of Porphyrian source. But see Apul. *DPD* 1.5, 190, where the highest god is already described as *nihil indigens*. The description, moreover, is echoed in Marius Victorinus' description of the god as *nullius egens* at *Adversus Arium* 1.13, 13, 1047d.
[111] Cal. *Comm. in Tim.* 176, 204 5–9.

In this earlier context of the commentary, Calcidius' emphasis is on the relation between providence and fate. According to Plato, 'providence comes first, fate follows' (*iuxta Platonem praecedit providentia, sequitur fatum*, 143, 380, 1). This asymmetrical relationship between providence and fate is reinforced at 146, 382, 18–19, where fate 'draws its origin (*originem*) from providence' (cf. providence as the *initium* of fate at 151, 386, 3).[112] Crucially, providence and fate are assigned to different metaphysical levels. Divine and intelligible things (*divina atque intellegibilia*, 145, 382, 4–5) are governed by providence, while corporeal and 'natural' things are governed by fate (ibid. ll. 5–6).[113]

In the same chapter 143, we learn that there are two aspects of fate, its essence and its active impact upon the universe (143, 380, 8–9). In its essential nature (*in substantia positum*, 144, 380, 17–18, cf. 149, 384, 19–20), fate is the world soul. In terms of its active impact upon the cosmos, on the other hand, fate is described as an 'inevitable decree' (*scitum inevitabile*) familiar from Plato's *Phaedrus* (*Phaedr.* 248c),[114] the laws announced by the Timaean demiurge to human soul (cf. *Tim.* 41d), and the 'word of Lachesis' of *Rep.* 617d8.[115] Providence, in turn, is described as god's will in the subsequent chapter (144, 380, 25–7).[116]

In these earlier chapters of Calcidius' treatment *de fato* we notice much similarity with Apuleius, who defines the relationship between providence and fate in similar terms. Apuleius' highest god at *DPD* 1.12, 205[117] issues his divine 'thought' (*sententia*), subsequently identified as providence. Likewise, on the material plane, providence is turned into fate, defined

---

[112] Cf. Apuleius at *DPD* 1.12, 205; Ps.-Plut. *Fat.* 573b1–3; Nem. *Nat. hom.* 38, 753b; 44, 800a.

[113] This dualistic providential framework is, to some extent, mirrored in Apuleius, as I have argued above, pp. 148–56. While Nemesius, like Ps.-Plutarch, assumes a tripartite hierarchy of providential powers, the tasks he assigns to the first providence is the management of intelligible ideas and universals, merging Platonic ontology with the Aristotelian categories (*Nat. hom.* 43, 126, 1–4,). Unlike Den Boeft 1970: 16, I see little overlap between the scope of influence ascribed to the primary providence by Calcidius and Nemesius.

[114] Cf. Ps.-Plut. *Fat.* 574b; Nem. *Nat. hom.* 38.

[115] The same group of Platonic textual references appear in Ps.-Plut. *Fat.* 568c–d.

[116] Cf. Nem. 42, 125, 6; Ps.-Plut. *Fat.* 572f6.

[117] Cf. p. 151.

as divine 'law' (*lex*), and like Calcidius, Apuleius stresses the asymmetrical relationship between (primary) providence in the divine sphere and fate in the material sphere. Such parallels between the two authors are found also Nemesius' *De natura hominis* and Ps.-Plutarch's *De fato*. But despite such common ground, important differences emerge. While Calcidius' commentary, in chapters 143–75, betrays more parallels with these Greek texts than does Apuleius' *DPD* I.11–12,[118] his interpretation diverges from chapter 176 onwards, where he continues to set out a system of divine hypostases. His earlier descriptions of providence and fate are now integrated into the framework of these hypostases, of which the *summus deus* is the first, as noted previously.

Instead of dwelling on the highest god in chapter 176, we saw earlier, Calcidius descends to the inferior levels of divinity, identifying the intermediately subordinate hypostasis as 'providence', 'second power', and 'intellect' (*providentia, secunda eminentia, nous*).[119] *Providentia* is an *intellegibilis essentia* and imitates the first god's goodness, being unremittingly turned towards him (*aemulae bonitatis propter indefessam ad summum deum conversionem*).[120] *Providentia* draws upon the highest

---

[118] To a large extent, this is certainly due to the sheer exhaustiveness of Calcidius' full-blown commentary over against the extent of Apuleius' *DPD*. Aside from the parallels to Ps.-Plut. and Nemesius listed in the previous notes, Calcidius picks up the reference to fate as the 'word' of Lachesis (Cal. chapter 143, Nem. *Nat. hom.* chapter 38), fate as ἐξ ὑποθέσεως (Ps.-Plut. *Fat.* 569d–e, 570a–b, Cal. 144, 176, Nem. *Nat. hom.* 38), fate as substantiated by the tripartite world soul (Cal. 144, Ps.-Plut. *Fat.* 568e), and fate as a cycle (Cal. chapter 149, Ps.-Plut. *Fat.* 569a–c). Further, Nemesius, like Calcidius in chapters 160–74, frames his treatment of fate in *De natura hominis* 35 with a discussion of the Stoic doctrine on fate, a refutation of which requires more detailed argument; similarly also Ps.-Plut. *Fat.* 574c–f.
[119] Den Boeft 1970: 90 and Bakhouche 2011: *comm. ad loc.* Note that it is Plotinus who first identifies νοῦς with the second hypostasis only. Numenius (fr. 16, ed. Des Places, p. 57) distinguishes between a first and a second νοῦς. Ps.-Plutarch at *Fat.* 572f–573a speaks of a πρόνοια that is the νόησις of a first god. Reydams-Schils 1999: 212–15 and 2002: 194 perceives Calcidius' commentary as 'ethicized (meta-)physics' with an emphasis on ethical matters concerning providence, free will, and the problem of evil. Reydams-Schils argues that this is likely to have been influenced by a Stoic perspective on physics and ethics as disciplines that are closely bound up with each other.
[120] A possible echo of the Plotinian ἐπιστροφή, 'conversion', cf e.g. *Enn.* 4.8.4. But, as pointed out by Bakhouche, *comm. ad loc.*, the notion also appears in the *Didaskalikos*, 10.3, 16, as well as Plutarch, *Proc. an.* 1024c–d.

god's goodness, by which it is adorned, just as everything else is adorned by his doing (*estque ei ex illo bonitatis haustus*[121] *quo tam ipsa ornatur quam cetera quae ipso auctore honestantur*, 176, 408, 19–22).[122] The activity of the highest two levels is described as a kind of 'adornment'. Finally, in the subsequent chapter the third hypostasis is introduced as 'fate', the 'divine law announced by the wise harmony of intellect for the sake of governing all things' (*lex divina promulgata intellegentiae sapienti modulamine ad rerum omnium gubernationem*, 177, 408, 27–8). Fate is obeyed by the 'second mind',[123] the tripartite world soul ... just as one might call 'law' the soul of an experienced law-giver' (*huic obsequitur ea quae secunda mens dicitur, id est anima mundi tripertita ... ut si quis periti legum latoris animam legem vocet*, ibid. 28–30).

Calcidius' triadic metaphysical structure is rather easily aligned with the three Neoplatonic hypostases.[124] However, we detect a triadic scheme already in Numenius,[125] who proposes a divine triad in fr. 11, whose first godhead is transcendent, while the two lower godheads appear to be on a par.[126] In fr. 16 Numenius describes a νοῦς that he identifies with the Good,

---

[121] Literally 'it has a draft from him', i.e. it imitates his goodness. On parallels in Neoplatonism, but also in Numenius, cf. Den Boeft 1970: 91f.

[122] See Den Boeft's detailed discussion at 1970: 85–98. Calcidius' triadic structuring is discussed by Reydams-Schils 2002: 196–201. Reydams-Schils 2007b examines the relationship between three elements in Calcidius' triadic schema in greater detail and stresses the Stoic character of Calcidius' theology. Cf. also Dillon 1996: 403–4.

[123] In chapter 188, Calcidius' emphasis on the second mind is slightly different. While it 'obeys' fate in the present context, it is later said to be the 'preserver' (*custos*, 418, 188, 12) of eternal fate.

[124] Plot. e.g. *Enn.* 5.1.8. Cf. den Boeft 1970: 90, and Bakhouche 2011: 774 n. 354.

[125] Hadot 1968 vol. 1: 459–60 points to close parallels also in Macrobius, advancing Numenius (transmitted via Porphyry) as a possible common source for this Latin writer and Calcidius.

[126] 'The first god, being in himself, is simple, because becoming one with himself he is never divided. But the second and the third god are one' (ὁ θεὸς ὁ μὲν πρῶτος ἐν ἑαυτοῦ ὤν ἐστιν ἁπλοῦς, διὰ τὸ ἑαυτῷ συγγιγνόμενος διόλου μή ποτε εἶναι διαιρετός· ὁ θεὸς μέντοι ὁ δεύτερος καὶ τρίτος ἐστὶν εἷς·). Proclus expands on this in fr. 21, explaining that Numenius called the first god 'father', the second the 'maker', and the third 'that which is made' (= the cosmos), but aligns the second and third god instead of the first and the second.

as well as a second divinity of generation, which imitates its superior.[127]

An element that is not found in the authors who show the closest parallels to Calcidius' treatment of fate in chapters 143–57, Apuleius, Ps.-Plutarch, and Nemesius – all of whom assign the executive function of fate to multiple divine agents on the material realm – is Calcidius' assignment of this role to the third hypostasis, the world soul. Yet, despite this divergence, Calcidius' discussion *de fato* from chapters 143–90 is fused into what is, for the most part, a clear interpretative line that delivers the same envisaged result as the other authors. The transcendent divinity remains free from any contact with the material sphere. It is Calcidius' peculiar manner of exegetical syncretism that is the most original feature of his commentary.

A Note on Demons

Before I turn to other contexts in the commentary to examine the nature and role Calcidius assigns to the more elevated levels of his divine triad, let me add a brief discussion of his demonology, the subject of a further sub-treatise in his work. We saw in the preceding chapter that Apuleius' complex network of divine powers provides the necessary material framework that transmits the effects of the god's providence throughout the cosmos. Apuleius' doctrines on providence and on demons are thus intrinsically linked. Despite the similarities in both authors' treatment of fate and providence, Calcidius' demonology plays a rather different role in his exegesis.

It is true that we find notable parallels with Apuleius, such as Calcidius' definition of demonic nature in chapter 135 of his commentary: 'A demon is a rational animal. It is immortal,

---

[127] The first god is unmoved, but the second is in motion. The first god is tied to the intelligible, the second to both the intelligible and the physical sphere (ὁ μὲν οὖν πρῶτος περὶ τὰ νοητά, ὁ δὲ δεύτερος περὶ τὰ νοητὰ καὶ αἰσθητά). Similarly in fr. 12 we learn that the first god is inactive and the second god's father, the second god being referred to as the demiurge and described as 'moving through heaven'. See Dillon 1996: 367–72 for a discussion of these and further fragments.

susceptible to passions, and made from aether, and bestows care upon humans' (*daemon est anima rationabile, immortale, patibile, aethereum, diligentiam hominibus impertiens*, 135, 372, 3–4).[128] To compare, Apuleius' *DDS* 13, 148 describes demons as animals with rational thought, with a soul that is susceptible to passions, a body made from air and immortal endurance (*genere animalia, ingenio rationabilia, animo passiva, corpore aeria, tempore aeterna*). What is more, both authors point to the role of the demons as guardians and protectors of humankind. The god, according to Calcidius, wished for the demons to ensure human soul's safeguarding (*tutela*, 374, 136, 1).[129] What is more, his assertion that god's will has given demons to humans as 'guardians' (*custodes*, 135, 372, 10)[130] is mirrored, for instance, in Apuleius' *DPD* 1.12, 206 and *DDS* 16, 155.

Nevertheless, it is crucial to note that Calcidius' demons are not introduced in the context of his discussion of fate and providence in chapters 158–74. And with good reason: Calcidius, we saw above, assigned the executive function of fate to the lowest of his three hypostases, the world soul. The demons do not feature in Calcidius' providential structure such as it is set up in his discussion *de fato*. Instead, they appear in the course of his discussion of the 'Four Kinds of Living Creatures', building on *Tim.* 39e10–40d5, at the beginning of the second part of Calcidius' commentary, starting at chapter 119.

Calcidius' primary interest there is the creation of the heavenly bodies (cf. *Tim.* 39d87), and of the things 'the world

---

[128] Plutarch, *Is. et Os.* 25, 360d–e (= F 145, F147 IP 2012 = fr. 225, 227 IP 1982) credits Xenocrates, along with Plato, Pythagoras, and Chrysippus, with the view of a demon as a being subjected to passions. Cf. Plut. *Def. orac.* 12, 416c–d = F 142 IP 2012 = fr. 222 IP 1982. The description of demons as beings that are immortal and subject to passions appears also in Origen, *Contr. Cels.* 8.35; cf. Maximus of Tyre's *Discourse* 9.1–6.

[129] A similar sentiment appears at 132, 372, 8–9. Given the feebleness of human nature, there is need for a better, nobler one, Calcidius explains, wherefore the 'creator and preserver of all things, wishing the human race to exist, set before them angels or demons, with whose help they would be suitably guided'. Cf. Ps.-Plut. *Fat.* 573a5, Nem. *Nat. hom.* 43, 126, 12.

[130] On the term *custos*, see Timotin 2012: 270–1.

comprises, so that the universe would be full and complete, and the living being, [consisting of] the sensible world, would achieve close similarity to the perfect intelligible world' (119, 356, 7–9). Calcidius duly reports one celestial kind and three terrestrial kinds, of which one is winged, another swims, the third is earth-bound. He next explains that Plato was, however, not content with these kinds, but mentioned a further, aetherial kind he called 'demons', itself divided into those made from aether, air, and a 'humid substance'.[131] His mention of the demons picks up Timaeus' reference to the gods of popular religion at *Tim.* 40d6–41a3, which, in the original dialogue, contains no description of the elemental make-up of these gods. Calcidius thus relates the gods of popular religion, such as they appear in the original dialogue at 40d6–41a3, to the preceding discussion of the four kinds of living creatures that are all assigned to a specific habitat in the world, and duly supplies information regarding their elemental make-up, which is not provided in the Greek text.

As noted above, Calcidius next accounts for this omission in Plato's text by the fact that the latter postponed a separate discussion on demons (*quem tractatum necessario differt*), since he considered this topic to be 'loftier and beyond the subject of physics', the current context in Plato's dialogue (*elatior et ultra naturae contemplationem*, 120, 356, 21–2).[132] Nevertheless, Calcidius explains, Plato did address the topic 'briefly and cursorily' (127, 364, 18–19), for fear that the world would remain incomplete in some part should he remain silent on such a topic.[133] Plato's separate discussion on demons is, presumably,

---

[131] *humecta essentia.* Calcidius at 129, 366, 18 uses the underlying Greek ὑγρὰ οὐσία to refer to a type of air breathed by humans, as opposed to the less compressed air of the heavens. The expression appears in the context of the creation of living beings also in Plutarch, *Quaest. conv.* 730e1 and Philo, e.g. *Opif. mund.* 132, 3 and 12, but not in connection with demons.

[132] Cf. also the discussion of Calcidius' expression *epoptica* by Somfai 2003: 134–5; Moreschini 2003: 717.

[133] This echoes Calcidius' statement at 120, 356, 20–1, where he ascribes to Plato the view that the existence of demons was necessary to ensure that no region of the world was left uninhabited (cf. *Tim.* 39e3–7). Calcidius connects Plato's authorial agenda, such as he perceives it, to the contents of the dialogue.

the *Epinomis*, where Plato, according to Calcidius at 128, 364, 30–1, elaborated on the subject of demons 'with the highest diligence and utmost attention'. Following Plato, Calcidius perceives it to be his task as an exegete to address this topic, albeit cursorily (*breviter*, 129, 366, 12), in the present context of his commentary, and in the ensuing discussion sets out the nature of the different kinds of demons by leaving heavily on the *Epinomis*.[134] It is noteworthy, however, that Calcidius' discussion of demons, even though its subject matter might be termed epoptical according to his earlier characterization, is undertaken by him in a manner that is very much appropriate to a *disputatio naturalis*. Its main focus, as will become obvious, is the demons' elemental make-up,[135] as it was the case previously with the other living creatures mentioned by Calcidius in chapter 119.

Calcidius at 129, 366, 14–21 illustrates the demons' various habitats (*differentes positiones*) and bodily make-up (*differentia corporum*), with reference to physical density[136] and spatial extension. What is more, he explains in chapter 131 the need for demons in the cosmos not by pointing to the god's desire to protect humans, but by appealing to the mathematical principle of continued geometrical proportion that he appealed to in his

---

[134] The author of *Ep.* at 984b–985b also classifies demons according to their elemental make-up. As in this work, Calcidius integrates the element of aether, which does not appear in the *Timaeus*, below that of fire, contrary to the exalted place it holds in Aristotle and in Apuleius, *DDS* 8, 138, who places it within the material cosmos but above fire; similarly perhaps Alc. *Didask.* 15, 3. For the detailed parallels between Calcidius and the *Epinomis*, cf. Bakhouche's and Den Boeft's extensive *comm. ad loc.*

[135] Underlined by Calcidius' translation of 'nature' (*natura*) instead of 'coming to be' (γένεσις) in his translation of *Tim.* 40d6: 'to discover and declare the coming to be of the demons is beyond us', noted by Somfai 2003: 133. I disagree with Somfai that Calcidius believed Plato to have considered the topic of demons one of 'insignificance' (ibid. n. 33). If so, Calcidius would have been hard pressed to explain why Plato devoted an entire different discussion to this subject in the *Epinomis* (cf. 364, 128, 30). Instead, Calcidius associated with Plato the belief that this topic was 'out of place' in the context of *Tim.* 40d.

[136] The notion of varying degrees of density associated with the material elements is associated with Xenocrates by Plutarch, *De facie* 29, 943e–944a (= F81 IP 2012 = fr. 161 IP 1982). As noted by Timotin 2012: 134, the density or πύκνωσις associated with the material elements does not occur in the *Timaeus*, but appears in Aristotle, e.g. *Gen. et corr.* 330b9–13.

exegesis of *Tim.* 32a7–32c4, the god's creation of the three-dimensional elements according to harmonious proportions.[137] What is more, Calcidius had made it clear in the same context that adjacent elements shared specific properties that allowed for the formation of a continuous chain, inspired by *Tim.* 31c–32d. This principle is now applied to the various habitats of the world. Since there is a species that is immortal (the stars) as well as a species that is of temporal existence and susceptible to affects (the terrestrial kind), there necessarily has to be an intermediate kind that connects both extremes by partaking of both natures (immortal/mortal, susceptible to passions/unsusceptible), something that is perceptible in harmonics as well as in the world (*necesse est esse inter haec duo medietatem aliquam conectentem extimos limites, sicut in harmonia videmus et in ipso mundo*, 131, 368, 13–14). This same emphasis on an intermediate connector of two extremes continues in chapter 134, where the demons that inhabit the middle region of the heavens (*mediam mundi sedem*) render services to the heavens while attending to the earth (*caelo praebentibus, etiam terrena curantibus*, 134, 370, 21–2) in mutual exchange. Even though Calcidius subsequently comments on the textbook definition (*definitio*, 135, 372, 3) of demons discussed earlier, he immediately aligns their various characteristics with their elemental make-up and habitat. While the same definition applies to aetherial[138]

---

[137] Cf. *Tim.* 32a7–32c4, where Timaeus explains that, in mathematics, two middle terms are needed to ensure the continuous proportion of cubic numbers. Accordingly, to ensure harmonious proportions in the creation of the world, the demiurge required intermediary elements between the outermost elements fire and earth, air and water. Calcidius' application of this passage as evidence for the need of the demonic race in the cosmos is close to Maximus of Tyre, *Dissertation* 9, 24–6, as pointed out by Den Boeft 1977: 27: 'just as, in harmonic sounds, the mean brings two extremes into agreement' (ὥσπερ ἐν ἁρμονίᾳ φθόγγων τὴν πρὸς τὰ ἄκρα ὁμολογίαν ἡ μέση ποιεῖ); see also *Epinomis* 984e5–985a2. A thematic discussion of Calcidius' application to the cosmic habitats in his demonology is Somfai 2003: esp. 130–1. The standard *loci* in Plato for the intermediary function of demons are *Symp.* 202e3–6 and *Rep.* 620d8–e1; further *Leg.* 717b.

[138] Calcidius identifies the aetherial demons, highest in the hierarchy, with 'angels', likely a gesture to his Christian dedicatee. Cf. Somfai 2003: 137–41; Timotin 2012: 138–41.

and aerial demons, the latter 'dwell in the air and, inasmuch as [they are] closer to earth, to that same extent their disposition is more susceptible to passion' (ibid. ll. 10–12). Similarly in chapter 136, while Calcidius notes the god's wish for the demons to give protection (*tutela*, 136, 374, 1) to humans, as noted above, he immediately proceeds to explain the relationship between human souls and demons in terms of their elemental nature. Deserving human souls may on occasion assume an aerial or even an aetherial nature, and thus exceed their natural earthly habitat.[139]

We note once again the idiosyncratic character of Calcidius' Platonic exegesis, this time in the context of his demonology. In the context of Plato's doctrine on providence and fate, Calcidius had assigned the executive function, which is associated by Apuleius and Ps.-Plutarch with different kinds of demons, to the world soul. While, in his role as an interpreter, he feels called upon to address this important part of Platonic doctrine, he aligns his source material in accordance with his exegetical programme and explains the presence of demons in the cosmos by drawing primarily on the notion of a necessary intermediate elemental layer between the other habitats, fire and earth. Calcidius' appropriation of his sources in the context of demonology is thus carefully adjusted in accordance with his overall interpretative line that understands this part of the *Timaeus*, primarily, as a discussion of physics.

Theology: Providential νοῦς

Continuing our examination of Calcidius' Platonic theology, let us turn to other contexts in his commentary that offer details on the nature and role he assigns to the individual elements of his divine triad. Towards the end of his commentary,

---

[139] The context is Calcidius' attempt to discredit the notion that human souls are classed as a species of demons, a view he associates with 'most of those coming from Plato's school' (*plerique tamen ex Platonis magisterio*, 372, 136, 21), among whom we may count Apuleius, *DDS* 15, 150–16, 156; cf. Plutarch, *De genio Socratis* 593d7 and *De defectu oraculorum* 431e1–8; cf. Maximus of Tyre, *Dissertation* 9.

Calcidius reveals additional information concerning the second hypostasis, νοῦς or *providentia*, first identified in chapter 176. It is this *hypostasis* which is responsible for the creation of the material cosmos. In chapter 269, we learn that the 'world is made up by the rational deliberations of providential intellect [cooperating with] necessity, with providence being the active agent' ([*mundus*] *consultis providae mentis et necessitatis rationibus constitit operante quidem providentia et agente*, 269, 498, 17–18). Matter, in turn, is passive and lends itself willingly to adornment, with the divine intellect permeating and bestowing form upon it (*silva vero perpetiente exornationique se facilem praebente, penetratam siquidem eam usque quaque divina mens format plene*, 269, 498, 18–20). In other words, the role of the providential divine intellect is such as to persuade matter (equivalent to necessity in Calcidius' description) by force to undergo whatever form he intends for it (*opus dei tale est, ut vi persuadeat*, 270, 500, 2). *Providentia*, identified as the second of three metaphysical hypostases in the context of Calcidius' discussion *de fato*, is interpreted in the present context of the creation process with the activity of 'adorning' or 'embellishing' (*honestari, exornatio*) matter, rather than with the providential maintenance of the lower cosmic spheres.

Regarding the creative activity of a secondary divine hypostasis described as intellect (ultimately going back to Timaeus' description of the demiurge as νοῦς, e.g. *Tim.* 48a1), I would point to chapter 10 of the *Didaskalikos*. In a much-discussed passage, Alcinous distinguishes between 'potential intellect' (νοῦς ἐν δυνάμει) that is 'superior to soul' (ψυχῆς ἀμείνων),[140] and 'actualized intellect' (ὁ κατ᾽ ἐνέργειαν) that is, in turn, superior to potential intellect. He then hints at an even higher metaphysical entity, 'finer than actualized intellect, being its cause' (τούτου δὲ καλλίων ὁ αἴτιος τούτου). This Alcinous describes somewhat opaquely: 'whatever it is that exists still prior to these, this would be the primal god' (ὅπερ ἂν ἔτι ἀνωτέρω

---

[140] Chapter 10.2.1. Dillon 1993: *comm. ad loc.*, conjectures that this is human intellect, taking the actualized intellect to be that of the universe in its entirety.

τούτων ὑφέστηκεν, οὗτος ἂν εἴη ὁ πρῶτος θεός).[141] Section 3 of the same chapter ends with the statement that the 'first intellect' (ὁ πρῶτος νοῦς) is the father who 'lends order to the heavenly intellect and to the soul of the universe' (κοσμεῖν τὸν οὐράνιον νοῦν καὶ τὴν ψυχὴν τοῦ κόσμου), and who 'has filled by his own will all things with himself' (κατὰ γὰρ τὴν ἑαυτοῦ βούλησιν ἐμπέπληκε πάντα ἑαυτοῦ). The soul's intellect, 'put into order by the father' (κοσμηθεὶς ὑπὸ τοῦ πατρός), is what 'lends order to all nature in this world' (διακοσμεῖ σύμπασαν φύσιν ἐν τῷδε τῷ κόσμῳ, 10.3.18). The last statement suggests that it is the intellect of the world soul which is responsible for creating the cosmos, a function that is similar to that of the νοῦς identified as the second hypostasis of Calcidius' metaphysical structure, *providentia*.[142]

Theology: The Cosmological Principles

Let us consider a final context in Calcidius' commentary to explore further the relationship between the individual elements of his hierarchical metaphysics. In chapters 302–4 the Calcidian god appears in an exegetical context that identifies

---

[141] Chapter 10.2.3-4. With Dillon 1993: *comm. ad loc.*, I take ὅπερ ἂν ἔτι ἀνωτέρω τούτων ὑφέστηκεν, οὗτος ἂν εἴη ὁ πρῶτος θεός to be the same object as is referred to also as ὁ αἴτιος of actualized intellect.

[142] We also note the mention in Alcinous of the 'will of the highest god', by which the latter has filled everything (κατὰ γὰρ τὴν ἑαυτοῦ βούλησιν ἐμπέπληκε πάντα ἑαυτοῦ), possibly an alternative manner of describing the activity of the world soul's intellect that διακοσμεῖ σύμπασαν φύσιν ἐν τῷδε τῷ κόσμῳ. Calcidius associates *providentia* with the god's will at 144, 380, 24-8: 'some people believe that a difference between providence and fate is assumed, although, in truth, it is one, since providence is the will of god, and his will, in turn, is a series of causes. And it is called providence, since his will is providence, and also fate, because it is itself a series of causes'. Bakhouche 2011: 774 n. 356 points to a similar description of providence as adorning or embellishing the physical cosmos in Ps.-Plutarch, *Fat.* 9.573a. It is unclear what role exactly Alcinous associates with that of the demiurge in Timaeus' narrative. Has he been incorporated into the entity that is the first intellect and father (this appears to be Dillon's opinion at 1995 *comm. ad loc.*, esp. 106), or should we understand him as corresponding to the heavenly intellect that is κατ' ἐνέργειαν, the intellect of the world soul? In view of the fact that it is the latter who 'orders all nature in the cosmos', the second possibility appears the more likely; but this is not stated explicitly in Alcinous' discussion.

him as one of the cosmological principles of the Timaean universe.[143] These are discussed in the context of Calcidius' lengthy excursus on Plato's (and his adversaries') doctrine of matter. Without diving into the complexities of this discussion,[144] we note that Calcidius identifies three metaphysical principles in Plato's doctrine: god, matter, and form.[145] While matter, *silva*, is the only principle whose nature is discussed at length by Calcidius, we nevertheless are able to gather the following information regarding the principle Calcidius identifies as god.

In chapters 302–4, Calcidius describes how one may attain a grasp of these metaphysical principles, *initia*. Matter is arrived at by a 'mental process'[146] termed *dissolutio* (*analusis*), god with the help of *compositio* (*sunthesis*); finally, the intelligible paradigm (*exemplum*) can be grasped by contemplating god's creation, presumably by inferring from the physical universe the intelligible blueprints according to which the demiurge fashioned the cosmos (304, 532, 25–7).

'*Compositio*', Calcidius explained previously, 'follows *resolutio* as aggregation follows segregation' (*sequitur quippe resolutionem compositio et discretionem concretio*). In a reversal of the *resolutio*, in which the mind abstracts an object's attributes and qualities so as to arrive at the underlying principle of *silva*, *compositio* restores these attributes, but in an orderly fashion (*cum cultu et ordine*, 304, 532, 14–17). The actual process of *compositio* is then described in the following manner: 'order cannot be without harmony, and harmony associates with

---

[143] Cf. Apul. *DPD* 1.5, 190.
[144] The most comprehensive study of this topic remains van Winden 1959; see further Gersh 1986 vol. 2: 445–51.
[145] Cal. *Comm. in Tim.* 307, 536, 1–3: 'There are the principles god, matter, and the paradigm, and god is the primary origin in an executive and active role, while matter is that from which that which becomes first comes to be' (*sunt igitur initia deus et silva et exemplum, et est deus quidem origo primaria moliens et posita in actu, silva vero ex qua prima fit quod gignitur*). Calcidius offers the standard Middle Platonic doctrine on principles we find also in the *Didask.* 8–10, Seneca, *Ep.* 58, 16–25, Plut. *Quaestiones convivales* 720a; cf. Bakhouche 2011 *comm. ad loc.*; Moreschini 2015: 220 with n. 5. See also Dillon 1993: 93–4. Concerning Apuleius, cf. p. 124 with n. 75.
[146] Van Winden's expression, 1959: 132.

analogy. Analogy, in fact, associates with reason, and reason, in turn, is bound up with providence (*ratio comes individua providentiae reperitur*). Providence does not exist without intellect (*sine intellectu*), nor intellect without mind (*sine mente*). 'The god's mind thus has arranged, ordered, and adorned the entire corporeal structure [of the universe]': *mens ergo dei modulavit, ordinavit, excoluit omnem continentiam*[147] *corporis*. And finally: 'The divine principle of the craftsman (*opificis divina origo*) has thus been found.'[148] I shall return to this opaque line of reasoning in a moment. For now, we note that the divine *initium*, a conception of which can be attained by *compositio*, is identified as the demiurge, the *deus opifex*.[149]

The closest parallels to Calcidius' description of these reasoning processes is the *Didaskalikos*. For Alcinous, it is the first intellect that may be grasped either by a process of mental abstraction (ἀφαίρεσιν, 10.5.1), by analogy (ἀναλογίαν, 10.5.4), or by a third way in which a concept of Beauty and Good is formed initially by the contemplation of beauty in the sensible world, followed by that of beauty in the soul (10.6.2).[150] These methods correspond to what became known among later Latin authors as the *via negativa*, *via analogia*, and *via eminentia*, respectively.[151] Calcidius' *compositio*, however, does not appear to correspond to any of the methods used by Alcinous. What is more, the Calcidian *resolutio* and *compositio* bear a superficial similarity to a different type of logical argument mentioned in the *Didaskalikos*, more precisely the second type of analysis referred to in chapter 5 of this work.[152] But this type of argument is characterized as 'an ascent through

---

[147] Cf. his use of *continentia* for σύστασις at *Tim.* 32c6, as noted also by Bakhouche 2011: *comm. ad loc.*
[148] Cal. *Comm. in Tim.* 304, 532, 17–24.
[149] Cf. n. 145.
[150] Cf. Plat. *Symp.* 210–11.
[151] The *via eminentia* bears similarities to the method described by Calcidius at 304, 532, 27, where, admittedly, its aim is to arrive at the *exemplum*, not god: *ex operibus porro dei opificis exemplum* [*reperitur*].
[152] *Didask.* 5.5.6; as noted already by van Winden 1959: 134–5. This second type of analysis is further described as initially moving from a given proposition to propositions antecedent to it, demonstrating these antecendent propositions by ascending from logically posterior propositions to more primary ones until that is arrived

what can be demonstrated and indicated to propositions which are indemonstrable and immediate' (ἡ δὲ διὰ τῶν δεικνυμένων καὶ ὑποδεικνυμένων ἄνοδος ἐπὶ τὰς ἀναποδείκτους καὶ ἀμέσους προτάσεις), somewhat different from the line of reasoning demonstrated by Calcidius as a method of grasping the divine *origo*.

As noted previously, Calcidius' process of reasoning apparently does not aim at a conception of the highest divine entity such as is identified in his own exegesis.[153] Instead, we recall, it is the *deus opifex* that is grasped by Calcidius' method of *compositio*, and that is identified in chapter 304 as one of the cosmological principles: 'The divine principle of the craftsman (*opificis divina origo*, 304, 532, 21–2) has thus been found.' With regard to the divergent mental processes described by Alcinous and Calcidius, we perhaps fare best by conjecturing that both writers were drawing upon a pool of various logical and dialectical methods, and that Calcidius may have combined for his own purposes several methods of reasoning he drew from different contexts of philosophical exegesis.[154] What remains

at which is primary and agreed upon. Starting out from this, in turn, one arrives at what is being sought by the (reverse) method of synthesis (συνθετικῷ τρόπῳ). This twofold process appears to be similar, at least to some extent, to Calcidius' *resolutio* and *compositio* (cf. 304, 532, 14: *sequitur quippe resolutionem compositio et discretionem concretio*). For this passage of chapter 5 of the *Didaskalikos*, I am relying greatly on the translation offered by Dillon 1993: *ad loc.*

[153] Neither does the method described by Alcinous at *Didask.* 10.5.1–4, which leads to the first intellect. We recall that Alcinous hints at a first god that is finer than, and the cause of, the first, actualized intellect, at *Didask.* 10.2.3–4, cf. p. 207.

[154] I suggest that Calcidius somehow had in mind a combination of Alcinous' first and second types of ἀνάλυσις, one describing an ascent from logically posterior propositions to more primary ones, which would correspond to Calcidius' description of *resolutio* in chapter 302, and another describing an ascent from sense-objects to the primary intelligible, similarly to the manner in which *resolutio* is described in chapter 303. The fact that Calcidius uses *dissolutio* as a synonym for *resolutio* at the end of chapter 304 may give away his erroneous association of Aristotelian ἀφαίρεσις (with its Latin equivalent: *resolutio*) and Platonic ἀνάλυσις (with its Latin equivalent *dissolutio*). But how may we account for the switch from *syllogismus* to *compositio*? A further look at the *Didaskalikos* may help. Remaining with the same discussion of Platonic dialectic, the author describes as a contrary method to ἀνάλυσις that of σύνθεσις through which one arrives *from* the primary premises to the sought-after conclusions. The Latin equivalent of σύνθεσις, of course, is *compositio* – which might explain Calcidius' sudden switch from *syllogismus* in chapter 302 to *compositio* in chapters 304–5. Regarding the difficult notions of Calcidius' *resolutio* and *compositio*, I have benefited greatly from the comments

Calcidius

problematic, however, is the characterization of the providential *deus opifex*, identified in the discussion *de fato* as the second metaphysical principle in Calcidius' theology, as the divine *initium* that is grasped with the help of *compositio*, a role one might assume to be held by the highest god. This difficulty emerges more poignantly at 137, 374, 10–15, a passage in which Calcidius discusses the creation of the human soul and body: '[Plato] says that a twofold faculty of the soul has been given to the soul of the universe ... by the highest and intelligible god (*a summo et intellegibili deo*); [the irrational parts of the human soul ... and the entire body] have been bestowed upon mortals by those powers generated by himself (i.e. the lesser divinities) on the command and the order of the divine architect (*iussu et ordinatione architecti dei*) lest the perfection of the All be incomplete had these [parts] also been given to them by the craftsman and the divine intellect' (*si haec etiam ab opifice et intellegibili deo forent*). The *intellegibilis deus*, a discussion of whom Calcidius had envisaged for *liber* 27 of his commentary, is identified as the *summus deus* as well as the *architectus deus* and the *opifex deus*. It thus appears that the two highest metaphysical hypostases are merged.[155]

Let us revisit the exegetical contexts in which these seemingly contradictory representations of the divinity appear. The highest god is separated sharply from the subordinate spheres in Calcidius' discussion *de fato*. The emphasis in these chapters is on minimizing the contact between the highest divinity and the lower spheres, all with a view to absolving it from any responsibility for evil arising in the human realm, an issue explicitly addressed by Calcidius[156] in the chapters leading up to the summary of his system of hypostases in chapters 176 and following. We recall from chapter 149 that the highest god issues the divine law, *fatum*, which is substantiated by the

by John Magee and Gretchen Reydams-Schils. Both conclude that we find in this part of the commentary a mixture of Platonic and Peripatetic methodologies that are intertwined and sometimes wrongly associated with each other. See further Bakhouche 2011: n. 1099.
[155] This is pointed out also by Reydams-Schils 2007b: 247–50.
[156] Cal. *Comm. in Tim.* 174, 406, 12: *unde ergo mala?*

world soul, the third hypostasis.[157] In the context of Calcidius' treatment *de silva*, however, the highest god and the second hypostasis, the *providentia* or *mens provida dei*, appear less as separate entities than as different aspects of one and the same divine essence.[158] In other words, in the context of the creation, the adornment of matter, a more inclusive interpretation of the first and second metaphysical hypostases appears to be at work, perhaps because this context, unlike the discussion *de fato*, may have posed a somewhat smaller risk of associating the highest god with the negative aspects of the material realm.

Conclusion

The above analysis of Calcidius' exegesis has revealed a translator and interpreter who approaches Plato's doctrine from an pedagogical angle. His sensitivity to the Platonic curriculum, which by his time had become rather compartmentalized, is reflected in his frequent observations on the scope of the Timaean creation account, which he primarily considers a discussion of physics. Calcidius adjusts his own commentary accordingly, but, taking seriously his exegetical role, exceeds the scope of this discipline where he feels that the comprehensiveness of Plato's doctrine may be improved by additional excursus into other subjects, such as fate and providence, matter, and demons. The translation forms an intrinsic part of Calcidius' educational agenda by providing a creation account that depicts the creation of the cosmos in temporal terms,

---

[157] Ibid. 149, 384, 17–20: *ergo scitum inevitabile vocat [Plato] fatum, inevitabilem vim potentiamque intellegens principalem causam omnium quae in mundo consequenter continueque fiunt. Haec porro anima est mundi tripertita, quod in substantia positum fatum in superioribus diximus.* Nevertheless, the choice whether to conform with this law remains with the individual, who is thus responsible for his own actions. This is in accordance with the principle *si hoc erit, sequetur illud*, discussed in detail by Calcidius in chapters 152–5, which already forms a part of his discussion *de fato*.

[158] Den Boeft 1970: 90–1 notes that providence and the highest god are not clearly distinguished in the discussion *de silva* and criticizes van Winden's close correlation between the *providentia* of Calcidius' discussion *de fato* and the *providentia* of the discussion *silva*.

before the exegete offers to his readers a more complex interpretation in his commentary. In those parts of the commentary
that go beyond the contents of the original dialogue in terms
of complexity and subject matter, in particular his discussions
of fate, demons, and his triadic metaphysical system of hypostases, the most notable feature of Calcidius' exegetical method
is his idiosyncratic appropriation and combination of source
material. The overall character of his commentary is that of a
patchwork of various Platonic sources that has been integrated,
at times with some difficulty, to form a coherent Platonic doctrinal line offered to readers in the form of a comprehensive
study course.

CHAPTER 5

AUGUSTINE

Preliminaries: Manichaeism, Neoplatonism, Christianity

With Augustine we turn to the final author of our study. While the impact of Neoplatonism on Augustine's thought has been studied extensively, I aim to show in the present chapter the extent to which specific aspects of his creation theory and his soteriology, in particular, have been informed also by the Timaean tradition. It is in Augustine's writings that a direct influence of Cicero and Apuleius becomes noticeable. At the same time, parallels with Calcidius emerge in Augustine's exegesis of Gen. 1.1, which suggest that the two authors were drawing on the same pool of sources. I will discuss Augustine's relationship with all three authors in the course of the present chapter.

In view of the vast scholarly output concerning Augustine's life, I will keep the biographical details on our author to a minimum.[1] Instead, I begin by sketching a very basic outline of the development of Augustine's thought with specific reference to the systems of belief he engaged with throughout his career. Thereafter, I examine a number of references to Plato and Platonism throughout the Augustinian corpus and assess the author's relationship with Plato and his successors, vis-à-vis the Christian faith, along the various stages of his intellectual journey. The third section of this chapter will illustrate the Timaean echoes in Augustine's creation narrative and parts of his soteriology. My particular emphasis here will be on those topics that exhibit similarities with the Timaean exegesis of

---

[1] Helpful general studies are Bonner 1986, Brown, 2000, Chadwick 1986, Clark 1994, Kirwan 1989, O'Donnell 1985, O'Meara 1997, Rist 1994. For the chronology of Augustine's works, I am following Brown 2000: 3, 64, 178, 280, 380.

Cicero, Apuleius, and Calcidius: Augustine's view on temporal and external existence, his view on matter, his metaphysics, and his critique of Platonic demonology.

Augustine was born in Thagaste, in present-day Algeria, in 354 CE. The rhetorical skills he developed as a young man would later yield a prestigious employment at the imperial court of Milan where he was appointed a Master of Rhetoric. Augustine's mind, however, had from a young age engaged with the Christian faith, strengthened by the efforts of his devout Christian mother, Monica. In what he famously describes as a key event in his intellectual development, Augustine was encouraged to give renewed attention to questions of faith through his encounter with Cicero's *Hortensius*, which turned him from mundane affairs towards the search for wisdom.[2] We shall see in the course of this chapter that Cicero's influence was to remain with Augustine throughout his career, notably so the Ciceronian translation of the *Timaeus*, which would become for him an important means of accessing Platonic cosmology.

The first port of call on Augustine's intellectual journey, on which he departed equipped with a basic Christian frame of mind thanks to his mother, was Manichaeism, which was to delay him for almost a decade.[3] Mani's uncompromisingly dualistic cosmos, divided into a 'good' and an equally powerful, 'evil' substance,[4] bound Augustine's mindset to a materialist conception of two realms, opposed yet intertwined. One was ruled over by a good, the other by an evil demiurge, their struggle being set against the background of a fantastic

---

[2] Aug. *Conf.* 3.4.7: 'This book changed my frame of mind and turned my prayers towards you yourself, lord, and made me long for and desire other things. At once, all empty hope became worthless to me and I began to desire with an unimaginable fire in my heart the immortality that is brought by wisdom, and I began to rise up, so I would return to you.'

[3] Brown 2000: 46–60.

[4] Aug. *Conf.* 4.15.24, cf. 5.10.20. The Platonic tinges are noticeable in Augustine's labelling of the 'good' substance as the monad, the 'evil' substance as the dyad, further associating the former with virtue, unity, and rationality, the latter with vice, discord, and irrationality.

array of semi-divine and human creatures that each fulfilled a specific supporting role in this cosmic contest.[5] Augustine's loyalty initially remained with the Manichaeans during the years he spent in Rome as a teacher of rhetoric. The strength of his conviction, however, was counteracted by Augustine's acquaintance with the sceptical Academy's policy of refuting their opponents' positive doctrines.[6] One of the difficulties that weakened his faith in Mani's teachings, Augustine reflects in his *Confessions*, was his search for a conception of god that was neither burdened by the properties of a physical existence nor limited in its power by an evil counterpart.[7] The sceptics now provided him with the tools to question the Manichaean cosmology and to establish the most 'probable' viewpoint with the help of his own reasoning:

> Concerning the very body of this world, and all of nature that is touched by the senses of our body, as I increasingly considered and compared them, I judged that many philosophers had held more probable views. Therefore, I decided I ought to abandon the Manichaeans, doubting and wavering between all things in the manner of the Academics, such as they are believed to be …[8]

The sceptics of old provided the springboard for Augustine's leap away from Manichaean constraints and towards an engagement also with the dogmatic philosophical tradition. Nevertheless, he stopped short of swearing allegiance to the philosophers: 'And yet I refused to commit the cure of my ailing soul to the philosophers entirely, since they were without the saving name of Christ.'[9] Even though he found the philosophers' wisdom superior to the Manichaean tales

---

[5] Helpful general overviews of Manichaean doctrine are Decret 1970, Lieu 1985. On Augustine's relationship with Manichaeism see e.g. Maher 1979, Koenen 1978.
[6] Aug. *Conf.* 5.10.18–19.
[7] Aug. *Conf.* 5.10.20.
[8] Aug. *Conf.* 5.14.25: *verum tamen de ipso mundi huius corpore omnique natura, quam sensus carnis attingeret, multo probabiliora plerosque sensisse philosophos magis magisque considerans atque comparans iudicabam. itaque Academicorum more, sicut existimantur, dubitans de omnibus atque inter omnia fluctuans Manichaeos quidem relinquendos esse decrevi …*
[9] Ibid.: *quibus tamen philosophis, quod sine salutari nomine Christi essent, curationem languoris animae meae committere omnino recusabam.*

(*fábulae*), they were unable to discover the creator due to their haughty perception of themselves as having conquered the heavens by their knowledge.[10] They were largely correct about their theory of creation, but failed to recognize the grandeur of its creator and to render pious service to Jesus Christ.

They say much that is true concerning the creation, yet the truth, the artificer of creation, they do not seek piously, and so they do not find him. If they do find him, they recognize that he is god but do not honour him as god, do not render him thanks. They are absorbed by their reasoning, and they believe themselves to be wise, crediting themselves with what is yours.[11]

His connections at Rome procured Augustine a post in Milan under Bishop Ambrose,[12] a man who would shape Augustine's intellectual outlook most effectively. Raised on the elegant parataxis of Cicero, Augustine had deplored the crude and unsophisticated style of the *Vetus Latina* and the episodes of violent atrocity in the Old Testament.[13] Through Ambrose Augustine discovered a welcome instrument to access the Christian faith on a different level: exegesis through allegory.[14] Augustine now actively countered the Manichean ridicule of the Old Testament's barbarism and, moreover, was able to distance himself also from a sceptical outlook, having obtained a new confidence in asserting a positive Christian identity. His newly found confidence in Christian wisdom would soon prompt the composition of his *Contra Academicos* at Cassiciacum, a country estate outside of Milan. What had previously sparked his confidence, however, was a decisive event that occurred around 384 CE. In Book 7 of the *Confessions* we find the notorious reference to some 'Platonic readings', translated into Latin by Marius

---

[10] Aug. *Conf.* 5.3.3; cf. *Conf.* 5.7.13.
[11] Aug. *Conf.* 5.3.5: *et multa vera de creatura dicunt et veritatem, creaturae artificem, non pie quaerunt et ideo non inveniunt, aut si inveniunt, cognoscentes deum non sicut deum honorant aut gratias agunt et evanescunt in cogitationibus suis et dicunt se esse sapientes sibi tribuendo quae tua sunt* (Rom. 1.21–2).
[12] Aug. *Conf.* 5.13.23.
[13] Aug. *Conf.* 3.5. On Augustine's relationship with Cicero, cf. DiLorenzo 1982, Foley 1999, Brittain 2012.
[14] Aug. *Conf.* 5.14.24.

Victorinus,[15] that would provoke a major development in Augustine's Christian identity:

You made available to me, with the help of a person bursting with immeasurable pride [i.e. a philosopher], certain books by the Platonists that had been translated from Greek into Latin. In these books I read, perhaps not expressed in the same words, but supported by many and manifold arguments, altogether the very same content, that in the beginning there was the word, that the word was with god and the word was god. I learned that the word was with god in the beginning, and all things are created by him, and nothing is created without him ... And I learned that he was in this world and that this world was made by him; still, the world did not know him. But that he has come to his kin and they did not receive him, and that, however many did receive him, to those he gave the power to become the children of god if they believed in his name, this I did not read in the books of the Platonists.[16]

It was this encounter with Neoplatonic teaching that revealed to Augustine an immaterial reality and, more crucially, that helped him conceive of the Christian god as an immaterial divinity:

But then, after I had read those books of the Platonists, and by them had been advised to seek an incorporeal truth, I discerned your invisible works, works that are understood through visible objects and, even though I was cast back, I understood what, through the shadows of my soul, I had been prevented from seeing. I was certain that you were infinite, and yet not dispersed through finite and infinite space, and that you truly were who is the same and himself forever, that you were no other, in any other way, not in any part nor through any motion. I was certain that all other things, in turn, were from you, because of this single strongest evidence, that they were.[17]

[15] '... certain books of the Platonists that Victorinus had translated into Latin; [Victorinus,] the orator of Rome who, I had learnt, had died a Christian' (*ubi autem commemoravi legisse me quosdam libros Platonicorum, quos Victorinus quondam, rhetor urbis Romae, quem Christianum defunctum esse audieram, in latinam linguam transtulisset, Conf.* 8.2.3).
[16] *Conf.* 7.9.13: *procurasti mihi per quendam hominem immanissimo typho turgidum quosdam Platonicorum libros ex graeca lingua in latinam versos, et ibi legi non quidem his verbis, sed hoc idem omnino multis et multiplicibus suaderi rationibus, quod in principio erat verbum et verbum erat apud deum et deus erat verbum: hoc erat in principio apud deum; omnia per ipsum facta sunt, et sine ipso factum est nihil ... et quia in hoc mundo erat, et mundus per eum factus est, et mundus eum non cognovit. quia vero in sua propria venit et sui eum non receperunt, quotquot autem receperunt eum, dedit eis potestatem filios dei fieri credentibus in nomine eius, non ibi legi.*
[17] *Conf.* 7.20.26: *sed tunc lectis Platonicorum illis libris posteaquam inde admonitus quaerere incorpoream veritatem invisibilia tua per ea quae facta sunt intellecta conspexi et repulsus sensi, quid per tenebras animae meae contemplari non sinerer, certus esse te et infinitum esse nec tamen per locos finitos infinitosve diffundi et vere te*

Augustine does not tell us which translated works, by which Platonic authors, he had accessed,[18] nor do we know with certainty which works were translated by Marius Victorinus, although we may assume that he counted among Augustine's most important Latin sources for translations of Plotinus' and Porphyry's writings. No conclusive evidence points to a direct acquaintance with Plato's dialogues either, and in the case of the *Timaeus* it is clear that Augustine read the dialogue through Cicero's translation, as I shall discuss below.[19] Elsewhere, Augustine uses the label *Platonici* to refer to authors now classed as Middle and Neoplatonists, Apuleius, Plotinus, Iamblichus, and Porphyry (*Civ.* 8.12), and there is one direct mention of a few *libri Plotini* in his *De beata vita* 1.4.

It has become the prevailing view[20] that Augustine's knowledge of Greek, after somewhat humble beginnings, improved throughout his career to the extent that, during roughly the final two decades of his life, he was able to access Greek source material directly. The development is mirrored by the growing number of Greek references in late works such as the *Tractatus in Ioannem* (414–ca. 417 CE), *Ennarationes in psalmos* (finished ca. 420 CE), his *Locutionum in heptateuchum libri septem*, and his *Quaestiones in heptateuchum* (both 420 CE).[21] The relative lack

esse, qui semper idem ipse esses, ex nulla parte nulloque motu alter aut aliter, cetera vero ex te esse omnia, hoc solo firmissimo documento, quia sunt. In the remainder of the passage, Augustine expresses his belief that it was God's will that he should encounter the Platonic teachings before Ambrose' allegorical exegesis. Had the order been reversed, his piety and faith in Scripture might have been dampened by the new Platonic ideas, or else he might have rested content with Scripture alone, without having received the inspiration for an allegorical exegesis.

[18] O'Donnell 1992 vol. 2: 421–43.

[19] *Tim.* 29c is quoted via Cicero's translation in an important passage in Augustine's *De consensu evangelistarum* 1.35.53 = *De trinitate* 4.18.24, cf. 256. Augustine, moreover, quotes Cicero's translation of the demiurge's address to the created gods at *De civitate* 13.16.1, where he explicitly refers to his source: 'Indeed, these are Plato's words, as Cicero translated them into Latin' (*nempe Platonis haec verba sunt sicut ea Cicero in Latinum vertit*). The same Timaean passage appears at *Civ.* 22.26 and in Augustine's *Sermo* 241.8. The subordinate Timaean gods, created by the demiurge, and their own activities are referred to at *Civ.* 6.1.1, 9.23.1, and 12.24.26. The passages Augustine quotes from Cicero's translation are listed in Hagendahl 1967: 131–8, cf. Courcelle 1969: 169–70.

[20] Courcelle 1969: 149–65 remains a useful analysis of Augustine's use of Greek; see also Bartelink 1987, Altaner 1967.

[21] Cf. Courcelle 1969: 151–2.

of a thorough discussion of Greek terminology in Augustine's earlier work does not necessarily indicate a corresponding lack of expertise, but may be explained at least in part also by taking into account Augustine's audience. For sermons directed at his Latin-speaking audience, for instance, he would presumably have felt little need to supplement his thoughts with foreign technical terminology. In his later works, nevertheless, it is rather more obvious that Augustine has gained sufficient confidence in the language to deliver passing comments on various grammatical features in the Greek biblical texts,[22] to set these out alongside the relevant Latin grammatical patterns,[23] and even to spot errors that had occurred in his source texts during the translation process from Greek into Latin.[24] With increased expertise comes a greater appreciation of the language. Having owned up, famously, to his immense dislike of Greek at a young age,[25] Augustine has come to admire the language after a more thorough acquaintance in his mature writings.[26]

The close parallels, both doctrinal and linguistic, between Plotinus and his disciple Porphyry make it notoriously difficult to untangle the numerous allusions to Neoplatonic doctrine in Augustine. To produce a confident verdict on the question of Plotinus vs. Porphyry in the various contexts of Augustinian exegesis would exceed the frame and focus of the present discussion, and I will at this point discount neither master nor disciple as a possible source, as has been done by some scholars,[27]

---

[22] E.g. *Enn. ps.* 67.16, 118.15.

[23] E.g. *Quaest. heptat.* 2.116.

[24] *Quaest. heptat.* 3 90, where Augustine accounts for the Latin rendering *confirmatio* in his source by a confusion of the terms βεβαίωσις and βεβήλωσις, cf. Courcelle 1969: 158–60, with n. 60.

[25] 'Why did I hate Greek grammar …?' (*cur ergo graecam etiam grammaticam oderam …?, Conf.* 1.14.23).

[26] *Quaest. heptat.* 7.37: 'Among the languages of the gentiles, Greek excels to such an extent that, with the help of this language, everyone can express themselves suitably.'

[27] The views of Theiler 1953, O'Meara 1959, O'Connell, e.g. 1963, and Béatrice 1989, are among the strongest pro-Porphyrian stances. Béatrice limits Augustine's source material to Porphyry's *Philosophy from oracles*, following O'Meara 1959, and identifies this with Porphyry's lost *Contra Christianos*. Courcelle 1950 suggests that Porphyrian material may have reached Augustine through Ambrose. More recently, Rist 1996 has made a case for Plotinus. For a more detailed review of the controversy, see O'Donnell 1992 vol. 2: 412–43.

but will comment on parallels between Augustine and the two Neoplatonists as appropriate to the context. Important to take away at this point is the fact that Augustine's encounter with dogmatic Neoplatonic philosophy, an encounter likely made possible through his contacts with Ambrose's teachings, allowed him to develop his Christian identity by appropriating the allegorical method for his biblical exegesis. We find an attempt to justify the appropriation of philosophical wisdom in his *De doctrina Christiana* 2.40.60. There Augustine defends the similarities between Platonic and Christian teaching against the charge of unoriginality on the part of the Christians with the parallel of the Egyptian riches the Hebrews took upon their flight of the country, 'to put them to a better use' (*ad usum meliorem*). Accordingly, as foreshadowed by this episode, Christians ought to take over valuable non-Christian teachings and put them to a 'better' use: to worship Christ.

In the following section I will draw attention to several passages in the Augustinian corpus that provide further evidence for his changing relationship with Platonic philosophy. We will find that his references to Plato and the Platonists must be carefully placed within the timeline of his career, with Plato and his various followers fulfilling different functions in Augustine's argument. Sometimes ally, sometimes antagonist, we will encounter the Platonic doctrine in a variety of contexts, its role being carefully adapted in each case to underline Augustine's message.

Augustine's Plato and Platonism

Augustine's portrayal of Plato and the Platonists may appear as a downward-pointing vector that, from an enthusiastic high in his early career, steadily descends before settling on a selective, at times begrudging, recognition of the veracity of certain elements in their teaching. Our graph becomes more nuanced if we consider the contexts in which Augustine invokes Plato or his successors. In his early *Epistle* 1.1 (late 386 CE) he refrains even from playful criticism of the school,[28] while in

---

[28] Aug. *Ep.* 1.1: 'I would not dare attack the Academics, not even in jest. For when would the authority of such eminent men not move me?' (*Academicos ego ne inter*

his *Contra Academicos*, written in the same period of his life, Augustine distances himself from the negative epistemology of the sceptics but expresses a high regard for what he considers to have been the true Platonic doctrine. Plato, he believes, had learnt about physics and theology from Pythagoras, and he credits him with developing a coherent philosophical system that included Socratic ethics and dialectic.[29] While he acknowledges that Plato did not wear his doctrinal heart on his sleeve, he remains convinced that Plato did maintain a more or less fixed philosophy[30] at whose centre Augustine places the two familiar realms, one sensible, one intelligible.[31] Parallels such as the belief in an immaterial, providential creator and the immortal human soul moved Augustine, even at a later stage in his career, to single out the Platonists as the noblest of all philosophers.[32] Elsewhere he goes as far as acknowledging that, with only a few verbal alterations, Platonists could become Christians and vice versa:

If those men could relive this life in our company, they would certainly see by whose authority men receive counsel more easily, and by changing only a few words and sentences they could become Christians, just like a great many Platonists of our more recent times have done.[33]

---

iocundum quidem umquam lacessere auderem – quando enim me tantorum virorum non moveret auctoritas?).

[29] Aug. *Contra Academicos* 3.17.37. At *Civ.* 8.4. Augustine attributes to Plato the merging of the two branches of philosophy, practical and theoretical, and the perfecting of the discipline by implementing a new threefold division into a moral part, a natural part, and a logical part. Among these, the natural branch is associated by Augustine with theoretical philosophy (*contemplationi deputata*). Cf. p. 107 with n. 20, p. 157 with nn 54, 55. Cf. also Gioia 2008: 50–8.

[30] Aug. *Contr. Ac.* 3.17.37.

[31] Still noted in his late *Retractationum libri duo* 1, especially 1.3: 'Nor did Plato err on this matter, in saying that there is an intelligible world' (*nec Plato quidem in hoc erravit, quia esse mundum intellegibilem dixit*).

[32] Aug. *Civ.* 10.1.1 (composed between 413 and 427 CE): 'we have rightly chosen the Platonists as the noblest of all philosophers, since they were able to understand that human soul, even if it is immortal and rational or has understanding, cannot be blessed unless it partakes of the light of god by whom soul itself and the world has been created' (*elegimus enim Platonicos omnium philosophorum merito nobilissimos, propterea quia sapere potuerunt licet inmortalem ac rationalem vel intellectualem hominis animam nisi participato lumine illius dei, a quo et ipsa et mundus factus est, beatam esse non posse*).

[33] Aug. *De vera religione* 4.7 (ca. 390/391 CE): *ita si hanc vitam illi viri nobiscum rursus agere potuissent, viderent profecto, cuius auctoritate facilius consuleretur hominibus,*

How did Augustine's dogmatic Plato fit in with his sceptical successors? In his *Epistle* 1 to Hermogenianus, in his *Contra Academicos*, and even in his later *Epistle* 118 (410 CE) he credits Plato with the belief in the divine father and son, but asserts that, given the lack of an authoritative figure to convince the crowds, he and his successors were unable to spread their teachings. Consequently, they decided on the official policy of refuting their opponents' views only, and of withholding any positive doctrinal views from the multitude. Their knowledge concerning the divine was entrusted to secrecy and accessible only to a few wise people.[34] It is possible that Augustine's approval of this view may have been prompted, at least as regards his earlier writings, by an intuitive wish to establish strong parallels between Platonism and the Christian creed, given the immense significance Platonic doctrine had upon his own intellectual development. A genuinely sceptical outlook, he argues throughout the *Contra Academicos*, would deny humans the possibility of obtaining blessedness. The validity of living by what merely resembles the truth is reduced to nought, Augustine argues, if one recognizes that knowledge of a thing's likeness is impossible without knowledge of said thing itself.[35] This is, however, as far as Augustine's arguments against the sceptics go. No attempt is made throughout his works to establish a coherent epistemological programme on his own initiative.[36] We should note, moreover, that Augustine later abandoned his theory of a secret knowledge and came to consider the sceptics truthful proponents of a negative

et paucis mutatis verbis atque sententiis Christiani fierent, sicut plerique recentiorum nostrorumque temporum Platonici fecerunt.

[34] At *Contr. Ac.* 3.20.43 Augustine points to Cicero as an authority on the matter. See further *Ep.* 118.5. The view may have been inspired by Cicero, *Ac.* 2.78, who reports that Philo, having distanced himself from the strict scepticism of Clitomachus, came to follow some of the views espoused by Metrodorus.

[35] Aug. *Contr. Ac.* 3.18.40: 'For how does the sage approve of anything, or follow that which is truth-like, if he does not know what the truth itself is? It follows that [the Academics] knew the truth, yet approved of falsehoods in which they perceived some praiseworthy imitation of the truth' (*quomodo enim approbat sapiens aut quomodo simile sequitur veri, cum ipsum verum quid sit ignoret? ergo illi norant et approbabant falsa, in quibus imitationem laudabilem rerum verarum advertebant*).

[36] See Matthews 1972 passim; O'Daly 1987: 171; Rist 1994: 53.

epistemology that had been eclipsed by the Christian revelation. The sceptics really were mere sceptics, a conclusion that on one occasion moved the mature Augustine to retract his former praise not only for Plato's successors, sceptics and dogmatists alike, but even for Plato himself.[37]

In contexts where Augustine's focus is not on Platonist–Christian parallels but on proving the superiority of the Christian faith, Augustine's tone is frequently one of polemical contempt. Neither Plato nor Pythagoras is credited with discovering divine wisdom. In his *De doctrina Christiana*, Augustine assumes that Plato may have obtained his knowledge from Scripture.[38] What is more, addressing doctrinal details in the New Testament, he acknowledges that Plato was the first to label the intelligible ideas 'ideas', but is unconvinced that nobody would have recognized their existence beforehand.[39] In his *Sermon* 68 (ca. 425–30 CE), moreover, Augustine groups Plato with the arrogant philosophers who err in their technical discussions and remove themselves from the possibility of forming a personal relationship with the divine. Since Plato showed neither reverence nor gratitude to the creator, divine wisdom was not revealed to him: 'Peter trembles at [god's] words, Plato did not. May the fisherman acquire what the most noble disputant (*nobilissimus disputator*) has lost.'

At *Civ.* 8.5 Augustine concedes that no other philosophers came closer to the Christian faith than the Platonists (*nulli nobis quam isti propius accesserunt*), while soon after at *Civ.* 8.10.1,

---

[37] Aug. *Retractationum libri duo* 1.1 (ca. 426 CE). 'And the very praise with which I extolled Plato, or the Platonists or Academics, more than what is appropriately bestowed on impious men, displeased me not undeservedly, especially those against whose immense errors the Christian doctrine must be defended' (*laus quoque ipsa qua Platonem vel Platonicos sive Academicos philosophos tantum extuli, quantum impios homines non oportuit, non inmerito mihi displicuit, praesertim contra quorum errores magnos defendenda est Christiana doctrina*).

[38] Aug. *De doctrina Christiana* 2.28.43. Augustine there conjectures that Plato had learned his wisdom from Jeremiah on his travels to Egypt, a view he later came to reject. Cf. p. 235 Vols. 1–3 of this work are dated to 397 CE; Augustine composed a fourth volume in 426 CE.

[39] His further remarks on the intelligible ideas identify them as the thoughts of the creator (*in ipsa mente creatoris*), as was standard in later Platonism, cf. *De diversis quaestionibus octoginta tribus*, *Quaestio* 46.

admonishing them with one of his favourite scriptural passages, Romans 1.21–2, he adds: 'Even though they recognized god, they did not glorify him as god nor give thanks to him, but lost themselves in their arguments, and their foolish heart became darkened. Pronouncing themselves as wise men, they became fools ...'.[40] Nevertheless, he acknowledges that they got it right on one important account: 'however, insofar as they share our view concerning the one creator god of this universe, who not only surpasses all corporeal objects because he is incorporeal, but also surpasses all souls because he is incorruptible, our beginning, our light, our good – in that respect, we prefer them to the other [philosophers]'.[41]

What was missing from the Platonists' teachings was any reference to faith in the incarnation of god in Jesus and in the redemption of the world's sins through his sacrifice.[42] As for the individual Platonists, Augustine places Plotinus in a close doctrinal relation with Plato and, at least in his *Epistle* 118, holds the Neoplatonist and his disciples in high regard while hinting, with a thinly veiled reference to Porphyry,[43] that some have been led astray by their curiosity about magical arts. Elsewhere, in turn, Porphyry is acknowledged to have improved upon Plato and Plotinus in dispensing with the doctrine of metempsychosis between human and animal bodies.[44] Augustine's approval or disapproval of Plato and his followers is dependent on the author's agenda, either that of underlining Christian teaching by an appeal to reasoned philosophical arguments, or that of undermining Platonic teaching by appeal to its failure to arrive at the truth Augustine perceives as represented by Christ.

[40] *quoniam cognoscentes deum non sicut deum glorificaverunt, aut gratias egerunt, sed evanuerunt in cogitationibus suis et obscuratum est insipiens cor eorum. Dicentes enim se esse sapientes stulti facti sunt ...*
[41] *in quo autem nobis consentiunt de uno deo huius universitatis auctore, qui non solum super omnia corpora est incorporeus, verum etiam super omnes animas incorruptibilis, principium nostrum, lumen nostrum, bonum nostrum, in hoc eos ceteris anteponimus.*
[42] Aug. *Conf.* 7.20.26.
[43] Aug. *Ep.* 118.5.33: *... aliqui [Platonici] magicarum artium curiositate depravati sunt ...*
[44] Aug. *Civ.* 10.30.

Augustine and the *Timaeus*

Augustine had access to Plato's *Timaeus* through Cicero's translation. Hagendahl in his detailed study of the traces of Latin Classical authors in Augustine's writings identified twenty-eight quotations from Cicero's Latin translation.[45] A perhaps self-evident, yet important, point to make is that Augustine, while acknowledging Cicero's mediating effort, considers the contents of the translation as essentially Platonic.[46] I will draw on a number of these quotations in various contexts in the remainder of the present chapter.

Augustine's Creation Narrative

I will frame the present part of my analysis by sketching some basic components of Augustine's creation narrative, drawing from Augustine's *De Genesi contra Manicheos* (388 CE), the *De Genesi ad litteram liber imperfectus* (composed ca. 393), Books 11–13 of his *Confessions* (ca. 400), the *De Genesi ad litteram* (between 401 and 415),[47] and Books 11–12 of the *De civitate Dei* (ca. 415). My focus will be on the doctrinal parallels Augustine perceived between Christian dogma and Timaean doctrinal elements. A brief excursus will discuss Augustine's distinction between temporal and eternal existence, and a further excursus his interpretation of matter. In this latter context, I will explore similarities in Augustine's writings and Calcidius' commentary on the *Timaeus*.

In his *De civitate Dei* 12.12 Augustine points to the *Timaeus*, identified with Plato's own doctrinal stance, in order to attack

---

[45] Hagendahl 1967: 131–8.

[46] We saw above, p. 20 n. 19, that in the context of *Tim.* 41a–b, his most frequently quoted passage from Cicero's translation, Augustine reports at *Civ.* 13.16.1 that 'Indeed, these are Plato's words, such as Cicero translated them into Latin' (*nempe Platonis haec verba sunt sicut ea Cicero in Latinum vertit*). This is the only reference to Cicero in Augustine's Timaean quotations, whose contents he invariably presents as Plato's own views.

[47] Augustine finished this work two years before returning to the creation narrative again in Book 11 of *Civ.* It is assumed that Augustine's main sources were Basil's *In hexaemeron*, via Eustathius' Latin translation, and Origen's *In Genesim homiliae* via Rufinus' Latin version. Cf. Taylor 1982: 6.

his Neoplatonic heirs while defending a created universe. He recruits Plato to corroborate the Christian stance on creationism:

Regarding the question about the world's origin my response to those who refused to believe was that it had not always existed, but that it began to exist, as even Plato acknowledges openly.[48]

Augustine had already touched on the subject in the earlier context of *Civ.* 10.31, where he argued that soul's having been created in time does not entail its perishability, and then extended the validity of his reasoning also to the createdness of the world. Let us trace his train of thought in this earlier context. Attacking the Neoplatonic stance that only that which has existed always (and is uncreated) can have everlasting existence, he points to the *Timaeus* as a dialogue that sees the world and the created gods obtaining everlasting existence warranted by the will of the demiurge.

Plato clearly says, concerning the world and the gods within the world he describes as created by god, that these came to be and have a beginning [to their existence], but that they will have no end. Instead, he asserts that they endure throughout eternity through the creator's most powerful will.[49]

With Plato's authority Augustine in the ensuing statement rejects the stance adopted by the Neoplatonists, according to which the world has no temporal beginning, but a beginning 'of causation' (*non esse hoc videlicet temporis, sed substitutionis*[50] *initium*). He next points to the fact that soul,

---

[48] Aug. *Civ.* 12.12: *quod autem respondimus cum de mundi origine quaestio verteretur eis qui nolunt credere non eum semper fuisse, sed esse coepisse, sicut etiam Plato apertissime confitetur.*

[49] *de mundo et de his quos in mundo deos a deo factos scribit Plato, apertissime dicat eos esse coepisse et habere initium, finem tamen non habituros, sed per conditoris potentissimam voluntatem in aeternum mansuros esse perhibeat (Civ. 10.31).*

[50] *substitutio* appears to reproduce the Greek σύστασις, 'coming into existence', a term that occurs e.g. at *Tim.* 32c6, where it describes the 'construction' of the cosmic body from the four material elements. In Porphyry's no longer extant *Commentary on the Timaeus* (2.49, Sodano), however, the term is used for an image that likens the impact of God on his creation to the impact of a foot that leaves a print in the dust (ibid. 2.50). Porphyry thus argues that the σύστασις of the cosmos is not the same as the σύστασις of a body. I therefore take Augustine's *substitutio* to denote a specific type of creation that acts like an external impulse whose impact is comparable to a footprint, rather than a physical creation. Cf. Courcelle 1969: 187.

having suffered throughout its time on earth, will find eternal blessedness, an emotion that will itself replace the previous state of unblessedness and continue eternally through its union with the divine.[51] Augustine equates the condition of soul, eternal blessedness, with soul's existence itself, inferring from the fact that soul's blessedness began 'at a certain moment in time' (*coepit ex tempore*) but nevertheless, endures eternally, the temporal beginning and everlasting existence of soul itself. Thus, according to Augustine, a temporal creation, whether of soul or of the entire universe, does not entail perishability.

By thus advocating a temporal creation, however, Augustine finds himself entangled by another anti-creationist argument. At *Civ.* 11.4.2 he builds upon the previous discussion about the soul in order to continue his case for a universe created in time. Here he has to deal with a charge against the creator, more particularly with the familiar anti-creationist argument intended to show that a creation at any point in time would suggest either that the supposedly immutable divinity was idle prior to creating or underwent a change in the transition from non-creating to creating. This argument *could* be countered by the assumption that god created the soul not temporally but causally, as held by some Platonists,[52] thereby giving it a non-temporal origin that would preclude any questions concerning the creator's prior activity. Yet there are other ways to avoid the charge of a divine *novum consilium* that do not force Augustine to give up on a creation of the world in time. It is possible to argue that the creation has been the creator's 'eternal will'

---

[51] At this point Augustine points to Porphyry's (*iste*) own view for support of his argument.

[52] I take Augustine to refer to a 'causal' origin in his phrasing **non tamen eum temporis volunt habere, sed suae creationis initium** at *Civ.* 11.4.2. Cf. Sorabji 1983: 268–83, esp. 281–2. Those Platonists who maintain the theory of a causal origin, not unlike Augustine himself, would disagree that '[the idea] of creating the world, an idea he had never thought of before, had suddenly occurred to god, and that a new resolve had befallen him, even though he is entirely and in every respect immutable' (*subito illi venisse credatur in mentem quod numquam ante venisset, facere mundum, et accidisse illi voluntatem novam, cum in nullo sit omnino mutabilis*).

(*aeterno consilio*). Augustine expands on the creator's eternal will also at *Civ.* 12.16–17. There he reinforces his stance by arguing that the divinity abides in immutable eternity and that no temporal framework, including questions such as 'What was the creator doing before he created?', and no charge of a *novum consilium*, applies to the divine realm.[53] In the context of *Civ.* 11.4.2, after his appeal to the difference between god's eternity and temporal existence as indicators of diverging ontological levels, Augustine is confident in summing up the success of his argumentative strategy that originated with his 'proof' that soul was created yet is everlasting:

> If they concede in turn that [soul] was created in time but will not perish in any time to come ... they will certainly not doubt that this occurred with the unchangeability of god's will remaining intact. Let them believe likewise, then, that it was possible for the universe to come into existence in time, but that [in creating the universe] god still did not, for this reason, change his eternal will and purpose.[54]

Temporal and Eternal Existence

The preceding discussion is indicative of the significance of Augustine's distinction between temporal and eternal types of existence for his creation theory, and it will be useful at this point to take a closer look at his understanding of these concepts.[55] At *Civ.* 12.15.1 Augustine distinguishes between the

---

[53] *Civ.* 12.17. The creative act is the god's eternal resolve, the creator has therefore 'always' willed to create; this will to create was predestined and no change of mind has taken place: 'in his eternity and in his own word, coeternal with him, there was already pre-determined that which would exist in its own time' (*in eius aeternitate atque in ipso verbo eius eidem coaeterno iam praedestinatione fixum erat, quod suo tempore futurum erat*). The rival assumption of a 'new resolve' is erroneously based on human behaviour, more precisely, on the fickleness and presumptuousness of the philosophers who, jumping from one argument to the next, arrogantly assume a similar behaviour to apply to the divine.

[54] *porro si ex tempore creatam [animam fatentur], sed nullo ulterius tempore perituram ... non utique dubitabunt hoc fieri manente incommutabilitate consilii dei. sic ergo credant et mundum ex tempore fieri potuisse, nec tamen ideo deum in eo faciendo aeternum consilium voluntatemque mutasse.* Cf. also *Civ.* 12.15. Cf. O'Daly 1999: 137–8.

[55] On Augustine's theory of time, cf. e.g. the more recent works by Flasch 1993, Teske 1996, Knuuttila 2001: 81–97, Sorabji 1983: 17–32. Carter 2011 identifies nine different views on the nature of time in Augustine. Disqualifying a number

common notion of time associated with the movement of the heavenly bodies that lend us the structural pattern of days, months, weeks, and years, and a different time, preceding the former, that is associated with the movements of the angels prior to the creation of the heavenly bodies.[56] At *Conf.* 11.23.29–30, in turn, Augustine offers a more nuanced explanation, clarifying that time is not to be identified with the celestial movements:

I heard it from a learned man that the motions of the sun, the moon, and the stars themselves are time. I did not agree with him. For why should not rather the motions of *all* bodies be time? If the celestial bodies ceased their movements, but the potter's wheel continued to move, would there be no time to measure its rotations? ... Well then, let nobody tell me that the motions of the celestial bodies are time, seeing that, when the sun had stood still upon the wish of a certain man[57] to allow him to carry through his campaign victoriously, the sun stood still yet time continued. Indeed, that fight was carried through and finished in its own, adequate timespan. I, therefore, see (*video*) time as a kind of distention (*distentio*).[58]

of often-cited passages as indicative of the ontological status Augustine assigns to time, Carter concludes that he viewed time as 'an accidental condition of substances which makes possible (through time numbers) the successive distribution of a substance's accidents' (321). Nightingale 2011 distinguishes between 'psychic' time and time that applies to bodies.

[56] Ibid. 12.15.1: '[I am not referring to the time measured in] hours, days, months, or years, for these extensions of temporal intervals are commonly termed "times" and clearly take their beginning from the movements of the planets ... [instead, I am referring to the time] that is marked by some changing movement ... if, therefore, there was such a kind of time in the angelic movements before the creation of the heavens, and time, therefore, already existed, and the angels' movements, from the moment of their creation, were in time: in this manner, indeed, they existed at all times, seeing that the units of time came to be with them' ([*tempus non quidem*] *in horis et diebus et mensibus et annis, nam istae dimensiones temporalium spatiorum, quae usitate ac proprie dicuntur tempora, manifestum est quod a motu siderum coeperint ... sed* [*tempus*] *in aliquo mutabili motu ... si ergo ante caelum in angelicis motibus tale aliquid fuit et ideo tempus iam fuit atque angeli, ex quo facti sunt, temporaliter movebantur: etiam sic omni tempore fuerunt, quando quidem cum illis facta sunt tempora*).

[57] A reference to Jos. 10.13–14. Joshua is helped by god and granted the wish to delay sunset so Israel could defeat the Amorites.

[58] *audivi a quodam homine docto quod solis et lunae ac siderum motus ipsa sint tempora, et non adnui. cur enim non potius omnium corporum motus sint tempora? an vero, si cessarent caeli lumina et moveretur rota figuli non esset tempus quo metiremur eos gyros ... nemo ergo mihi dicat caelestium corporum motus esse tempora, quia et cuiusdam voto cum sol stetisset, ut victoriosum proelium perageret, sol stabat, sed tempus ibat. per suum quippe spatium temporis, quod ei sufficeret, illa pugna gesta atque finita est. video igitur tempus quandam esse distentionem.* Philo at *Opif. mund.* 26.4 describes time as the διάστημα of cosmic motion, a Stoic notion, cf. e.g. Chrysippus at *SVF* II 509. Cf. Runia 2001: 158; O'Daly 1977.

It is important to note that Augustine here indicates the manner in which he perceives (*video*) time, instead of giving us an actual definition thereof.[59] Augustine subsequently makes it clear that time is to be identified neither with celestial movement, nor with the movement of any other body. Temporal extensions are merely a manner of measuring the duration of physical movement:

> Do you command me to agree if someone claims that time be the motion of a body? You do not. For I hear that a body moves in time only; you tell me so. But I do not hear that the motion of a body itself is time; this you do not tell me. For when a body is moved, I measure with the help of time how long it is moving, from the moment it begins to move until it ceases to move.[60]

While time is not to be identified with movement, but rather serves to measure its duration, it cannot 'be' without it, Augustine explains at *Civ.* 11.6:

> If eternity and time are distinguished correctly, [meaning that] there is no time without change and mutability, while there is no mutability in eternity, who would not see that there would have been no temporal extensions unless something had been created that would bring about change through some kind of motion? The process of its various movements and changes happens in stages, one after the other, because they cannot all happen simultaneously. Time comes about in the shorter or longer intervals of these stages.[61]

Elsewhere, at *In Ioh. ev. tract.* 38.8,[62] Augustine aligns the temporal extensions 'past' and 'future', specifically, with the motion and change of created things. Importantly, however, he

---

[59] Cf. the useful discussion by Carter 2011: 312–14.

[60] Aug. *Conf.* 11.24.31: *iubes ut approbem, si quis dicat tempus esse motum corporis? non iubes. nam corpus nullum nisi in tempore moveri audio: tu dicis. ipsum autem corporis motum tempus esse non audio: non tu dicis. cum enim movetur corpus, tempore metior quandiu moveatur, ex quo moveri incipit, donec desinat.*

[61] *si enim recte discernuntur aeternitas et tempus, quod tempus sine aliqua mobili mutabilitate non est, in aeternitate autem nulla mutatio est: quis non videat quod tempora non fuissent nisi creatura fieret, quae aliquid aliqua motione mutaret, cuius motionis et mutationis cum aliud atque aliud, quae simul esse non possunt, cedit atque succedit, in brevioribus vel productioribus morarum intervallis tempus sequeretur?*

[62] *In Ioh ev. tract.* 38.8 (Joh. 8:21–5): *nam in omnibus actionibus et motibus nostris, et in omni prorsus agitatione creaturae duo tempora invenio, praeteritum et futurum. praesens quaero, nihil stat: quod dixi, iam non est; quod dicturus sum, nondum*

denies the past and future any real existence, since the future 'is not yet' and the past is 'no more'. There is no true present in our actions. But 'in the truth that abides, I see neither past nor future, only the present. It is also incorruptible, which is not the case in created things. Examine the changes of things, and you will find "was" and "will be". Consider god, and you will find "is", since "was" and "will be" cannot exist.'[63] Only the creator dwells and forever abides in the present. This sentiment appears also at *Conf.* 11.14.17: 'No times are coeternal with you, because you persist, but if [times] persisted like you, they would not be times' (*nulla tempora tibi coaeterna sunt, quia tu permanes; at illa si permanerent, non essent tempora*).

The creator's immutability and eternity is of central importance also in Augustine's polemic against the Arians in his *De trinitate dei*. At *Trin.* 5.5.6, Augustine reasons that any accidental property must necessarily imply mutability: 'There is no

---

est: quod feci, iam non est; quod facturus sum, nondum est: quod vixi, iam non est; quod victurus sum, nondum est. praeteritum et futurum invenio in omni motu rerum: in veritate quae manet, praeteritum et futurum non invenio, sed solum praesens, et hoc incorruptibiliter, quod in creatura non est. discute rerum mutationes, invenies fuit et erit: cogita deum, invenies est, ubi fuit et erit esse non possit. Cf. *Conf.* 11.13–14.

[63] At *Conf.* 11.20.26 Augustine deals with the riddle of how time can, at least in some manner, be said to 'be' if past, present, and future seemingly 'are not' but can be measured, thought of, remembered, and anticipated: 'Perhaps one might say correctly: "there are three kinds of time, a present [moment] of the past, a present [moment] of the present, and a present [moment] of the future. For these three kinds are in the soul, and I do not see them elsewhere. The present [moment] of the past is memory, that of the present is contemplation, that of the future is expectation." If it be granted that one say so, I see three kinds of time and declare that they are' (*fortasse proprie diceretur: tempora sunt tria, praesens de praeteritis, praesens de praesentibus, praesens de futuris. sunt enim haec in anima tria quaedam et alibi ea non video, praesens de praeteritis memoria, praesens de praesentibus contuitus, praesens de futuris expectatio. si haec permittimur dicere, tria tempora video fateorque tria sunt.*) Once again, Augustine focuses on the experience rather than the ontology of time. It is the soul that makes possible the 'existence' of three kinds of time, of the past via memory, of the present via contemplation, and of the future via hopes, plans, or expectations. When we experience memory or hope, past and future become 'present' as it were, or appear presently in the mind. Time is experienced in the mind through the comparison of the various durations of particular events. Yet, the only way in which we may explain that past and future somehow 'exist' is by lending them a platform, our soul, that allows them to resurface and to be experienced.

accidental property in god, because there is nothing mutable or nothing that can be lost' (*nihil itaque accidens in deo, quia nihil mutabile aut amissibile*). In the case of created and changeable things, 'all things that can be lost or diminished are accidents to them, both magnitudes and qualities, and likewise things that are said in relation to something, such as friendships, relations, services, similarities, equalities ... and also locations, times, deeds, and passions'.[64]

God's immutable eternity is his very essence, no mere accidental property of the kind that time is to mutable objects. At *Enn. ps.* 101.2.10, Augustine stresses:

Eternity is the very essence of god in which there is no change ... do not despair, fragile humankind. He says 'I am the god of Abraham, the god of Isaac, and the god of Jacob (Ex. 3.13–14). You have heard what I am to myself; hear now what I am to you. This eternity has called upon us, and the word has erupted from eternity.[65] There was eternity, there was the word, but time was not yet ... Oh, the word is before time, through him all time is made. He, too, was born in time, even though he is eternal life. Calling upon creatures of time, he makes them eternal.[66]

Significant for the purpose of the present discussion is the fact that Augustine at *Civ.* 8.11 notes that Plato's description of the highest god almost had him fully convinced that Plato knew Scripture:

The strongest evidence [that Plato was familiar with Scripture] is the following point, which convinced me the most, so that I more or less agree that Plato was not ignorant of the Bible. When the words of God were announced to holy Moses by an angel, responding to his question after the name of the one who had instructed him to make haste and lead the Hebrew people out of Egypt

---

[64] *omnia enim accidunt eis, quae vel amitti possunt vel minui et magnitudines et qualitates, et quod dicitur ad aliquid sicut amicitiae, propinquitates, servitutes, similitudines, aequalitates ... et loca et tempora et opera atque passiones.* Carter 2011: 317–19 describes 'time as the accident of a substance' in greater detail.

[65] Cf. Johnson 1972.

[66] *... aeternitas ipsa dei substantia est quae nihil habet mutabile ... noli desperare, humana fragilitas. ego sum, inquit deus Abraham, et deus Isaac, et deus Iacob. audisti quid sim apud me, audi et quid sim propter te. haec igitur aeternitas vocavit nos, et erupit ex aeternitate verbum. iam aeternitas, iam verbum, et nondum tempus. O verbum ante tempora, per quod facta sunt tempora, natum et in tempore, cum sit vita aeterna, vocans temporales, faciens aeternos!* Cf. Teske 1985b for a thorough examination of Augustine's exegesis in this and other expositions.

the answer was 'I am who I am (*ego sum qui sum*), and tell the sons of Israel: he who is (*qui est*) has sent me to you' [Ex. 3.14]; so that in comparison with him who truly is because he is immutable, the things that are created as mutable, are not (*tamquam in eius comparatione, qui vere est quia incommutabilis est, ea quae mutabilia facta sunt non sint*). To this view Plato held steadfastly and commended it [to others] most assiduously.[67]

It is important to note that Augustine, in his statements preceding this passage, in the same chapter *Civ*. 8.11, had pointed to parallels between the creation account of Gen. 1.1–2 and Plato's *Timaeus* specifically. Augustine here reverses his earlier view that Plato may have obtained his wisdom from Jeremiah, concluding that it would have been impossible for the two men to meet.[68] Plato could not have met Jeremiah nor have read the Scriptures, which at the time had not yet been translated into Greek ...

... unless, perhaps, since he was exceedingly studious ... Plato studied Scripture through an interpreter; not that he might write down a translation of them ... but that he might learn as much as he could about their contents through conversation. There appears to be evidence that suggests this assumption is correct. For instance, the book of Genesis begins as follows: 'In the beginning God created heaven and earth. But earth was invisible and in disorder, and darkness was above the abyss, and the spirit of god was stirring above the water.' In the work *Timaeus*, in which Plato wrote about the creation of the world, he says that god during this work first joined together earth and fire [cf. *Tim*. 31b–32c]. Now, Plato clearly situates fire in the heavens. This view, then, has some similarity with the view that 'in the beginning, god created heaven and earth'. What is more, Plato talks about two intermediate elements, water and air, that are positioned between the two extremes [heaven and earth] and thus join these together. This may have been his interpretation of 'the spirit of god stirred above the water'. Since he did not pay enough attention to the manner in which Scripture regularly refers to the spirit of god, and since 'air' is often referred to as 'spirit', it may seem that he believed that the passage [from Genesis] describes four elements.[69]

---

[67] *maxime illud (quod et me plurimum adducit, ut paene assentiar Platonem illorum librorum expertem non fuisse) quod cum ad sanctum Moysen ita verba dei per angelum perferantur, ut quaerenti quod sit nomen eius, qui eum pergere praecipiebat ad populum Hebraeum ex Aegypto liberandum, respondeatur: ego sum qui sum, et dices filiis Israel: qui est, misit me ad vos, tamquam in eius comparatione, qui vere est quia incommutabilis est, ea quae mutabilia facta sunt non sint, vehementer hoc Plato tenuit et diligentissime commendavit.*

[68] Cf. p. 225 n. 38.

[69] *nisi forte, quia fuit acerrimi studii ... istas per interpretem didicit, non ut scribendo transferret ... sed ut colloquendo quid continerent, quantum capere posset, addisceret.*

Augustine is clearly referring to *Tim.* 31b–32c for this passage, and I think it likely that he has the *Timaeus* in mind also in the remainder of this chapter, cited in the previous passage, in which he refers to Plato's description of the creator god. More specifically, I think it likely that Augustine associated the announcement 'I am who I am' (*ego sum qui sum*), and the comparison (*comparatio*) between the god 'who truly is because he is immutable' (*qui vere est quia incommutabilis est*) and things 'that are not' because they 'have been created as mutable' (*quae mutabilia facta sunt non sint*), with Timaeus' distinction of being and coming to be at *Tim.* 27d6–28a4: 'what is that which always is, having no coming to be, and what is that which is always coming to be, but never truly is? ... the first is always self-same, the other comes to be and perishes and never truly is'. This passage, we recall, is rendered by Cicero in the following manner: *quid est quod semper sit neque ullum habeat ortum, et quod gignatur nec umquam sit ... quod unum atque idem semper est, alterum ... gignitur et interit nec umquam esse vere potest.* Admittedly, the lack of a direct overlap in the terminology used by Cicero for this part of the translation, and that used by Augustine's for his present discussion, ultimately leaves unclear the extent to which Cicero's translation of the *Timaeus* might have helped draw Augustine's attention towards those passages of the dialogue as are relevant to the present context.

I will continue to discuss Augustine's views on god's eternal being[70] in due course. As we return to the more immediate

---

hoc ut existimetur, illa suadere videntur indicia, quod liber Geneseos sic incipit: 'in principio fecit deus caelum et terram. terra autem erat invisibilis et incomposita, et tenebrae <erant> super abyssum, et spiritus dei superferebatur super aquam'. in Timaeo autem Plato, quem librum de mundi constitutione conscripsit, deum dicit in illo opere terram primo ignemque iunxisse. manifestum est autem, quod igni tribuat caeli locum: habet ergo haec sententia quandam illius similitudinem, qua dictum est: in principio fecit deus caelum et terram. deinde ille duo media, quibus interpositis sibimet haec extrema copularentur, aquam dicit et aerem; unde putatur sic intellexisse quod scriptum est: spiritus dei superferebatur super aquam. parum quippe attendens quo more soleat illa Scriptura appellare spiritum dei, quoniam et aer spiritus dicitur, quattuor opinatus elementa loco illo commemorata videri potest.

[70] The god's eternal being and Augustine's further characterizations of the creator is an extensive topic. See, for instance, Teske 1981, 1985a, 1985b, 1986; Mann 1987. On Augustine's interpretation of οὐσία, cf. Gioia 2008: 56–7.

context of his creation narrative, he reiterates at the end of *Confessions* 11 that no temporal framework can apply before the creative act: 'May they see, therefore, that there cannot be any time without creation, and may they desist from speaking such falsehood ... may they recognize that you are before all time, you, the eternal creator of all time, and that no time nor creation is coeternal with you ...'.[71]

Augustine's Creation Narrative, Continued

In the works listed above, the *De Genesi adversus Manicheos*, the *De Genesi ad litteram liber imperfectus*, Books 11–13 of his *Confessions*, the *De Genesi ad litteram*, and Books 11–2 of the *De civitate dei*, Augustine discusses the six days of creation and the creator's rest on the seventh day. At the outset of the *De Genesi ad litteram*, Augustine professes his intention to produce a 'literal' or 'historical' interpretation of the first chapters of Genesis. It has been noted that 'literal' and 'historical' to Augustine meant to express 'a trustworthy portrayal of events' (*secundum fidem rerum gestarum*), as opposed to a figurative understanding (*figurarum intellectum, Gen. litt.* 1.1.1).[72] That said, Augustine admits that certain elements represented by him as historical facts can have an additional allegorical meaning, and even a 'literal' piece of exegesis, we will find, may well appear 'allegorical' to us.

At the outset of his discussion, Augustine suggests that, in the statement *in principio fecit deus caelum et terram*, *principio* may be understood not as a temporal beginning, (Gen. 1.1),[73]

---

[71] *Conf.* 11.30.40: *videant itaque nullum tempus esse posse sine creatura et desinant istam vanitatem loqui ... intellegant te ante omnia tempora aeternum creatorem omnium temporum neque ulla tempora tibi esse coaeterna nec ullam creaturam ...* Cf. *De natura boni* 39.
[72] See e.g. the introduction by Agaësse and Solignac 1972; further, Taylor 1982: 9–12; Torchia 1999: 102, 104–5. In the present work Augustine remains with his literal course and chooses as his exegetical method a commentary concerned with individual words, phrases, and verses as appropriate, at times interlaced by contemplative detours.
[73] Alexandre 1988: 75–6 gives an overview of Patristic interpretations of Gen. 1.1.

but as referring to the word that is Jesus Christ.[74] No temporal framework can apply to this initial part of the creative process since, as of yet, no creature exists whose activity would be measurable by time.[75] Even though the universe, the final product of the creative process, is temporal, the *principium*, Christ itself, is non-temporal.[76]

Augustine in the subsequent passages, and throughout similar contexts in the above-named works, repeatedly deliberates the correct interpretation of the phrase *caelum et terram*, 'heaven and earth'. At *Gen. litt.* 1.9.15 he notes that *caelum* may be associated with the 'heaven of heavens' of Ps. 105.16, and 'the spiritual creation that had already been made and formed' (*caeli nomine intellegatur spiritalis iam facta et formata creatura, tamquam caelum caeli huius, quod in corporibus summum est*),[77] in other words, the angels, who were made on the first 'day' of creation. At *Civ.* 8.11, a passage we just encountered (pp. 235–6), Augustine had suggested, we recall, that his creation account may have been known already to Plato. What is more, Augustine had ascribed to Plato a biblical exegesis according to which 'heaven and earth' at Gen. 1.1–2 are understood to be the material elements earth and fire of the visible cosmos. He does not, in this context, associate the 'earth' of

---

[74] John 1.3–4. Similar interpretations of the phrase *in principio* appear in Origen's *In Genesim homiliae* 1.1 (likely the source behind chapters 276–8 in Calcidius' commentary) and Marius Victorinus' *Liber de generatione divini verbi* 27. Origen's christological exegesis at Gen. 1.1 is analysed by Köckert 2009: 240–7. Jerome in his *Liber hebraicarum quaestionum in Genesim* 1.1, however, is unable, after an analysis of the Hebrew, to corroborate this interpretation with a reference to the original. Ambrose, similar to Augustine and a likely influence on the latter, understands the phrase to refer to the word through which everything was made, cf. *Hexameron* 1.4.

[75] Cf. Aug. *Conf.* 12.9.9: 'But the spirit, the teacher of your servant, did not mention time or days when he instructed me that in the beginning (*in principio*) you had created heaven and earth.'

[76] Torchia 1999: 106–9 discusses the manner in which Augustine illustrates the role of the divine trinity in the creation process in greater detail than he had done in his earlier *De genesi ad litteram liber imperfectus* (ca. 393 CE). He specifically points to the son (*principium*) and the holy spirit that was 'hovering over the deep' (Gen. 1.2). Cf. *Gen. litt.* 1.5.11, 1.7.13.

[77] Aug. *Conf.* 12.2.2. Cf. Pépin 1953 and van Winden 1991.

Gen. 1.1–2, described above as *informis materia*, with Plato's receptacle. Now, Cicero's translation of the *Timaeus* breaks off at *Tim.* 52, ending with the eulogy to vision and before the introduction of the receptacle into the narrative. If Augustine did refer to Cicero's Latin text in the context of *Civ.* 8.11, a view that cannot be corroborated by any close textual parallels,[78] it is possible that Augustine did not associate unformed matter with Plato himself since he was unable to access Plato's 'own words' on the topic through Cicero's translation.

Matter

Let us remain for a moment with Augustine's interpretation of 'heaven and earth' at Gen. 1.1, which yields close parallels with Calcidius' review of the Hebraic concept of matter in chapters 276–8 in his commentary on the *Timaeus*. A debate has been sparked by Augustine's exegesis of 'heaven' at Gen. 1.1. In the context of *Conf.* 13.1–12, an actual process of formation[79] is described in which the previously unformed angelic substrate, referred to as 'heaven', is given form. Such a process of formation, it appears, was not envisaged earlier in the work, notably so at *Conf.* 12.13, where the angelic substrate was created as already formed (cf. *Gen. litt.* 1.9.15, *creatura iam facta et formata*).[80] During the process of formation described in the context of *Conf.* 13.1–12, the word 'light' in the creator's utterance 'Let there be light' (Gen. 1.3) is explained as referring to the angels who have received form, having been illuminated by the divine wisdom that is Jesus Christ.[81] I shall

---

[78] Cf. pp. 236–7.
[79] A view that also emerges from Augustine's discussion in *Gen. litt.* 1. On the various solutions that have been offered to account for Augustine's divergent views, cf. Pépin 1953: 198–202, 1977: xxii, 1997: 158–61, against whom see van Winden 1973: 104–5; see also Pelland 1972: 68, and Tornau 2014: 209–14.
[80] In the context of Augustine's interpretation of the 'heaven of heavens' of Ps. 105.16.
[81] The illumination of angels is described by Augustine as the three-step process *creatio, conversio, formatio*, a type of 'conversion' to Christ (with resounding

return to this apparent contradiction in Augustine's exegesis in due course. For now, we note that the scenario in which there was a point at which the angelic substrate had not yet been formed is also among the views reported by Calcidius in his subtreatise *De silva* (chapters 268–355), in the context of a survey of opinions leading up to Plato's own. In chapter 276[82] Calcidius begins with a survey of opinions associated with the Hebrews (matter is created) by listing the readings of Aquila, Symmachus, and Origen, with particular focus on the possible meanings of 'beginning' (*initium* – interpreted non-temporally throughout) and 'wisdom' (*sapientia*, 276, 504, 24–276, 506, 10). In chapters 277 and 278, in turn, Calcidius reports the different interpretations of 'heaven'. Those who push their investigations beyond the literal interpretation realize that what was in fact created from the beginning (*ab initio*) was light (*lumen*), referred to as [the first] 'day' (*dies*); thus, the 'heaven' and 'earth' created *ab initio* are not to be understood as material entities (277, 506, 14–21). With regard, specifically, to this non-material 'heaven', Calcidius reports a view he ascribes to Philo (*Opif. mund.* 3, 15–4, 16; 46, 134), according to which we are to understand heaven and earth as incorporeal and intelligible essences, the paradigms (*exemplaria*) of material heaven and earth. Others, however, believed that Moses used 'heaven' to refer to intelligible nature (*incorpoream naturam*) and 'earth' to the substance underlying corporeal objects (*substantia corporum, prius quam efficta dei opificis sollertia sumeret formas*, 278, 506, 30–2) referred to as ὕλη. Calcidius soon after conjectures that, alongside substance underlying corporeal objects, we may assume that there was also intelligible matter

---

echoes of Plotinus, *Enn.* 2.4.5 and 6.7.17) that allows the yet unformed angelic 'substrate' to attain the knowledge of eternal truth and perfect its form. On the similarities between these processes and the process Plotinus ascribes to the relationship between νοῦς and the One, cf. Tornau 2014: 202–9 and Vannier 1991.

[82] Chapters 276–8 in Calcidius' commentary are discussed by Köckert 2009: 229–37 and Bakhouche 2011. Both view Origen as Calcidius' primary source for this part of Calcidius' exegesis, pointing to Origen's *De principiis* (2.3.6, 2.9.1) and his *In Genesim homiliae* 1.1. Origen is assumed to be behind Calcidius' interpretation also by van Winden 1973: e.g. 64–5.

(*intellegibilis silva incorporei generis*, 278, 508, 11) referred to as 'heaven',[83] an interpretation that is close to one of the possible exegetical views we find in Augustine's *Confessions*.[84] The similarities in Calcidius' and Augustine's exegesis of 'heaven and earth' are likely due to the fact that both authors were probably drawing on material by Origen, rather than due to a direct connection between Calcidius and Augustine.[85]

Returning to Augustine's portrayal of matter in his creation theory, let us sum up thus far: 'heaven' and 'earth' in the first verse of Gen. 1.1 may refer to matter both spiritual and material, the products of creation that were made *in principio*, through Christ, who is co-eternal with the creator, and are

---

[83] Despite Calcidius' phrase 'as I think' (*opinor*), which is encouched in his report of the view that unformed intelligible matter may indeed have existed, it is unlikely that Calcidius himself, as opposed to his source Origen, is endorsing this type of created matter, given our conclusions from the previous analysis of Calcidius' view on the createdness of the cosmos. There, he had explained that the literal reading that is supported by his translation carries a pedagogical function only, while the type of creation we ought to associate with the creator is, in fact, one of ontological causation. What is more, Calcidius, of course, stresses on numerous occasions that, in line with Plato's thought, matter is uncreated (cf. e.g. chapters 268 and 350–4 in his commentary), a view opposed to that associated with him by Origen.

[84] Cf. van Winden 1973: 377. At *Conf.* 12.20.29 Augustine includes such a view also among those held by rival interpreters: 'in the beginning, god made heaven and earth, that is, he created in his own word, coeternal with him, the unformed matter of his spiritual and corporeal creation' (*in principio fecit deus caelum et terram, id est in verbo suo sibi coaeterno fecit informem materiam creaturae spiritalis et corporalis*).

[85] In the context of Augustine's *Confessions*, similarities emerge between both authors' description of matter, noted most recently by Tornau 2014: 191 n. 40. Augustine had described his difficulties in conceiving of matter at *Conf.* 12.6.6, where he states that he found it easier 'to imagine that which would be deprived of all form to have no being than to think of something between form and nothing, something that neither had form nor was nothing, but that was formless and thus almost nothing' (*citius enim non esse censebam, quod omni forma privaretur, quam cogitabam quiddam inter formam et nihil nec formatum nec nihil, informe prope nihil*). This description of matter is close to that given by Calcidius in chapter 334 of his commentary, where it is 'invisible form' (*invisibilem speciem*), 'formless capacity' (*informem capacitatem*), that is located, in some miraculous and incomprehensible fashion, between non-being and a kind of being (*ratione inter nullam et aliquam substantiam*), and as 'evidently [!] neither intelligible nor unintelligible' (*nec plane intellegibilem <nec plane sensibilem> positam*, 334, 560, 14–17). The similarity between both authors' descriptions may be due to their common source, but Calcidius is, in fact, here quoting his own translation of *Tim.* 51a7–b1, with very minor differences.

therefore exempt from temporality. More precisely, 'heaven' refers to the substrate, formed or unformed at the point of its creation, of the angelic creation. In the utterance 'Let there be light', 'light' refers to the fully formed angelic spirits. 'Earth', in turn, is the shapeless substrate from which the universe was to be formed.

Augustine's Creation Narrative, Continued

We turn to Augustine's creation theory in the specific context of Book 5 of the *De Genesi ad litteram*. At its outset we find the author accounting for the fact that Scripture contains two differing creation accounts, at Gen. 1.1–2.4a and Gen. 2.4b–25, respectively.[86] While Gen. 1.1 sets out: 'In the beginning god created heaven and earth' (*in principio deus fecit caelum et terram*); Gen. 2.4b begins: 'This is the book of the creation of heaven and earth. After day had been created, god created heaven and earth and all the green of the field, before it came above the earth, and all the fruit of the field, before it started to grow.'[87] At *Gen. litt.* 5.5.13–16 Augustine accounts for the presence of two creation accounts with the view that the creation of the universe had been a 'layered' process. Gen. 1.1–2.4a reports a causal, non-temporal act in which god created amorphous matter and the angelic substrate *ex nihilo*:[88]

---

[86] The so-called 'priestly' account ('P'), Gen. 1.1–2.4a, which recounts the six days of creation and a seventh day of divine rest, is dated to the fifth or fourth century BCE. The 'Yahwist' account ('J', from the German 'Jahwist'), Gen 2.4b–25, receives its name from the fact that god is referred to as Yahweh. This account, which reads rather more like a 'story', puts greater emphasis on the creation of humans in Eden. It is thought to go back as far as the tenth century BCE. See e.g. Bloom and Rosenberg 1990, Carr 1996, Garrett 2003.

[87] Augustine's Latin text of Gen. 2.4a reads as follows: *hic est liber creaturae caeli et terrae, cum factus est dies, fecit deus caelum et terram et omne viride agri, antequam esset super terram, et omne fenum agri, antequam exortum est.* The translation illustrates his hesitation concerning the punctuation between *hic est liber creaturae caeli et terrae* and *cum factus est dies*, where the second clause may be read either as the continuation after the preceding *et terrae* ('after day had been created'), or as the beginning of a new clause. Cf. Agaësse and Solignac 1972 *BA* 48.668–70.

[88] Augustine stresses that no pre-existing matter could have preceded the creation at *De fide et symbolo* 2.2, *De Genesi adversus Manicheos* 1.55–7.

It was not according to a temporal order, but according to a causal order, that matter, still formless yet awaiting form, both the spirited kind and the corporeal kind, was first created. From this [still formless matter] all that was to be created was made, but it did not exist itself before it was created.[89]

Gen. 2.4b–25, in turn, falls into the period *after* this initial causal creative act, but *before* the creation of conventional time. Augustine explains at *Gen. litt.* 5.2.4:

But if we reflect on the order according to which created things were made, we will see that all the green of the field was made on the third day, before the sun came to be which was created on the fourth day. It is due to the sun's presence that day as we know it is completed. Therefore, when we hear: 'After day had been made, god created heaven and earth and all the green of the field', we are told to think of that [other] day that we attempt to investigate with our intellect either as some sort of corporeal entity made possible by some source of light unfamiliar to us, or as a spiritual essence that is the society of the angels in union, not as the kind of day with which we are familiar.[90]

At this point, it may be helpful to review the 'timeline' of Augustine's creation theory. *In principio* refers to the medium of the word through which the two types of formless prime substrate, 'heaven and earth', were created in an 'initial' causal process, according to Gen. 1.1. This causal process, which I shall refer to as t_0, was followed by 'day', according to Gen. 2.4b–25. We are not to conceive of this 'day' as one familiar to us, for temporality, as we know it, did not begin to exist until the creation of the celestial bodies on the fourth 'day' of creation. I shall refer to this 'day' as t_1, as opposed to temporality as we know it: t_2. Instead, Augustine suggests that t_1 should be considered 'the spiritual essence that is the society of the angels in union'.[91] Any effort of analyzing the creative process

---

[89] *non ... temporali sed causali ordine prius facta est informis formabilisque materies, et spiritalis et corporalis, de qua fieret, quod faciendum esset, cum et ipsa, priusquam instituta est, non fuisset ...* Aug. *Gen. litt.* 5.55.13. Cf. further ibid. 1.15.29 and *Conf.* 12.99. The point is discussed also by Sorabji 1983: 31 with n. 53.

[90] *sed cum creaturarum conditarum ordinem recolimus et invenimus omne viride agri tertio die creatum, antequam sol fieret, qui quarto die factus est, cuius praesentia dies iste cotidianus usitatusque peragitur, quando audimus: cum factus est dies, fecit deus caelum et terram et omne viride agri, admonemur de ipso die cogitare, quem sive corporalem in nescio qua luce incognita sive spiritalem in societate unitatis angelicae non tamen talem, qualem hic novimus, intellectu vestigare conemur.*

[91] Aug. *Gen. litt.* 5.5.15: 'This day [i.e. the angelic spirits] knew the entire series of the creatures in their subsequent order ...'. At ibid. 5.4.9 the day is defined as the

in to its component parts, however, is immediately tempered by Augustine's statement at *Gen. litt.* 5.3.6:

> ... the earlier version [i.e. Gen. 1.1–1.2a] of the narrative had taught that everything was created and completed in the succession of six days; now everything is said to have happened in the space of one day, termed 'heaven and earth' ... to prove the fact that God created everything at the same time we need not look to another book of Scripture, but proof is close by, on the very next page, and it reminds us: 'after day had been made, god created heaven and earth and all the green of the field', so that you are to understand that the same day was repeated seven times in order to arrive at seven days, and so that, when you hear that everything was created once [the one] day had been made, you may comprehend, if you are able to, that this six- or sevenfold repetition happened without an interval or lapse of time.[92]

In truth, we are to understand that the material universe was created 'simultaneously' with the initial causal creative act: 'There is no doubt that this unformed matter, however much it resembles non-being, was made by god alone, and simultaneously with the objects that were [then] created from it.'[93] It remains unclear how, following the creation of t_2 on the fourth day, the remaining days five, six, and seven, a period that was already measured by the movements of the newly created celestial bodies, can be 'simultaneously' with the non-temporal, causal creation t_0 as well as with t_1, a period we must not understand along conventional temporal lines. While

---

'society and union of the supercelestial heavens and virtues' (*dies que ille societas atque unitas supercaelestium angelorum atque virtutum*). Augustine's explanation that this 'day one' (as opposed to 'the first day', which implies temporal succession) is not to be understood temporarily has been traced back to Philo's *De opificio mundi* 15, 35; cf. the detailed study by Pépin 1977. A similar interpretation is found in Basil's *Homilies on the Hexaemeron* 2.8 21A–C. On Philo's influence on Basil, cf. Runia 1993: 235–41.

[92] ... *narrationis illa contextio, cum sex dierum ordine creata cuncta et consummata memorasset, nunc ad unum diem omnia rediguntur nomine caeli et terrae ... ita iam non ex alio sanctae scripturae libro profertur testimonium quod omnia simul deus creaverit, sed vicina testificatio paginae consequentis ex hac re nos admonet dicens, cum factus est dies, fecit deus caelum et terram et omne viride agri, ut istum diem et septies intellegas repetitum, ut fierent septem dies et, cum audis tunc facta omnia, cum factus est dies, illam senariam vel septenariam repetitionem sine intervallis morarum spatiorumque temporalium factam, si possis, adprehendas.*

[93] *non itaque dubitandum est ita esse utcumque istam informem materiam prope nihil, ut non sit facta nisi a deo, et rebus quae de illa factae sunt simul concreata sit, Gen. litt.* 1.15.29 and see ibid. 4.33.52; cf. *De genesi ad litteram imperfectus liber* 7.28 and *Conf.* 13.33.

the relation between t_0, t_1, and t_2 during the creation process remains somewhat blurred, Augustine does clarify, at *Gen. litt.* 5.4.11, how the creator ensured the future existence of all creatures 'simultaneously' with the creation of the unformed substrate ('earth'), yet without compromising his divine transcendence. In the word that is Jesus Christ everything was *causaliter*,[94] meaning 'earth received the capacity of producing (*producendi virtutem*) [the creatures that were to be]'. In 'the roots of time' (*radices temporum*) the creator created what was to spring forth from the earth at its own appropriate moment during t_2. What is more, Augustine explains that it was during t_0 that the non-physical seeds of god's future creation were sown:

In that first creation (*conditio*) of the world when god created everything simultaneously he created man who was to exist in the future: [he created the] causal principle (*ratio*, transl. Taylor 1982) of the man who would exist, not man actually created ... in some regard [created things] are in the [physical] seeds (*seminibus*) where they are found to be, as it were, primordial causes (*quasi primordiales causae*) that derive, in turn, from the creation that has come forth in accordance with those [truly primordial] causes that god first built [into the substrate] ... In all these things creatures that had already been created had taken on the modes and activities (*modos et actus*) at their own time, and these developed, from the hidden and invisible [truly primordial] reasons (*rationibus*) that are latent in creation and that work in a causal manner (*causaliter*), into visible shapes and natures ... But [the corporeal living things], in turn, have duplicates of themselves [i.e. the physical seeds, transl. Taylor 1982] that are carried in themselves invisibly through some hidden power of generation which they have extracted from these primordial causes in which they were inserted into the created world when day was made; before they grew into a visible shape of their own proper kind.[95]

---

94 In response to his own question at ibid. 5.4.9: 'Where then were the creatures prior to their coming into existence? Were they inside the earth itself, in the causes and reasons (*causaliter et rationaliter*), just as all things exist already in their seeds before they develop in whatever form and unfold their intrinsic nature through the course of time?'

95 *Gen. litt.* 6.9.16–6.10.17: *in illa enim prima conditione mundi, cum deus omnia simul creavit, homo factus est qui esset futurus, ratio creandi hominis, non actio creati ... aliter in seminibus, in quibus rursus quasi primordiales causae repetuntur, de rebus ductae quae secundum causas, quas primum condidit, exstiterunt ... in quibus omnibus ea iam facta modos et actus sui temporis acceperunt, quae ex occultis atque invisibilibus rationibus, quae in creatura causaliter latent, in manifestas formas naturasque prodierunt ... sed etiam ista secum gerunt tamquam iterum seipsa invisibiliter in occulta quadam vi generandi, quam extraxerunt de illis primordiis causarum suarum,*

Two important points emerge. First, t_0 and t_1 are to be under-stood as '[actual] creation', *conditio*, whereas the unfolding of the material universe in t_2 is termed *administratio* (*Gen. litt.* 5.4.10). At 5.12.28 Augustine, even more explicitly, distinguishes three parts of the creation process: 1) the 'planting' of the seeds: the causal reasons, in the word of god (*omnium creaturarum rationes incommutabiles in verbo dei*) inside the yet unformed material substrate [t_0]; 2) the subse-quent works created during the six 'days' of creation, which really coincided with the creation of the angels on 'day one' [t_1]; and 3) his work as it manifests itself now in the reproduction of the material creatures [within t_2]. Of these three parts, the 'first two are beyond our sense perception and beyond human knowledge'. They must be believed first, putting one's faith in the authority of god. Only then are some able to attain a par-tial knowledge of divine activity preceding t_2, if granted by god. To return, briefly, to Augustine's varying interpretations of 'heaven', either as created angels or as yet uninformed angelic substrate. The creation of the angels marked 'day one', which marked a non-temporal, causal creation.

Although we do not find a time before [the angelic creature], since what has been created before all things precedes also the creation of time, before (*ante*) this creature there is, nevertheless, the eternity of the creator, from whom it has taken its origin; albeit not an origin of time, because time did not yet exist, but the origin of its creation (*conditionis*).[96]

In line with Augustine's creation account, as set out above, it is possible to infer that we ought to imagine the process of angelic formation, i.e. the angels' illumination through Christ, in the same manner as Augustine had described the creation pro-cess that preceded the creation of time. Scripture may imagine individual days, or individual steps within the angels' process

in quibus creato mundo cum factus est dies, antequam in manifestam speciem sui gen-eris exorirentur, inserta sunt. Cf. ibid. 5.4.9–11. Cf. Taylor 1982: *comm. ad loc.*, on whose guidance I rely greatly for the present passage.
[96] *Conf.* 12.15.50: etsi non invenimus tempus ante illam, quia et creaturam temporis antecedit, quae prior omnium creata est, ante illam tamen est ipsius creatoris aeternitas, a quo facta sumpsit exordium, quamvis non temporis, quia nondum erat tempus, ipsius tamen conditionis suae.

of formation, but this is merely to help us imagine a certain order. In reality, god created everthing simultaneously.[97] What is more, while the creation of the 'heaven of heavens' did mark the beginning of 'time', t_1, this is not to be understood as the temporal extensions with which we are familiar.[98]

A second point emerges from Augustine's creation theory. With the help of the seed metaphor that is woven throughout his exegesis, he is able to explain the impact of a providential power that originates with the eternal god, yet steers the future course of its creation without restricting it by too rigid a system of determinism. With regard to the seed metaphor already encountered in Calcidius,[99] we note that Augustine distinguishes immaterial causes, which he further identifies as the primordial causes inserted during the 'first' creation (*conditio*),[100] from the physical seeds from which the living creatures eventually were to rise. A subtle yet most effective difference between Augustine's *causae* and *semina*, in comparison with those of Calcidius, is the fact that Augustine makes the physical seeds the 'copies' of the underlying primordial causes, thereby establishing a connection between the divine and the physical realm. According to Augustine, the living physical things can therefore be directly traced back to the creator's agency during the *prima conditio*, the first creation, all the while his distance to the physical realm is ensured. Some Aristotelian overtones of the seed metaphor become apparent at *Gen. litt.* 5.23.45:

[97] Tornau suggests that we are to understand the uninformed state of angelic substrate as something that has never existed in reality, but 'as if they were written in the subjunctive' (2014: 211). Augustine illustrates this interpretation, nevertheless, in order to emphasize the role of the holy spirit in the act of grace that made possible the illumination of the angels.

[98] Augustine comments on the difference between 'angelic' time and our time at *Civ.* 12.5.2, where he explains that the angels existed 'at all times' (*omni tempore*) and that their 'changing motions' (*mutabilibus motibus*) allowed time to progress. At the same time, the angels' immortal being (*immortalitas*) does not progress through time (*non transit in tempore*), and it cannot be said to be in the past nor in the future at any moment (*nec praeterita est quasi iam non ist, nec futura quasi nondum sit*).

[99] Cf. p. 182; cf. p. 148 n. 135.
[100] *Gen. litt.* 5.23.44–5.

In the seed itself were the works, invisible and present all at once, that would grow into a tree over time. In this manner we ought to imagine that the world, when god created all things simultaneously, had all things at once that were made in and with it when he created 'day' ... even those creatures that water and earth brought forth causally, in potentiality, before they grew in the course of time, such as they are known to us now in the works that god creates even until now.[101]

The Augustinian creation theory leaves the overall impression of a patchwork of Greek philosophical and Judaeo-Christian dogma. We re-encounter the causal interpretation of γένεσις, a traditional component of Plato's successors proved and tested throughout the centuries. Augustine's creation theory successfully integrates both intelligible *causae* and physical *semina* into the framework of a 'twofold' creation process.[102] At the same time, Augustine anchors this, as it were, layered creation theory in Scripture itself, where the two different creation accounts should not be understood as inconsistent with, but as complementing, one another.

The type of layered creation process we find in Augustine looks back on a rich exegetical tradition that, to judge from our extant sources, emerged in the first century CE. Philo of Alexandria[103] appears to be one of its earliest proponents. His *De opificio mundi*, which betrays the influence of Platonism, Stoicism, and Neopythagoreanism, with an overall heavy dependence on the *Timaeus*, explains that a 'first' creation was the intelligible image of the creation-to-be, formed in the creator's mind. The creator formed the intelligible world so he would be able to create a *'newer* cosmos, as the likeness of the *former'* (πρεσβυτέρου νεώτερον ἀπεικόνισμα, *Opif. mund.* 16).

---

[101] *autem in ipso grano invisibiliter erant omnia simul quae per tempora in arborem surgerent; ita ipse mundus cogitandus est, cum deus simul omnia creavit, habuisse simul omnia quae in illo et cum illo facta sunt, quando factus est dies ... etiam illa quae aqua et terra produxit potentialiter atque causaliter, priusquam per temporum moras ita exorerentur, quomodo nobis iam nota sunt in eis operibus, quae deus usque nunc operatur.*

[102] The *causae* or *semina* are mentioned frequently in the *Gen. litt.*, e.g. 2.15.39, 4.33.52, 6.11.18–19, 6.14.25–15.26, 6.16.27, 6.18.29, and 9.17.21.

[103] On Philo's influence on the early Christian writers, East and West, see the extensive study by Runia 1983. The strongest support for this view is Wolfson 1956 who is frequently criticized for his attempt to ascribe to the work of all prominent Church Fathers a distinctive Philonic influence.

The six days of creation are not to be thought of as temporal, but the god made all things 'simultaneously' (ἅμα, ibid. 13), the six days being mentioned simply because a certain 'order was required for the things that came into existence' (τοῖς γιγνομένοις ἔδει τάξεως, ibid.). Subsequently he explains that the first, intelligible world was nothing other than the 'λόγος[104] of god, who was already creating' (οὐδὲν ἂν ἕτερον ... τὸν νοητὸν κόσμον εἶναι ἢ θεοῦ λόγον ἤδη κοσμοποιοῦντος, ibid. 24.6).[105] The most important parallels to Augustine appear at Philo, *Opif. mund.* 16–36, 69 and 134–5; the concept of a double creation that is structured through the order of the six 'days' emerges at 16–25.[106] What is more, we find a reference to 'seeds' at Philo's *Opif. mund.* 42–3:[107]

[104] Philo's concept of the λόγος is complex. It may be described as the rational aspect of god, or a 'reason-principle' (Runia) that is concerned with creation. It is unclear if the λόγος presents an entity separate from god. For discussions of the Philonian λόγος, see Runia 1986: 446–51; Tobin 1992. In any case, the identification of the Philonian λόγος with the Christian 'word' or λόγος that is Jesus Christ is ready at hand.

[105] Similarly the second-century apologist Tatian of Syria distinguishes a first stage of the creation process during which the divine λόγος was created. Thereafter, in turn, the λόγος created the universe by creating matter (ἀντεγέννησε τὴν καθ' ἡμᾶς ποίησιν ... τὴν ὕλην δημιουργήσας, *Oratio* 5).

[106] See also Philo's explanations concerning the role of the number six (six days) in the creation process at ibid. 13; we find a similar interpretation by Augustine at *Gen. litt.* 4.32.49–50. Cf. Agaësse and Solignac 1972 vol. 2: 612; Runia 1993: 325–6; Runia 1986: 416–20.

[107] Philo refers to Chrysippus' notion of a seed from which the universe is created at *Aet. mund.* 94.1–4 (*SVF* 2.618). After Philo, we find a reference to the demiurge who sows a part of himself into matter with Plutarch at *Plat. quaest.* 2.1, 1000e–1001b. Köckert 2009: 39–40 with n. 151 discusses the Aristotelian imagery in Plutarch, pointing to Aristotle's *Gen. an.* 1.2, 716a4–7; 1.21, 1.20, 729a9–13; 729b16–18. But we recognize in Augustine's theory of seminal reasons embedded in the created earth, which ensured the successive creation of living things, not only the echo of a Stoic λόγος that permeates the universe, but also the echo of Plotinian metaphysics. The seeds mentioned by Plotinus at *Enn.* 3.1.7 appear to be closer to the Stoic, physical seeds. Yet elsewhere, Plotinus explains that the coming to be of material objects is ultimately prompted by their emanation from the One (cf. *Enn.* 3.2.2; 5.1; 5.3; 5.6). See O'Meara 1997: 122–3 for a more detailed discussion. The One's 'thought' or 'thinking' is the λόγος while its first emanation is 'intellect' or νοῦς, imagined as the actualized state of the potential One. νοῦς, itself remaining immutable, passes on intelligible notions, the λόγοι, to the third hypostasis, soul. It is soul that is regarded as the mediatory link between the intelligible and the physical realms, passing on, in its own turn, the λόγοι to the individual souls, thereby enabling humans to participate in reason. It is soul, in this universal function, that is responsible for the creation of the physical world. In its contemplative function soul turns towards and meditates over νοῦς, fashioning in our material realm an image of the intelligible λόγοι or patterns it perceives in

In the first creation (ἐν δὲ τῇ πρώτῃ γενέσει) of all things ... the god sends forth the entire stock of plants, already matured, from the earth ... he then assigns to the earth the task of bringing them forth. Earth, in turn, as if it had been pregnant and in labour for a long time, gives birth to all that has been sown (τίκτει πάσας μὲν τὰς σπαρτῶν) ... But the fruits were not only nourishment for living creatures, but also a means of provision for the eternal coming to be (πρὸς τὴν τῶν ὁμοίων ἀεὶ γένεσιν) of their kind, holding within them the seed substances (τὰς σπερματικὰς οὐσίας transl. Colson/Whittaker) in which there are the principles (οἱ λόγοι τῶν ὅλων) of all things, hidden and invisible.

In the Eastern tradition parallels with Philo's exegesis are found, for instance, in Theophilus of Antioch, who likewise mentions a double creation at *Ad Autolycum* 2.10.32–4,[108] and a similar interpretation of the six days of creation at ibid. 2.11–18.[109] The role of the *Timaeus* as a point of reference for Theophilus' exegesis becomes explicit in his criticism of the 'Platonic' doctrine that leaves matter to be uncreated and therefore on an ontological par with the creator.[110] As for the Western Church Fathers, it was Augustine's mentor Ambrose of Milan who extended the reach of Philo into the Latin world[111] and may have been a further channel of transmission for the Timaean elements of creationism that helped

νοῦς (*Enn.* 4.1.3.). νοῦς is thus considered to be the blueprint of our familiar physical world. The λόγοι that are thereby distributed and immanent throughout the sensible realm may to some extent be paralleled with Augustine's seminal reasons which are immanent in our universe. After Augustine, Boethius at *Cons.* 3 m.9 presents Philosophia's creation theory, where God is invoked as 'the one who has sown (*sator*, l. 2) the earth and the heaven', 'ruling the world by eternal reason' (*ratione*, l. 1), who orders time to 'proceed from eternity' (*ire ab aeterno*, ll. 2–3). Boethius' *sator* may be a reference to Augustine's creation theory, the inspiration behind Boethius' thought at *Opuscula sacra* 1.29–32.

[108] ταῦτα ἐν πρώτοις διδάσκει ἡ θεία γραφή, τρόπῳ τινὶ ὕλην γενητήν, ὑπὸ τοῦ θεοῦ γεγονυῖαν, ἀφ' ἧς πεποίηκεν καὶ δεδημιούργηκεν ὁ θεὸς τὸν κόσμον.

[109] This is the case also in Ps.-Justin's *Cohortatio ad Graecos*, likewise associated with Philonian influence. Cf. Runia 1993: 184–9.

[110] Theophilus, *Ad Autolycum* 2.4: Πλάτων δὲ καὶ οἱ τῆς αἱρέσεως αὐτοῦ θεὸν μὲν ὁμολογοῦσιν ἀγένητον καὶ πατέρα καὶ ποιητὴν τῶν ὅλων εἶναι. εἶτα ὑποτίθενται θεὸν καὶ ὕλην ἀγένητον καὶ ταύτην φασίν συνηκμακέναι τῷ Θεῷ. A further significant link in the intellectual chain of a double creation is Origen of Alexandria (185–253 CE). As noted above in the case of Calcidius, it is most unfortunate that Origen's commentary on Genesis is no longer extant. Pépin 1977 has shown the exegetical link between Philo, Origen, and Augustine in the context of the latter's interpretation of the *caelum* of Gen. 1.1.

[111] Ambrose employed Philonian exegesis more extensively than any other Church Father. See Runia 1993: 291–311.

shape Augustine's own narrative. While we may be confident that Augustine had access at least to Philo's *Quaestiones in Genesim*,[112] he refers to him by name only once. In his *Contra Faustum* at 12.39 he notes Philo's elegant style but chastizes him for failing to recognize Jesus in his scriptural interpretation. Nevertheless, the continuity of a 'twofold' creation, and its unmistakeable parallels with the Timaean tradition, in particular the notions of an intelligible creature, of a causal creation, and the distinction between temporality and atemporal eternity as markers of diverging ontological realms between creator and creation, become an integral part of the Christian creation narrative that developed over the first centuries of our era. At the same time, we note that no passage is found within Scripture that would warrant a multi-layered creation process that begins with a 'causal' act. I therefore suggest that it was the controversy regarding the createdness of the Timaean cosmos, already stretching over many centuries, that helped inspire this specific interpretation.

Metaphysics: Christ the Mediator

We saw in the preceding chapters that Middle Platonic authors found various solutions for reconciling the creator's transcendence with providential material cosmos. This difficulty was a part of the Platonic heritage that came along with the relationship between the intelligible forms and their sensibles, between τὸ ὄν and τὸ γιγνόμενον (*Tim.* 27d6) or οὐσία and γένεσις (*Tim.* 29c3). In what manner could the ontological divide be bridged so as to allow for the intelligible realm to impact on the nature of our material world while, at the same time, maintaining its transcendence? We find echoes of a familiar Timaean passage that exhibits the underlying dualism of Plato's metaphysics in Augustine's *De consensu evangelistarum* (ca. 400 CE), and in his *De trinitate* 4.18.24 (399–ca. 427 CE). In both works, Augustine puts Timaeus' words to an astonishing exegetical use. Both contexts share the broad overall aim of

---

[112] Cf. Altaner 1967 and see Runia 1993: 322–6 for a summary of the evidence.

justifying Christ's full divinity. In his *Retractationes*, Augustine delivers a survey of his works intended to rectify his doctrinal stance on the many issues he had dealt with in his writings over decades. At *Retr.* 2.16 he groups the *De consensu evangelistarum* with his *De trinitate:*

> During the same years, while I was gradually composing the books on the trinity, I wrote with continuing effort also other books during times that were devoted to the former. Among [these other works] are the four books on *The Harmony of the Evangelists*, [addressing] those who falsely accuse the Evangelists, as if they were in disagreement. The first volume was written against those who either honour, or pretend to honour, Christ as a man of supreme wisdom, and are unwilling to believe in the gospels, precisely because they were not written by himself but by his disciples, whom they believe to have attributed to him his divinity, through which he is now held to be god, by mistake.[113]

The most systematic criticism of the gospels, at the time Augstine composed the *De consensu evangelistarum*, had been a part of Porphyry's no longer extant work *Contra Christianos*, which had already provoked Eusebius of Caesarea to defend the veracity of the gospels in his *Praeparatio evangelica*, *Demonstratio evangelica*, and in his *Historia ecclesiastica*. Augustine's *De consensu evangelistarum*, likewise, may have been primarily in response to Porphyry's arguments against the evangelists' accounts. While the Neoplatonist remains the primary target in this work, Augustine occasionally directed similar criticism also at prominent Manichaean voices who had equally questioned Christ's divinity. His *Against Faustus the Manichaean*, composed around the same time as the *De consensu evangelistarum*, shows that Augustine had to wrestle with the following hostile arguments:

> Do you accept that [Christ] was born [i.e. incarnate]? Indeed, I tried for a long time to convince myself of this, whatever it may mean, that god was born. But I was put off by the disagreement especially between two of the evangelists

[113] *per eosdem annos, quibus paulatim libros de trinitate dictabam, scripsi et alios labore continuo interponens eos illorum temporibus, in quibus sunt libri quattuor De consensu evangelistarum propter eos qui tamquam dissentientibus calumniantur. quorum primus liber adversus illos conscriptus est, qui tamquam maxime sapientem Christum vel honorant vel honorare se fingunt, et ideo nolunt evangelio credere, quia non ab ipso illa conscripta sunt sed ab eius discipulis, quos existimant ei divinitatem qua crederetur deus errore tribuisse.* On Porphyry as Augustine's target, cf. Dodaro 2004: 64 and Madec 1992.

who wrote about his genealogy, Luke and Matthew, and I was stuck, uncertain which one to follow over the other.[114]

In Book 4 of his *De trinitate*, Augustine's immediate concern lies with soteriology. Christ participates in human nature to allow us to share in his divine nature, a process that would not be possible if the nature of father and son were distinct. I shall use Augustine's discussion in the *De consensu evangelistarum* as my primary point of reference, with frequent references to *Trin.* 4.18.24.

In chapter 35.53 of Book 1 of the *De consensu evangelistarum*, Augustine explains that a prophecy made to the ancients, and now revealed through the gospel to Christians, had already spoken of Christ as a mediator between the divine and human realms. Let us examine the relevant passage in full:

Table 29. *Augustine,* De consensu evangelistarum *1.35.53*

1	§1: *cum sit ipse Christus sapientia dei per quam creata sunt omnia, cumque nullae mentes rationales sive angelorum sive hominum nisi*	Since Christ himself is the wisdom of god, through which all things were created, and since no rational minds, whether of angels
5	*participatione ipsius sapientes fiant cui per spiritum sanctum, per quem caritas in cordibus nostris diffunditur, inhaeremus, quae trinitas unus deus est,*	or men, become wise except by participation in this very wisdom to which we cling through the holy spirit through whom charity is diffused in our hearts, −[and this is] the trinity that is the one God−,
10	§2: *consultum est divina providentia mortalibus quorum temporalis vita in rebus orientibus et occidentibus occupata tenebatur,*	divine providence decreed, for the sake of mortals whose temporal life was restrained and occupied by things that come to be and die,

(continued)

[114] *Contr. Faust.* 3.1: *accipis ergo generationem? equidem conatus diu sum hoc ipsum qualecumque est persuadere mihi, quia sit natus deus: sed offensus duorum maxime evangelistarum dissensione, qui genealogiam eius scribunt, Lucae et Matthaei, haesi incertus quemnam potissimum sequerer.*

Table 29 (*continued*)

15	§3: *ut eadem ipsa dei sapientia ad unitatem personae suae homine assumpto, in quo temporaliter nasceretur, viveret, moreretur, resurgeret, congrua saluti nostrae*	that this same wisdom of god, having received the [nature] of man into the oneness of his person, [a nature] in which he would be born in accordance with a temporal existence, in which he would
20	*dicendo et faciendo, patiendo et sustinendo fieret et deorsum hominibus exemplum redeundi, qui sursum est angelis exemplum manendi.*	live, die, and rise again, should through word and deed effect things becoming to our salvation, and through endurance and perseverance would become to men on earth a paradigm of returning [to heaven], and to the angels above a paradigm of remaining in heaven.
25	§4: *nisi enim et in animae rationalis natura temporaliter aliquid oriretur, id est inciperet esse quod non erat, numquam ex vita pessima et stulta ad*	For unless something came to be also in the nature of a rational soul, in accordance with a temporal existence, – that is, unless that began to be which was not before –
30	*sapientem atque optimam perveniret.*	soul would never attain, from a life of utmost calamity and ignorance, to a life of wisdom and excellence.
	§5: *ac per hoc, cum rebus aeternis contemplantium veritas perfruatur, rebus autem ortis fides*	For this reason, since the truth of those who behold it rejoices in things eternal, while the faith of believers is owed to things created,
35	*credentium debeatur, purgatur homo per rerum temporalium fidem, ut aeternarum percipiat veritatem.*	man is purified through the faith in temporal things, that he may perceive the truth of things eternal.
	§6: *nam et quidam eorum*	For likewise a certain man, the
40	*nobilissimus philosophus Plato in eo libro, quem Timaeum vocant, sic ait: quantum ad id quod ortum est aeternitas valet, tantum ad fidem veritas.*	philosopher Plato, most noble among them, speaks in the book they call the *Timaeus*: 'To the same degree as eternity impacts upon things made, in the same manner truth impacts upon faith.'
45	§7: *duo illa sursum sunt, aeternitas et veritas, duo ista deorsum, quod ortum est et fides. ut ergo ab imis ad summa revocemur atque id quod ortum est recipiat*	Those two things, eternity and truth, are associated with [the heavens] above; these other two things, that which is made and faith, are associated with [the

254

Table 29 (*continued*)

50 *aeternitatem, per fidem veniendum* *est ad veritatem.*	earth] below. Therefore, that we may be called away from the lowest up to the highest, and that what is made may attain to eternity, we must arrive at truth through faith.

§8: *et quia omnia quae in*
       contrarium pergunt per aliquid
       medium reducuntur, ab aeterna
 55   *iustitia temporalis iniquitas*
       nos alienabat, opus ergo erat
       media iustitia temporali, quae
       medietas temporalis esset de
       imis, iusta de summis, atque ita
 60   *se nec abrumpens a summis et*
       contemperans imis, ima redderet
       summis.
	And since all that strives towards opposite extremes is held [in balance] by some mediating element, as the lack of righteousness of a temporal existence alienated us from eternal righteousness, there was need of some mediating righteousness of a temporal nature. This mediating element would be of a temporal nature from the lowest perspective, but righteous from the highest perspective, and thus, by adjusting itself to the former without breaking from the latter, it would restore what is lowest to what is highest.

§9: *ideo Christus mediator dei et*
       hominum dictus est inter deum
 65   *immortalem et hominem mortalem*
       deus et homo, reconcilians
       hominem deo, manens id quod
       erat, factus quod non erat.
	For this reason, Christ was named the mediator between god and men, between the immortal god and mortal man, himself being both god and man who reconciled man to god and who, remaining what he was, was made what he was not.

§10: *ipse est nobis fides in rebus* 70 *ortis, qui est veritas in aeternis.*	He himself for us is the faith in things that are made, and the truth that belongs to things eternal.

§11: *hoc magnum et inenarrabile*
       sacramentum, hoc regnum
       et sacerdotium antiquis per
       prophetiam revelabatur, posteris
 75   *eorum per evangelium praedicatur.*
	This grand and unerring revelation, this kingdom and Christ's mediating office,[115] was revealed through prophecy to the ancients, and is preached through the gospel to their descendants.

---

[115]   Cf. Vulg. Heb. 7,12 and 7,24.

In §1 Christ himself is recognized as the wisdom of god (*sapientia dei*) which illuminates and brings to perfection the angelic spirits and human intellect that, through their conversion to the wisdom that is Christ, themselves receive wisdom (*nullae mentes rationales sive angelorum sive hominum nisi participatione ipsius sapientes fiant*).[116] We are united with this wisdom by the holy spirit that spreads charity into our hearts. This trinity, Christ, god, and the holy spirit, at the same time constitutes one god.

§§2–3: Divine providence (*divina providentia*), in its care for humankind, decreed that this wisdom of god (*ipsa dei sapientia*), having taken on human form and a temporal existence (*homine assumpto, temporaliter*) and having lived, died, and risen, should serve as a paradigm (*exemplum*) for followers to show them the path to salvation (*saluti*). §4: Unless, in the nature of a rational soul, too, something began to rise up, to exist, that had not existed before (*aliquid oriretur, id est inciperet esse quod non erat*), soul would never be able to arrive from a life of utter corruption and ignorance at one of wisdom and goodness. §5: While the truth of those able to contemplate it rejoices in things eternal (*veritas perfruatur*), those who believe owe faith (*fides credentium debeatur*) to things pertaining to the temporal realm. Through the faith they hold in the temporal world (*per rerum temporalium fidem*) humans are purified (*purgatur*), a necessary condition for an individual's access to eternal truth (*ut aeternarum percipiat veritatem*).

Augustine underlines his explanation by pointing to the *Timaeus*, and quotes the dialogue almost verbatim via Cicero's translation:

Table 30. *Plato,* Tim. *29c3*

ὅτιπερ πρὸς γένεσιν οὐσία, τοῦτο πρὸς πίστιν ἀλήθεια.	As being is in relation to becoming, so truth is in relation to convincingness.

---

[116] For the purpose of the present study I shall discuss Augustine's concept of *sapientia* primarily in the context of his hierarchical metaphysics. While this trinitarian structure is immediately tied to Augustine's epistemology, I am unable to

Table 31. *Augustine,* De consensu evangelistarum *1.35.53*

quantum ad id quod ortum est aeternitas valet, tantum ad fidem veritas.	To the same degree as eternity impacts upon what has come to be, truth impacts upon faith.

Table 32. *Cicero's translation of Plato,* Tim. *29c3 (Cic.* Tim. *3.8, 1–2)*

quantum enim ad id quod ortum est aeternitas valet, tantum ad fidem veritas.	B§3: For to the same degree as eternity impacts upon what has come to be, truth impacts upon faith.

Aligning eternity (*aeternitas*) and truth (*veritas*), notions that belong to 'above' (*sursum*) or the divine realm, over and against temporal creatures and faith, notions of 'below' (*deorsum*) or the material realm,[117] Augustine in §7 offers his interpretation of the prophecy revealed by the gospel, after Plato, who lacked in Christian illumination, had failed to interpret it correctly. Faith in Christ provides for humans, who are anchored in temporality throughout their human lives, the bridge that enables them to be led from the lowest to the highest realm (*ab imis ad summa*), and that enables the temporal to participate in the eternal (*quod ortum est recipiat aeternitatem*). Christians must come through faith to truth (*per fidem veniendum est ad veritatem*). *Fides*, in Augustine's understanding of Timaeus' analogy, is not a mere epistemological plane that necessarily pertains to the material realm, but is the one quality that makes possible the transition between material and divine realms.

We continue in §8 of our passage: As contraries may be united through an intermediate element (*per aliquid medium*), there was a need for a mediating, temporal source of righteousness (*media iustitia temporali*), itself partaking

---

address his understanding of the role of wisdom in this latter context in greater detail. For a recent general study on the subject, see Gioia 2008; see also Doull 1988. Lorenz 1979: 137 gives a summary of the Christian wisdom tradition.

[117] Cf. Origen's *Hom. ps.* 36.5,4; *Princ.* 2.3.6.

of temporality *and* eternity (*se nec abrumpens a summis et contemperans imis ima redderet summis*), to make possible the path from a lack of righteousness within the temporal realm (*temporalis iniquitas*) to eternal righteousness (*aeterna iustitia*). Accordingly, Augustine explains in §9, Christ was pronounced this mediating link between humans and the divine (*Christus mediator dei et hominum dictus est*), himself both human and god, thereby reconciling one to the other. In §10 Christ himself, who *is* faith for us in the material realm (as the son of god incarnate), and who is at the same time the truth of things eternal: *ipse est nobis fides in rebus ortis qui est veritas in aeternis.* Christ remains that which 'was' even while he was made into something that 'was not' (*quod non erat*). This mediating link, to humans, at one and the same time represents an object of faith within the material realm (as the son of god incarnate), and the truth of things eternal (as god himself): *ipse est nobis fides in rebus ortis qui est veritas in aeternis.* This grand and unerring revelation (*sacramentum*) of Christ's mediating office was revealed to the ancients through a prophecy (*per prophetiam*), now proclaimed to their descendants through the gospel.

Some notes are in order. The immediate context of this passage, we recall, is Augustine's aim of defending the validity of Christ's divinity against those who denied him an equal role in the godhead, given his incarnate form. By pointing to the revelation (*sacramentum*) to which Plato's *Timaeus* bears witness – even though Plato had lacked the Christian wisdom required for decoding it – Augustine now launches his defence of Christ's divinity by interpreting this revelation in accordance with his Christian faith. From the beginning the emphasis is on Christ's mediatory role, and on the necessary impact this role has on human salvation. Both aspects are announced in the first paragraph: the trinitarian god is one; human soul is transformed by participating (*participatione*) in the very wisdom that is Christ himself.

In §3 Augustine elaborates on Christ's mediating impact. Having assumed human form in the temporal realm, he serves as our *exemplum*, a paradigm, of behaviour that will lead us to salvation. At the same time, he exemplifies the ontological change that will be undergone by humans: he is born, dies, and rises again (*exemplum redeundi*). Having witnessed this change in him allows us to have *faith* – *fides* appears in Augustine's interpretation in §5 – in him and faith in the process of transformation he represents. Faith will ultimately enable us to quit the temporal sphere. Unlike the notion of πίστις at *Tim.* 29c3, a term that denotes a level of cognitive reliability, Augustine's faith is a necessary cognitive activity[118] that prepares for the next step towards a higher level of cognitive activity, the contemplation of truth. What is more, while the objects of the Timaean πίστις are those that have γένεσις, that come to be and perish, the object of faith such as it is described by Augustine, Christ, participates in both ontological levels γένεσις and οὐσία, or, in Augustine's (Cicero's) words, in both *aeternitas* and *quod ortum est*. Christ who, as god, had already participated in *aeternitas*, became 'something he was not before' (§4): he became *quod ortum est*. Let me summarize Augustine's line or reasoning thus far: Christ has a mediatory impact on us by providing an *exemplum* of ontological change. Unlike the intelligible *exempla* of Platonic doctrine, the paradigm of Christ is more accessible as a model for human ontological change given that it is both eternal and has come to be. Witnessing his *exemplum* allows for a change in the cognitive activity in our soul, the exercise of faith. Exercising faith purifies our soul, which allows us to access truth in the eternal realm.

---

[118] Cf. *De diversis quaestionibus octoginta tribus, Quaestio* 57,2. On the above passage in general, cf. Ayres 2010: 142–70; Gioia 2008: 68–9, 78–83. At ibid. 79 Gioia notes that 'faith is a mode of participation in this [earthly] life'; cf. ibid. 175 and ibid. 76: 'faith and vision have the same object and are both a real form of knowledge of God, the only difference between the two is in the modality of this knowledge' (Gioia's rendering of Plato's πίστις in the context of our *Timaeus* passage as 'faith' is slightly misleading). In addition to understanding Augustine's meaning of *fides* as an epistemological mode, I would stress the fact that it is an 'activity', cf. McGrath 1986: 27, who notes that the 'act of faith in itself is a divine gift, in which god acts upon the rational soul in such a way that it comes to believe'. Yet, despite its origin from god, 'the acts of receiving and possessing themselves can be said to be man's'. Camelot 1956: 167 picks up Augustine's use of Cicero's translation in this passage but does not comment on its portrayal as a *mysterium* received by Plato. It appears that Camelot, interpreting the term *fides*, erroneously transfers Cicero's sceptical nuance to Augustine: 'on n'entend pas pour autant qu'il soit "vraisemblable", conjectural et incertain.'

In §6 we encounter the Timaean passage that is of central importance to Augustine's metaphysical viewpoint at *De consensu evangelistarum* 1.35.53: 'For likewise a certain man, the philosopher Plato, most noble among them, speaks in the book they call the *Timaeus*: "To the same degree as eternity impacts upon things made, in the same manner truth impacts upon faith"' (*quantum ad id quod ortum est aeternitas valet, tantum ad fidem veritas*). In what follows, Christ himself is shown to be the mediating link that establishes a connection not only between the two ontological realms, temporal and divine, but also between these ontological realms and their associated cognitive activities *fides* and *veritas*. He represents truth and eternity, notions associated with above (*sursum*) while, at the same time, he participates in the material realm and, as the son incarnate, inspires faith in our souls.

At *De trinitate* 4.18.24, where *Tim.* 29c3 is equally quoted by Augustine, he reveals that Christ himself is the truth:

Table 33. *Augustine,* De trinitate *4.18.24*

...	...
ipsa veritas patri coaeterna de terra orta est cum filius dei sic venit ut fieret filius hominis et ipse in se exciperet fidem nostram qua nos perduceret ad veritatem suam qui sic suscepit mortalitatem nostram ut non amitteret aeternitatem suam.	the truth itself, co-eternal with the father, took a beginning from earth, when the son of God so came as to become the son of man, and to take to himself our faith, that he might thereby lead us to his own truth, and he assumed our mortal existence in such a way as allowed him not to lose his own eternity.

As we return to our passage *De consensu evangelistarum* 1.35.53 (Table 29), Augustine paves the way for his view concerning Christ's mediating role with the help of a familiar argument originally borrowed from geometry. In §8 a mediating element is required in order to reduce opposite extremes to unity. It is likely that this part of Augustine's exegesis was ultimately inspired by *Tim.* 31b4–32c4 – covered by Cicero's translation – where Timaeus establishes the significance of the geometrical proportion in the context of the four material elements that make up the cosmos, an idea we have previously encountered in the context of Apuleius' and Calcidius' demonology. Let us remind ourselves of the most salient features of Timaeus' explanation. The universe, as something that has come to be, must be of a corporeal nature and be made up from fire (ensuring the cosmic body's visibility) and earth (ensuring its tangibility, *Tim.* 31b4). To unite the two elements fire and earth, a third mediating element was required, as a bond to unify the two extremes (δεσμὸν γὰρ ἐν μέσῳ δεῖ τινα ἀμφοῖν συναγωγὸν γίγνεσθαι, 31c1–2).[119] The most effective bond for achieving true unity is that which is able to assimilate itself to the two extremes it unites (ὃς ἂν αὑτὸν καὶ τὰ συνδούμενα ὅτι μάλιστα ἓν ποιῇ, 31c2–3), which is brought about by proportion (ἀναλογία): 'Whenever the middle term of three numbers … between any two of them is such that what the first term is to it, it is to the last, and, conversely, what the last term is to the middle term, it is to the first, then, since the middle term turns out to be both first and last, and the last and the first likewise both turn out to be middle terms, they will all of necessity turn out to have the same relationship to each other, and, given this, will be unified' (*Tim.* 31c4–32a7, transl. Zeyl).[120]

In Augustine' exegesis, we may conjecture, Christ assumes the role of a middle term, unifying the two 'extremes', eternal divine existence above and temporal coming to be below, in his own incarnate nature, thereby fulfilling the same unifying role that had been assigned to the demons by Apuleius and Calcidius.[121] At this point, it is worth pointing out, moreover, that we find in Augustine's passage *Consens.* 1.35.53 the notion of a 'divine providence' (§2) that takes care of the lower ontological realm, similarly to the effects of divine

---

[119] Compare Cicero's translation: *omnia autem duo ad cohaerendum tertium aliquid anquirunt et quasi nodum vinculumque desiderant.* On Christ as mediator, cf. Dodaro 2004: 94–107, O'Daly 1999: 120–2.

[120] ὁπόταν γὰρ ἀριθμῶν τριῶν … ὡντινωνοῦν ᾖ τὸ μέσον, ὅτιπερ τὸ πρῶτον πρὸς αὐτό, τοῦτο αὐτὸ πρὸς τὸ ἔσχατον, καὶ πάλιν αὖθις, ὅτι τὸ ἔσχατον πρὸς τὸ μέσον, τὸ μέσον πρὸς τὸ πρῶτον, τότε τὸ μέσον μὲν πρῶτον καὶ ἔσχατον γιγνόμενον, τὸ δ' ἔσχατον καὶ τὸ πρῶτον αὖ μέσα ἀμφότερα, πάνθ' οὕτως ἐξ ἀνάγκης τὰ αὐτὰ εἶναι συμβήσεται, τὰ αὐτὰ δὲ γενόμενα ἀλλήλοις ἓν πάντα ἔσται.

[121] Cf. pp. 148–58 with n. 140; pp. 201–6.

providence in the Apuleian cosmos and in the Calcidian cosmos.[122] Nevertheless, while both Apuleius and Calcidius had clearly pointed to the role of intermediary agents from the perspective of the world's material continuity, Augustine's description of the 'middle term' in §8 of the above passage is couched not so much in the terms of material continuity, but is made rather with reference to the pairs temporality–lack of righteousness and eternity–righteousness. The two extremes (*contraria*) that are held together by some mediating element (*per aliquid medium*) are eternal righteousness (*aeterna iustitia*) associated with above (*summa*) and the lack of righteousness that is inherent in a temporal existence (*temporalis iniquitas*) associated with below (*ima*).[123]

A note on the translation of the Timaean analogy at *Tim.* 29c3.[124] As noted above, Augustine's translation is quoted almost verbatim from Cicero's partial Latin translation of the *Timaeus*. While Augustine may be drawing on various other sources for his exegesis in the present context, there is no question that the phrasing he found in the Latin text fits rather seamlessly with the interpretative stance he is developing. We saw that Cicero's *valere*, 'to have an impact upon', does not faithfully capture the purely relational description between the ontological realms and their associated epistemological planes 'truth' and 'convincingness' that we find in the original Greek. Nevertheless, Cicero's rendering lends itself beautifully

---

[122] Cf. pp. 150–8, 196–200.

[123] Teske 1985b emphasizes Augustine's views of time and eternity in relation to *Enn.* 3.7, where Plotinus associates the origin of time with soul's entering the temporal world through sin.

[124] Augustine's description has certainly lost the geometrical character of Timaeus' original statement, which is retained by Cicero; cf., for instance, the latter's translation of Timaeus' introduction of the geometrical ἀναλογία: *id optime adsequitur, quae Graece analogia, Latine (audendum est enim, quoniam haec primum a nobis novantur) comparatio proportiove dici potest.* While there are no close terminological similarities between Cicero's translation of *Tim.* 31b–32c (cf. also my discussion above, pp. 236–7) and Augustine's §8, Timaeus' description at *Tim.* 32c2 of the cosmic body having obtained 'friendship', φιλία, from the four bonded elements, is translated by Cicero with the tautological (*quaedam*) *amicitia et caritas*. It is possible that Cicero's choice of terminology was on Augustine's mind for his description of the holy spirit's diffusing of *caritas* into mortals in §1 of the above passage *Consens.* 1.35.53.

to Augustine's reinterpretation of Plato's text, according to which Christ's eternity (*aeternitas*) has an impact upon (*valet ad*) our temporal existence. Furthermore, we recall that Cicero translated *aeternitas* for οὐσία, likely due to his erroneous interpretation of Timaeus' eternal intelligible paradigm as the Form of Eternity:[125]

Table 34. *Plato,* Tim. *29a2–4*

εἰ μὲν δὴ καλός ἐστιν ὅδε ὁ κόσμος ὅ τε δημιουργὸς ἀγαθός, δῆλον ὡς πρὸς τὸ ἀίδιον [παράδειγμα] ἔβλεπεν· εἰ δὲ ὃ μηδ᾽ εἰπεῖν τινι θέμις, πρὸς γεγονός.	If this cosmos is beautiful and the demiurge good, it is clear that he was looking towards the **eternal paradigm**. If not – an unlawful thing even to utter – he was looking towards a created model.

Table 35. *Cicero's translation of Plato,* Tim. *29a2–4 (* Cic. Tim. *2.6, 1–5)*

atqui si pulcher est hic mundus et si probus eius artifex, profecto **speciem aeternitatis** imitari maluit; sin secus, quod ne dictu quidem fas est, generatum exemplum est pro aeterno secutus.	But if this cosmos is beautiful and its maker is good, he certainly preferred to imitate the **form of eternity**. If not – even to utter this is unlawful – he followed a created instead of an eternal model.

As a consequence, we noted that Cicero's translation of the Timaean analogy at *Tim.* 29c3, which appears also in Augustine, seems to express the relation to each other not of the realm of being (οὐσία), taken as an ontological class, to becoming, but as referring to the Form of Eternity (*species aeternitatis*; *aeternitas*) as a particular representative of the intelligible realm. On this interpretation, Cicero makes our universe a copy or an image of the Form of Eternity (eternity being only *one* of the qualities possessed by a generic Platonic form). Be that as it may, Cicero's translation of οὐσία as *aeternitas* had an impact on Augustine's understanding of the *Timaeus*. οὐσία, the ontological class of intelligible being, is

[125] Cf. pp. 99–101.

associated by Augustine with the eternal type of existence that is obtained through salvation.[126]

[126] Boethius' *De consolatione philosophiae* offers a more expansive interpretation of the Timaean analogy at *Tim.* 29c3. In Philosophia's discourse the correlated pair time and eternity appear alongside other pairs that serve to explain the divine nature in relation to its manifestations in the human sphere. At the centre is again the image of a circle that may be collapsed into its central point, an image used by Philosophia to connect the metaphysical and physical frameworks that underlie her reasoning. At 4 pr. 5 Philosophia draws up a number of correlated pairs that relate immutable, all-encompassing unity to mutable, limited plurality: 'As reasoning stands in relation to intellect, so that which comes to be stands in relation to that which is, [likewise] time stands in relation to eternity, a circle to its central point; in a like manner, the moving series of fate is in relation to the steadfast simplicity of providence' (ibid. 4 pr. 5: *igitur uti est ad intellectum ratiocinatio, ad id quod est id quod gignitur, ad aeternitatem tempus, ad punctum medium circulus, ita est fati series mobilis ad providentiae stabilem simplicitatem*). Philosophia thus transforms Timaeus' analogy and expands it to include also cognitive method (all-encompassing, immutable intellect – progressive, discursive reasoning); the category 'ontological status' (being, coming to be) appears next to the pair 'eternity and time' that has been introduced first by Philosophia in order to grasp the nature of the divine. The pair 'truth and convincingness', which in the *Timaeus* appears in the context of the speaker's reflection on the epistomololgical status of his own account, is not part of Philosophia's modified analogy. With good reason: as their conversation proceeds, her patient comes to realize the truth of her statements, induced by the kinship she establishes between her subject matter and the literary forms and argumentative method she employs. In the present context, instead, Philosophia includes the geometrical relation between a point and its moving sphere, and the relation between divine providence and the fatal series of events in the temporal realm (at 5 p. 3 providence is not merely the mechanical foreseeing of events but takes on the role of a cognitive faculty that is opposed to human opinion. If providence did not foresee everything, how would it 'surpass human opinion'? This is in line with the definition of providence previously at 4 pr. 6 as 'the divine reason itself'). The individual elements that are part of the transformed analogy of the *De consolatione* serve the specific purpose of settling Philosophia's patient's troubles and of curing his soul. Through Philosophia the dualistic Timaean relational analogy of *Tim.* 29c is transformed into an inclusive one-way embrace in which the lower realm (represented by discursive reasoning, coming to be, temporality, the image of a sphere and fate) is embraced and contained by the higher (intellect, being, eternity, point, divine providence). Philosophia includes the correlated pair 'point and circle' in order to make clear that the individual qualities and facilities associated with the higher sphere must be conceived of as the essential unity that is god. All members of the related pairs in the higher sphere are, indeed, aspects of one and the same divine essence. The differentiation between these aspects is necessary only from our perspective since we are unable to understand divine simplicity. Philosophia merges the issues that are discussed by Timaeus at *Tim.* 37e–38a, time and eternity, with those discussed at *Tim.* 29c, the relational analogy between being and coming to be, in her explanation of the *divina substantia*. While 'intellect', 'being', 'eternity', and 'providence' all describe the divine nature, they cannot be expressed through one word alone that would convey to us their self-identity and unity. We cannot grasp the divine nature save through the correlational analogies that make

With Cicero's unassuming help, Augustine finds in Plato's very own words the promise of *aeternitas*, eternal existence, achieved through faith, *fides*. Based on our previous findings that saw Augustine stressing the creator's eternity as a mark of his immutable ontological essence, we may take *aeternitas* as a reference to the divine realm and to the essence of the creator himself, who has been identified as true being. In our present context Augustine couples *aeternitas* with *veritas* as a further attribute that pertains to the realm of eternal being (cf. above, *ut aeternarum percipiat veritatem*).[127] This association is expressed even more clearly in Augustine, *In Ioh. ev. tract.* 38.10:

What is it that is proper to you and that you have retained as your own being, that you have not given to others, so that you alone are [that which is proper to you]? ... Oh truth, it is you that truly is. In all our activities and motions, certainly in every stirring of created things I find two times, the past and the future. I seek the present, and nothing stands still. What I have said is no more. What I shall say is not yet. What I have done is no more. What I shall do is not yet. The life I have lived is no more. The life I shall live is not yet. I find the past and the future in every motion of things. In truth, which abides, I do not find the

it comprehensible for us with the help of a set of labels: 'intellect', 'being', 'eternity', and 'providence' set in relation to their manifestations in our human sphere. The relational pair fate–providence is the final key element of Philosophia's argumentation intended to heal her patient. The image of a sphere circling its centre is applied again in Books 4 and 5 of the *De consolatione* to explain the exact relation between *providentia* and *fatum*. At 4 pr. 6 Philosophia explains that no randomness exists in the cosmos since the All is ruled by omniscient, divine providence. Providence is defined as 'divine reason itself '(*divina ratio*, 4 pr. 6, 9), yet the understanding of precisely how this rule of reason manifests itself in the cosmos depends upon the cognitive abilities of the observer. If observed from the perspective of divine intelligence itself, the workings the divine mind are, simply, 'providence': rational order leading to the best possible outcome. From a human perspective, however, this same force is 'what the ancients called fate' (4 pr. 6, 8), a seemingly random and incoherent chain of events. Providence is 'the unfolding of this temporal order [of events], unified into the foresight of the divine mind', while fate is 'the same unity broken up and unfolded in time' (4 pr. 6, 10). As the circumference of a circle may be collapsed ino its centrepoint, in the same manner the causal chain of fate collapses into simple providential unity. Philosophia effectively transfers the distinction between providence and fate as forces operating in two distinct ontological spheres, such as we see it in Calcidius and Apuleius, to the distinction between two different cognitive modes – one divine, the other human – that operate in the same sphere.

[127] Augustine associates god with the term *veritas* e.g. at *Conf.* 10.23.33; *De libero arbitrio* 3.16.

past nor the future, but only the present, and this I find to be incorruptible, which is not a characteristic of created things.[128]

Let us continue with our notes on the previous passage *Consens.* 1.35.53. A further conspicuous term that appears in the context of Augustine's interpretation of the analogy passage (Table 29, §8) is *iustitia*. We recall: as contraries may be united through a mediary middle term (*per aliquid medium*), there was a need for a mediating, temporal source of righteousness (*media iustitia temporali*), itself partaking of temporality *and* eternity (*se nec abrumpens a summis et contemperans imis ima redderet summis*), to make possible the path from a lack of righteousness associated with the temporal realm (*temporalis iniquitas*) to righteousness associated with eternal existence (*aeterna iustitia*). The appearance of the term *iustitia* in the context of our familiar analogy is at first sight unexpected; its Greek equivalent δικαιοσύνη is not a part of the Timaean analogy at *Tim* 29b3.

It is important to place Augustine's mention of *iustitia* in the context of his concept of justification.[129] In Christian theology the term describes the process of transformation that is undergone by a person being restored from a sinful state to a right relationship with god through the mediation of Christ, the redeemer of human sin. One transitions from a state of *in*justice, in the sense of non-righteousness (being morally wrong), to a state of *iustitia*, 'righteousness', the state of being morally right. This concept of justification, which was to emerge as one of Augustine's most important legacies in the subsequent theological tradition, first became significant for him in his altercation with the Pelagians, Christian heretics who maintained that morally upright deeds were sufficient to

---

[128] *quid est quod tibi proprium quiddam tenuisti ipsum esse, quod aliis non dedisti, ut tu solus esses? ... O veritas quae vere es. nam in omnibus actionibus et motibus nostris, et in omni prorsus agitatione creaturae duo tempora invenio, praeteritum et futurum. praesens quaero, nihil stat: quod dixi, iam non est; quod dicturus sum, nondum est: quod feci, iam non est; quod facturus sum, nondum est: quod vixi, iam non est; quod victurus sum, nondum est. praeteritum et futurum invenio in omni motu rerum: in veritate quae manet, praeteritum et futurum non invenio, sed solum praesens, et hoc incorruptibiliter, quod in creatura non est.*

[129] Useful studies on Augustine's theory of justification by faith are Bammel 1996 (who stresses the influence of Origen on Augustine's view); cf. further, Scheck 2008, Christes 1980, and McGrath 1986: 23–36.

bring about a person's salvation. According to Augustine's view, humans lacked the intrinsic power to bring about this transformation without the grace of god.[130] This grace was, however, bestowed only upon those individuals who exercised faith (*fides*), to which I shall return shortly.

The term *iustificare* was a calque employed by Latin Christian authors for the Greek δικαιοῦν (Rom. 3.23–4), after it emerged with the *Vetus Latina* translation of the Septuagint. Augustine resorts to *iustus* + *facere* in order to explain this concept to his readers:[131] 'What else could it mean [to describe persons as] "justified" (*iustificati*) than that they "have been made just" (*iusti facti*) by him who renders just the impious,[132] so a just person emerges from an impious one?'[133] To Augustine, then, *iustitia*, 'righteousness', is a divine attribute bestowed upon what had previously lacked this quality once the ascent to the divine sphere, through the mediating power of Christ, has been achieved. At this point, let us briefly recall Cicero's translation of *Tim.* 29e4:

Table 36. *Plato,* Tim. *29e4–30a2*

ταύτην δὴ γενέσεως καὶ κόσμου μάλιστ' ἄν τις ἀρχὴν κυριωτάτην παρ' ἀνδρῶν φρονίμων ἀποδεχόμενος ὀρθότατα ἀποδέχοιτ' ἄν.	Whosoever accepts this [i.e. the fact that the creator was 'good'] as the most authoritative principle [obtained] from wise men will do so most justly.

Table 37. *Cicero's translation of Plato,* Tim. *29e4–30a2 (Cic.* Tim. *3.9, 15)*

haec nimirum gignendi mundi causa iustissima.	This [i.e. the fact that the creator was 'good'] is without doubt the most just cause for the creation of the world.

---

[130] E.g. Aug. *Spir. et litt.* 9.15.

[131] It first appears in the Latin *Vulgata* at Num. 9.3. Augustine may have been familiar with the term through his mentor Ambrose, who uses it e.g. at Luc. 1.21. Cf. Dodaro 2004: 73 with n. 4; McGrath 1986 vol. 1: 30–1.

[132] Cf. Romans 3.24; 4.5.

[133] Aug. *Spir. et litt.* 26.45; see further ibid. 9.15; *Expositio quarundarum propositionum ex epistula ad Romanos* 16.22; *Ad Simplicianum* 1.2.3; *Sermo* 131,9; *De gratia et libero arbitrio* 6.13.

Certainly, the context in which Cicero uses the term *iustitia* is a cosmological one. Nevertheless, it is possible that Augustine found the appearance of the term 'justice' in the Ciceronian version of the dialogue to be a further keyword that confirmed him in his specific interpretation of *Tim.* 29c3.[134] Back to our passage *Consens.* 1.35.53. While in Plato's text the diverging pair πίστις and ἀλήθεια had denoted different epistemological planes, *fides* to Augustine is bound up with *iustitia* in his theory of justification. It is through faith, *fides*, in conjunction with love,[135] that one merits the divine gift of righteousness. In his exegesis of Romans 3.22 (Septuagint: δικαιοσύνη δὲ θεοῦ διὰ πίστεως Ἰησοῦ Χριστοῦ; Augustine: *iustitia autem dei per fidem Iesu Christi*), Augustine identifies *fides* as 'that through which one believes in Christ'.[136] At *Spir. et litt.* 11.18, he explains:

The righteousness of god is revealed ... through faith, in faith, as it is written: 'The righteous person lives through faith' (Rom. 1.16–17). This is the righteousness of god, obscured in the Old Testament but revealed in the New Testament (Hab. 2.4). It is likewise called the righteousness of god because he makes [individuals] righteous by bestowing it upon them ... And 'faith' is the faith through which and in which [god's righteousness] is revealed, that is: through the faith of those who prophesy it, and in the faith of those who heed [their word] ...[137]

---

[134] Note, of course, that the meaning of Augustine's *iustitia* differs from that of Cicero: 'But god's justice is without law (*sine lege*), [the justice] god bestows upon the believer through the spirit of grace without the aid of the law' (*sine adiutorio legis, Spir. et litt.* 9.15). On Cicero's concept of *iustitia* vis-à-vis Augustine, cf. Dodaro 2004: 10–19.

[135] Faith is a gift from god; without love, however, it is unable to effect a true conversion to god, cf. Aug. *Trin.* 15.18.32 (Acts 8.20), and see further *Epistolae ad Galatas expositio* 5–6, 44. Other gifts are bestowed by the holy spirit (1 Cor. 12.8), but they are useless without love (*sine caritate*, cf. 1 Cor. 13.3). Cf. n. 124 on the possible connection between *caritas* and Timaean φιλία in the context of Augustine's *De consensu evangelistarum* 1.35.53. See Gioia 2008: 125–46, 175, and see TeSelle 1996–2002: 1335 on the role of faith in justification in the context of the Pelagian controversy.

[136] Aug. *Spir. et litt.* 9.15. Cf. Louth 2002 on Augustine's association of the trinity with the notion of 'love'.

[137] *iustitia enim dei in eo revelatur ex fide in fidem, sicut scriptum est: iustus autem ex fide vivit. haec est iustitia dei, quae in Testamento Vetere velata, in Novo revelatur; quae ideo iustitia dei dicitur, quod impertiendo eam iustos facit ... et haec est fides, ex qua et in quam revelatur, ex fide scilicet annuntiantium in fidem oboedientium.*

A final note on the different contexts in which the Timaean analogy at *Tim.* 29c3 appears in Augustine's *De consensu evangelistarum* and the *De trinitate dei*. In the former work, Augustine commends the authority of Plato, the *nobilissimus philosophus*. In countering Porphyry, a central target of Augustine's development in the *De consensu evangelistarum* due to his doubts concerning the divinity of Christ, the fact that Augustine resorts to Plato's own words (via Cicero) is a significant move that undermines Porphyry's doctrinal stance by pitting him against his own master. In Book 4 of *On the Trinity* Augustine's agenda is somewhat more complex. In the chapters preceding his Timaean exegesis, Augustine offers a sharp invective against the philosophers who, despite being ...

... more proficient than others in these eminent and eternal matters, have [not] been able to behold such subjects with their understanding. Otherwise, they would ... be prescient also about the future. Those who are [prescient about the future] are called 'soothsayers' by them, but by us they are called 'prophets'.[138]

At *Trin.* 4.17.23, he suggests that non-believers might have heard about Christ through the announcements of demonic intermediaries:

The proud and deceitful aerial powers, even, if they are found to have said something through their soothsayers concerning the fellowship and city of the saints, and about the true mediator, things they heard from the holy prophets or the angels, they did this in order that they might attract with these truths, which were not their own, even those faithful in god and, if they could, draw them to their own falsehoods. But god brought it about with the help of those who were ignorant, that truth might resound from all sides, aiding the faithful, but a witness to the impious.[139]

I shall return to Augustine's invective against the Platonic demons shortly. At 4.18.24, Augustine finally introduces the

---

[138] *Trin.* 4.16.21: *isti philosophi ceteris meliores in illis summis aeternisque rationibus intellectu talia contemplati sunt; alioquin ... potius et futura praenoscerent quod qui potuerunt ab eis vates, a nostris prophetae appellati sunt.*

[139] *potestates autem aereae superbae atque fallaces etiam si quaedam de societate et civitate sanctorum et de vero mediatore a sanctis prophetis, vel angelis audita per suos vates dixisse reperiuntur id egerunt, ut per haec aliena vera etiam fideles dei si possent ad sua falsa traducerent. deus autem per nescientes id egit, ut veritas undique resonaret, fidelibus in adiutorium, impiis in testimonium.*

Timaean analogy, discussed above, as something that was maintained even by one 'of those who were once considered wise among the Greeks'. Augustine agrees with the contents of the analogy at *Tim.* 29c3, yet not without 'translating' Plato's (or Cicero's) terminology into a Christian one: 'This statement is certainly correct. For what we call temporal, this he describes as that "which has come to be"' (*et profecto est vera sententia. quod enim nos temporale dicimus, hoc ille 'quod ortum est' appellavit*). Augustine thus avoids naming Plato as the source of *Tim.* 29c3, perhaps so as to align his tone with that of the preceding chapters, in which he denies the Platonists any real understanding of even their own wisdom.

To Augustine, Plato anticipated aspects of the Christian doctrine, such as the eternal essence of god, or the role of the mediator Christ, with astonishing accuracy. Nevertheless, since Plato himself lacked faith in the mediatory effort of Christ, faith that was required for arriving at the 'true' Christian interpretation of this and other passages we find in Plato's writings, he was unable to attain true wisdom and remained removed from god. Augustine thus appropriates the originally dualistic Timaean framework that is illustrated by the passage *Tim.* 29c3 and, with the help of very few words, portrays the text as a *sacramentum*, a revelation and an assertion of Christ's mediation, sounded of old, but misunderstood by Plato himself.

Theology: Augustine on Demons and Angels

In the context of Augustine's metaphysical structure of the universe, which emphasizes the mediatory role of Christ incarnate, it is to be expected that any other mediating elements that had been identified by the Platonic tradition as bridging the gap between the mortal and the divine spheres are denounced as inadequate by Augustine. Thus at *Civ.* 8–9 Augustine delivers a harsh polemic against Apuleius' demonology that aims at proving the unsuitability of Apuleius' demons as mediators between humans and god. Augustine's portrayal, which, of course, at no time strives for a fair representation of the rival demonology, sets up Apuleius' creatures in such a way as to perform abysmally when compared to Christ, the 'true' mediator. It is clear from several almost verbatim quotations, to which I shall point in due course, that Augustine had at his disposal a text that differs only minimally from the readings of Apuleius' *DPD* and *DDS* that have reached us. This is not surprising, given that the two authors, while separated by a couple of centuries, were fellow countrymen, and Apuleius' fame had reached Augustine, if not before, during the few years he spent in African Madauros, Apuleius' native city.[140]

At the outset of the discussion at *Civ.* 8.5, Augustine stresses that the Platonists, given their shared belief in an immutable creator god, have close affinities with the Christians, for which reason they deserve his particular attention. Soon after, following a survey of the various philosophical schools that begins with the Presocratics, Augustine at *Civ.* 8.12 names as the 'noblest' (*nobilissimi*) philosophers the more recent (*recentiores*) disciples of Plato, Plotinus, Iamblichus, Porphyry, and his fellow countryman, the African Apuleius. This initial respectful commendation, in stark contrast to Augustine's increasingly polemical and hostile references to Apuleius throughout Books 8 and 9, serves a specific purpose. By thus commending Apuleius' and his fellow Platonists' insights, he will later be able to claim that the Christian faith, once the Platonic doctrines have been shown to be erroneous, triumphs over even those of the brightest among Plato's own followers. Augustine's invective begins with the question directed at the Platonists, are both good and evil gods to be worshipped? From the start, Augustine sows discord between the Platonists and Plato, noting that, according to Plato himself, there were, in fact, no evil gods.[141] But if not gods, who, then,

---

[140] Cf. Aug. *Ep.* 138.4.19. See Hunink 2003: 83–5 for further discussion of the numerous references Augustine makes to Apuleius. Cf. also Den Boeft 1996–2002: 213–14; Pépin 1977: 29–37. A thorough discussion of Augustine's polemic in the present context is Moreschini 2015: 348–63; see also Karfíková 2004: 162–89; O'Daly 1999: 115–22; cf. Gioia 2008: 89–90; Rémy 1979: 206–34; Den Boeft 1996–2002: 219–20; Ciarlantini 1983, 1984, 1985; Siniscalco 1990; and Fuhrer 1997. Cf. also O'Daly 1999: 101–34.

[141] Cf. e.g. Plat. *Symp.* 202c–d; *Rep.* 379a–383c; *Tim.* 42d.

were the creatures mentioned by the Platonists who 'love the-atrical plays and demand for these to be added to divine rituals and performed in their honour?' (*qui ludos scaenicos amant eosque divinis rebus adiungi et suis honoribus flagitant exhiberi, Civ.* 8.13).[142] Augustine decides to let the Platonists answer this riddle. In what follows, he will argue that it is Apuleius' demons who enjoy the theatre, spectacles, and depravities of all sorts.[143]

Augustine's attack on Apuleius proper begins at *Civ.* 8.14.1, where he refers to the Apuleian tripartite hierarchy (*tripartita divisio*) of living beings – gods, men, and demons. Each kind is assigned their own habitat – heaven, air, and earth, respect-ively – and their habitat is also indicative of their ontological classification. 'Just as their habitats differ in excellence, so do their natures' (*sicut eis diversa dignitas est locorum, ita etiam naturarum*). The demons, whom the Platonists place in the middle position in terms of both habitat and excellence, share

---

[142] In this context Apuleius mentions the story of a certain Roman, Titus Latinius, charged by the demons, who insisted on cheerful displays of worship to be performed in their honour, to deliver to the Roman senate the message of how certain religious rites had displeased them and ought to be repeated. Augustine recounts the story in fuller detail at *Civ.* 4.26. Different versions of the same story are mentioned also by Cicero, *Div.* 1.55, Livy 2.36, and Valerius Maximus 1.7.4. It is also possible that Varro may have been Augustine's source for this anecdote.

[143] While the specific connection of demons with a partiality for stage plays does not appear to be a part of Apuleius' demonology, Augustine may have in mind, for instance, Apul. *DDS* 147–8: 'For, just as we are, they can be subject to all types of mental calming and excitement, with the consequence that they are roused by anger, moved by pity, enticed by gifts, softened by prayers, irritated by insults, soothed by honours, and are thoroughly changeable in all other matters in a similar way to ourselves.' See further ibid. 148–50: 'As a consequence of the different practices of religions and the various offerings of cults, we should believe that there are some divine beings of this class who take pleasure in the various sacrifices, ceremonies, and rites ... all these are customary and established in accordance with the trad-ition of each place, just as we know, largely through dreams, visions, and oracles, that deities have often shown indignation if any element of their cult is omitted through human negligence or arrogance' (trans. Harrison). Augustine may have connected the Apuleian demons with the stage plays mentioned in the context of Plato's critique of poetry in the *Republic* in order to establish a doctrinal link between master and student that, at the same time, allowed Augustine to exhibit the differences between the two: while Plato rightly banned demons from the just city, Apuleius seems intent on reinstalling them, according to Augustine's por-trayal. Cf. n. 144 and, further, Moreschini 2015: 353–4.

with their superiors, the gods, an immortal body, while sharing with humans a soul that is subject to passions (*habent enim cum diis communem immortalitatem corporum, animorum autem cum hominibus passiones*). It is their susceptibility to emotions that allows Augustine to link them with the impassioned demons mentioned earlier, whom he had described as being fond of obscene spectacles so that even Plato himself expelled them from the city.[144] The demons' delight in depravity, caused by their passionate soul, is used by Augustine as a central line of attack that allows him to dismantle Apuleius' doctrine.

Augustine at *Civ.* 8.4 continues to associate these ideas with Apuleius' doctrine and begins to single him out for his particular focus on the topic. 'While these things are certainly found also in other Platonists, Apuleius, the Platonist from Madaura, was the only one to have written a book on the subject, for which he chose the title "On the God of Socrates"'. Despite the misleading title, Augustine explains, Apuleius makes clear in this work that it was really a demon, not a god, who accompanied Socrates. Given that Apuleius portrays this demon in a positive light, it must be the case either that he himself incorrectly classified Socrates' demon as a god, or that Plato contradicted himself (*Civ.* 8.14.2) by honouring creatures whose festivals he later banished from the city. Once again, Plato is pitted against Platonists by Augustine, with the ultimate aim, as we will find, of proving the superiority of the Chrisian doctrine.

According to Augustine at *Civ.* 8.15.2, Apuleius failed to mention any redeeming qualities in his description of the

---

[144] *Civ.* 8.14.1: It is no surprise, then, they say, if the [demons] also rejoice in obscene plays and the poets' phantasms, given that they are in the grip of human passions. From these [passions] the gods are far removed and are in every way alien to them. From this we may conclude that Plato, when he denounced poetry and prohibited fiction, did not strip the pleasures of stage plays from the gods, who are all good and excellent, but from the demons. (*quapropter non est mirum, inquiunt, si etiam ludorum obscenitatibus et poetarum figmentis delectantur, quando quidem humanis capiuntur affectibus, a quibus dii longe absunt et modis omnibus alieni sunt. ex quo colligitur, Platonem poetica detestando et prohibendo figmenta non deos qui omnes boni et excelsi sunt privasse ludorum scaenicorum voluptate, sed daemones*).

demons. The only praiseworthy aspect he reports is the 'subtlety and vigour of [their] bodies and their eminent habitat'. Given Apuleius' failure to list any positive demonic characteristics, it is clear that Plato's elemental hierarchy really serves to indicate the opposite conclusion to that drawn by Apuleius, namely that a superior mind can inhabit an inferior body, and inferior mind a superior body (*ut inferius corpus anima melior inhabitet deteriorque superius*). Since Plato places water above earth, any other view would surely lead us to conclude that fish were worthier than men! Instead, Augustine reasons, Plato's hierarchy of living beings can apply to their habitat only, not to their 'dignity' (*dignitas*). Augustine, by proving himself knowledgeable of the various elements of Platonic doctrine (*Tim.* 31b–32d, 39e–40a), with which he was familiar through Cicero's translation, undermines the teachings of one of Plato's finest disciples.

Augustine next makes use of Apuleius' own definition of the demonic kind in order to attack his stance in greater detail, quoting *DDS* 13 almost verbatim. According to Apuleius, demons are 'living creatures in kind, have a mind subjected to passions, a rational soul, an aerial body, and an eternal existence. Of these five characteristics, they share the first three with us, the fourth is theirs only, while they share the fifth with the gods.'[145] In what follows, however, Augustine points out that the demons share the first two characteristics, those of being a living creature and of possessing a rational mind, also with the gods superior to them. Therefore, in fact, it is only their immortality that they share exclusively with the gods, and only a soul susceptible to passions that they share exclusively with us. Crucially, by extracting from Apuleius' own work the combination of these two characteristics for the demons, a mind

---

[145] *Civ.* 8.16: *daemones esse genere animalia, animo passiva, mente rationalia, corpore aeria, tempore aeterna. horum vero quinque tria priora illis esse quae nobis, quartum proprium, quintum eos cum diis habere commune.* Cf. Apul. *DDS* 13, 148: *daemones sunt genere animalia, ingenio rationabilia, animo passiva, corpore aeria, tempore aeterna. ex his quinque, quae commemoravi, tria a principio eadem quae nobis, quartum proprium, postremum commune cum diis immortalibus habent, sed differunt ab his passione.*

susceptible to passions and an immortal existence, Augustine is able to damage considerably the eminent existence Apuleius had ascribed to them. Reminding us that Apuleius himself (on Augustine's view) had ascribed no positive qualities to the demonic soul, Augustine confirms that the demonic condition is inferior even than the human condition: 'how much less deserving of divine honours are the aerial creatures, since they possess rationality for the purpose of being miserable, are subject to passions for the purpose of being miserable, and have an eternal existence to render them unable to end their misery' (*quanto minus nunc honore divino aeria digna sunt animalia, ad hoc rationalia ut misera esse possint, ad hoc passiva ut misera sint, ad hoc aeterna ut miseriam finire non possint*, *Civ.* 8.16).

It is thus preposterous to suggest that a 'chaste man, unfamiliar with the crimes of magic, would make those creatures his advocates who take pleasure in these things, and with whose aid the gods may perceive him … If human decency is so worthless as not only to esteem depravities, but to believe, moreover, that [depravities] are welcome to divine beings, we may refer them, against such views, to their own master Plato, who has considerable authority among them.'[146] Augustine inverts the positions of demons and humans in Apuleius' demonic hierarchy, having rejected the idea that there is an intrinsic connection between the ranking of elemental make-up and habitat, on the one hand, and the eminence of being, on the other. Augustine underlines his attack, further, by pointing to Plato's own pious prudence and philosophical dignity (*religiosa prudentia, philosophica gravitas*, *Civ.* 8.21.2). Note that, thus far, Augustine has been arguing exclusively within Apuleius' own doctrinal framework, without having yet introduced the Christian view on demonic nature.

---

[146] *Civ.* 8.18: *homo castus et ab artium magicarum sceleribus alienus eos patronos adhibeat, per quos illum dii exaudiant, qui haec amant, quae ille non amando fit dignior, quem facilius et libentius exaudire debeant … habemus contra ista magistrum eorum et tantae apud eos auctoritatis Platonem, si pudor humanus ita de se male meretur, ut non solum diligat turpia, verum etiam divinitati existimet grata.* On Augustine's aim of pitting Plato against the Platonists in the present context, cf. Moreschini 2015: 362.

It is the sorry state of their passionate souls that disqualifies Apuleius' demons from the mediating role he so avidly assigned to them. Augustine next moves to evaluate them for this very role according to the criteria of the Christian doctrine. Initially, he identifies the demons with the fallen angels of Scripture who had been rejected from the superior heavenly habitat (*de caeli superioris sublimitate deiecti merito*, Civ. 8.22). Further, he returns to the notion that humans are, in fact, superior to demons despite their earthly body, but due to possessing a pious mind (*pia mente*), once they have chosen god (*electo deo*), instead of demons, as their aid.

At the same time, Augustine now cashes in on his earlier analysis according to which demons, occupying a middle position, share one quality with each of the extremes they serve to connect: immortality with the gods and a passionate soul with humans. Given the specific coincidence of these characteristics in their own nature, demons turn out to be forever bound to their eternal, yet miserable, existence, while humans can be 'healed' and become like the angels (*sanamur, ut quales ipsi* [angeli] *sunt simus*, Civ. 8.25), thus transcending their own level of existence once they have cultivated their soul. Yet we are not to rely on the angels to mediate actively between human and divine spheres. Instead, we can approach them through our faith during our mortal existence, if we believe that we become blessed through him (i.e., through Christ) through whom the angels themselves have obtained blessedness, while they themselves also act on our behalf (*fide illis interim propinquamus, si ab illo nos fieri beatos, a quo et ipsi facti sunt etiam ipsis faventibus credimus*, Civ. 8.25). To Augustine's Christian audience the mention of *fides*, even without the earlier reference to god who ought to be chosen as an aid by humans, would have announced the arrival of Christ on Augustine's polemical stage.

The demons' unsuitability for a mediating role, on account of their passionate souls, is explored further in Book 9 of the *De civitate*. At Civ. 9.6 Augustine reasons: 'their mind, that is, the superior part of their soul, which makes them rational and in which virtue and wisdom (if they have any) would subdue the tempestuous passions of their soul's inferior parts that are to be reined in and regulated – their very mind, I say, and this Platonist affirms it, is tossed about in an ocean of perturbance'.[147] Since it is the supposedly superior part by virtue of which the demons have proved to be inferior to humans, Augustine shows that Apuleius' demons are, 'as it were, bound and hung upside down' (*tamquam in perversum ligati atque suspensi*), 'their servile [part, their] body, they share with the gods, the dominating [part, their soul], they share with humans in their state of misery. They are thus elevated by their inferior part, but are subdued due to their [supposedly] superior part (*servum corpus cum diis beatis, dominum animum cum hominibus miseris, parte inferiore exaltati, superiore deiecti, Civ.* 9.9). The one quality they share exclusively with the gods, their immortal body, becomes their doom since it prevents them from escaping the one quality they share exclusively with men: misery, caused by a passionate soul. Their body is not an 'eternal vessel' (*aeternum vehiculum*), but an 'eternal prison' (*aeternum vinculum*).

Having turned Apuleius' demonology on its head, Augustine further sharpens a familiar argument he mentioned previously.[148] In order to join together two extremes, a mediator must necessarily share one quality with each of these extremes. A mediator between immortal blessed gods and mortal miserable humans, then, must be either blessed and mortal or immortal and miserable (*cum quaerimus medium inter beatos immortales miserosque mortales, hoc invenire debemus, quod aut mortale sit beatum, aut immortale sit miserum, Civ.* 9.13.3). Significantly, the angels do *not* fulfil this requirement since they are immortal *and* blessed (*angeli inter miseros mortales et beatos immortales*

---

[147] *mens eorum, id est pars animi superior, qua rationales sunt, in qua virtus et sapientia, si ulla eis esset, passionibus turbulentis inferiorum animi partium regendis moderandisque dominaretur; ipsa, inquam, mens eorum, sicut iste Platonicus confitetur, salo perturbationum fluctuat.*
[148] See also Karfíková 2004: 182–6.

medii esse non possunt, quia ipsi quoque et beati et immortales sunt, Civ. 9.15.1). It is Christ alone who fulfils it, as he agreed to a temporary mortal existence while remaining blessed in eternity (*miseriam et mortalis esse ad tempus voluit, et beatus in aeternitate persistere potuit*). He situated himself in between the earthly and divine kinds of existence, at once mortal and blessed, so that, once his mortal existence had come to an end, he would make mortals immortal, as shown by his own resurrection, and would make miserable humans blessed, a quality he himself has never lost (*Civ.* 9.15.2).

In a final blow against Apuleius, Augustine suggests that only a person who has already been tempted by the demons might think otherwise: 'Who could believe [such consequences of the Platonists' doctrine], unless the deceptive demons had already tricked him?' (*quis talia sentiat, nisi quem fallacissimi daemones deceperunt?, Civ.* 9.16.2).

The Platonists erred in assuming that mediators would carry out their role with the help of some material participation in the extremes they unite. Rather, it is through spiritual, incorporeal loftiness that we ascend to god (*quoniam non per corporalem altitudinem, sed per spiritalem, hoc est incorporalem similitudinem ad deum debemus ascendere, Civ.* 9.18). In fact, as Augustine points out rather casually, Christians had been made aware all the while through the language of Scripture that, while there are good and bad angels, there can never be good demons. Fortunately, this negative connotation with the term 'demon' has become so widespread (*hanc loquendi consuetudinem in tantum populi usquequaque secuti sunt, Civ.* 9.19), even among pagans, that hardly anybody would use the term with a positive connotation, a view that explains Calcidius' pointed effort, in his commentary, to convince his Christian dedicatee Osius that the term δαίμων does not carry any such negative undertones.[149]

[149] Cf. p. 162 n. 15.

Conclusion

Augustine on several occasions appropriates Cicero's Latin translation of Plato's *Timaeus* for the purpose of corroborating the Christian doctrine, most frequently in order to prove wrong Plato's disciples, the Middle Platonists and Neoplatonists. 'Plato's' view of a created soul and universe is held against either Plotinus' or Porphyry's view of an uncreated universe that demotes the Timaean creator god. What is more, Timaeus' dualistic framing of his creation account is interpreted by Augustine in such a manner as to allow him to conclude that Plato possessed knowledge which would later be divulged through the gospel. Timaeus' τὸ ὄν may have been associated with Moses' god at Ex. 3.14, who declares *ego sum, qui sum*. Key terms that appear in Cicero's translation of Timaeus' ontological–epistemological analogy at *Tim.* 29c3 – *aeternitas, fides, veritas* – are interpreted by Augustine in such a manner as to align Timaeus' dualistic metaphysics with his Christian metaphysics, where Christ the mediator is shown to be the crucial link to bridge the boundaries between divine and human existence. What is more, the *Timaeus* was used by Augustine to fatally undermine Apuleius' demonology, whose foundation, the tripartite ontological hierarchy of living beings, is shown by Augustine to be 'upside down' and inferior to his own Christian exegesis, which he finds corroborated in the *Timaeus*. While Augustine's writings betray no evidence for a direct acquaintance with Calcidius' writings, noteworthy similarities between the two authors appear that betray a common exegetical background. Despite the fact that, overall, Augustine's own outlook has been shaped most significantly by the Neoplatonists, it was Cicero's translation that allows the *Timaeus* to exert a considerable influence upon his view of Plato and his 'original' doctrine.

CONCLUSION

Plato's *Timaeus* provides the foundation for the continuous intellectual discourse we have witnessed in the work of our authors by gathering into one narrative the fundamental questions that pertain to human existence, questions concerning the origin and nature of our world, and the overall metaphysical framework in which to place our own existence.

The Latin authors we have examined transfer these questions into various new environments with the help of their chosen language, form of expression, literary genre, and setting. In the case of Cicero and Apuleius, in particular, rhetorical skill is integrated into the authors' wider philosophical project. Cicero transfers Greek philosophy into fictitious learned conversations delivered through the voices of illustrious Roman contemporaries, as a strategy of appropriating the Greek intellectual heritage. He summons his combined expertise as an authority on Hellenistic philosophical doctrines, as a scholar of the Greek language, and as an orator, to create a Roman genre of philosophical writing that centres around his role as a *doctus declamator*.[1] Apuleius, likewise, is a *doctus declamator*, yet instead of relying on a thorough expertise in the various Hellenistic philosophical schools, he relies on his authority as a priest and initiate into the divine wisdom revealed through Platonic doctrine. For both Cicero and Apuleius, their philosophical projects are exclusive rather than inclusive in that they are aimed at an erudite audience capable of accessing philosophical knowledge through the specific channel of communication the two authors themselves create: learned, urbane discourse.

---

[1] Cf. Cic. *Or.* 15.47.

Conclusion

Calcidius, I assume, would lay no particular claim to being a *doctus declamator*, but is more concerned to carve out for himself the role of exegete and educator who breaks down barriers between those versed and those unversed in Platonic dogma. Among our authors he is the most pedagogically minded and underlines his role as an educational guide by creating a twofold learning device for the student, translation in combination with commentary, that is tailored to support the reader's growing expertise in Platonic teaching. Augustine, in turn, harvests the intellectual crop of the preceding centuries to create a coherent theory of creation and of the relationship between human and divine nature. Like Calcidius he is concerned to make his intellectual project an inclusive one aimed at recruiting others for his cause. Timaean doctrine not only allowed Augustine to negotiate his own doctrinal stance against Plato's very own heirs, the Middle and Neoplatonists, but, moreover, helped him express a theoretical foundation for the Christian creed that would remain authoritative for centuries to come.

A Timaean motif that has invited many diverse and original responses is that of an ontological–epistemological kinship between a specific object of investigation and the explanatory accounts that treat thereof. We recall Timaeus' statement at *Tim.* 29b4–5: '[we ought to determine that] the accounts bear a kinship to the subject matter of which they serve as exegetes'. The immediately ensuing remarks set out the dualistic ontological–epistemological framework in which Timaeus operates. Our authors make use of this passage to reveal their understanding of the Timaean narrative and of their role as participants in Platonic thought. Cicero's use of the dialectical–rhetorical *disputatio in utramque partem* aligns him with the sceptical Academy while showcasing the suitability of rhetorical skill for discussions of fundamental philosophical import. Apuleius' interpretation of the same passage reveals that 'faith', *fides*, understood to be the highest degree of trustworthiness, characterizes the Platonic *doctrinae* contained in the *Timaeus*. Calcidius manipulates the passage in his translation in order to stress his own authority, which at

281

times merges with that of Plato's protagonist Timaeus, as an exegete while identifying this part of the dialogue primarily as a *mediocris explanatio*, an investigation in the field of natural philosophy, despite his complex digressions into related disciplines elsewhere in his commentary. Augustine expands the Timaean relational analogy at *Tim.* 29c3 between the two pairs, being–becoming, truth–belief, which expresses the ontological and epistemological divide at the centre of Timaeus' account, to describe a Christian metaphysical outlook in which *fides*, 'faith', represents the bridge that makes possible a personal relationship between humans and the Christian god.

Concerning one of the most contentious interpretative issues in the dialogue, the createdness of the cosmos, we found that Cicero, with the help of specific modifications in his Latin translation, exploits the controversy for his setting of a *disputatio in utramque partem*, in which the contending parties would have clashed in their views on a created or uncreated world. Both Apuleius and Calcidius, in turn, represent the majority view among the later Platonic tradition, according to which Timaeus' creation account is to be understood in non-temporal terms. Calcidius, in particular, credits Plato's description of a creator god at work with the purpose of facilitating a student's understanding of the world's nature. Accordingly, Calcidius presents his translation of the dialogue in temporal terms while setting out in his commentary Plato's reasons for such a portrayal. Augustine, in a fascinating exegetical synthesis, appropriates the non-temporal solutions that had been developed throughout the centuries preceding him, in order to account for the two seemingly differing creation accounts in the Book of Genesis. His appropriation of the exegetical strategies that had originated in the Greek philosophical tradition allows him, crucially, to disambiguate and thereby to strengthen the Christian creation narrative.

Our examination has opened windows on different stages in the development of Platonic doctrine throughout the early centuries of our era. Apuleius reflects the increased effort of Middle Platonic thinkers to emphasize the centrality of the highest divinity removed from the physical realm, while integrating this concept of the divine with the idea of a providential force that permeates and oversees all aspects of human existence. At times, the figure of the demiurge merges with that of a supramundane transcendent divinity, but this relationship is not clearly negotiated by Apuleius. Nevertheless, this divinity's providential impact upon the physical sphere is rendered possible by proxy administrative agents that are given a detailed treatment by him and also by Calcidius, even though the latter appears to de-emphasize the role of demons as the caretakers of human affairs to some extent, instead stressing the need for their presence in the cosmos from the perspective of material continuity.

Alongside the heightened transcendence of the *summus deus*, the metaphor of divine *semina*, 'seeds', is employed already by Calcidius to remove the divinity from the physical scene while explaining his lasting impact on the continued changes within nature. Calcidius maintains Timaeus' strict dualistic framework, but clarifies that seeds, as the origins of the works of nature, are merely the physical equivalent to the intelligible *causae* underlying the works of god. These mysterious *causae* we are unable to grasp save with the help of the guidance provided by the exegete. Augustine develops the seed metaphor in a most resourceful manner that allows him to argue for a *created* cosmos. The physical seeds that are the origins of living things on the earth are the duplicates of non-physical, primordial 'seeds' or *causae* that were sown by the creator during a causal creation which provided the impulse also for the birth of the physical realm. The creator creates, yet remains removed from his corporeal creature.

What is more, Augustine's creation theory integrates elements we encounter in his non-Christian intellectual predecessors in a manner that allows him to bridge successfully the ontological divide between the human and the divine spheres through the figure of Christ. The mediatory function of the Apuleian and Calcidian demons is assigned by Augustine to Christ, thereby linking it to the very same trinitarian God who is responsible also for creating the universe. Transcending the limitations of a human life is possible through the exercise of faith in

Christ, a faith that brings about the purification of the human mind and body, the necessary prerequisites that grant humans access to an immortal life. At the same time, the mediatory agency of Christ allows for a personal relationship between humans with the creator.

Each author finds his own approach to Plato's *Timaeus* and, with his individual contribution to its history of transmission, prolongs the enduring significance of Plato's cosmology.

BIBLIOGRAPHY

Editions and Translations of Plato's *Timaeus*

Archer-Hind, R.D. (ed., trans.) (1888) *The Timaeus of Plato*. London: McMillan & Co. (Reprinted: Salem, NH: Ayers Co. Publishers, 1988).

Brisson, L. (2001) *Platon: Timée; Critias. 5th edition*. Paris: G.F. Flamarion.

Burnet, J. (ed.) (1902) *Platonis Opera, Vol. 4*. Oxford: Clarendon Press.

Bury, R.G. (1966) *Plato, with an English Translation: Timaeus; Critias; Cleitophon; Menexenus; Epistles*. London: W. Heinemann; Cambridge, MA: Harvard University Press.

Cornford, F. (1937) *Plato's Cosmology: The Timaeus of Plato. Translated with a Running Commentary*. London: Routledge & Kegan Paul.

Lee, H.D.P. (transl.) (1965) *Plato, Timaeus*. Harmondsworth: Penguin Books.

Schleiermacher, F., Susemihl, F. (1977) *Platon: Philebos; Timaios; Kritias*. Munich: Goldmann.

Zeyl, D.J. (2000) *Plato: Timaeus*. Indianapolis, IN, Cambridge, MA: Hackett Pub. Co.

Editions of Cicero's Translation

Ax, W., Plasberg, O. (eds.) (2011) *M. Tulli Ciceronis De Divinatione; De Fato; Timaeus*. Revised Edition. Stuttgart: Teubner.

Giomini, R. (ed.) (1975) *M. Tulli Ciceronis Scripta Quae Manserunt Omnia: De Divinatione, De Fato, Timaeus*. Leipzig: Teubner.

Editions of Apuleius' Works

Beaujeu, J. (1973) *Apulée: Opuscules Philosophiques (Du Dieu de Socrate, Platon et sa Doctrine, Du Monde) et Fragments*. Paris: Les Belles Lettres.

Hunink, V.J.C. (1997) *Apuleius of Madauros: Pro Se De Magia, Apologia*. Amsterdam: J. C. Gieben.

Lee, B.T. (2005) *Apuleius' Florida: A Commentary*. Berlin: De Gruyter.

Moreschini, C. (1991) *Apulei Platonici Madaurensis Opera Quae Supersunt, Vol. 3: De Philosophia Libri*. Berlin: De Gruyter.

Bibliography

Editions and Translations of Calcidius' Translation and Commentary:

Bakhouche, B. (ed.) (2011) *Calcidius: Commentaire au Timée de Platon. Texte Établi, Traduit et Annoté. Tome 1: Introduction Générale, Introduction à la Traduction du Timée, Traduction du Timée et Commentaire (c. 1–355); Tome 2: Notes à la Traduction et au Commentaire, Indices, Annexes, Bibliographie Générale.* Paris: Vrin.

Magee, J. (ed., transl.) (2016) *Calcidius: On Plato's Timaeus.* Cambridge, MA: Harvard University Press.

Waszink, J.H., Jensen, P.J. (eds.) (1962) *Plato: Timaeus a Calcidio Translatus Commentarioque Instructus.* Leiden: Brill, Warburg Institute.

Wrobel, J., (ed.) (1876) *Platonis Timaeus Interprete Chalcidio.* Leipzig: Teubner.

Editions of Augustine's Works

Corpus Christianorum, Series Latina (= Library of Latin Texts) (1954–) Turnhout.

Corpus Scriptorium Ecclesiasticorum Latinorum (1866–) Vienna.

Migne, J.P. (ed.) (1844–64)*Patrologiae Cursus Completus, Series Latina, Vols.* 32–47. Paris.

Secondary Sources

Adams, J.N. (2003) *Bilingualism and the Latin Language.* New York: Cambridge University Press.

Agaësse, P., Solignac, A. (eds.) (1972) *Oeuvres de Saint Augustin: La Genèse au Sens Litéral. BA* 48/49. Paris: Desclée de Brouwer.

Alexandre, M. (1988) *Le Commencement du Livre Genèse 1–IV : La Version Grecque de la Septante et sa Réception.* Paris: Beauchesne.

Algra, K. (1995) *Concepts of Space in Greek Thought.* Leiden, New York: Brill.

Allen, J. (1994) "Academic Probabilism and Stoic Epistemology," *Classical Quarterly* 44: 85–113.

 (1995) "Carneadean Argument in Cicero's Academic Books," in *Assent and Argument: Studies in Cicero's Academic Books*, eds. Inwood, B. and Mansfeld, J. Leiden: Brill: 217–56.

Altaner, B. (1967) *Kleine Patristische Schriften.* Berlin: Akademie Verlag.

Annas, J. (1992) "Plato the Sceptic," in *Oxford Studies in Ancient Philosophy*, *Suppl. Vol.* 43–72. Oxford: Clarendon Press.

Aronadio, F. (2008) "L'Orientamento Filosofico di Cicerone e la sua Traduzione del *Timeo*," *Méthexis* 21/1: 111–29.

Atzert, K. (1908) *De Cicerone Interprete Graecorum.* Dissertation: Göttingen.

Ayres, L. (2010) *Augustine and the Trinity.* Cambridge University Press.

Bibliography

Bakhouche, B. (2003) "Éternité et Temps dans le 'Commentaire au *Timée*' de Calcidius," in *Hommages à Carl Deroux 5: Christianisme et Moyen Âge, Néo-Latin et Survivance de la Latinité*, ed. Defosse, P. Brussels: Latomus: 10–19.

(2008) "Tradition Graphique et Tradition Textuelle dans le 'Commentaire au *Timée*' de Calcidius," *Revue Belge de Philologie et d'Histoire* 86/1: 97–113.

Baltes, M. (1976) *Die Weltentstehung des Platonischen Timaios nach den Antiken Interpreten, Vol. 1.* Leiden: Brill.

(1979) *Die Weltentstehung des Platonischen Timaios nach den Antiken Interpreten, Vol. 2: Proklos.* Leiden: Brill.

(1996) "Gegonen (Platon, *Tim.* 28b7): Ist die Welt Real Entstanden oder Nicht?" in *Polyhistor: Studies in the History and Historiography of Ancient Philosophy: Presented to Jaap Mansfeld on His Sixtieth Birthday*, eds. Algra, K., van der Horst, P. W., Runia D. T. Leiden: E.J. Brill: 76–96.

Baltes, M., Dörrie, H. (eds.) (1998) *Die Philosophische Lehre des Platonismus: Text, Übersetzung, Kommentar, Vol.* 2. Stuttgart-Bad Cannstatt: Frommann Holzboog.

(2002) *Die Philosophische Lehre des Platonismus: Text, Übersetzung, Kommentar, Vol. 3.* Stuttgart-Bad Cannstatt: Frommann Holzboog.

(2008) *Die Philosophische Lehre des Platonismus: Text, Übersetzung, Kommentar, Vol. 4.* Stuttgart-Bad Cannstatt: Frommann Holzboog.

Baltzly, D., Runia, H., Share, M., Tarrant, H. (eds.) (2006–9) *Proclus: Commentary on Plato's Timaeus, Vols.* 1–4. Cambridge University Press.

Bammel, C.P. (1996) "Justification by Faith in Augustine and Origen," *Journal of Ecclesiastical History* 47: 223–35.

Barnes, J., Mansfeld, J., Schofield, M. (eds.) (1999) *The Cambridge History of Hellenistic Philosophy.* Cambridge University Press.

Barra, G. (1963) "La Biografia di Platone nel '*De Platone et Eius Dogmate*' di Apuleio," *RAAN* 40: 35–42.

Bartelink, G. (1987) "Die Beeinflussung Augustins durch die Griechischen Patres," in *Augustiniana Traiectina. Communications Présentées au Colloque International d'Utrecht 13–14 Novembre 1986*, eds. Den Boeft, J., van Oort, J. Paris: Etudes Augustiniennes: 9–24.

Barwick, K. (1963) *Das Rednerische Bildungsideal Ciceros: Abhandlungen der Sächsischen Akademie der Wissenschaften zu Leipzig 54.3.* Berlin: Akademie Verlag.

Bassnett-McGuire, S. (1991) *Translation Studies.* London: Routledge.

Beatrice, P.F. (1989) "*Quosdam Platonicorum Libros*: The Platonic Readings of Augustine in Milan," *Vigiliae Christianae* 43: 248–81.

Beaujeu, J. (1973) *Apulée: Opuscules Philosophiques (Du Dieu de Socrate, Platon et sa Doctrine, Du Monde) et Fragments.* Paris: Les Belles Lettres.

(1983) "Les dieux d'Apulée," *Revue de l'Histoire des Religions* 200: 385–406.

Bibliography

Bénatouïl, T. (2009) "How Industrious Is the Stoic God?," in *God and Cosmos in Stoicism*, ed. Salles, R. Oxford University Press: 23–45.

Bernard, W. (1994) "Zur Dämonologie des Apuleius zu Madaura," *Rheinisches Museum* 137: 358–73.

Bertolini, M. (1990) "Aspetti Letterari del Commentarius di Calcidio al *Timeo*," *Koinonia* 14: 89–112.

Betegh, G., Annas, J. (eds.) (2015) *Cicero's De Finibus: Philosophical Approaches*. Cambridge University Press.

Betegh, G., Gregoric, P. (2014) "Multiple Analogy in Ps.-Aristotle, *De Mundo* 6," *Classical Quarterly* 64/2: 574–91.

Bett, R. (1989) "Carneades' *Pithanon*: A Reappraisal of its Role and Status," *Oxford Studies in Ancient Philosophy* 7: 59–94.

Blatt, F. (1938) "Remarques sur l'Histoire des Traductions Latines," *Classica et Medievalia* 1: 217–42.

Bloom, H., Rosenberg, D. (1990) *The Book of J*. New York: Grove Press.

Bonazzi, M., Opsomer, J. (eds.) (2009) *The Origins of the Platonic System: Platonisms of the Early Empire and Their Philosophical Contexts*. Collection d'Études Classiques 23. Louvain, Namur, Paris, Walpole, MA: Éditions Peeters; Société des Études Classiques.

Bonner, G. (1986) *St. Augustine of Hippo: Life and Controversies*. Norwich: The Canterbury Press.

Boyancé, P. (1970) "Le Platonisme à Rome: Platon et Cicéron," *Etudes sur l'Humanisme Cicéronien*. *Latomus* 121: 222–47.

Boys-Stones, G.R. (2001) *Post-Hellenistic Philosophy: A Study of its Development from the Stoics to Origen*. Oxford University Press.

Brandwood, L. (1990) *The Chronology of Plato's Dialogues*. Cambridge University Press.

Brisson, L. (1974) *Le Même et l'Autre dans la Structure Ontologique du Timée de Platon*. Paris: Éditions Klincksieck.

(2003) "Plato's *Timaeus* and the Chaldean Oracles," in *Plato's Timaeus as a Cultural Icon*, ed. Reydams-Schils, G. University of Notre Dame Press: 111–32.

(ed.) (2005) *Porphyre, Sentences. 2 Vols. Études d'Introduction, Texte Grec et Traduction Française. Commentaire par l'Unité Propre de Recherche Nr. 76 du Centre National de la Recherche Scientifique*. Paris: Vrin.

Brittain, C. (2001) *Philo of Larissa: The Last of the Academic Sceptics*. Oxford University Press.

(2012) "Augustine as a Reader of Cicero," in *Tolle Lege: Essays on Augustine and on Medieval Philosophy in Honor of Roland J. Teske SJ*, ed. Taylor, R. et al. Milwaukee, WI: Marquette University Press: 81–112.

(2016) "Cicero's Sceptical Methods: The Example of the *De Finibus*," in *Cicero's De Finibus: Philosophical Approaches*, eds. Betegh, G. and Annas, J. Cambridge University Press: 12–40.

Broadie, S. (2012) *Nature and Divinity in Plato's Timaeus*. Cambridge University Press.

Bibliography

Brown, P. (2000) *Augustine of Hippo: A Biography. 2nd Edition.* Berkeley, CA: University of California Press.

Bryan, J. (2012) *Likeness and Likelihood in the Presocratics and Plato.* Cambridge University Press.

Buckley, M.J. (1970) "Philosophical Method in Cicero," *Journal of the History of Philosophy* 8: 143–54.

Burkert, W. (1965) "Cicero als Platoniker und als Skeptiker," *Gymnasium* 72: 175–200.

Burnyeat, M. (1983) *The Skeptical Tradition.* London: University of California Press.

(2002) "*De Anima* II.5," *Phronesis* 47/1: 28–90.

(2009) "Εἰκώς Μῦθος" in *Plato's Myths*, ed. Partenie, C. Cambridge, New York: Cambridge University Press: 167–86.

Burton, P. (2001) "Christian Latin," in *A Companion to the Latin Language*, ed. Clackson, J. Malden, MA: Wiley-Blackwell: 485–501.

Camelot, T. (1956) "A l'Éternel par le Temporel (*De Trinitate*, IV, XVIII, 24)," *Revue d'Études Augustiniennes et Patristiques* 2: 163–72.

Carone, G.-R. (2005) *Plato's Cosmology and its Ethical Dimensions.* Cambridge University Press.

Carr, D.M. (1996) "Canonization in the Context of Community: An Outline of the Formation of the Tanakh and the Christian Bible," in *A Gift of God in Due Season: Essays on Scripture and Community in Honor of James A. Sanders*, eds. Weiss, R.D. and Carr, D.M. Sheffield: Sheffield Academic Press: 22–64.

Carter, J.W. (2011) "St. Augustine on Time, Time Numbers, and Enduring Objects," *Vivarium* 49/4: 301–23.

Chadwick, H. (1986) *Augustine.* Past Masters Series. Oxford University Press.

Cherniss, H. (1944) *Aristotle's Criticism of Plato and the Academy, Vol. 1.* Baltimore: Johns Hopkins University Press.

Chroust, A.H. (1975) "Some Comments to Cicero, *De Natura Deorum* II.37, 95–96: A Fragment of Aristotle's *On Philosophy*," *Emerita* 43: 197–205.

Ciarlantini, P. (1983) "Mediator: Paganismo y Christianismo en *De Civitate Dei* 7.12–11.2 de San Agustín," *Revista Agustiniana* 24: 9–62.

(1984) "Mediator: Paganismo y Christianismo en *De Civitate Dei* 7.12–11.2 de San Agustín," *Revista Agustiniana* 25: 6–69.

(1985) "Mediator: Paganismo y Christianismo en *De Civitate Dei* 7.12–11.2 de San Agustín," *Revista Agustiniana* 26: 5–47, 301–32.

Clackson, J., Horrocks, G. (eds.) (2007) *The Blackwell History to the Latin Language.* Malden, MA; Oxford: Blackwell.

Clark, M.T. (1994) *Augustine.* Washington, D.C.: Georgetown University Press.

Cornford, F.M. (1937) *Plato's Cosmology: The Timaeus of Plato.* London: Routledge & Kegan Paul.

Cottier, J.-F. (2002) "La Paraphrase Latine, de Quintilien à Érasme," *Revue des Études Latines* 80: 237–52.

Bibliography

Couissin, P. (1929) "Le Stoicisme de la Nouvelle Academie," *Revue d'Histoire de la Philosophie* 3: 241–76.

Courcelle, P. (1950) *Recherches sur les Confessions de Saint Augustin.* 2nd edition. Paris: Boccard.

(1967) *La Consolation de Philosophie dans la Tradition Littéraire.* Paris: Études Augustiniennes.

(1969) *Late Latin Writers and their Greek Sources* (transl. Wedeck, H.E.). Cambridge, MA: Harvard University Press.

(1973) "Ambroise de Milan et Calcidius," in *Romanitas et Christianitas*, eds. Den Boer, W., van der Nat, P.G., van Winden, J.C. Amsterdam: North-Holland Publishing Company: 45–53.

Dal Pra, M. (1975) *Lo Scetticismo Greco.* 2 vols. Bari: Laterza.

Decret, F. (1970) *Aspects du Manichéisme dans l'Afrique Romain: Les Controverses de Fortunatus, Faustus et Felix avec Saint Augustin.* Paris: Études Augustiniennes.

(1974) *Mani et la Tradition Manichéenne.* Paris: Edition de Seuil.

Della Casa, A. (1962) *Nigidio Figulo.* Roma: Ed. Dell'Ateneo.

Den Boeft, J. (1970) *Calcidius on Fate: His Doctrine and Sources. Philosophia Antiqua* 18. Leiden: Brill.

(1977) *Calcidius on Demons.* Leiden: Brill.

(1996–2002) "*Daemon(es)*," in *Augustinus-Lexikon*, eds. Mayer, C., Müller, C., Dodaro, R. Basel: Schwabe: 213–22.

Dillon, J. (1989) "Tampering with the *Timaeus*: Ideological Emendations in Plato, with Special Reference to the *Timaeus*," *American Journal of Philology* 110: 50–72.

(1993) *The Handbook of Platonism: Alcinous.* 2nd Edition. Oxford: Clarendon Press.

(1996) *The Middle Platonists: A Study of Platonism 80 B.C. to A.D. 220.* 2nd edition. London: Duckworth.

(2003) *The Heirs of Plato: A Study of the Old Academy, 347–274 BC.* Oxford: Clarendon Press.

DiLorenzo, R.D. (1982) "Ciceronianism and Augustine's Conception of Philosophy," *Augustinian Studies* 13: 171–6.

Dobell, B. (2009) *Augustine's Intellectual Conversion: The Journey from Platonism to Christianity.* Cambridge University Press.

Dodaro, R. (2004) *Christ and the Just Society in the Thought of Augustine.* Cambridge, New York: Cambridge University Press.

Donini, P. (1988) "Il *Timeo*: Unità del Dialogo, Verosimiglianza del Discorso," *Elenchos* 9: 5–52.

(1994) "Testi e Commenti, Manuali e Insegnamento: La Forma Sistematica e i Metodi della Filosofia in Età Postellenistica," *Aufstieg und Niedergang der Römischen Welt* 2, 36.7: 5027–100.

Dörrie, H. (1974) "Le Renouveau du Platonisme à l'Époque de Cicéron," *Revue de Théologie et de Philosophie* 24: 13–29.

Bibliography

Doull, J.A. (1988) "What Is Augustinian *Sapientia*?," *Dionysius* 12: 61–7.

Dragona-Monachou, M. (1994) "Divine Providence in the Philosophy of the Empire," *ANRW II* 36/7: 4417–90.

Dubuisson, M. (1992) "Le Grec à Rome à l'Époque de Cicéron: Extension et Qualité du Bilinguisme," *Annales. Economies, Sociétés, Civilisations* 47/1: 187–206.

Dunkel, G.E. (2000) "Remarks on Code-Switching in Cicero's Letters to Atticus," *Museum Helveticum* 57: 122–9.

Dutton, P.E. (2003) "Medieval Approaches to Calcidius," in *Plato's Timaeus as a Cultural Icon*, ed. Reydams-Schils, G. Notre Dame: University of Notre Dame Press: 183–205.

Dyck, A.R. (1996) *A Commentary on Cicero, De Officiis*. Ann Arbor: University of Michigan Press.

Effe, B. (1970) *Studien zur Kosmologie und Theologie der Aristotelischen Schrift "Über die Philosophie"*. Munich: Beck.

Elders, L. (1966) *Aristotle's Cosmology: A Commentary on De Caelo*. Assen: Van Gorcum.

Engelbrecht, A. (1912) "Zu Ciceros Übersetzungen aus dem Platonischen *Timaeus*," *Wiener Studien* 34: 216–26.

Ernesti, J.C.G. (1983) *Lexicon Technologiae Graecorum Rhetoricae*. Hildesheim: Georg Olms.

Falcon, A. (2012) *Aristotelianism in the First Century BCE: Xenarchus of Seleucia*. Cambridge University Press.

Festugière, A.J. (1949) *La Révélation d' Hermès Trismégiste, Vol. 2: Le Dieu Cosmique*. Paris: Gabalda.

Finamore, J. (2006) "Apuleius on the Platonic Gods," in *Reading Plato in Antiquity*, eds. Tarrant, H. and Baltzly, D. London: Duckworth: 33–48.

Flamant, J. (1977) *Macrobe et le Néo-Platonisme Latin, à la Fin du IVe Siècle*. Leiden: Brill.

Flasch, K. (1993) *Was ist Zeit? Augustinus von Hippo: Das 11. Buch der Confessiones*. Frankfurt am Main: Klostermann.

Flashar, H. (ed.) (1983) *Die Philosophie der Antike, Vol. 3: Ältere Akademie, Aristoteles, Peripatos*. Basel, Stuttgart: Schwabe & Co. AG.

(1994) *Die Philosophie der Antike, Vol. 4: Die Hellenistische Philosophie*. Basel: Schwabe & Co. AG.

Fletcher, R. (2014) *Apuleius' Platonism: The Impersonation of Philosophy. Cambridge Classical Studies*. Cambridge; New York: Cambridge University Press.

Foley, M.P. (1999) "Cicero, Augustine, and the Philosophical Roots of the Cassiciacum Dialogues," *REA* 45: 51–7.

Fortenbaugh, W.W., Steinmetz, P. (1989) *Cicero's Knowledge of the Peripatos*. New Brunswick, NJ: Transaction Publishers.

Fraenkel, E. (1916) "Zur Geschichte des Wortes *Fides*," *Rheinisches Museum* 71: 187–99.

291

Bibliography

Frede, M. (1983) "Stoics and Sceptics on Clear and Distinct Impressions," in *The Skeptical Tradition*, ed. Burnyeat, M. Berkeley, CA: University of California Press: 65–93.

Fuchs, C. (1982) *La Paraphrase*. Paris: Presses Universitaires de France.

Fuhrer, T. (1993) "Der Begriff von *Veri Simile* bei Cicero und Augustin," *Museum Helveticum* 50: 107–24.

    (1997) "Die Platoniker und *Civitas Dei* (Buch 8–10)," in *Augustinus, De Civitate Dei*, ed. Horn, C. Klassiker Auslegen 11. Berlin: Akademie: 87–108.

Furley, D. (1989) "Aristotelian Material in Cicero's *De Natura Deorum*," in *Cicero's Knowledge of the Peripatos*, eds. Steinmetz, P. and Fortenbaugh, W.W. New Brunswick, NJ: Transaction Publishers: 201–19.

Furley, D., Foster, E.S. (eds., transl.) (1965) *Aristotle: On Sophistical Refutations. On Coming to be and Passing Away. On the Cosmos.* Cambridge, MA: Harvard University Press.

Gallop, D. (2003) "The Rhetoric of Philosophy: Socrates' Swan-Song," in *Plato as Author: The Rhetoric of Philosophy*, ed. Michelini, A. Leiden: Brill: 313–32.

Galonnier, A. (2009) "Cosmogenèse et Chronocentrisme chez Chalcidius," *Philosophie Antique* 9: 189–207.

Garrett, D. (2003) *Rethinking Genesis: The Source and Authorship of the First Book of the Pentateuch.* Fearn, UK: Christian Focus Publications.

Gersh, S. (1986) *Middle Platonism and Neoplatonism: The Latin Tradition.* 2 Vols. Notre Dame, IN: University of Notre Dame Press.

Gill, C. (1977) "The Genre of the Atlantis Story," *Classical Philology* 72: 287–304.

Gioia, L. (2008) *The Theological Epistemology of Augustine's De Trinitate.* Oxford University Press.

Gloy, K. (1986) *Studien zur Platonischen Naturphilosophie im Timaios.* Würzburg: Königshausen, Neumann.

Glucker, J. (1978) *Antiochus and the Late Academy.* Hypomnemata 56. Göttingen: Vandenhoeck and Ruprecht.

    (1988) "Cicero's Philosophical Affiliations," in *The Question of Eclectism: Studies in Later Greek Philosophy*, eds. Dillon, J. and Long, A.A. Berkeley, CA: University of California Press: 34–69.

    (1995) "*Probabile, Veri Simile* and Related Terms," in *Cicero the Philosopher*, ed. Powell, J.G.F. Oxford: Clarendon Press: 115–43.

Görler, W. (1992) "Ein Sprachlicher Zufall und seine Folgen: Wahrscheinliches bei Karneades und bei Cicero," in *Zum Umgang mit Fremden Sprachen in der Griechisch-Römischen Antike: Kolloquium der Fachrichtungen Klassische Philologie der Universitäten Leipzig und Saarbrücken am 21. und 22. November 1989 in Saarbrücken*, eds. Müller, C. et al. Stuttgart: Steiner: 159–71.

Bibliography

(1994a) "Karneades," in *Die Philosophie der Antike, Vol. 4: Die Hellenistische Philosophie*, ed. Flashar, H. Basel: Schwabe & Co. AG: 849–97.

(1994b) "Philon aus Larissa," in *Die Philosophie der Antike, Vol. 4: Die Hellenistische Philosophie*, ed. Flashar, H. Basel: Schwabe & Co. AG: 915–37.

(1995a) "Cicero's Philosophical Stance in the *Lucullus*," in *Assent and Argument: Studies in Cicero's Academic Books*, eds. Inwood, B. and Mansfeld, J. Leiden: Brill: 36–57.

(1995b) "Silencing the Troublemaker: *De Legibus* 1.39 and the Continuity of Cicero's Scepticism," in *Cicero the Philosopher*, ed. Powell, J.F.G. Oxford: Clarendon Press: 85–113.

Grimaldi, W.M.A. (1957) "A Note on the πίστεις in Aristotle's *Rhetoric* 1354–1356," *The American Journal of Philology* 78: 188–92.

Habermehl, P. (1996) "*Quaedam Divinae Potestates*: Demonology in Apuleius' *De Deo Socratis*," in *Groningen Colloquia on the Novel, Vol. 1*, ed. Hofmann, H. Groningen: Egbert Forsten: 117–42.

Hadot, I. (1991) "The Role of the Commentaries on Aristotle in the Teaching of Philosophy According to the Prefaces of the Neoplatonic Commentaries on the *Categories*," in *Aristotle and the Later Tradition*, eds. Blumenthal, H. and Robinson, H. Oxford: Clarendon Press: 175–89.

Hadot, P. (1968) *Porphyre et Victorinus*. 2 *Vols*. Paris: EA.

(1982) "Die Einteilung der Philosophie im Altertum," *Zeitschrift für Philosophische Forschung* 36: 422–44.

(1995) *Philosophy as a Way of Life: Spiritual Exercises from Socrates to Foucault* (transl. Chase, M.). Oxford: Blackwell.

(2002) *What Is Ancient Philosophy?* Cambridge, MA: Belknap Harvard.

Hagendahl H. (1947) "Methods of Citation in Post-Classical Latin Prose," *Eranos*: 114–28.

(1967) *Augustine and the Latin Classics*. 2 *Vols*. Göteborg: Almquist and Wiksell.

Hampton, C. (1990) *Pleasure, Knowledge and Being*. Albany, NY: SUNY Press.

Happ, H. (1968) "Weltbild und Seinslehre bei Aristoteles," *Antike und Abendland* 14: 77 84.

Harrison, S.J. (2000) *Apuleius: A Latin Sophist*. Oxford University Press.

Heinze, R. (1982) *Xenokrates: Darstellung der Lehre und Sammlung der Fragmente*. Leipzig: Teubner.

Helm, R. (1955) "Apuleius' Apologie: Ein Meisterwerk der Zweiten Sophistik," *Das Altertum* 1: 86–108.

Hijmans, B.L. (1987) "Apuleius Philosophus Platonicus," *ANRW II*.36.1: 395–475.

Hirzel, R. (1877–83) *Untersuchungen zu Ciceros Philosophischen Schriften*. 3 *Vols*. Leipzig: Hirzel.

Hoenig, C. (2013) "Εἰκὼς λόγος: Plato in Translation(s)," *Methodos. Savoirs et Textes* 13: *Interpréter en Contexte.*

(2014) "Calcidius and the Creation of the Universe," *Rhizomata* 2/1: 80–110.

(2018a) "Calcidius," in *A Companion to the Reception of Plato in Antiquity,* eds. Tarrant, H., Baltzly, D. et al. Leiden: Brill: 433–47.

(2018b), Review of Stover, Justin A., A New Text of Apuleius: The Lost Third Book of the De Platone. Oxford University Press, 2016. Pp. xviii + 216. *Classical Philology* 113/2: 227–32.

Hölscher, L. (1986) *The Reality of Mind: Augustine's Philosophical Arguments for the Human Soul as a Spiritual Substance.* London: Routledge and Kegan Paul.

Horsfall, N. (1979) "Doctus Sermonis Utriusque Linguae?" *Échos du Monde Classique* 23: 79–95.

Howald, E. (1922) "Eikōs Logos," *Hermes* 57: 63–79.

Hunink, V. (2003) "'Apuleius, Qui Nobis Afris Afer est Notior': Augustine's Polemic against Apuleius in *De Civitate Dei*," *Scholia N.S.* 12: 82–95.

Hyers, C. (1984) *The Meaning of Creation: Genesis and Modern Science.* Atlanta, GA: John Knox Press.

Inwood, B., Mansfeld, J. (eds.) (1995) *Assent and Argument: Studies in Cicero's Academic Books: Proceedings of the 7th Symposium Hellenisticum Utrecht, August 21–25.* Leiden: Brill.

Isnardi Parente, M., Dorandi, T. (ed.) (2012) Senocrate e Ermodoro: Testimonianze e Frammenti. Pisa: Edizioni della Normale.

Isnardi Parente, M. (ed.) (1982) *Senocrate e Ermodoro: Frammenti.* Naples: Bibliopolis.

Jocelyn, H.D. (1973) "Greek Poetry in Cicero's Prose Writing," *YCS* 23: 61–111.

Johansen, T.K. (2004) *Plato's Natural Philosophy: A Study of the Timaeus–Critias.* Cambridge University Press.

Johnson, D.W. (1972) "*Verbum* in the Early Augustine (386–397)," *RA* 8: 25–53.

Jones, D.M. (1959) "Cicero as a Translator," *Bulletin of the Institute of Classical Studies of the University of London* 6: 22–34.

Kahn, C. (2010) "The Place of Cosmology in Plato's Later Dialogues," in *One Book, The Whole Universe: Plato's Timaeus Today*, eds. Mohr, R., Sanders, K., and Sattler, B. Las Vegas: Parmenides Publishing: 69–78.

Kajanto, I. (1972) "Fortuna," *RAC* 8: 182–97.

Karamanolis, G. (2006) *Plato and Aristotle in Agreement? Platonists on Aristotle from Antiochus to Porphyry.* Oxford University Press.

Karfíková, L. (2004) "Augustins Polemik gegen Apuleius," in *Apuleius: De Deo Socratis. Über den Gott des Sokrates*, eds. Baltes, M., Lakman, M.-L., Dillon, J., Donini, P., Häfner, R., and Karfíková, L. Darmstadt: Wissenschaftliche Buchgesellschaft: 162–89.

Kirwan, C. (1989) *Augustine: The Arguments of the Philosophers*. London: Routledge.

Knuuttila, S. (2001) "Time and Creation in Augustine," in *The Cambridge Companion to Augustine*, eds. Stump, E. and Kretzmann, N. Cambridge University Press: 103–15.

Köckert, C. (2009) *Christliche Kosmologie und Kaiserzeitliche Philosophie: Die Auslegung des Schöpfungsberichtes bei Origenes, Basilius und Gregor von Nyssa vor dem Hintergrund Kaiserzeitlicher Timaeus-Interpretationen.* Studien und Texte zu Antike und Christentum 56. Tübingen: Mohr Siebeck.

Koenen, L. (1978) "Augustine and Manichaeism in Light of the Cologne Mani Codex," *Illinois Classical Studies* 3: 154–95.

Kouremenos, T., Parássoglou, G.M., Tsantsanoglou, K. (eds.) (2006) *The Derveni Papyrus*. Florence: Leo S. Olschki.

Krafft, P. (1979) "Apuleius' Darstellung der *Providentia Tripertita*," *Museum Helveticum* 36: 153–63.

Krämer, H.J. (1971) *Platonismus und Hellenistische Philosophie*. Berlin: de Gruyter.

Kroll W. (1903) "Studien über Ciceros Schrift *De Oratore*," *Rheinisches Museum* 58: 552–97.

Kytzler, B. (1989) "*Fides Interpres*: The Theory and Practice of Translation in Classical Antiquity," *Antichthon* 23: 42–50.

Lambardi, N. (1982) *Il "Timaeus" Ciceroniano: Arte e Tecnica del "Vertere"*. Florence: Le Monnier.

Ledger, G.R. (1989) *Re-counting Plato: A Computer Analysis of Plato's Style*. Oxford: Clarendon Press.

Lemoine, M. (1998) "Innovations de Cicéron et de Calcidius dans la Traduction de *Timée*," in *The Medieval Translator: Traduire au Moyen Age, Vol. 6*, eds. Ellis, R., Tixier, R., and Weitemeier, B. Turnhout: Brepols: 72–81.

Leonhardt, J. (1999) *Ciceros Kritik der Philosophenschulen*. Munich: Beck.

Lévy, C. (1985) "Cicéron et la Quatrième Académie," *Revue des Études Latines* 63: 32–41.

　(2003) "Cicero and the *Timaeus*," in *Plato's Timaeus as Cultural Icon*, ed. Reydams-Schils, G. Notre Dame, IN: University of Notre Dame Press: 95–110.

Lienhard, J.T. (1966) "A Note on the Meaning of ΠΙΣΤΙΣ," *The American Journal of Philology* 87/4: 446–54.

Lieu, S.N.C. (1985) *Manichaeism in the Later Roman Empire and Medieval China: A Historical Survey*. Manchester University Press.

Lilla, S.R. (1997) "The Neoplatonic Hypostases and the Christian Trinity," in *Studies in Plato and the Platonic Tradition: Essays Presented to John Whittaker*, ed. Joyle, M. Aldershot: Ashgate: 127–89.

Bibliography

Liuzzi, D. (ed.) (1983) *Nigidio Figulo, Astrologo e Mago: Testimonianze e Frammenti.* Lecce: Milella.

Loenen, J.H. (1956) "Albinus' Metaphysics: An Attempt at Rehabilitation," *Mnemosyne* 9: 296–319.

Löfstedt, E. (1912) "Plautinischer Sprachbrauch und Verwandtes," *Glotta* 3: 171–91.

Long, A.A. (1974) *Cicero, Academica.* London: Duckworth.

(1995) "Cicero's Plato and Aristotle," in *Cicero the Philosopher*, ed. Powell, J.G.F. Oxford: Clarendon Press: 37–61.

Long, A.A., Sedley, D. (eds.) (1987) *The Hellenistic Philosophers, Vol. 1: Translation of the Principal Sources with Philosophical Commentary; Vol. 2: Greek and Latin Texts with Notes and Bibliography.* Cambridge University Press.

Lorenz, R. (1979) *Arius Judaizans? Untersuchungen zur Dogmengeschichtlichen Einordnung des Arius.* Göttingen: Vandenhoek and Ruprecht.

Lorimer, W.L. (ed.) (1933) *Aristotelis Qui Fertur Libellus De Mundo.* Paris: Les Belles Lettres.

Louth, A. (2002) "Love and the Trinity: St. Augustine and the Greek Fathers," *Augustinian Studies* 33: 1–16.

Maas, W. (1974) "Unveränderlichkeit Gottes: Zum Verhältnis Griechisch-Philosophischer und Christlicher Gotteslehre," *Paderborn Theologische Studien* 1. Munich: Schöningh.

Macdonald, S. (2001) "The Divine Nature," in *The Cambridge Companion to Augustine*, eds. Stump, E. and Kretzmann, N. Cambridge University Press: 71–90.

Madec, G. (1992) "Le Christ des Païens d'après le *De Consensu Evangelistarum* de Saint Augustin," *Recherches Augustiniennes* 26: 3–67.

Magee, J. (ed., transl.) (2016) *Calcidius: On Plato's Timaeus.* Cambridge, MA: Harvard University Press.

Maher, J.P. (1979) "Saint Augustine and the Manichaean Cosmogony," *Augustinian Studies* 10: 91–104.

Mann, W.E. (1987) "Immutability and Predication: What Aristotle Taught Philo and Augustine," *International Journal for Philosophy of Religion* 22/1–2: 21–39.

(2014) *Augustine's Confessions: Philosophy in Autobiography.* Oxford, New York: Oxford University Press.

Mansfeld, J. (1979) "Providence and the Destruction of the Universe in Early Stoic Thought, with Some Remarks on the Mysteries of Philosophy," in *Studies in Hellenistic Religions*, ed. Vermaseren, M.J. Leiden: Brill: 129–88.

(1990) "Doxography and Dialectic," *ANRW* II.36.4: 3056–229.

(1994) *Prolegomena: Questions to Be Settled before the Study of an Author, or a Text. Philosophia Antiqua 61.* Leiden: Brill.

Marouzeau, J. (1947) "Latini Sermonis Egestas," *Eranos* 45: 22–4.

Bibliography

Marrou, I. (1956) *A History of Education in Antiquity* (transl. Lamb). New York: Sheed and Ward.

Marti, H. (1974) *Übersetzer der Augustin-Zeit*. Munich: Fink.

Matthes, D. (1958) "Hermagoras von Temnos," *Lustrum* 3: 1904–55.

Matthews, G.B. (1972) "*Si Fallor, Sum*," in *Augustine: A Collection of Critical Essays*, ed. Markus, R.A. Garden City, NY: Anchor Books: 156–67.

McGrath, A. (1986) *Iustitia Dei: The History of the Christian Doctrine of Justification, Vol. 1: From the Beginning to 1500*. Cambridge University Press.

Menn, S. (1995) *Plato on God as Nous*. Carbondale, IL: Southern Illinois University Press.

Meyer-Abich, K.M. (1973) "Eikōs Logos: Platons Theorie der Naturwissenschaft," in *Einheit und Vielheit: Festschrift für C.-F. von Weizsäcker*, eds. Scheibe, E. and Süssmann, G. Göttingen: Vandenhoeck und Ruprecht: 22–44.

Michel, A. (1960) *Rhétorique et Philosophie chez Cicéron*. Paris: Presses Universitaires de France.

Mohr, R., Sanders, K., Sattler, B. (eds.) (2010) *One Book, The Whole Universe: Plato's Timaeus Today*. Las Vegas: Parmenides Publishing.

Moorhead, J. (2009) "Boethius' Life and the World of Late Antique Philosophy," in *The Cambridge Companion to Boethius*, ed. Marenbon, J. Cambridge University Press: 13–33.

Moraux, P. (1949) "L'Exposé de la Philosophie d'Aristote chez Diogène Laërce v.28–34," *Extr. de la Revue Philosophique de Louvain* 47: 5–43.

(1968) "*La Joute Dialectique* d'après le Huitième Livre des *Topiques*," in *Aristotle on Dialectic: The Topics*, ed. Owen, G.E.L. Oxford: Clarendon Press: 277–311.

Moreschini, C. (1964) "La Posizione di Apuleio e della Scuola di Gaio nell' Ambito del Medioplatonismo," *Annali della Scuola Normale Superiore di Pisa, Classe di Lettere e Filosofia* 33: 17–56.

(1966) *Studi sul 'De Dogmate Platonis' di Apuleio*. Pisa: Nistri-Lischi Editori.

(1978) *Apuleio e il Platonismo*. Florence: L.S. Olschki.

(2003) *Calcidio: Commentario al "Timeo" di Platone*. Milan: Bompiani.

(ed.) (2005) *De Consolatione Philosophiae: Opuscula Theologica*. Leipzig: K.G. Saur.

(2015) *Apuleius and the Metamorphoses of Platonism*. Turnhout: Brepols.

Morford, M.P.O. (2002) *The Roman Philosophers: From the Time of Cato the Censor to the Death of Marcus Aurelius*. London: Routledge.

Mortley, R. (1972) "Apuleius and Platonic Theology," *AJPh* 93: 584–90.

Neschke-Hentschke, A. (ed.) (2000) *Le Timée de Platon: Contributions à l'Histoire de sa Réception*. Bibliothèque Philosophique de Louvain 53. Louvain, Paris: Peeters.

Bibliography

Nida, E. (1964) *Toward a Science of Translating: With Special Reference to Principles and Procedures Involved in Bible Translating*. Leiden: Brill.

Nightingale, A. (2011) *Once out of Nature*. Chicago, London: University of Chicago Press.

Nisbet, R.G.M. (1992) "The Orator and the Reader," in *Author and Audience in Latin Literature*, eds. Woodman, A.J. and Powell, J.G.F. Cambridge, New York: Cambridge University Press: 1–17.

O'Connell, R.J. (1963) "*Ennead* VI. 4 and 5 in the Works of St. Augustine," *Revue des Études Augustiniennes* 9: 1–39.

O'Daly, G. (1977) "Time as Distention and St. Augustine's Exegesis of Philippians 3,12–14," *Revue des Études Augustiniennes* 23: 265–71.

(1987) *Augustine's Philosophy of Mind*. Berkeley, CA: University of California Press.

(1999) *Augustine's City of God*. Oxford: Clarendon Press.

O'Donnell, J. (1985) *Augustine*. Twayne's World Author Series. Boston, MA: Twayne Publishers.

(1992) *Augustine: Confessions. Text and Commentary*. 3 vols. Oxford University Press.

(2006) *Augustine: A New Biography*. New York: Harper Perennial Books.

O'Meara, J.J. (1959) *Porphyry's Philosophy from Oracles in Augustine*. Paris: E.A.

(1997) *Understanding Augustine*. Dublin: Four Courts Press.

Patillon, M., Bolognesi, G. (1997) *Aelius Theon, Progymnasmata*. Paris: Les Belles Lettres.

Peetz, S. (2005) "Ciceros Konzept des *Probabile*," *Philosophisches Jahrbuch* 112/1: 99–133.

Pelland, G. (1972) *Cinq Études d'Augustin sur le Début de la Genèse*. Théologie, Recherches 8. Montreal: Ballarmi.

Pépin J. (1953) "Recherches sur le Sens et les Origines de l'Expression *caelum caeli* dans le Livre XII des *Confessions* de S. Augustin," *Archivum Latinitatis Medii Aevi* 23: 185–274.

(1964) *Théologie Cosmique et Théologie Chrétienne: Ambroise, Exam. I. I. I–4*. Paris: Bibliothèque de Philosophie Contemporaine.

(1977) *Ex Platonicorum Persona: Études sur les Lectures Philosophiques de Saint Augustin*. Amsterdam: A.M. Hakkert.

(1997) *Libro Dodicesimo in Sant'Agostino, Confessioni, Vol. 5: Libri XII–XIII* (trans. Chiariti, G., comm. Pépin, J., Simonetti, M.). Milan: Mondadori, Fondazione Lorenzo Valla: 149–229.

Petit, A. (1988) "Le Pythagorisme à Rome à la Fin de la République et au Début de l'Empire," *Annales Latini Montium Arvernorum* 15: 23–32.

Petrucci, F.M. (2012) *Teone di Smirne: Expositio Rerum Mathematicarum ad Legendum Platonem Utilium*. Sankt Augustin: Academia Verlag.

(2016) "Argumentative Strategies for Interpreting Plato's Cosmogony: Taurus and the Issue of Literalism in Antiquity," *Phronesis* 61: 43–59.

Bibliography

(2018) *Taurus of Beirut: The Other Side of Middle Platonism*. Oxford, New York: Routledge.

Pini, F. (1960) "Varianti del Codice Vossiano Latino Q 10 al testo del *Timeo*," *Ciceroniana* 1–2: 161–3.

Poncelet, R. (1957) *Cicéron Traducteur de Platon*. Paris: De Boccard.

Portogalli, B.M. (1963) "Sulle Fonti della Concezione Teologica e Demonologica di Apuleio," *Studi Classici e Orientali* 12: 227–41.

Powell, J.G.F. (1995) "Cicero's Translations from the Greek," in *Cicero the Philosopher*, ed. Powell, J.G.F. Oxford: Clarendon Press: 273–300.

Puelma, M. (1980) "Cicero als Platonübersetzer," *Museum Helveticum* 37: 137–78.

Ratkowitsch, C. (1996) "Die *Timaios*-Übersetzung des Chalcidius," *Philologus* 140: 139–62.

Redfors, J. (1960) *Echtheitskritische Untersuchungen der Apuleianischen Schriften De Platone und De Mundo*. Lund: Gleerup.

Regen, F. (1971) *Apuleius Philosophus Platonicus: Untersuchungen zur Apologie und De Mundo*. Berlin: De Gruyter.

(1999) "Il *De Deo Socratis* de Apuleio," *Maia* 51: 429–56.

(2000) "Il *De Deo Socratis* de Apuleio (II Parte)," *Maia* 52: 41–66.

Reiff, A. (1959) *Interpretatio, Imitatio, Aemulatio: Begriff und Vorstellung literarischer Abhängigkeit bei den Römern*. Doctoral Thesis. Universität Köln.

Reinhardt, T. (2000) "Rhetoric in the Fourth Academy," *Classical Quarterly* 50/2: 531–47.

(2003) *Marcus Tullius Cicero: Topica*. Oxford University Press.

Rémy, G. (1979) *Le Christ Médiateur dans l'Oeuvre de Saint Augustin*. Doctoral Thesis. Paris, Lille.

Rener, F.M. (1989) *Interpretatio: Language and Translation from Cicero to Tytler*. Amsterdam, Atlanta, GA: Rodopi.

Reydams-Schils, G. (1999) *Demiurge and Providence: Stoic and Platonist Readings of Plato's Timaeus*. Turnhout: Brepols.

(2002) "Calcidius Christianus? God, Body, and Matter," in *Metaphysik und Religion: Zur Signatur des spätantiken Denkens*, eds. Kobusch, T., Erler M., and Männlein-Robert, I. Munich, Leipzig: Saur: 193–211.

(ed.) (2003) *Plato's Timaeus as Cultural Icon*. Notre Dame, IN: University of Notre Dame Press.

(2007a) "Meta-discourse: Plato's *Timaeus* according to Calcidius," *Phronesis* 52: 301–27.

(2007b) "Calcidius on God," in *Platonic Stoicism – Stoic Platonism: The Dialogue between Platonism and Stoicism in Antiquity*, eds. Bonazzi, M. and Helmig, C. Leuven: Leuven University Press: 243–58.

(2010) "Calcidius," in *The Cambridge History of Philosophy in Late Antiquity*, ed. Gerson, G.L. Cambridge University Press: 498–508.

Riposati, B. (1944) "Quid Cicero de Thesi et Hypothesi in Topicis Senserit," *Aevum* 18: 61–71.

Bibliography

Rist, J. (1994) *Augustine: Ancient Thought Baptized.* Cambridge University Press.

(1996) *Man, Soul, and Body: Essays in Ancient Thought from Plato to Dionysius.* Aldershot: Variorum.

Robinson, T.M. (2004) *Cosmos as Art Object: Studies in Plato's Timaeus and Other Dialogues.* Binghamton, NY: Global Academic Publishing.

Rowe, C. (2003) "The Status of the 'Myth' in Plato's *Timaeus*," in *Plato Physicus: Cosmologia e Antropologia nel Timeo*, eds. Natali, C. and Maso, S. Amsterdam: Adolf Hakkert: 21–31.

Ruch, M. (1969) *"La Disputatio in Utramque Partem* dans le *Lucullus* et ses Fondements Philosophiques," *Revue des Etudes Latines* 47: 310–35.

Runia D.T. (1986) *Philo of Alexandria and the Timaeus of Plato.* Leiden: Brill.

(1993) *Philo in Early Christian Literature.* Assen: Van Gorcum.

(ed.) (2001) *Philo of Alexandria: On the Creation of the Cosmos According to Moses. Introduction, Translation and Commentary.* Philo of Alexandria Commentary Series 1. Leiden: Brill.

(2003) "The King, the Architect, and the Craftsman: A Philosophical Image in Philo of Alexandria," in *Ancient Approaches to Plato's Timaeus*, ed. Sharples, R.W., and Sheppard, A. Bulletin of the Institute of Classical Studies Supplement. London: Institute of Classical Studies: 89–106.

Ryle, G. (1965) "Dialectic in the Academy," in *New Essays on Plato and Aristotle,* eds. Anscombe, G.E.M. and Bambrough, R. London: Routledge and Kegan Paul: 69–79.

Sandwell, I. (2010) "Pagan Conceptions of Monotheism in the Fourth Century: The Example of Libanius and Themistius," in *Monotheism between Pagans and Christians in Late Antiquity,* eds. van Nuffelen, P. and Mitchell, S. Cambridge University Press: 101–26.

Sandy, G. (1997) *The Greek World of Apuleius: Apuleius and the Second Sophistic.* Mnemosyne Suppl. 175. Leiden: Brill.

Scheck, T.P. (2008) *Origen and the History of Justification: The Legacy of Origen's Commentary on Romans.* Notre Dame, IN: University of Notre Dame Press.

Schofield, M. (1983) "The Syllogisms of Zeno of Citium," *Phronesis* 28/1: 31–58.

(1986) "Cicero for and against Divination," *Journal of Roman Studies* 76: 47–65.

Schütrumpf, J. (1990) "Cicero's *De Oratore* and the Greek Philosophical Tradition," *Rheinisches Museum* 133: 310–21.

Schweinfurth-Walla, S. (1986) *Studien zu den Rhetorischen Überzeugungsmitteln bei Cicero und Aristoteles.* Mannheimer Beiträge zur Sprach- und Literaturwissenschaft 9. Tübingen: Gunter Narr.

Sedley, D. (1983) "The Motivation of Greek Skepticism," in *The Skeptical Tradition,* ed. Burnyeat, M. Berkeley, CA: University of California Press: 9–29.

Bibliography

(1996) "Alcinous' Epistemology," in *Polyhistor: Studies Presented to Jaap Mansfeld*, ed. Algra, Keimpe A., van der Horst, P.W., and Runia, D.T. Leiden, New York: Brill: 300–12.

(1997) "Plato's *Auctoritas* and the Rebirth of the Commentary Tradition," in *Philosophia Togata II: Plato and Aristotle at Rome*, eds. Barnes, J. and Griffin, M. Oxford: Clarendon Press: 110–29.

(ed.) (2003) *The Cambridge Companion to Greek and Roman Philosophy*. Cambridge University Press.

(2007) *Creationism and its Critics in Antiquity*. Berkeley, CA: University of California Press.

(2010) "The Status of Physics in Lucretius, Philodemus and Cicero," in *Miscellanea Papyrologica Herculanensia, Vol.* I, eds. Antoni, A. and Delattre, D. Pisa: Fabrizio Serra: 63–8.

(2012) *The Philosophy of Antiochus*. Cambridge University Press.

(2013) "Cicero on the *Timaeus*," in *Aristotle, Plato and Pythagoreanism in the First Century BC*, ed. Schofield, M. Cambridge University Press: 187–205.

Sedley, D., Bastianini, G. (1995) "Commentarium in Platonis *Theaetetum*," in *Corpus dei Papiri Filosofici Greci e Latini (CPF): Testi e Lessico nei Papiri di Cultura Greca e Latina. Commentari*, Vol. 3. Florence: Olschki: 227–562.

Seele, A. (1995) *Römische Übersetzer*. Darmstadt: Wissenschaftliche Buchgesellschaft.

Sharples R.W. (1982) "Alexander of Aphrodisias on Divine Providence: Two Problems," *Classical Quarterly* 32: 198–211.

(1995) "Counting Plato's Principles," in *The Passionate Intellect: Essays on the Transformation of Classical Traditions Presented to Professor I.G. Kidd*, ed. Ayres, L. New Brunswick, NJ: Transaction Publishers: 67–82.

(2003) "Threefold Providence: The History and Background of a Doctrine," in *Ancient Approaches to Plato's Timaeus*, ed. Sharples, R.W., and Sheppard, A. Bulletin of the Institute of Classical Studies Supplement. London: Institute of Classical Studies: 107–27.

Sharples R.W., Van der Eijk, P.J. (eds., transl.) (2008) *Nemesius: On the Nature of Man*. Liverpool: Liverpool University Press.

Sheppard, A., Sharples, R.W. (eds.) (2003) *Ancient Approaches to Plato's Timaeus*. London: Institute of Classical Studies, University of London.

Siniscalco, P. (1990) "Dai Mediatori al Mediatore: La Demonologia di Apuleio e la Critica di Agostino," in *L'Autunno del Diavolo*, ed. Corsini, E. Milan: Bompiani: 279–94.

Sinko, T. (1905) *De Apulei et Albini Doctrinae Platonicae Adumbratione*. Krakow: Akademie der Wissenschaften.

Somfai, A. (2002) "The Eleventh-Century Shift in the Reception of Plato's *Timaeus* and Calcidius' Commentary," *Journal of the Warburg and Courtauld Institutes* 65: 1–21.

Bibliography

(2003) "The Nature of Demons: A Theological Application of the Concept of Geometrical Proportion in Calcidius' Commentary to Plato's *Timaeus* (40d–41a)," in *Ancient Approaches to Plato's Timaeus*, eds. Sharples, R.W. and Sheppard, A. London: Institute of Classical Studies, University of London: 129–42.

(2004) "Calcidius' Commentary on Plato's *Timaeus* and its Place in the Commentary Tradition: The Concept of *Analogia* in Text and Diagrams," in *Philosophy, Science and Exegesis in Greek, Arabic and Latin Commentaries*, eds. Adamson, P., Baltussen, H., and Stone, M.W.F. London: Institute of Classical Studies, University of London: 203–20.

Sorabji, R. (1983) *Time, Creation and the Continuum: Theories in Antiquity and the Early Middle Ages*. London: Duckworth.

Steiner, G. (1998) *After Babel: Aspects of Language and Translation. 3rd edition*. Oxford University Press.

Steinheimer, E. (1912) *Untersuchungen über die Quellen des Chalcidius*. Aschaffenburg: Werbrun.

Steinmetz, P. (1989) "Beobachtungen zu Ciceros Philosophischem Standpunkt," in *Cicero's Knowledge of the Peripatos*, eds. Steinmetz, P. and Fortenbaugh, W.W. New Brunswick, NJ: Transaction Publishers: 201–19.

Stemplinger, E. (1912) *Das Plagiat in der Griechischen Literatur*. Leipzig, Berlin: Teubner.

Stover, J. (2016) *A New Work by Apuleius: The Lost Third Book of the De Platone. Edited and Translated with an Introduction and Commentary*. Oxford, New York: Oxford University Press.

Striker, G. (1980) "Skeptical Strategies," in *Doubt and Dogmatism: Studies in Hellenistic Epistemology*, eds. Schofield, M., Burnyeat, M., and Barnes, J. Oxford University Press: 54–83.

Strohm, H. (1952) "Studien zur Schrift *Von der Welt*," *Museum Helveticum* 9: 137–75.

Stump, E., Kretzmann, N. (eds.) (2001) *The Cambridge Companion to Augustine*. Cambridge University Press.

Sullivan, M.W. (1967) *Apuleian Logic: The Nature, Sources, and Influences of Apuleius' Peri Hermeneias*. Amsterdam: North-Holland Publishing Co.

Swain, S. (2002) "Bilingualism in Cicero? The Evidence of Code-Switching," in *Bilingualism in Ancient Society: Language Contact and the Written Text*, eds. Adams, J.N., Janse, M., and Swain, S. Oxford University Press: 128–67.

Switalski, B.W. (1902) *Des Chalcidius Kommentar zu Platons Timaios: Eine Historisch-Kritische Untersuchung*. Münster: Aschendorff.

Swoboda, A. (ed.) (1964) *Nigidius Figulus: Operum Reliquiae*. Amsterdam: A.M. Hakkert.

Tarrant, H. (1985) *Scepticism or Platonism? The Philosophy of the Fourth Academy*. Cambridge University Press.

Tatum, J. (1979) *The Golden Ass*. Ithaca, NY: Cornell University Press.

Bibliography

Taylor, A.E. (1928) *A Commentary on Plato's Timaeus*. Oxford: Clarendon Press.

Taylor, J.H. (1982) *The Literal Meaning of Genesis/ St. Augustine*. 2 vols. (Ancient Christian Writers, vol. 41, 42). New York: Newman Press.

TeSelle, E. (1996–2002) "*Fides*," in *Augustinus-Lexikon*, eds. Mayer, C. et al. Basel: Schwabe: 1333–40.

Teske, R. (1981) "Properties of God and the Predicaments in *De Trinitate* v," *Modern Schoolman* 59/1: 1–20.

(1985a) "Augustine's Use of *Substantia* in Speaking about God," *Modern Schoolman* 62/3: 147–63.

(1985b) "*Vocans Temporales, Faciens Aeternos*: St. Augustine on Liberation from Time," *Traditio* 41: 29–47.

(1986) "The Aim of Augustine's Proof that God Truly Is," *International Philosophical Quarterly* 26/3: 253–68.

(1996) *Paradoxes in Time in St. Augustine*. Milwaukee, WI: Marquette University Press.

Theiler, W. (1953) "Porphyrios und Augustin," *Schriften der Königsberger Gelehrten Gesellschaft, Geisteswiss. Klasse 10/1*. Halle: Niemeyer.

(1964) *Die Vorbereitung des Neuplatonismus*. Berlin: Weidmann.

Throm, H. (1932) *Die Thesis: Ein Beitrag zu ihrer Entstehung und Geschichte. Rhetorische Studien 17*. Paderborn: F. Schoning.

Timotin, A. (2012) *La Démonologie Platonicienne: Histoire de la Notion de "daimon" de Platon aux Derniers Néoplatoniciens*. Leiden: Brill.

Tobin, T.H. (1992) "*Logos*," *ABD* 4: 348–56.

Torchia, N.J. (1999) *Creatio ex Nihilo and the Theology of St. Augustine: The Anti-Manichean Polemic and Beyond*. New York: Peter Lang.

Tornau, C. (2014) "Intelligible Matter and the Genesis of Intellect: The Metamorphosis of a Plotinian Theme in *Confessions* 12–13," in *Augustine's Confessions: Philosophy in Autobiography*, ed. Mann, W.E. Oxford, New York: Oxford University Press: 181–218.

Trapp, M.B. (2007) *Philosophy in the Roman Empire: Ethics, Politics and Society*. Aldershot: Ashgate.

Tull, A.C. (1968) *The Theology of Middle Platonism: A Study in the Platonism of the Second Century. Dissertation*. New York.

Ulacco, A., Celia, F. (eds.) (2012) *Il Timeo: Esegesi Greche, Arabe, Latine*. Atti dell'Incontro di Culture, GRAL, Pisa, 27–30. April 2010. Pisa: Plus.

Usener, H. (1873) "Vergessenes," *Rheinisches Museum* 28: 400–2.

van den Broeck, R. (1982) "Apuleius on the Nature of God (*De Plat.*, 190–191)," in *ACTVS: Studies in Honour of H. L. W. Nelson*, ed. den Boeft, J., and Kessel, A.H.M. Utrecht: Instituut voor Klassieke Talen: 57–72.

van der Stockt, L. (2012) "Plutarch and Apuleius: Laborious Routes to Isis," in *Aspects of Apuleius' Golden Ass 3: The Isis Book. A Collection of Original Papers*, eds. Hette Keulen, W. and Egelhaaf-Gaiser, U. Leiden: Brill: 168–82.

Bibliography

van der Stockt, L., Roskam, G. (eds.) (2011) *Virtues for the People: Aspects of Plutarchan Ethics.* Plutarchea Hypomnemata. Leuven: Leuven University Press.

Vannier, M.A. (1991) "*Creatio, Conversio, Formatio* chez Augustine," *Paradosis* 31 (Editions Universitaires): 83–9.

van Nuffelen, P., Mitchell, S. (eds.) (2010) *One God: Pagan Monotheism in the Roman Empire.* Cambridge, New York: Cambridge University Press.

van Winden, J.C.M. (1959) *Calcidius on Matter: His Doctrine and Sources. A Chapter in the History of Platonism.* Leiden: Brill.

  (1973) "The Early Christian Exegesis of 'Heaven and Earth' in Gen. 1," in *Romanitas et Christianitas*, eds. den Boer, W. et al. Amsterdam, London: North-Holland Publishing Company: 371–82.

  (1991) "Once Again *Caelum Caeli*: Is Augustine's Argument in *Confessions* XII Consistent?" in *Collectanea Augustiniana* 41. ed. Mélanges T.J. Van Bavel. Leuven: 905–11.

Venuti, L. (2008) *The Translator's Invisibility: A History of Translation.* London: Routledge.

Vlastos, G. (1965) "The Disorderly Motion in the *Timaeus*," *Classical Quarterly* 33: 71–83. Reprinted in *Studies in Plato's Metaphysics*, ed. Allen, R.E. London: Routledge and Kegan Paul Ltd: 379–421.

von Dyck, W., Caspar, M. (eds.) (1937) *Johannes Keppler: Gesammelte Werke.* Munich: C.H. Beck.

Waszink, J.H. (1964) *Studien zum "Timaioskommentar" des Chalcidius: Die Erste Hälfte des Kommentars.* Leiden: Brill, Warburg Institute.

  (1967) "Calcidius *Comm. in Tim.* 28," *Mnemosyne* 20: 441–3.

  (1972) "Calcidius: Nachtrag 243 zum *RAC*," *Jahrbuch für Antike und Christentum* 15: 236–44.

  (1986) "Calcidio, la Retorica nella Traduzione dal Greco al Latino," *Siculorum Gymnasium* 39: 51–8.

Whittaker, J. (1969) "Timaeus 27dff.," *Phoenix* 23: 181–5.

Wikramanayake, G.H. (1961) "A Note on the πίστεις in Aristotle's Rhetoric," *The American Journal of Philology* 82: 193–6.

Wisse, J. (1989) *Ethos and Pathos from Aristotle to Cicero.* Amsterdam: Hakkert.

Wolfson, H.A. (1956) *The Philosophy of the Church Fathers, Vol. 1.* Cambridge, MA: Harvard University Press.

Wrobel, J. (1876) *Platonis Timaeus Interprete Chalcidio.* Leipzig: Teubner.

Zgusta, L. (1980) "Die Rolle des Griechischen im Römischen Reich der Kaiserzei," in *Die Sprachen im Römischen Reich der Kaiserzeit*, eds. Neumann, G. and Untermann, J. Köln: Rheinland-Verlag: 121–45.

Zielinski, T. (1912) *Cicero im Wandel der Jahrhunderte.* Leipzig, Berlin: Teubner.

INDEX VERBORUM GRAECORUM

INDEX VERBORUM LATINORUM

INDEX LOCORUM

Index Locorum

Index Locorum

SUBJECT INDEX

Academic sceptics, 48–9
  dispute with Stoics, 67–8, *see also*
    Plato; scepticism; sceptics
Academy, Philo's, 70, 74
  influenced Cicero's *Timaeus*
    translation, 81, 82 (*see also*
    Cicero; scepticism)
  see also Academic sceptics; Academy,
    sceptical; assimilation; Philo
Academy, sceptical
  Cicero's affiliation with, 38, 39n.11
Aetius, 26
Alcinous, 208n.142, 211
  and demiurge in *Timaeus*, 208n142
  on highest god's will, 208n142
  on intellect, 207
  logical methods of, 208, 210–11
  on Plato, 27n37
  Platonism of, 119–20, *see also*
    Didaskalikos
All, the, 86
  everlasting, 98n135, *see also* cosmos;
    universe
allegory
  exegesis through, 218
    Augustine and, 222, 237
    see also Augustine
Ambrose
  influence on Augustine, 218, 222
  and Philo, 250–1, *see also* Augustine
analogy
  Augustine Christianizes, 257, 282
  military (*see under* Aristotle;
    Apuleius)
  and reason, 210
  Timaeus's, ontological/
    epistemological, 19, 121, 263,
    270, 279
    Boethius's expansion of, 264n126

Cicero's interpretation of, 84
  see also under Apuleius;
    Augustine
angelic substrate, 239, 242, *see also*
  angels
angels
  act on humans' behalf, 276 (*see also*
    Christ; mediator)
  Augustine on, 238, 270–8
  creation of, 246
  formation of, 239, 246–7
  as "light" in Genesis, 239
  see also angelic substrate; creation;
    god(s); humans
Annas, J., 6–7
Antiochus of Ascalon, 39, 54, 64, 106,
  175n54
Apollo, 33n50, *see also* gods: Olympian
Apuleius, 117
  Apology, 102, 113, 127
  Augustine and, 271, 272–7 (*see also*
    under Augustine; demonology;
    demons)
  accused of "magical" practices, 110
  and Cicero, 280
  cosmology of, 105–6
  De deo Socratis (*DDS*), 102, 129, 133,
    142, 271
    as oratorical, 104
    supports study of philosophy, 111
    and demons, 144, 261, 273 (*see also*
      under demons)
  De mundo, 102, 129, 132–5, 137,
    157–8
    cosmology in, 145
    and *DPD*, 106
    on highest god, 143
    on prophets, 111 (*see also*
      translation)

315

Subject Index

Subject Index

Subject Index

Christ (*cont.*)
  as mediator, 251, 253–70
    vs. Apuleius' demons, 271
  and non-believers, 269–70
  participates at both ontological
    levels, 259
  and trinity, 258
  as truth, 208n142
  as wisdom, 256, 258
  see also faith; god; Jesus; truth
Christian creed. *See* Christian faith
Christian faith
  Augustine's access to, 218–19
  Platonists closest to, among
    philosophers, 225
  superiority of (Augustine), 225,
    271, 273, *see also* Augustine;
    Christians
Christians
  come to truth via faith, 257
  and non-Christian authors, 165
  see also Augustine; Christ; Jesus;
    Christian faith
Chrysippus, 89n123, 98n135
Cicero, Marcus Tullius
  Academica, 39, 48–9, 81, 89, 91
  and creation of cosmos, 83–101
  De divinatione, 45, 54, 82
  De finibus, 39n11, 44, 48–9
    preface to, 33n50, 44
    and Timaeus translation, 52–3,
      54–5, 68–9, 70, 88
      (*see also* Plato, *Timaeus*;
      translation)
  De natura deorum, 48–9, 52–3, 55,
    69, 70, 88, (*see also* Plato,
    Timaeus)
  on emulating Greek orators, 41
  and fusion of rhetorical and
    philosophical methods, 64,
    65, 69
  historical reach of translations, 46
  Hortensius, 216
  on knowledge of god, 196n104
  language of
    rhetorical, 58–9 (*see also*
      assimilation)
    concurrence of, 64–5
    sceptical terms used by, 81

Partitiones oratoriae, 61, 66, 77
Philonean outlook of, 40n11, 93
philosophical treatises of, 83–93
Plato and Platonism of, 38–40
on Romans surpassing Greeks (in
    Tusculans), 42–3
"scepticisms" of, 38, 39
Somnium Scipionis, 167
speaking role in *Timaeus*,
    48–9, 56
Topics, 77
Tusculan Disputations, 87, 89, *see also*
    cynics; Plao, *Timaeus*; rhetoric;
    translation
Claudius Maximus (proconsul), 114–15,
    117
Clitomachus, 38, 62n78
coming to be
  and being, 22, 251, 259
  causal interpretation of, 248
  and convincingness, 19
  of universe, 96, *see also* cosmos;
    universe
compositio, 209, 210–11
convincingness, 19–20, 23, 60, 127
  see also fides;
Corpus Hermeticum, 33n50
cosmology, 61, 120–1
  Calcidius on Plato's, 208–13
  sceptical perspective on, 49, 52,
    87–8
  see also cosmos
cosmos, 27
  as "the All," 172
  Apuleian, 262
  Calcidian, 262
  createdness of, 179–86, 251, 283
  creation of
    Calcidius on, 177–94
    Cicero on, 80, 86–101
  divine intellect constructed, 84
  everlastingness of, 181, 183–4,
    189–90
  god and, 145–8
  Manichean, 216–17
  origins of, 15–17, 174n50
  temporal creation of, 95
    (*see also under* universe)
  three principles of, 35

318

Subject Index

Subject Index

mathematics
  within curricular hierarchy, 175n54
  proportion and, 204–5, 205n137
    (*see also* proportion)
matter
  Augustine and Calcidius's descriptions
    of, 241n85
  Augustine's portrayal of, 241–2
  chaotic vs. orderly (Plutarch), 28–9
  formation of, 238
  "heaven" as intelligible
    (Calcidius), 240–1
  Plato's doctrine of (*see under* Plato),
    see also under intellect
mediator(s)
  angels unsuitable as, 277–8
  Apuleius as, 109–10, 109n30
  demons unsuitable as, 276–7
  see also under Christ
metaphor
  Platonists and, 27
  of seed, 247, 283
    Aristotelian, 246–7
  Timaeus creation account as, vs.
    literal, 22–9
  see also allegory; Plato,
    Timaeus; seeds
metaphysics
  Apuleius's treatment of, 144
  in Calcidius's commentary, 208
  in Platonic curriculum, 107
  Plato's, in *Timaeus*, 251
    influence on Augustine, 249–50,
      251–70
  Plotinian, 249n107 (*see also* Plotinus)
  trinitarian, 252, 258, 279
  see also Augustine; Plato
metempsychosis, 226
methodology passage (in
    Timaeus), 169–77
  Apuleius's version of the original, 129
  Calcidius and, 172, 178
  Cicero's version of the original, 66
methods, logical, 211
  see also Alcinous; Calcidius
"middle term," 262
Middle Platonists
  on highest divinity, 282
  move towards monotheism, 3

and Platonic heritage, 251
on providence, 151, *see also* Apuleius;
  Neoplatonists; Platonism;
  Platonists
modus coniecturae, 76, 77, 78
Mohr, R., 2
Moses, 279, *see also* Bible; Scriptures
motion/ movement
  and change, 232–3
  cosmic, Apuleius on, 136–8, 146–7
  disorderly, preceding time, 23, 25,
    263–4
  and heavenly apparatus (Apuleius),
    141n119, 147
  of heavenly bodies, Aristotle on, 51
  time and, 232, *see also* cosmos; time;
    universe
Musaeus, 17n6
μῦθος
  vs. λόγος, 21, 21n16
    see also λόγος; *see also under*
    Timaeus
myth, *see* μῦθος

nature
  creations of, perishable, 181
  "heaven" as intelligible, 240–1
  see also god; origins; seeds
necessity
  and intellect, 34
  see also intellect
Nemesius
  De natura hominis, 199
  on fate, 199n118, 201
Neoplatonists
  and Augustine, 227–8, 279
  and Jewish/ Christian thinkers,
    4–5
  Platonism of, 120
  translations by, from Greek, 219
  see also Augustine; Middle Platonists;
    Platonism; Platonists; Plotinus;
    Porphyry
Neopythagoreans, 47, 48
  see also Pythagoreans
Neschke-Hentschke, Ada Babette, 4
[P.] Nigidius Figulus, 46, 47, 48, 49, 50,
    70, 98n135
  works of, 47

324

philosophy
  Apuleius's "doing" of, 112–17
  Cicero as translator of Greek, 43
  god as beyond, 195
    (see also physics)
  natural, sceptical treatments of, 49,
    71, 176
  separate from theology, 174, 177–8
    (see also theology)
  Neoplatonic, influence on
    Augustine, 222
  Plato's (Unitarian vs.
    developmental), 24
    (see also Plato)
  theoretical vs. practical, 175
  three disciplines of, 175, 175n54,
    175n56
  see also philosophy, Roman
philosophy, Roman 5–8
  Greek influence on, 5–6
  history of, 5, see also philosophies,
    Hellenistic; philosophy
physics, 107, 176, 197
  Alcinous's Platonic, 120
  and "necessity," 34
  separate from theology (Platonists),
    175, 176, 178
    (see also under theology)
pithanê phantasia, 62, 62n78
pithanon, 60–70, and passim
  Aristotle uses as "persuasive," 60
Plato
  Apuleius quotes, 142 (see also god[s]:
    highest)
  and Cicero, 40, 48–9, 71
  concerned to reach all readers,
    179
  creationism of consistent with
    Christians' (Augustine), 227–8,
    238
  curricular agenda of, 178
    (Calcidius), 223n29 (Augustine)
  on demons, 271
  as "divine," 85, 108–12, 116
  development of, 282
  on the elements, 274 (see also
    elements)
  Epinomis, 204
  on highest god, 192–3

(Calcidius), 212, 258 (see also god:
    highest)
  as ineffable (Apuleius), 142
  lacks Christian wisdom, 225, 256,
    258, 270
  Laws, 25
  Parmenides, 178
  Phaedrus, 24, 107, 198
  vs. Platonists, 273, 275
  Republic, 2, 149n137
    Divided Line in, 33
    Timaeus as sequel to, 178–9
  and Sceptics, 225
  "swan song" of, 116
  Symposium, 107
  as "that man," 143, see also under
    Apuleius; Calcidius; Cicero;
    Sceptics
Plato, Timaeus, 9–13 and passim
  Apuleius and, 117–59
  Augustine and, 227–78
    (see also under Augustine)
  beginning of, 14–18
  Calcidius commissioned to
    translate, 164–5
  Cicero translates, 45–50, 52, 66,
    237, 239, 262–3
    and De natura deorum, 68–9
    in monologue form, 49
    (see also under Cicero;
    translation)
  creation account in, 15, 88–9, 177
    ambiguity of, 21
    Apuleius interprets, 121–8
    and Christianity, 165
    didaskalias charin and, 26, 193–4
    discrepancies in, 23–5
    dualism in, 279
    and Genesis, 235
    inaccessibility of, 44–6, 166n27
    interpretive controversies in, 22–9,
      36
    legacy of, 280
    as likely, 22–3
    literal interpretation of, 25–9, 119
    on mortality of god's
      creations, 187
    as myth, 18
    as natural philosophy, 18

Subject Index

as physics, 213
and *Republic*, 14–15, 178–9
technical jargon in, 165–6,
    see also Apuleius; Augustine;
    Calcidius; Middle Platonists;
    Neoplatonists; Platonism;
    Platonists; translation
Platonism
Apuleius's, 105, 108–9, 139–45, 158
development of, in early centuries CE,
    106–8, 118
in first century, 106–8
in second century, 120
Plutarch's view of, 119
and Second Sophistic, 104, *see also*
    Plato; Platonists
Platonists
and Augustine, 223, 261, 269, 271
as dogmatic, 107
and Christians, 223, 271
on cosmos, 26–7
curriculum of, 107, 177
Timaeus defining dialogue of Middle
    and Neo-, 163
see also Middle Platonists;
    Neoplatonists; Plato;
    Platonism
Plotinus, 26, 220, 221–2, 226, 249n107
Plutarch
Aristotelian imagery in, 249n107
cosmology, 28–9, 119
De Iside et Osiride, 119
on "epoptical" subject matter,
    108 (*see also* epoptical
    subject matter)
on Plato, 27n37
and Timaeus, 15, 119
    see also Atticus
Porphyry, 220
and Augustine, 221–2, 226, 269
Contra Christianos, 252
on creation, 180
criticizes gospels, 252
    see also creation
Powell, J. G. F., 6
power(s)
demonic, 194
divine, providential, 85–6, 157
preface

to Calcidius's commentary on
    Timaeus, 165–6, 166n27, 173
    (*see also under* Calcidius)
to Cicero's *De finibus*, 44
    De divinatione, 45
    Tusculan Disputations, 42
translation of *Timaeus*, 46, 50
    see also under Calcidius; Cicero;
    Plato, *Timaeus*
probabile (in Cicero's writings), 60
concurrence of philosophy and
    rhetoric in, 64, 65, 80, 81
and *disputatio in utramque
    partem*, 61
and εἰκὼς λόγος, 70
and *fides*, 70
Lucullus on, 61, 67–8
in philosophical writings, 61–5
and *pithanon*, 61
in rhetorical writings, 60
and *veri simile*, 64, 65, 69
    see also probability; *veri simile*
probability (*probabile*)
conveyed by εἰκὼς, 20
in rhetoric, 69
    see also probabile
Proclus, 26
prophecy
ancient, on Christ as mediator, 253–70
proportion, 262
geometrical, 261, 264n126, *see also*
    analogy; mathematics
providentia. See providence
providence
as "adorning" matter, 207–8
Apuleius's doctrine on, 134, 148–58
and Boethius, *De Philosophia*,
    264n126
diverging levels of, 194
divine, 261–2
and divine hierarchy, 196
and fate, 148–58, 208n142, 265n126
    Apuleius on, 198–9
    Calcidius on, 196–201, 208n142
and god's will, 198, 199n119, 208n142
and intellect, 210
primary, 151, 154
secondary, 152–3, 154, 156
    lacks definition in Apuleius, 152–3

327

Subject Index

time (*cont.*)

god precedes construction of, 182

as image of eternity, 135–6, 188

Kronos as personification of, 135n98
(*see also* gods: Olympian)

pre-cosmic "trace" of (Plutarch), 28

Timaeus on, 34, 184–5, *see also*
cosmos; eternity; extensions:
temporal; god(s); temporality

τὸ γιγνόμενον

Apuleius on, 125, 126

distinguished from τὸ ὄν, 15–16, 251

see also τὸ ὄν

τὸ ὄν

and Moses' god, 279

as "substance" (Apuleius), 125

and τὸ γιγνόμενον, 15–18, 126, 251

see also οὐσία; τὸ γιγνόμενον

translation

agendas of, 9, 55, and *passim*

Apuleius's compared with
Cicero's, 159

Apuleius and, 116, 121–9, 133–4, 147

Timaeus methodology
passage, 121–8

Calcidius and, 45, 164–8

and commentary on Plato,
Timaeus, 165–214

on creation as temporal, 192

on demiurge, 194–5

methodology of, 166–77

as self-reflection, 177

Cicero and, 41, 44, 45, 46, 54, 159

appropriates Greek intellectual
heritage, 280

Augustine and, 220, 220n19, 227,
256, 265, 279

quotes, 262–3

discontinues project, 52–5

methodology of, 70

"methodology passage" in, 56–71

paraphrase of *Timaeus*, 101

preface to, 46, 48–9, 52

reflections on, 41–2, 44

on temporality of cosmos (*see
under* cosmos)

varies from original, 68–9, 73, 282
(*see also under* Plato, *Timaeus*)

widespread use of, 45

Roman, 42–4, *see also under* Cicero;
Plato, *Timaeus*

trinity, 252, 256

truth

Christ represents, 257, 258, 260

faith identified with, 258

leads to, 161–257, 259

and *fides*, 127

found in Plato's works, 107

rejoices in the eternal, 256

Stoic criterion of, 62, *see also* Christ;
faith; god; soul

universe, 16, 17–18, 20, 34

as copy of something eternal, 27, 97,
98, 100–1, 263

cosmic soul and, 16

created from seed (Chrysippus),
249n107

created vs. uncreated, 86, 87–8,
92–3, 130–5, 183, 279 (*see also*
seeds; soul)

demiurge as creator of Timaean, 31–2

distinct from intelligible sphere, 177

as perishable but everlasting, 16, 98

possesses soul and intellect, 16

reason for creation of, 73, 79–80
(*see also under* question[s])

ruled by highest god, 197

Timaeus on, 14 (*see also* Plato,
Timaeus; Timaeus)

uncreated and everlasting
(Neoplatonists), 228, *see also*
cosmology; cosmos; creation

Velleius (Epicurean), 51n54, 54–5,
55n60, 88–9, 90–1

Venus

vulgar vs. celestial, 115n55

see also gods: Olympian

veri simile (in Cicero's writings), 60

and *fides*, 66, 78

in philosophical writings, 61–5

and *pithanon*, 61

in rhetorical writings, 60

types of, *see also* likelihood(s);
probabile

Vetus Latina, 218, 267

via analogia, 210

Ingram Content Group UK Ltd.
Milton Keynes UK
UKHW022029080623
423147UK00035B/700